Echoes from the Set

Volume II: 1967 - 1977

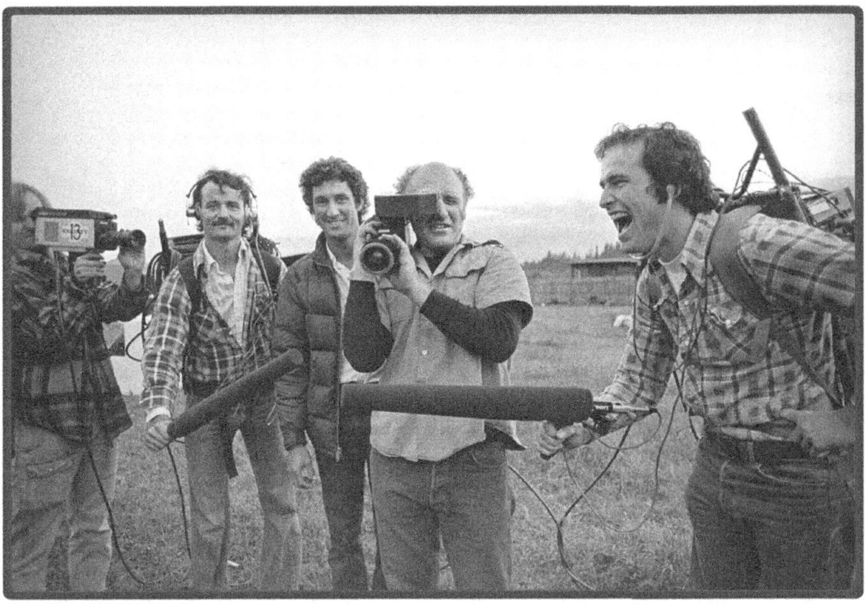

Shadows from the Underground: Cinema Under the Influence

Katherine Wilson

Foreword by Dr. Steve Rust, Film Instructor, University of Oregon

Echoes from the Set, Volume II (1967-1977) – Shadows from the Underground: Cinema Under the Influence

Published by:
Trine Day LLC
PO Box 577
Walterville, OR 97489
1-800-556-2012
www.TrineDay.com
publisher@TrineDay.net

Library of Congress Control Number: 2021942664

Wilson, Katherine
–1st ed.
p. cm.

Epub (ISBN-13) 978-1-63424-356-8
Print (ISBN-13) 978-1-63424-355-1
1. Motion pictures -- United States.. 2. Motion picture producers and directors. 3. Motion picture actor.. 4. Motion picture writers. 5. Motion pictures -- History . 6. Motion pictures -- History – Oregon. 7. Motion pictures -- Ken Kesey. I. Wilson, Katherine II. Title

First Edition
10 9 8 7 6 5 4 3 2 1

Printed in the USA
Distribution to the Trade by:
Independent Publishers Group (IPG)
814 North Franklin Street
Chicago, Illinois 60610
312.337.0747
www.ipgbook.com

Publisher's Foreword

But I remembered one thing: it wasn't me that started acting deaf; it was people that first started acting like I was too dumb to hear or see or say anything at all.

– Chief Bromden, *One Flew Over the Cuckoo's Nest,* Ken Kesey

The love of wicked men converts to fear, that fear to hate, and hate turns one or both to worthy danger and deserved death.

– King Richard II, *Richard II,* William Shakespeare

Can the Ethiopian change his skin, or the leopard his spots? then may ye also do good, that are accustomed to do evil.

– Jeremiah 13:23

Rhetoric wins votes. Votes get you into government. And in government, you can actually change the real world.

– Mark Forsyth, Ted Talk

I had to keep reminding myself that it had truly happened, that we had made it happen.

– Chief Bromden, *One Flew Over the Cuckoo's Nest,* Ken Kese

Where are we going, where have we been? Does it matter?

In the late sixties while living in Portland, Oregon some of my friends and I were putting on rock and roll dances. One of the bands was the Grateful Dead, and somehow we ended up with a reel-to-reel tape from the LA Acid Tests. On this tape there was a lady screaming, "Who cares? Who cares? My head is full of snot, snot, snot, snot, snot." This was repeated throughout the tape. It must have been quite an evening.

There were profound changes going on in the 1960s, and Katherine Wilson takes a deep dive as to the when, how, where and why of it all. *Echoes of the Set II, Shadows from the Underground: Cinema Under the Influ-*

ence is a tour de force delving in to one of the biggest questions of our age: Where did the hippies come from? Was it simply an outgrowth of a CIA MK-Ultra experiment, as some say? Or was there more to it?

I first met Katherine in the early 1970s when she picked me up hitchiking in Eugene, Oregon, and then, amazingly enough, we later reconnected after she gave me a ride in the late 1980s. It was unusual for a single woman to give rides, but then Katherine is unusual.

Because my father, a former intelligence officer, had told me some stuff I didn't understand, I began reading conspiracy literature in the early 1970s, especially a subject I call CIA-Drugs. I came across articles saying Ken Kesey and Jerry Garcia were FBI agents with the posit that us hippies and our flower power revolution were nothing but an intelligence operation. Being a member of the high school class of 1967, gave me a ringside seat to what was going on. And yes, "they" may have tried, but what was happening was beyond "their" control. LSD can be used to disrupt, but not control.

One day, while visiting at Kesey's office, I asked him about the report of him being an FBI agent or informant, he said it wasn't accurate. Yes, he had been interviewed by them after an arrest, but his word to me was "hijack." He had found something interesting and he had hijacked LSD from the hospital to share with his friends. In 1970, when the Kinney National Company (they ran parking garages, not the shoe company) that owned Warner Music Group tried to recreate Kesey's cross country bus trip and take along the San Francisco bands. The Dead and others demanded that Kesey would be in charge, Warner's refused and most of the bands pulled out. To run an "op" one needs control. The hippes were "out of control," and on their way to creating a deep-rooted counter-culture. Our heads were full of snot, snot, snot, snot, snot – and we needed a change.

Katherine Wilson's book, *Echoes of the Set II, Shadows from the Underground: Cinema Under the Influence* fills in some blanks, dots the i's and crosses the t's on the subject. I find her expositions and explanations very compelling and hope readers enjoy it as much as I do.

Onwards to the Utmost of Futures,
Peace,
RA "Kris" Millegan
Publisher
TrineDay
July, 7 2021

Dedicated to Scholar Anne Richardson (April 19, 1954- October 14, 2020)

Table of Contents

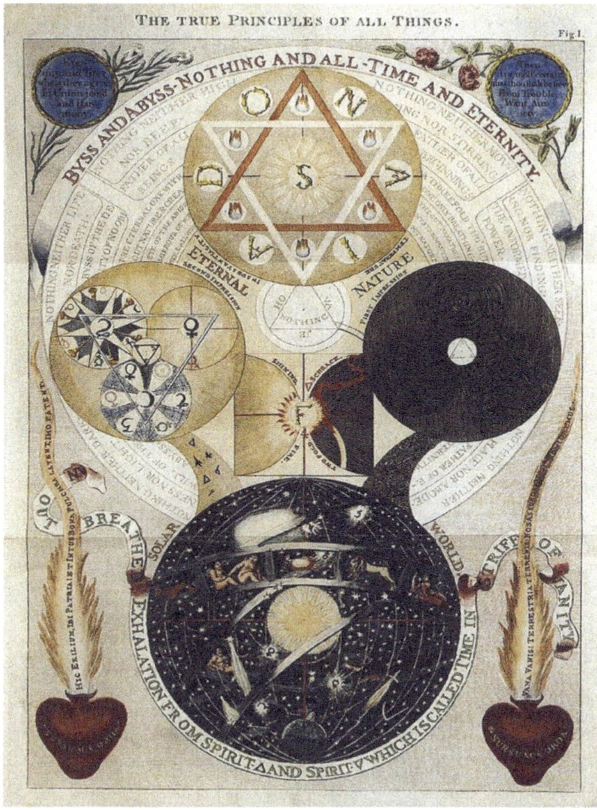

Aeonic Emanation

> *There are two offshoots from all the Aeons, having neither beginning nor end, from one root, and this root is a certain Power, an invisible and incomprehensible Silence. One of them appears on high and is a great power, the mind of the whole, who rules all things and is a male; the other below is a great Thought, a female giving birth to all things.*
>
> – Hippolytus.

The first 8 Aeons by generation: First generation – Bythos (the One) and Sige (Silence, Charis, Ennoea, etc.) Second generation, emanated from Bythos and Sige – Nous (Nus, Mind) and Aletheia (Veritas, Truth) Third generation, emanated from Nous and Aletheia --Sermo (the Word) and Vita (the Life) Fourth generation, emanated from Sermo and Vita – Anthropos (Homo, Man) and Ecclesia (Congregation). Mankind evolved, not from apes, but as an emanation from the Silence of the One."[1]

Foreword

by Dr. Stephen Rust

Shadows from the Underground is an ambitious combination of personal memoir, film history, and cultural theory that has blown my mind at every stage of its journey from concept to publication over the past year. Katherine Wilson, the Godmother of Oregon Film, has composed a detailed, provocative, and deeply insightful work of participatory history that will certainly shape a generation of scholarship on the history of underground independent filmmaking and film exhibition during the 1960s and 1970s, the history of female filmmakers, the study of Ken Kesey and the Merry Pranksters impact on popular culture during the period, and the role of biculturalism in the development of the distinctive cinematic literary voice of Oregon filmmakers. For readers of Katherine's first book, *Echoes from the Set,* get ready to take a deep dive into the years 1967-1977 when Eugene, Oregon became the capitol of Poetic Cinema in the United States and a center of independent and Hollywood film production. While *Echoes from the Set, Vol. I* explores Oregon film history from 1967-2017 and is more expansive in scope, *Echoes From the Set Vol. II: Shadows from the Underground* is a more ambitious work of literary theory and analysis blended with personal and professional 60s & 70s film history.

Katherine and I met in the summer of 2010 when she returned to the University of Oregon to finish the undergraduate degree that she had put on hold during the early 1970s to pursue her career in the film industry. After teaching high school for six years and spending another five pursuing a PhD, I was finally teaching my own Intro to Film Studies course for the first time and excited that Katherine seemed to know so much about film production and history for someone taking a first-year college course. After I screened a movie close to my heart to teach sound and editing, *The Empire Strikes Back* (1983), Katherine stayed after class to talk about William Kittridge's "silver bullet theory" that the *Star Wars* movies, like *Easy*

Rider (1969) and most New Hollywood films of that era, is a Western, that uniquely American genre of movies (like Jazz in music). We chatted about everything from Joseph Campbell to racial representations and Yoda's eastern mysticism and bonded immediately. I finally asked Katherine if she had worked in film or theater because she seemed to have such a keen understanding of the differences in how academics, students, and film reviewers analyze movies compared to the people who actually make them for a living. Humbly, she told me about her experiences as a location scout and casting agent for a little movie called *Animal House* (1978) that had been filmed on the University of Oregon campus and worked on productions like *One Flew Over the Cuckoo's Nest* (1975) and *Stand By Me* (1986).

We stayed in touch after the course, Katherine became a mentor and friend who is great fun to be around, in touch with the earth, and motivated like I am to help future generations of young people survive the technocratic corporatocracy that our country has become. We were both raised in rural Northwest communities where the blight of clear-cutting provided us both concrete examples of Western culture's seeming blindness to the consequences of unchecked resource extraction and white America's cultural and economic supremacy over its Indigenous communities. We both understand that real people and real interactions among people with racial ethnic, gender, sexual, political and other differences are far more meaningful than the politics of screen representation. We met for lunch one day at Taylor's near campus because I was curious to learn more about Katherine's work on *Animal House* and what it was like to work with John Belushi. I told Katherine that some people refused to teach the film anymore because they felt it presented negative stereotypes of black people, particularly in the scene where the fraternity brothers take their dates to a black dinner club by mistake. When she told me that the movie's producers had worried about the same thing, so they screened the scene for comedian Richard Pryor who told them he loved it and that they had to keep it in because it so effectively critiques the white privilege of the movie's protagonists. This is just one of many examples where Katherine has helped me to remember to avoid making any claims about textual representations or ideological critiques without attending to the production histories of movies and the stories of the people who make them in my own research.

Over the years, Katherine has visited several of my classes to share her experiences on *Animal House* and other local productions. These visits always helped my students understand that film and television are real industries where there are lots of different kinds of job opportunities and to remember that they may not necessarily have to move to Los Angeles or New York to pursue such professions (though it sure seems to help). At the end of a particularly engaging class discussion in a course on Pacific Northwest film history, Katherine connected with five students to work on a 5-10-minute documentary short about the making of *Animal House* for their class project. Over the next year, that project turned into *Animal House of Blues,* a feature-length documentary chronicling the making of *Animal House* and the meeting between John Belushi and local blues musician Curtis Salgado that led to the creation of the *Blues Brothers.* In 2019, the documentary's soundtrack was nominated for a Grammy. Most importantly, Katherine mentored these students and several others throughout the process, and they are all successfully pursuing careers in the media industry today. We call her the Godmother of Oregon Film because she mentors and develops the talents of those around her rather than exploiting them to make a profit.

Katherine wrote the first draft of *Shadows from the Underground* over the summer of 2020. Thanks to the University of Oregon Department of English support for her project, Katherine enrolled in three back-to-back terms of intensive independent study credits and won a small summer research grant to help with the cost of materials and books needed for the project. During the spring of 2020, she had taken a film history course from my amazing colleague Dr. Peter Alilunas. Peter had read Katherine's first book on Oregon film history and was so supportive of it I think for the first time she fully understood that her story and her writing abilities were being widely appreciated by film historians and cultural critics. With graduate school applications and other coursework looming in the fall, she knew that this summer would probably be her only opportunity to write this book. She worked at a breakneck pace for 12 weeks. We met for an hour every week to review her progress and my feedback. Undeterred by the Covid-19 pandemic and lockdowns, she took to Zoom and telephone working at all hours to accommodate her interviewees schedules and time zones. Most impressively, when I started reading her introductory chapters and recognized how she was weaving literary and cultural theory into her work of history and memoir my jaw hit the floor and the density and connection of the ideas, which resonated with everything I had read before about the history of the 1960s, the New Hollywood era in film, and the feeling that something very special and rare had taken place in America's cultural history during that era.

Introduction

While writing *Echoes From the Set Vol. I* in 2017, a single chapter on the author/filmmaker/icon of the 1960s, Ken Kesey; became five chapters because of the wealth of information I had from knowing Ken and working on the film version of his book, *One Flew Over the Cuckoo's Nest.* By the time I wrote Chapter 6 especially, *Echoes from the Set Vol. I* started raising larger questions than I was prepared to answer at the time in regards to that period; and I had too many other stories to tell to linger on these questions. Now, after attending the University of Oregon during 2019-2021, certain answers to those questions have revealed themselves to me, especially after studying contemporary literary theories and Indigenous, Race and Ethnic Studies. In addition, I submitted to the University's Research Symposium several abstracts on the 60s and 70s Cinema inspired by the early history of the Erb Memorial Union, a true microcosm of that particular time at the University of Oregon. The research I did for the symposium led me full circle, back to Chapter 6, and its unanswered questions; because by now several professors were essentially asking the same questions, and were working with me to answer them. It was then I decided a new book needed to be written to augment the first.

This new book is in response to questions raised about "Where did your anomalous 60s generation come from?" The answers were always peeking up from the shadows of the 1960s underground, which also held Cinema under its influence during the Hollywood Renaissance. As a screenplay writer, I instinctively looked for the "inciting incident." What caused the 1960s? What caused my generation to turn its back on our parent's trajectory of Post Modernism and Post-industrial life, and to create a whole new lifestyle that has profoundly altered American culture? I remember Dr. Stephen Rust first asked me to address what created the 1960s New Hollywood for a presentation to his Introduction to Film class back in the spring of 2012. And it was the same question that Dr. Alilunas asked in a different way about Cinema 7, an Arthouse from the 70s that I was a part of, and that he had completed a lot of research on before I met him in 2019. What those manifestations of our generation had in common was the Poetic Cinema genre of the 1960s. This poetic cinema was just one of many artistic expressions of the time, including the arts in music, literature, architecture, fashion, and film; but it was steeped in a massive counter-culture movement against every single tenet of "civilized society;" basically turning them all on their head in an 180-degree arc, and by doing so exposed their uncivilized dark sides.[2]

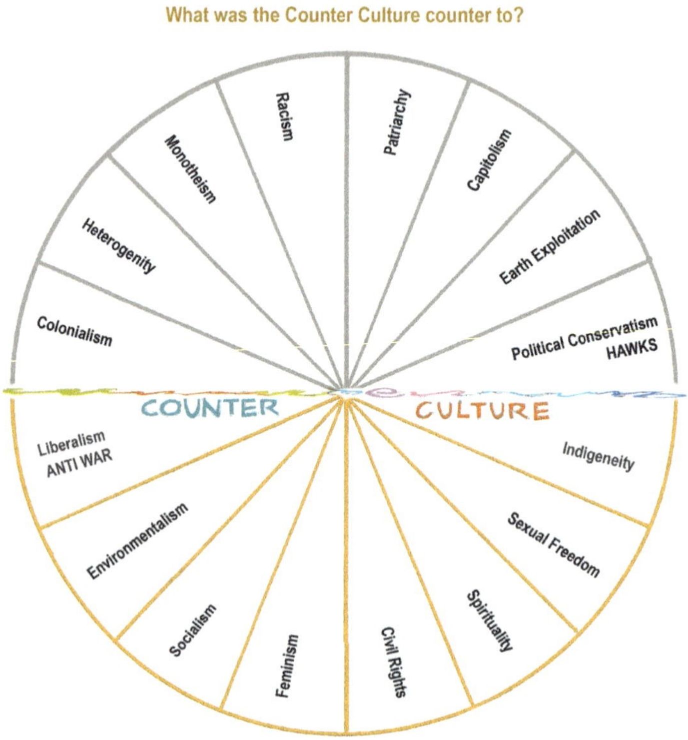

For instance, we turned away from Monotheism to Spiritualism, from a War Culture to a Peace Culture, From Capitalism to Socialism, from Patrimonialism to Feminism, from Conservatism to Liberalism, from Racism to Civil Rights, from exploiting the natural resources of the Earth to saving the Earth, and last but not least, from Colonialism to Indigeneity. It was by turning back from Modernism and Post-modernism to pre-industrial values, a return from the Age of Reason to Yeatsian Symbolism, a return from scientific values to human ones; that we found ourselves in direct opposition to our parents' generation.

But that is not all, our culture was brought together by protesting the war in Vietnam. The SDS supported the Student Strike sparked by Black Student Unions' demanding Black Studies at San Francisco State. The Black Panthers supported Vietnam War protesters; students of all colors came together to support the American Indian Student Union, all of us reeling under the pressures of a system that didn't work for us, and we were forced to became "subversives" by society. As Malcolm X said: " Europeanism has been such a strong poison for centuries it now becomes essential to emphasize Africanism to counteract it & Arabism to counteract Zionism, socialism to counteract capitalism etc."[3]

What also brought us together back then was our art, and the metaphors and symbolism in our art was what became the new language of our bicultural voice, a kind of code. That voice is what this book is going to focus on. And as a screenplay writer knows, it all began with an inciting incident, a conflict, one that set the trajectory of our generation (particularly in the U.S.) in reaction to the Apocalyptic assassinations of our generation's heroes, John F. Kennedy, Martin Luther King, Jr., Robert Kennedy; and the H-Bomb and resulting Bomb Shelters; the Cuban Missile Crisis and the Cold War. But there was something deeper than that. A lot of us children of the 40s and 50s could not relate to the pursuit of money and status, nor the religions of our fathers and mothers, to their love of plastic, to modernist architecture, Denny's restaurants; nor their music, their tv shows and especially, their movies. John Wayne was fine for the Post War reconstruction mythology of their generation. But while most of our parents' generation just heard about the WWII sirens in London and violence in far-away Pearl Harbor; as 50s children we were seeing sirens everywhere, and were building bomb shelters at home. And we needed more than they could give us, such as deeper understandings of Spirituality, including a new, more powerful American mythology; a new art, a new music, a new cuisine, a new politics and especially a new Cinema to embody all of that. The H-bomb in itself caused us to think on a sub-atomic level. The Space program also caused us to think about eternity, the Cosmos and the vastness of Space. All of this led to an openness to new ideas like quantum mechanics and astrology. And when we heard "One small step for man, and one giant step for Mankind" as we also saw, from space, a rather holistic image of our beautiful and fragile Earth, we immediately knew that we were all part of a cohesive whole, that our countries really had no borders, we were all one Family of Man.

And that was why the excuses for the Vietnam war, that my generation was asked to die for; did not make any sense. So if we look at this period from a microscopic quantum mechanics viewpoint, we see that "as below" is truly "as above." And that the "above" was being addressed by William Butler Yeats in his widely read yet terrifying poem "Second Coming"; it was being addressed by Walt Disney in his animated archetypal "children's stories" which borrowed from pre-Christian magic and Merlin and witches and even anthropomorphically animated objects such as brooms and teapots, a traditionally pagan premise of quantum level life-forms in all matter, including Yeats' Sphinx. And by reaching towards these metaphors from pre-history, to describe this understanding, we found ourselves astronomically aware of things like Plato's cave and his theory of the Aeon, a 2000 year old "widening gyre" which ruled the culture of the Age of Aries; and was countered by a new gyre 2000 years later in the Age of Pisces, whose spiritual emanation was coded as "The Divine Male, Christ, or Fisher of Men" and "the Fisher King."

"Not without reason do we date our era from the age of Augustus, for that epoch saw the birth of the symbolical figure of Christ, who was invoked by the early Christians as the Fish, the Ruler of the Aeon of Pisces which had just begun. He became the ruling spirit of the next two thousand years. Like the teacher of wisdom in Babylonian legend, Cannes, he rose up from the sea, from the primeval darkness, and brought a world-period to an end. It is true that he said, "I am come not to bring peace but a sword."[4]

Carl Jung was the first to coin "The Age of Aquarius." Here, Jungian Analyst Liz Green, with two PhD's in History and Psychology verifies my theory about Yeats' *Second Coming*:

> Aion, for Jung, also embodied an astrological age – that of Aquarius – which, in its imagery and meaning, combines the human form of the Water Bearer with its opposite constellation of Leo, the lion. W.B. Yeats, preoccupied with the same zodiacal polarity, described his own vision of the approaching New Age in his poem, "The Second Coming," written just after the Armageddon of the Great War, with a prophetic pessimism not unlike Jung's own: a terrifying being with a lion's body and the head of a man "slouching toward Bethlehem to be born" in the midst of chaos and social disintegration.[5]

If it is true that the Tarot Deck is a codex of the history of the world, as some Jungian analysts do, perhaps humanity in the next quote is the balance achieved between the masculine and feminine, as portrayed in the rather androgynous image of The Star, in the Tarot, which came right after the Tower depicting 911:

> The major theme of Jung's *Aion* is the shift in human consciousness and a simultaneous shift in the god-image, reflected in the ending of the Piscean age. In Jung's view, Pisces is associated with the Christian symbols of Jesus and Satan as the two fish. The advent of the Aquarian *aion* is associated with a new symbol: humanity as the Water Bearer. Jung believed that each of the great shifts represented by a new astrological *aion* is reflected in the imagery of the presiding zodiacal constellation and its planetary ruler:
>
> Apparently they are changes in the constellations of psychic dominants, of the archetypes, or "gods" as they used to be called, which bring about, or accompany, long-lasting transformations of the collective psyche. This transformation started in the historical era and left its traces first in the passing of the aeon of Taurus into that of Aries, and then of Aries into Pisces, whose beginning coincides with the rise of Christianity. We are now nearing that great change which may be expected when the spring-point enters Aquarius.[6]

According to gnostic philospher Samael Aun Weor, this spring point entered on Feb. 4th, 1962;[7] and led to where we are now in the great scheme of things, from where this emanation from the Universe began – the Age of Aquarius symbolically represented by an androgynous human as The Star in the Tarot Deck pouring out stars over the Universe, like blessings, from an alabaster jar. But it was affecting more than just the Youth of America; it was happening all over Europe; all over the Near East, in Africa and Asia, in Tibet, Bangladesh, and France. This "great change" started a few years before in the 50s as we came of age, created a crisis that the world found itself in, which also created subversive filmmakers in Czechoslovakia, like Milos Forman, who directed *Cuckoo's Nest* and Roman Polanski from Poland. It created Akira Kurosawa and *Rashomon*; it created Satyajit Ray, Jean Renoir, Italian Neo-realism, the Nouvelle Vague in France, and the German New Wave. Then what followed was the American Underground with counter-culture films exploring the clash between us and this crisis culture around drug deals: *Easy Rider*; Satanic Cults: *Rosemary's Baby*; Sex: *Midnight Cowboy* (the first X-rated movie to win an Academy Award); Violence: *Bonnie & Clyde* and more Sex: *The Graduate*. All of them utilizing Art Cinema's language for narrative clarity, like letting the camera, the soundtrack, the costumes, the location, the lighting and even the omniscient authorial commentary tell the story without words. *No Subtitles Necessary* is a great documentary about cinematographers like Vilmos Zsigmond and Laszlo Kovacs, from Hungary, who not only spoke this bicultural language, but let their cameras be "the poetic and bicultural third voice." If this book has an underlying thesis discovered while researching the project, I propose that what Kesey and the Eugene Poetic [underground] Cinema community he inspired helped us to better understand, is that before the beginning (before the word) was consciousness. The literary theory deconstructionists like Walter Benjamin, Jacques Derrida, Paul de Man, Peter de Bolla and Raymond Williams all danced around this word *consciousness*. And like them, when Ken Kesey tried to interpret this culture, (like everyone who tries to talk about archetype) he could "speak of it only in myth and allegory;" such as he did when writing *One Flew Over the Cuckoo's Nest* (1962).

In a nutshell, by looking to Plato for understanding the turning points of eons, to the poet Yeats to envision its timing, to Jung to unpack it symbolically and give it a name it, to Northrup Frye to see and understand it through Yeats' poetry, we can see how Ken Kesey later embodied Yeats' revolt against the Intellect. After all, it was The Age of Reason that had caused it, the post-industrial world, and the eve of mass of destruction during WWI, when man first murdered millions using machines, and escalated in WWII. Kesey took up that battle cry and as a new Meta-modernist, led us away from scientific logic and returned us to magic with archaic symbolism and ritual through the use of ancient modes of accessing primordial consciousness. As I said before, "As above, so below," because these events were all predicted by ancient astrological configurations, as if the Universe was indeed intelligence and had mathematically pre-ordained our generation as an anathema to the former ones. No other generation had been exposed to space travel and sub-atomic particles like this at the same time. And as a result of drug use we were able to grasp things like Unified Field theories of quantum mechanics; as was portrayed, using a Cinematic trope, "The Universe in a thumbnail" as in *Animal House*.

I started learning about this at the University of Oregon in the 80s when I worked on "The Annual Physics Super High Energy Conference" with the University of Oregon's Institute of Theoretical Science, and then with Dr. Linda Ettinger and her husband, Dr. Curt Lind coordinating conferences and filming debates on the ethics of Artificial Intelligence.

But it was Kesey who first helped us interpret this 1960s Platonian and Neo-Platonian "emanation from the Universe," that reigns over an "aeon or aion or eon"; as well as participating in fulfilling the prophesy of the Hopi Indians (*"This is the Eighth Sign:* You will see many youth, who wear their hair long like my people, come and join the tribal nations, to learn their ways and wisdom...")[8] and he even helped answer the rhetorical question from the final line of William Butler Yeats' *Second Coming*: "And what rough beast, its hour come round at last, Slouches towards Bethlehem to be born?"[9] And the answer is The Metamorphosized Sphinx. From animal to human to Jung's Paraclete.[10]

The youth movement was also fueled by Ken Kesey's Acid Trips, that Ken began in the Bay Area in 1962 (3 years after volunteering "to take part in a CIA-financed study named Project MKULTRA at the Menlo Park Veterans Hospital" in 1959) where he was given peyote and LSD. Kesey then continued to take the drugs while attending Stanford University, and said that the first chapter of *One Flew Over the Cuckoo's Nest* was written on Peyote, especially the mixed-race Indian who narrated the story. When the chemist Owsley manufactured LSD-25, private "Acid Trips" began with the Merry Pranksters, who then decided for the publishing of Kesey's second novel, *Sometimes a Great Notion,* they would take an "Intrepid Trip" to New York in 1964, in a Psychedelic-painted school bus. Upon returning, they organized the first of the "Acid Tests" at Ken Babbs' house on November 27th, 1965 with The Warlocks, who soon became the Grateful Dead.

LSD ART exploded, psychedelic bands blossomed, and filmmakers from San Francisco State were right there filming it. Soon, loving collectives began to foster collaboration, like the biggest psychedelic poster artists: Wes Wilson, Stanley Mouse, Alton Kelley, and Rick Griffin, who worked together to create the Haight/Ashbury Ballroom Music Posters, some of them worth more than $100,000 today. Rusty Goldman was born and raised in San Francisco, had a "Big Brother" who was involved in the scene, became a collector of these posters ever since he was 15. He was so knowledgeable about them that one of the Big 5 Artists, Wes Wilson named him Professor Poster, and he had this to say: "When the Music's finally finished and the crowd is all long gone.... Within the posters lie the memory that linger and live on ... "[11]

These bands that Rusty hung out with performed together at the Monterey Pop Festival, Woodstock, played on each other's albums, and for free especially for benefits like The Diggers Collective, who fed and nursed the young masses flocking to the Bay Area.

Honey Green was also there in 1965. She told me recently: "I was just fascinated with the idea of California, the beats and jazz, the politics. I always liked rock music as well. It was in 1965 that I met Bill Graham and became his first secretary, as my husband worked for him. I was a paralegal, got off work early and went to the Fillmore Auditorium. Bill asked me if I knew how to write a press release. Boom, I had a new job. Anyway I remained good friends with Bill for years." After 12 years, she found a new passion: "In 1977 I went to work for the Haight/Ashbury Free Medical Clinic for David Smith, the founder. During the next 12 years I worked all of Bill's shows as Rock Medicine, medical teams, and we always took time to talk about ourselves, our children, etc. Bill was very connected also to The Committee here in SF."[12] This kind of collaboration was everywhere, and film was at the heart of it all, documenting it. The film collective, Canyon Cinema was lucky enough to have my friend Loren Sears involved. Loren was an early computer engineer who became known for inventing the optical printer, and his films were recently shown at Cannes to celebrate their 50th Anniversary. Many of these films became important, documenting Native Tribes as well as the San Francisco scene in 1967.

Loren called them *Tribal Home Movies*[13] for a reason ... the American Indian Ethic inspired us: its ritual, spirituality, tolerance for people of all cultures, revered feminism, love and respect for the Earth, communal living, strong family values, and colorful creativity. Its culture embraced archaic songs, drums, totems, even occasional plant-based drug use and wisdom handed down from the eons. The infamous Lakota tribal member Russell Means, my dear friend, actor and musician (from the Pine Ridge Reservation; the first National Director of AIM, the American Indian Movement) used to call this ethic "The Great Mystery." It was that Great Mystery that my generation was looking for. And we found it, too, in Yeatsian symbolism and deconstructive language and poetry, that informed and created Poetic Cinema. Stan Brakhage tried to discuss this bicultural linguisticity when he said: "Imagine an eye untutored by man-made laws of perspective, an eye unprejudiced by compositional logic, an eye which does not respond to the name of everything, but which must know each object encountered in life through an adventure of perception ... imagine a world before (in the) beginning was the word."[14]

My theory is that Kesey and the Poetic Cinema Movement that he helped inspire allows us to perceive that which was before "in the beginning was the word," and that it was consciousness. And that consciousness was The Great Mystery which called to us. And expressed through us, through our music, our art, our lifestyles and our cinema. And that the 60s was just a beginning, just a window, to now, and that now and the immediate future is going to only be interpretable through this 60s bi-cultural voice, the "Metaphors of Vision" that is Yeatsian in its symbolism, and Shelley-like in its radical aestheticism. We hope it will overcome the bastardization *of the word* by human *unconsciousness*; during this Tower moment in history; this Babelian time when no one can understand each other, from all of the media spins of words, manipulated by money, of the very meanings of words, rendering most of them incomprehensible. There is a reason why young people are on a social platform that limits words to 240 characters; and on the primarily visual Snapchat, Facebook, and Instagram. They are tired of words. But every picture tells a story.

The truth is that we cannot separate images from consciousness, and we cannot manipulate words without consequences. They must be re-connected to the symbolism that birthed them. Which is why it is going to take the bicultural to straddle the gap between the archaic and the quantum future – the Alpha and the Omega – the primitive symbol and the quantum word; which requires a third language to bridge that gap, and a bicultural generation to find the equivalent of this "lost chord" of harmony between the linear word that is heard and seen and the visual that is seen and felt; the 1000 miles between the intellect and the heart. I want to help that happen by writing this book.

I hope you enjoy reading it as much as I did in writing it.

Katherine Wilson
03/30/21

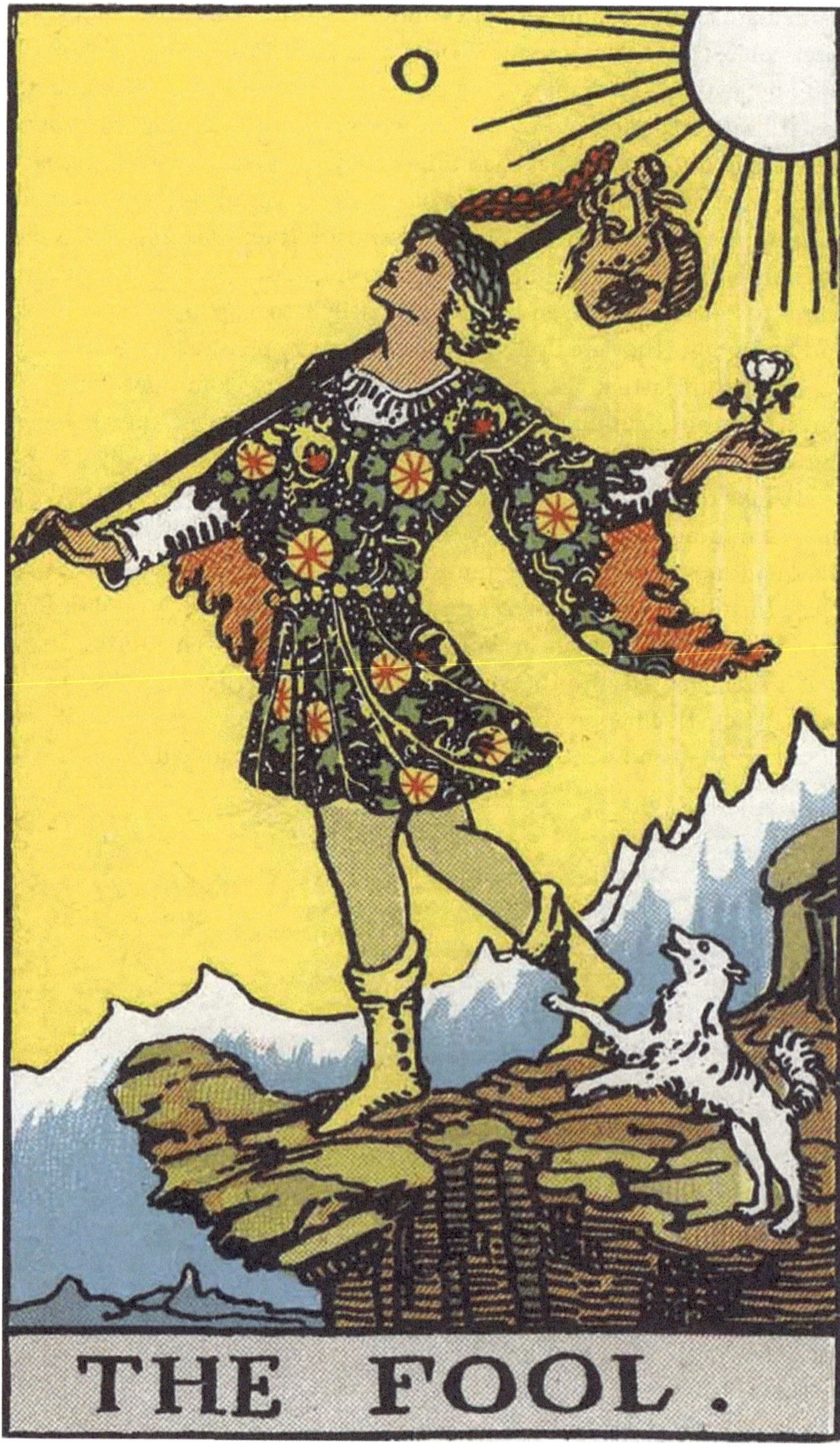

The Fool[15]

Chapter 0

The Archetype of the '60s Generation

What has most astonished me in even this most superficial study of Yeats's use of the symbolism of magic acquired through the Hermetic Society of the Golden Dawn is the great background of undisclosed knowledge from which he wrote. He gave away no secrets of the Order; and yet he used continually a method won by long and hard work in a language studied today by few, but intrinsically valid, and which will therefore outlast the ignorance of the time. Even since Yeats pursued truths in his time and in our own so unfashionable, that revolt of the soul against intellect which he himself predicted has manifested itself in many ways, and at the time of writing wears the aspect, even, of revolution among the younger generation, prepared to take the archetypal world by storm.

Truths so vital, so intrinsic to our very nature, cannot with impunity be denied. Jung wrote that "consciousness torn from its roots and no longer able to appeal to the authority of the primordial images, possesses a Promethean freedom, it is true, but it also partakes of the nature of a godless hybris.

– Kathleen Raine, *Yeats, The Tarot, and The Golden Dawn*[16]

Yes, it's true. We were like the Fool. My generation packed a knapsack and stuck out our thumbs hitch-hiking, and then stepped off the cliff into a different dimension when we heard a calling, a deep, resonating feeling that we needed to leave the life we had known and travel to San Francisco to find a new way of being in the world. Our childhoods in America were so full of trauma, we did not want to inherit the world. There had to be a better way. And we found it. We are still finding it. While the world rages on in post-industrial post-modernism, we have opted out. But I don't think we would have ever stepped off the cliff, if we weren't pushed by the Cuban Missile Crisis, sending us as chil-

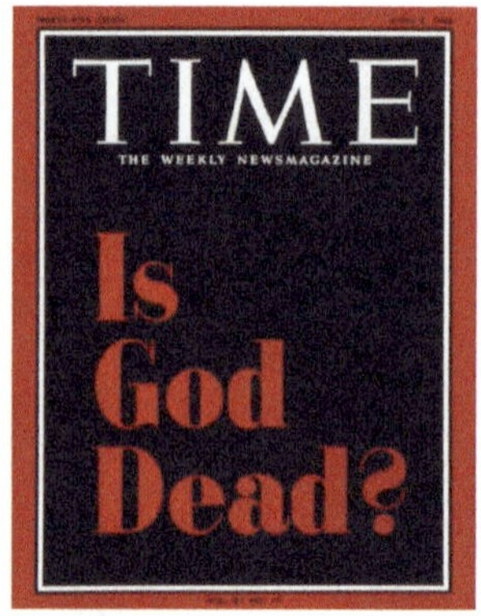

dren to create makeshift nuclear bomb shelters in our basements in 1962; by the murder of our heroes, John F. Kennedy, 1963; Martin Luther King, 1968; and Robert Kennedy; 1968, then the government drafting our classmates to die in the Vietnam war starting in 1961; our total disbelief in our own government after the Warren Commission Report was released in 1964; and the cover of *Time* magazine rhetorically asking us if "Is God Dead?" in 1966.[17]

Years later I found out that the *Time* magazine headline was a result of philosophical discussions in Europe, notably one provoked by Friedrich Nietzsche in 1882, and one that totally makes sense to me.

> Nietzsche used the phrase to sum up the effect and consequence that the Age of Enlightenment had had on the centrality of the concept of God within Western European civilization, which had been essentially Christian in character since the later Roman Empire. The Enlightenment had brought about the triumph of scientific rationality over sacred revelation; the rise of philosophical Materialism and Naturalism that to all intents and purposes had dispensed with the belief in or role of God in human affairs and the destiny of the world. Nietzsche recognized the crisis that this "Death of God" represented for existing moral assumptions in Europe as they existed within the context of traditional Christian belief.[18]
>
> When one gives up the Christian faith, one pulls the right to Christian morality out from under one's feet. This morality is by no means self-evident ... By breaking one main concept out of Christianity, the faith in God, one breaks the whole: nothing necessary remains in one's hands."[15] This is why in "The Madman," a passage which primarily addresses nontheists (especially atheists), the problem is to retain any system of values in the absence of a divine order.

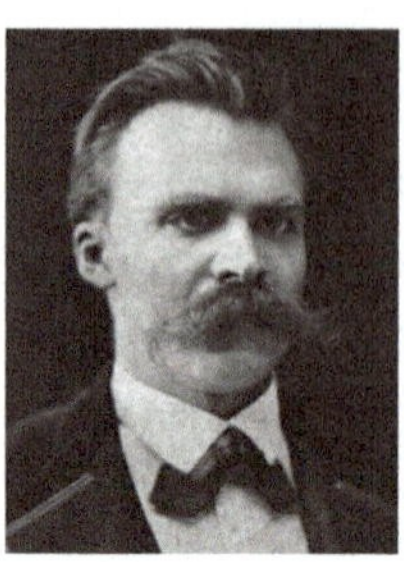
Nietzsche

> God is dead. God remains dead. And we have killed him. How shall we comfort ourselves, the murderers of all murderers? What was holiest and mightiest of all that the world has yet owned has bled to death under our knives: who will wipe this blood off us? What water is there for us to clean ourselves? What festivals of atonement, what sacred games shall we have to invent? Is not the greatness of this deed too great for us? Must we ourselves not become gods simply to appear worthy of it?[19]

This "Age of Enlightenment" was so misnamed, that we ended up calling it "The Age of Reason" and it was exactly what Yeats was revolting against in this quote in 1892:

> The mystical life is the centre of all that I do & all that I think & all that I write. It holds to my work the same relation that the philosophy of Godwin held to the work of Shelley & I have always considered myself a voice of what I believe to be a greater renaissance- the revolt of the soul against the intellect – now beginning in the world.[20]

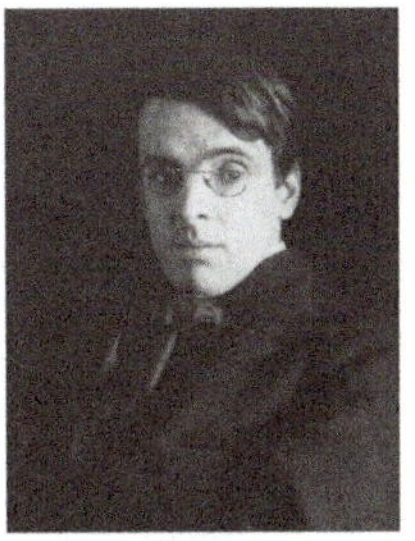

Yeats

Yeats' revolt was our revolt, Percy Blythe Shelley's poetry was our poetry, and William Godwin's philosophy was our philosophy, that of Anarchism.[21] Godwin was a publisher who married Mary Wollstonecraft. Their daughter, Mary Wollstonecraft Godwin, would marry the poet Shelley and then write *Frankenstein; or Modern Prometheus.* Her father William Godwin was a brilliant thinker, as was his wife, who wrote "The Vindications of Women" as a proto-feminist; but their daughter had both of their brilliances and wrote *Frankenstein* as an indictment of post-industrialism, as well as an indictment of the patriarchal imbalance, of denying the feminine intellect, and by trying to play God as Nietzsche had predicted. "Shelley's (Mary Wollstonecraft) works often argue that cooperation and sympathy, particularly as practiced by women in the family, were the ways to reform civil society."[21]

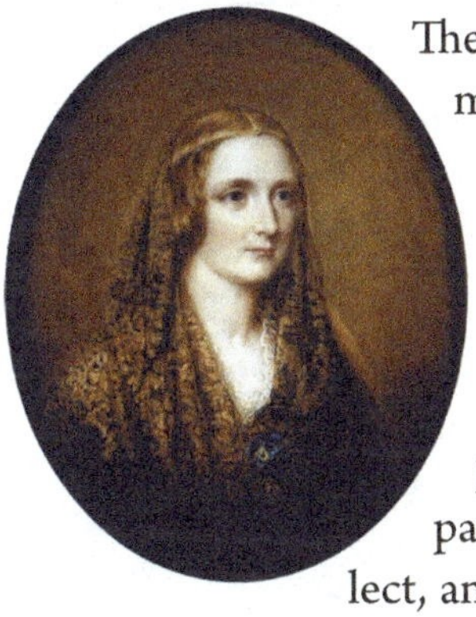

So, given the hell we were living in then, I stuck my thumb out underneath the "Weed/San Francisco" sign at the west end of Main Street where it joined Highway 97, in the town I was born in, Klamath Falls, Oregon; late November 1966. My Mom had left me and my Dad and my brothers and sister the week before. I was the oldest, 15, and had "complex" PSTD from growing up there, in a County with the most murders per capita in the nation for 6 years in a row, and when I was 5, had inadvertently watched my neighbor murder his wife over an argument about tuning in a different radio station in the car, next door. There

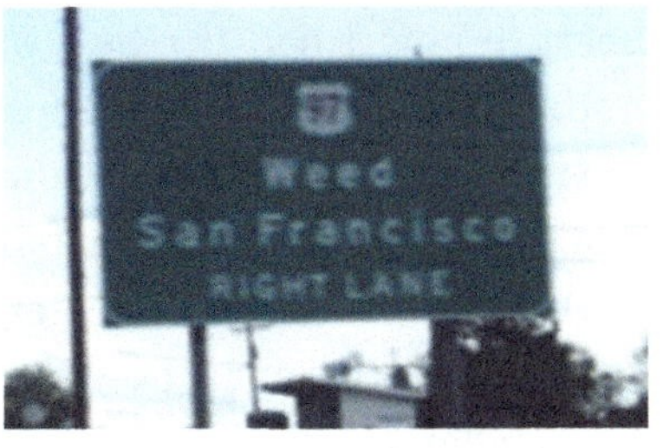

were 13 murders in one year in the tiny (500 people) American Indian Reservation town of Chiloquin, which was boarded up from the Government's Termination of the Klamath and Modoc Tribes, all of which broke my heart. But on that particular day in 1966, the cops picked me up trying to hitch-hike, and took me back down East Main street to Klamath Union High School, (which looked like a prison with a moat around it) and left me in the care of Hazel Todd, the School Dean.

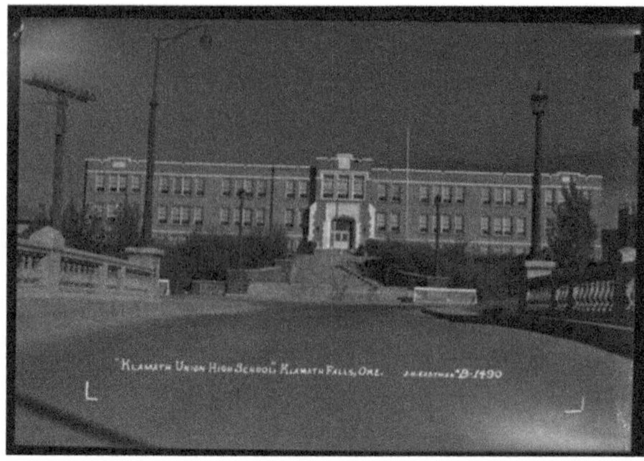

A few months later, things had become so bad at home I even decided to pray. My family's church was close to my high school. It was empty on a school day, and I went in, terrified. But I prayed. This act restored a faith I never really knew I had, because my prayers were answered when my Mom got in a car wreck, got the flu, and it made her come back. But I think it was under Mom's one condition, and that was that we moved to Eugene, near where her Dad and his 1870 family farm was. So I was then enrolled at South Eugene High School. And it turned out to be a much better way to get to San Francisco, to go North in order to go South; because now I had the best of both worlds, friends that took me to The City for shows at the Avalon, Fillmore, Matrix and Berkeley Community Theater, and in the Summer between High School and College, July 8th, 1969; Ken Kesey's Psychedelic Bus came by and I got on. San Francisco had come to me.

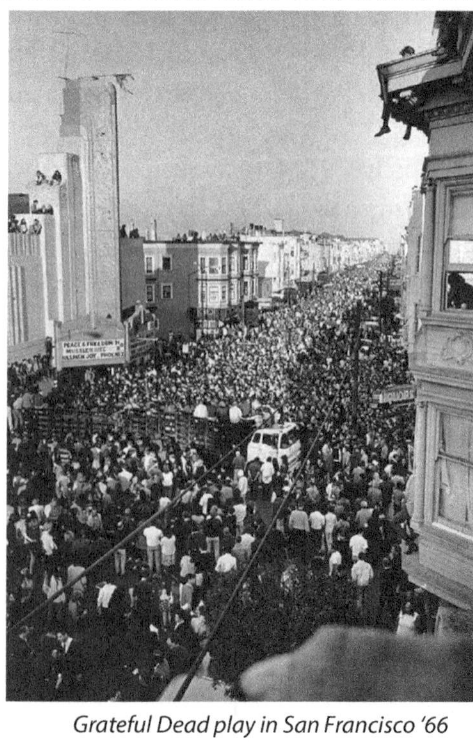

Grateful Dead play in San Francisco '66

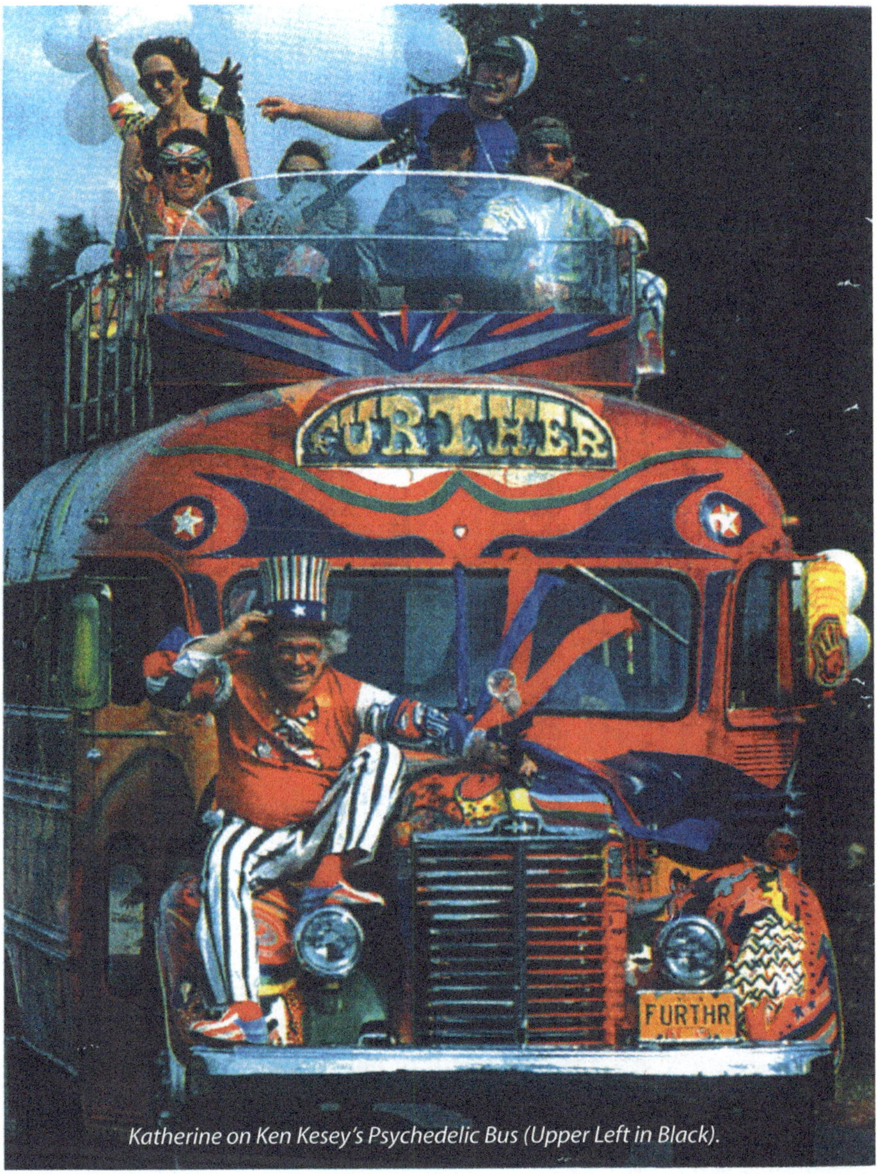

Katherine on Ken Kesey's Psychedelic Bus (Upper Left in Black).

This is my story, as seen through the eyes of an indigenous mixed breed bicultural on one side and a 6th generation settler colonial Oregonian on the other; who could sense that this step off the cliff would eventually realize all of her dreams from following that call; even leading her to future self, an archaic and quantum fueled filmmaker; one who worked with the 60s shadows from the underground to partake of a cinema under the influence of a force field that had called us to its own light. The light of a Platonic Aeon emerging from the 2000-year Piscean Age, the "widening gyre" of Aquarius.

> This phase must be brought to understand by *what means it has knowledge* of the thing it sees and warrant for what it affirms: if it became what it affirms, it would by that fact possess self-knowing. All its vision and affirmation being in the Supreme or deriving from it- There where itself also is – it will possess self-knowledge by its right as a Reason-Principle, claiming its kin and bringing all into accord with the divine imprint upon it.
>
> – Plotinus[22]

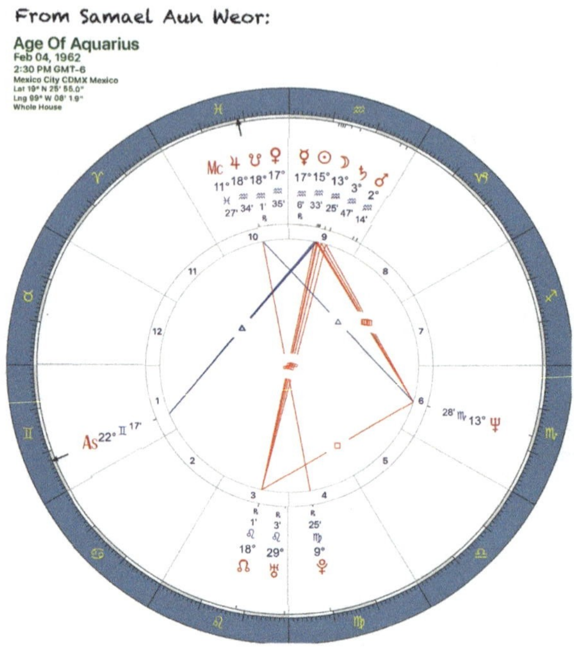

Our 60s generation was born[23] into a culture symbolically encoded with iconic images of both the atom and rockets to outer space; and as a result of being exposed to both the subatomic science that created the Nuclear Cuban Missile Crisis and the astrophysicist's skill in navigating the vastness of space (as accomplished in the Moon Landing) you could say that in trying to grasp such a vastness, we were forced to embrace a quantum level of what might be called consciousness.

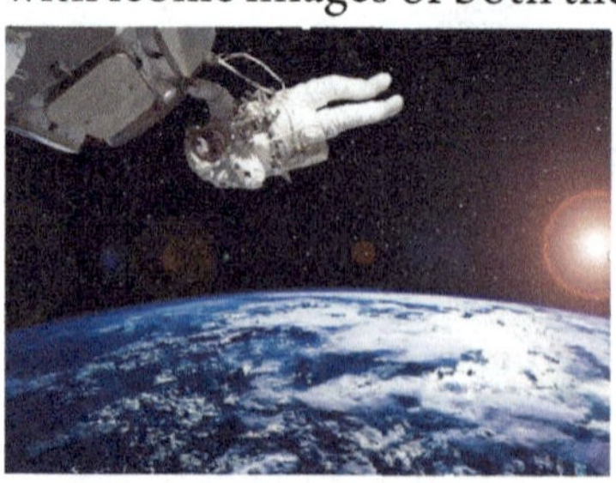

Like our ancient forefathers, (especially since we watched the skies a lot in the 60s) we looked to the skies to not only warily watch out for Armageddon, but to try to understand and interpret this thing called consciousness; specifically in the context of newer theoretical science and quantum mechanics, like the Heisenberg Principle of Uncertainty and the Higgs-Bosun; as well as those interpretations found in the I Ching, ancient religions like Buddhism, Hinduism, or even Religious Science; as well as prophesies and more archaic ways of understanding like Astrology, the *Egyptian Book of the Dead,* the Hopi Prophesies, the Tarot and Shamanic Psychotropic drug use, etc. that were also all about consciousness.

Literary theorist Raymond Williams seems to talk about this very thing in his "Dominant Residual and Emergent" theory when he was discussing how difficult it was for a new "culture" like ours to emerge during a Dominant mode like the 50s because: "... there is always other social being and consciousness which is neglected and excluded: alternative perceptions of others, in immediate relationships; new perceptions and practices of the material world." His theory is important because I hope to show how the pre- emergent 60s had not yet become dominant, nor is it now residual. It is just now beginning to widen as a gyre of time. Which means it is pre-emergent. Something that we need what Williams calls a "structure of feeling" to understand. Here is the structure:"[24,25]

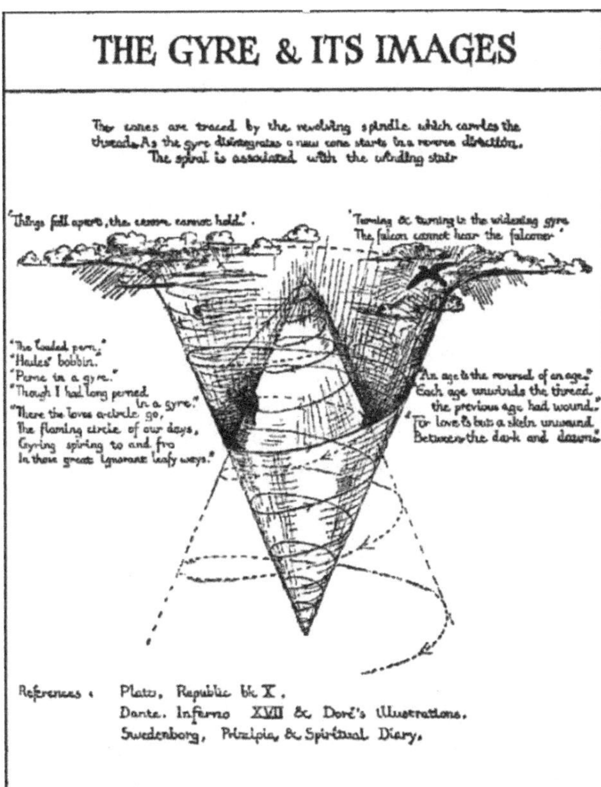

"The door to physical awareness comes through spiraling consciousness, gyres, if you will. Reality is simplicity, synchronicity, and simultaneity. Souls sometimes feel chosen … their mission echoing through the gyres from source consciousness."[26]

But at the time, in the early 60s when it was at its narrowest point, just a pin-prick coming from Pre-emergence, and not yet visible; and given that Quantum Mechanics was so rarefied in its understanding; we found that astrology provided a few ways that were helpful to understand what exactly it was that we were feeling; because it was also what helped us to find that elusive meaning, just like Yeats had found, and gave us what Literary deconstructionist Raymond Williams called "a structure of feeling,"[27] to describe it.

This curiosity was indeed induced and fostered by a certain feeling, a phenomenon that felt like an emanation of the Universe strongly calling from the future, the heavens, or perhaps even from the archaic past. I do not use the word feeling lightly, because feelings are not facts in the Post-industrial world, and cannot be used as proof in a court of law for instance, and therefore not very academic, but this is what Williams said in 1977:

> What matters, finally, in understanding emergent culture, as distinct from both the dominant and the residual, is that it is never only a matter of immediate practice; indeed it depends crucially on finding new forms or adaptations of form. Again and again what we have to observe is in effect a pre-emergence, active and pressing but not yet fully articulated, rather than the evident emergence which could be more confidently named. It is to understand more closely this condition of pre-emergence, as well as the more evident forms of the emergent, the residual, and the dominant, that we need to explore the concept of structures of feeling.[28]

It was also similar to the word "feeling," as another Literary theorist, de Bolla used, for "…intense moments of aesthetic experience" which "feel as if they are in the orbit of knowing, as if something has been barely whispered yet somehow heard."[29]

A current best-selling author and *NYT* Book Reviewer Sheila Weller recalled this particular feeling as "a high whistle audible only to hidden soulmates" by which "seekers in their 20s started moving to San Francisco."[23] Many of my friends and I can also agree with Stanley, a famous Rock-n-Roll Poster maker of the 60s, who said this about the feeling Weller describes:

> "Heading for the Bay Area was like a calling; it was very strong," says Stanley Mouse, a shy, rebellious painter of hot rods from Detroit. As he was crossing the Golden Gate Bridge, a friend with him asked, "How long you staying?" Mouse answered, "Forever."[30]

It was the artists, musicians, poets and philosophers, as always, who first heard that voice, that beat, that new archetype of expression emerging throughout the culture; artists like William Butler Yeats, who in his 1919 poem "Second Coming"; had predicted an event he believed would begin 50 years before the postmillennial 2000-year epoch of time, which was around 1962. Other expressions were from the Philosopher Nietzsche who declared "God is dead" even in the heydays of postmillennialism's eschatological faith in the 1950s; and from the more scientific thinkers who also predicted our Postmodernist Age 100 years before its arrival, like German Philosopher Karl Marx when he wrote "A spectre is haunting Europe."[31]

Marx's linguistic theory is encapsulated with this quote by Franco Moretti in *Dialectic of Fear*: "That 'must,' which for Marx is a scientific prediction of the nineteenth century bourgeois culture. The literature of terror (Frankenstein and Vampires) is born precisely out of the terror of a split society, and out of the desire to heal it."[32]

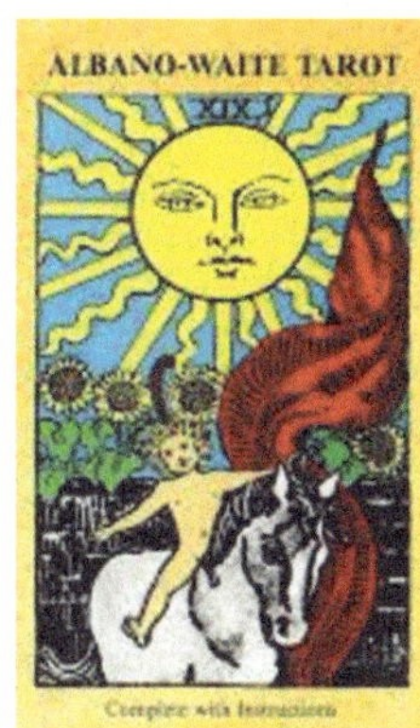

Yeats, who had been initiated in the Hermetic Order of the Golden Dawn, defied Marx's dialectics, however; and instead returned to the Platonic and Neo-platonic ancient theories of Aeons; including Egyptian ritual,27 and symbolism such as in "The Tarot deck created by A. E. Waite, (which) had been designed for the use of members of the Hermetic Society of the Golden Dawn, of which both Waite and Pamela Coleman-Smith (who executed the emblems) were members."[33]

As for the artists around the time of our generation's Grandfathers (when Yeats wrote "Second Coming") the Expressionist painters created "content by contradiction;"[34] filmmakers were making *The Golem (1920)*; and it seemed that around WWI, the whole world went into shock, and embraced Abstract Art. No wonder our parents' generation invented *Denny's* and loved the 1964 World's Fair which highlighted a totally plastic "Futurama" house with atomic aeriated food in the kitchen. But for some reason, we youth were not buying into that mass-manufactured culture. I propose a few theories as to why, below; because I believe the following is what created our generation and our art: recent epigenetics and DNA scientific experiments hint that what we have ancestral memory. Once again, science is embarrassed that what tribal people like John Trudell, have said all along is true:

> One of the objectives of this technologic reality has to do with erasing the memories of the human beings, because we have a common collective experience. We are all the descendants of tribes. Because we have ancestral memory. It's encoded in the DNA - it's a genetic memory...[35]

In the documentary *Reel Injuns* Trudell elucidates on the quote above by saying: "They (the hippies) were in a way trying to imitate us, but in another way they were trying to remember who they were. A time in their ancestry when they wore feathers, all right, wore beads, and shells. There was a time in their ancestry, all right, before this colonizing mentality, ... they are the descendants of Tribes."[36]

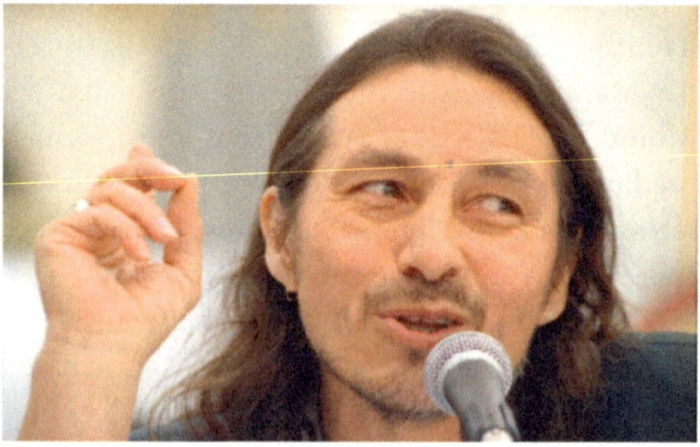

John Trudell Santee Dakota-American Poet, Author, Actor.

I believe that several things came together in the 60s to create in us this return (not unlike Yeats, or the Romantics did; perhaps even instinctively, but perhaps instinct IS ancestral memory) to archaic ways of understanding, expressing and surviving our culture. I owe this theory in part to literary critics Northrup Frye's work about Yeats, and Leslie Fiedler's about Kesey, in *Return of the Vanishing American*, published in January of 1967.

This new way of living was born in fertile soil, because San Francisco had always been a bit Bohemian historically, especially its Barbary Coast near North Beach, where prostitution, drug-dealing, alcohol and organized crime reigned during the turn-of-the-century. But even after it burned down in 1906 and was cleaned up, it still had something going on underground, perhaps something like an aura; a certain something that had called the Beat Poets there, even earlier than us. And in the Summer of 1967, an estimated 75,000 young people heard the same call to San Francisco and arrived enmasse. There were already an estimated 10,000 local concert goers alone at Kesey's Trip Festival in January of 1966. It is not hard to imagine how many other people had arrived since then, nor how many were not able to come to San Francisco, but were there in "spirit" or in consciousness. Two years later, as Joni Mitchell sang, "By the time we got to Woodstock" (in 1969) "we were half a million strong."[37] I, myself, had tried to hitchhike from Klamath Falls, Oregon to San Francisco the fall of 1966 when I was 15, and not just because of my personal life. In 1966, near my early home on the Klamath and Modoc Reservation, grief had taken its full toll as the Tribe was terminated by the US Government, and the tiny neighboring reservation town of Chiloquin, where I lived when I was 4, 5, & 6, was boarded up, and the Indians at my high school were snorting Watershed, a Boot Lacquer, to get high and numb the pain.

The year before, in 1965, the Native American Church was finally allowed to use its Peyote in its rituals.[38] Two years before that, in 1963, three men attended one of these ancient rituals with Indians who lived in the Comstock Hills of Central California, directly East from San Francisco, and said they came out of the ceremony "totally changed." However, even before that, in 1959, four years before the first San Franciscans went to the Comstock to partake of Peyote (and inadvertently start the Red Dog Saloon;) Ken Kesey, while attending Stanford University (after graduating from the University of Oregon) became a research subject for the CIA's MKULTRA program, and clinically ingested peyote, psilocybin, mescaline and LSD-25. He wrote *One Flew Over the Cuckoo's Nest* as a result, and it was released in January of 1962 to world-wide acclaim. Just two years later, after he wrote *Sometimes a Great Notion*, he is quoted by his Sky-Pilot friend Ken Babbs in his new unpublished book called *Cronies, a Burlesque*: "What happened, Ken, after you finished *Notion*? Were you burned out on writing?"

"Not that so much. I had proved myself once and then proved myself twice and so I asked myself what do I have to prove now? The answer was, prove nothing."

"You still write, then?"

"I'm not a writer anymore. I'm a storyteller. I use the tools of music and magic, of fire and smoke and smarting eyes. Nature abhors a hollow frame and if story doesn't fill that space, Pepsi will. And Chevrolet. And

Ronald McDonald. This is war, and story is one of our weapons. The innocent heart is the prize we battle for."[39]

Like Yeats, Kesey was an adept magician. And just like Kesey, who said that his writing was just one way he practiced magic,[40] Yeats was known for similar sentiments. "For Yeats, magic was not so much a kind of poetry, as poetry was a kind of magic, and the object of both alike was evocation of energies and knowledge from beyond normal Consciousness."[41]

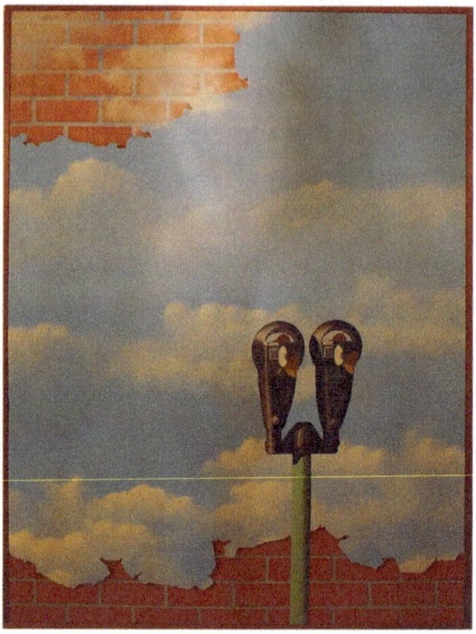

Painting by Philip Krysl

As for Kesey's impact on culture and our generation, Rick Dodgson sums it up nicely:

> The wave that Kesey rode in the sixties turned out to be a massive force for cultural change, one that washes over American society still. It has been more than fifty years since the decade dawned, and yet it still divides us, drawing a line across American society whether people know it or not. When conservatives speak of the culture war, it is the counterculture that they have in their sights. The conservative movement of the last forty years has been, in part, a generational backlash against the sixties and everything that the hippies stood for. But this movement is essentially a rearguard action attempting to recover lost ground with few prospects of success.[42]

Dodgson goes on talk about how if the Culture war was over, the hippies won. There is a yoga studio on every Main Street, the progressive values of America are Counter-cultural, Rock Music is now elevator music and marijuana is everywhere.

But more importantly, Dodgson shows how indelibly our generation countered our parents culture and made huge inroads into the change we wanted to see.

> Hippie values may not be the norm in every house- hold or every region of the country, but the fact that they exist as viable alternatives to traditional ways of thinking is an indication of their ultimate victory.[43]

Reading this is heady stuff for someone who thought our generation had failed the world because our Millennial children thought so. But then again, Rick Dodgson wrote this in 2013 when Obama was President, long before the Insurrection. We knew that the dawn of the Age of Aquarius would still bring up more darkness. We are not there yet, past all of it. Upon "furthur" reflection, the *je ne sais quoi* energy we felt and tried to interpret in our art in the early 60s has not really been made manifest, yet. It feels like the former period was just a beginning, to what is coming. The signal is getting stronger. More is being revealed.

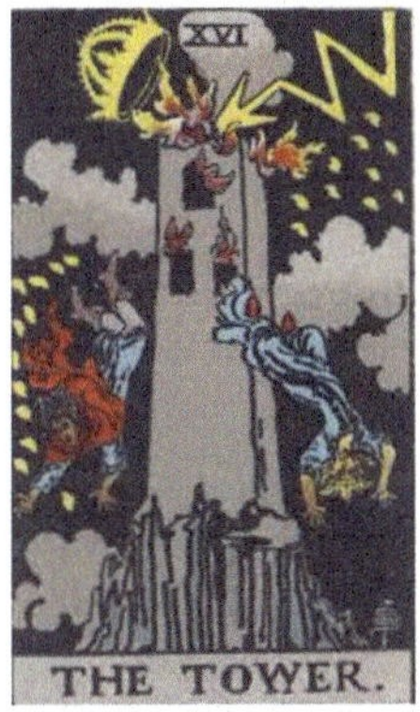

And as Yeats might tell you, we are still living in a Tower time, because such darkness always precedes the dawning, especially, of the New Age.[44]

And, the rather psychedelic 60s and 70s New Criticism or Deconstructionist Theories, although being taught, finally, in Academia, are still being fought by Professors in English on College Campuses. Form is still more important than content. Like me, U of O educated Hollywood alumni Stephen J. Cannell and Ken Kesey struggled in college because of it. Communication and Cinema Studies, Creative Writing and Contemporary Literary Theory professors saved us. I believe it is the dysfunctional, dyslexic, and/or poetic mind that can create 3D worlds in art, film, and literature. And can also understand theories, sometimes, because they too, seem to be created and understood in the third dimension.

Ken Kesey was not Postmodernist at all, but a Meta-modernist[45] (as Seth Abrahamson coined the phrase) an artist who heard the calling of the future age, and was able to express it by returning to Archaic modes of representation in his literature, using them in *One Flew Over the Cuckoo's Nest* and *Sometimes a Great Notion*; those very modes of representation that Literary Critic Leslie Fiedler found, which was the gestalt of the archaic psychedelics informing American Indian consciousness in his groundbreaking book, *The Return of the Vanishing American*. Kesey's books were coined "The New (Psychedelic) Western" by Fiedler, and not only did they create the "New Western Film" (Walter Hill said all of his movies were westerns, including Aliens) but they created a new culture that embraced the return of the vanishing American Indian's ways, some of which were contemporary tribal traditions such as circular time, community, and some more archaic, such as a reverence for Nature; including Her medicinal properties, and the mold and plant-based sacred ritual. The biculturality Kesey was exposed to in Oregon, his familial Oklahoma heritage, and his experiences with the local natives here were the perfect storm of elements to unpack this return to the past for us to get "back to the future."

Like Ken's favorite author Zane Grey who wrote *The Vanishing American* as one of the first indictments ever against Christian colonialism, and influenced Hollywood in the early 1920s, Kesey and his bicultural New (American Indian) Western *One Flew Over the Cuckoo's Nest* influenced the Haight/Ashbury scene, the "New Cinema," the "New Hollywood," the "New Politics," the "Sexual Revolution," "Environmentalism," "Feminism," "Activism," and even literary theory through his involvement; and he inspired the underground shadows of Poetic Cinema during the 60s and 70s, including the Beat poets, who influenced experimental filmmaker Stan Brakhage.

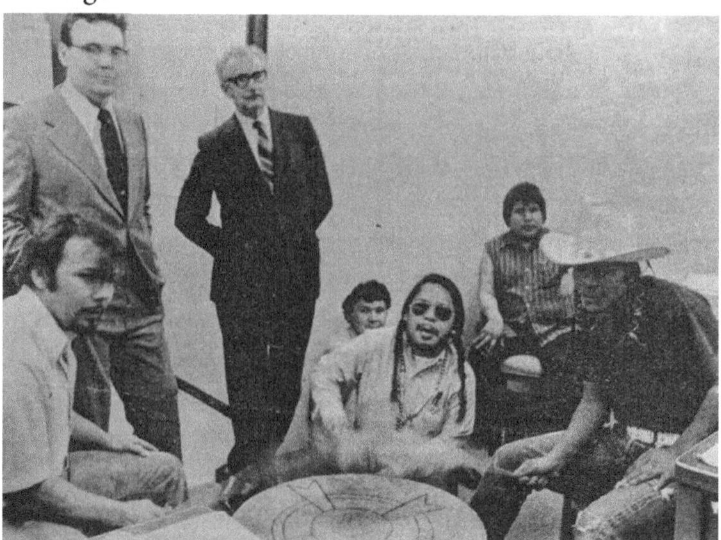

Ed Edmo occupying the Bureau of Indian Affairs.

Brakhage's close friend from CU Boulder, Professor Peter Michaelson's[46] groundbreaking books *The Aesthetics of Pornography* (1971) and *A Poetics of Obscenity* (1964) have all helped to create an academic language to unpack our Cinematic trajectory through history. I am grateful for the help of Dale Kesey, and especially my Prankster Partner Mike Hagen, (with whom I celebrated our 51-year Anniversary of being friends and filmmakers) to understand this, and also by my "Getting On The Bus," July 8th, 1969 at The U of O EMU. None of this would have been possible, either, without the prayers from my Nez Perce family, nor the encouraging support from Professors Alilunas, Rust, Bohls, Hatfield, Sayre & Pyle.

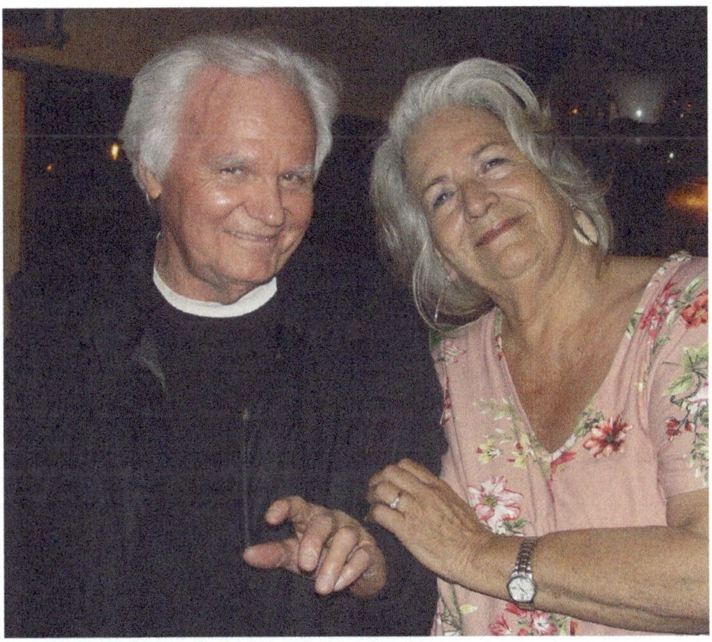

Mike Hagen and Katherine at OPB Premiere of *Animal House of Blues (2018)*

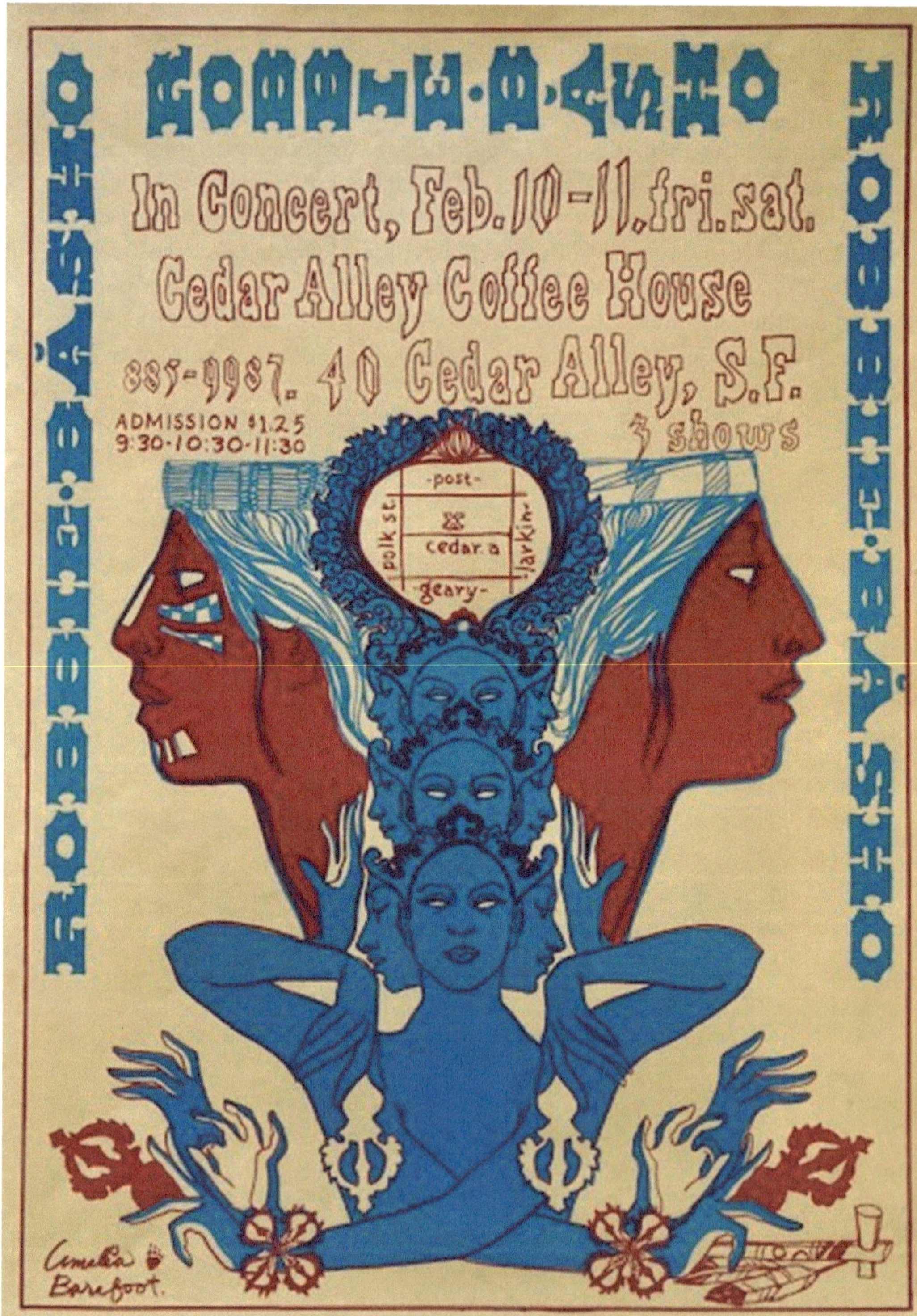

Poster by Camelia Barefoot Courtesy of Gary Westford

Chapter 1

The Subversive Shadows of the '60s Underground (1957 to 1966)

Thus we have shown that there exists that which in the strictest sense possesses self-knowing. But has our discussion issued in an Intellectual-Principle having a persuasive activity [furnishing us with probability]? No: it brings compulsion not persuasion... [47]

– Plotinus, *The Enneads*

Plato was right. In the 50s, post-industrial society's postmodernists were in a cave, and a generation was born that saw right through it. So we went out into the light and came back to try to convince our parents that the shadows on the wall were not "reality":

> In the famous image of the den, wherein mankind are the chained prisoners, with their eyes fixed upon the shadows of reality, Plato reminds us that even were our eyes opened to the upper world the light of reality would sear our vision. All that we can hope for is such intimations of the truth as we can gather from the allegory of nature.[48]

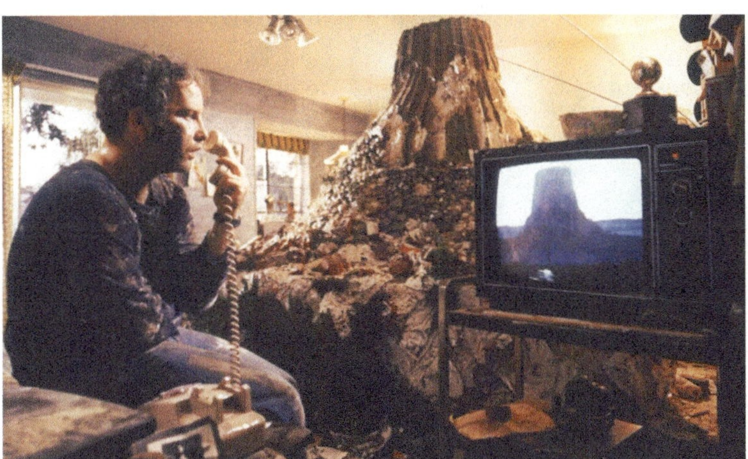

Richard Dreyfuss sees on TV the thing that has become his "Obsession."

And that was true, some of us became blinded looking at the sun and stars, but most of us turned to "the allegory of nature,"[49] for these "intimations of the truth."[50] And we found them in the building blocks of the Universe under a Microscope. As Plato also predicted, we Truth Tellers were threatening to our parents, teachers and society. So, instead, we sought to find solace in each other. But until we found each other, which back then was not so easy, our desire to know this archetype pressing against us had us making poetry and images. Because through our art, much like Richard Dreyfuss in *Close Encounters of the Third Kind,* who compulsively builds a "Mashed Potatoes Mountain"; our desire to know and express what we were experiencing first took shape.

At 11 years old, I was just like Richard Dreyfuss. On the Spring Equinox of 1963, in Jr. High, I drew this Sphinx, based on a painting called "Jaqueline Kneeling" by Picasso. You might even say I have been obsessed with The Sphinx, ever since.

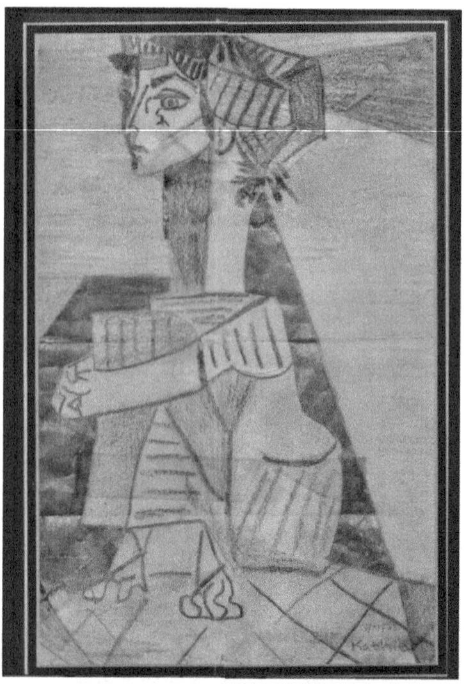

Drawing by Katherine Wilson dated 3/21/63

Imagine my surprise 42 years later in 2005; when the drawing seemed to be an exact replication of a Commemoration Ceremony and Repatriation of Bones (bones held in the Smithsonian for over 100 years) at the Bear Paw battlefield where Chief Joseph surrendered in 1877; with the native women wearing scarves, squatting, clasping their knees, and keening, against a backdrop of the pyramid-shaped Bear Paw mountains. When I first saw these mountains, while driving my best friend Etta Conner (Great-grand niece of Chief Joseph and great granddaughter of his brother, Alikut, who was killed there at Bear Paw) to our ceremony; I started weeping so hard I couldn't drive, and had to pull over. "Tacs, maii wee, la-ti-wah" she said. "You have been here before." As you look at this photo of my drawing, please also note that the Sphinx's Lioness-like feet look just like the Bear Paw shale these mountains are named for: Pyramid-like mountains, but made out of Bear Paw Shale.

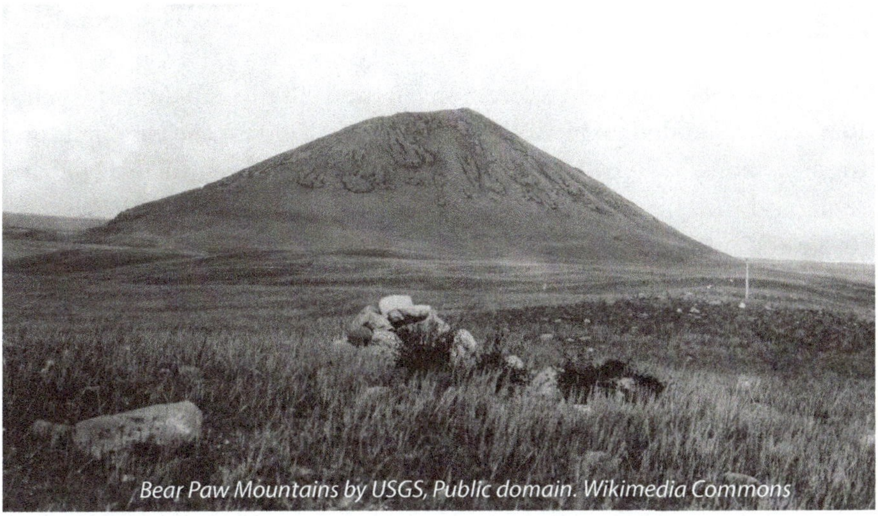

Bear Paw Mountains by USGS, Public domain. Wikimedia Commons

I had been researching a screenplay about Chief Joseph's nephew *Blanket of the Sun* with Etta ever since I had gained the Elders support in 2005. Before that, I had traveled from the Wallowas in Oregon to Big Hole, Montana several times, teaching my kids that the 1700-mile-long Lewis and Clark trail was really the Nez Perce Trail. My partner in my screenplays, Hoyt Axton, lived near there outside of Missoula, Montana. My husband had worked on *Return to Lonesome Dove* in Billings and *Don't Come Knocking* in Butte. But somehow, I could never seem to make myself go to Bear Paw. Perhaps it was because of what I experienced at Big Hole, another atrocious and murderous Battle site. Whatever I had experienced there was now being replicated and amplified at Bear Paw and was not a coincidence. They say that 3 is the lowest denominator of a pattern and

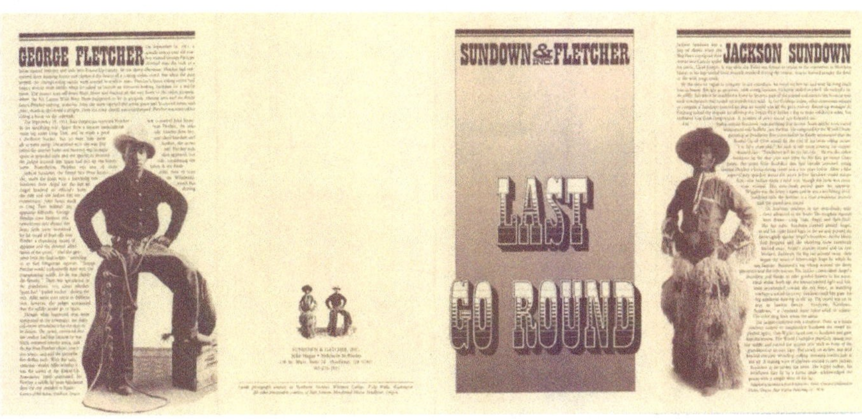

Last Go 'Round Promotional Foldout by Sundown Fletcher, Inc.
Copyrighted Text by Rick Steber.

is not a coincidence. These three powerful landscaped-based emotional reactions I had, first began when I heard that some of the Chief Joseph's Wallowa Band Elders held a ceremony in the 1990s to call their "lost children" home. I ended up in Wallowa County in 1990 for the very first time not really knowing why I was there, except possibly because in 1984 Ken Babbs and Ken Kesey had written a screenplay called "Last Go 'Round." On Feb. 22nd, 1990; I was down from Bainbridge Island, hiking on Mt. Pisgah close to Kesey's house, when "a voice" told me to call my old friend Mike Hagen. My rational mind asked why? After four years of being sober, I hadn't been on the bus, really. Besides, I doubted he had the same phone number that I had memorized years ago, and I even doubted he would be home. But when I used the pay phone at Mt. Pisgah, I found that Mikey did have the same number, and he was at home. And he told me about this screenplay idea he had brought Ken from his hometown of Pendleton; but it had been languishing on the shelf for six years. I asked if I could help to get it made. So, of course I would end up in the Wallowas, later in 1990. Because that was where Jackson Sundown was *from*. And if you are Indigenous, and want to know about someone, you know that where they are *from* is everything you need to know.

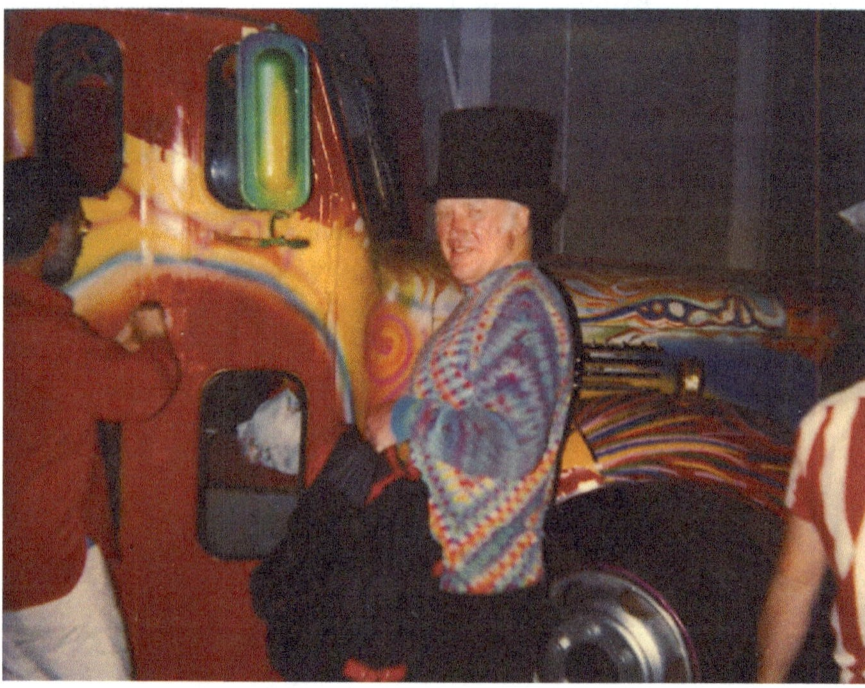

Photo of Ken Kesey by Katherine Wilson. June 1990, Las Vegas.

I picked up the screenplay from Hagen later than afternoon and read it. When I read it, I realized that Ken Kesey was not just a magician but a Literary Shaman.[51] Kesey said that his writing "was just one way he practiced magic."[52] Ken's close cousin Dale Kesey[53] said that as a child Ken was also fascinated with hypnosis, too; and once hypnotized his brother Chuck. It scared everybody, but evidently Chuck came out of it, because the brothers then used it to entertain themselves by scaring their cousins with the act. For instance, Ken would "hypnotize" Chuck into a Bear, who would roar on its hind legs and chase Dale under his bed. Ken was also a Ventriloquist, and had quite an act with his dummy. These two things remind me of Rod Serlings early *Twilight* T.V. shows from our childhood. One segment of the show I particularly remember was about a girl who hid under her bed, where a "4th wall" opened to another dimension. All of these stories contributed to thinking about that "other world" that we were all captivated by, these stories that our parents' good old logic, science and reason could never explain. So we were fascinated and wanted to find out for ourselves.

My favorite story of Dale's about Ken, however, was how as a boy, Ken got a tape recorder and taped the audio of his favorite western TV shows. One day, he invited friends over to watch one, but they did not know that Ken had turned the TV sound off, and was playing the audio from the week before. Dale said his timing was perfect, the commercials all lined up from the tape with the show, and the character's voices were the same, except it wasn't the same show. I imagine that twisted some young minds! Kesey's love for Westerns never left him. According to Steven L. Tanner in his article "The Western American Context of *One Flew Over the Cuckoo's Nest*" (from a Harold Bloom Edition of Ken Kesey's *One Flew Over the Cuckoo's Nest*):

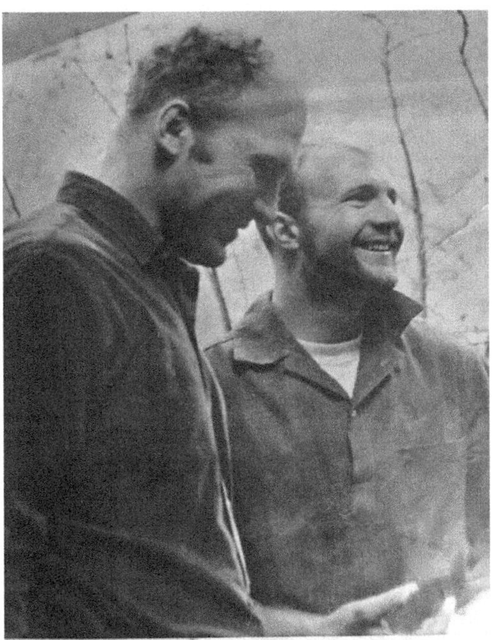

Photo of Ken Kesey and Dale Kesey courtesy of Dale Kesey

> The widow of Ernest Haycox hired him while he was at the University of Oregon to write plot summaries of her husband's novels. Haycox, a major figure in the genre, appeared in *Collier's* alone an average of thirteen times a year between 1931 and 1949 and did much to shape the nation's conception of the Western hero." Ernest Haycox, a Eugene, Oregon man, had a big movie made out of at least one of them: *Stagecoach*: The most noted of Haycox's stories, "Stage to Lordsburg" (*Collier's*, April 1937), became the basis of the landmark Western film *Stagecoach* (1939), directed by John Ford and starring John Wayne and Thomas Mitchell.[54]

This is the missing link I think, to Ken's bicultural vision, and to what I always thought, which is that being a novel writer was secondary to Ken. He majored in Speech and Communications at the U of O, wrote several screenplays, and bummed around Hollywood in the summers when school got out. It was after these summers failed to grant him any opportunities as an actor or screenplay writer that he switched his major to Creative Writing at the U of O under the tutelage of James Hall, who was known to grade his class based on creativity rather than the problematic spelling and grammar, something Ken, Stephen J. Cannell and I all struggled with and had in common.

The story that his cousin Dale told me about that first summer in college, was about how Ken came down to stay with them while Dale's Dad was trying to break into the country-western-music-band-as-entertainment market; was amazing to hear. As Dale said, Ken was an old hand at acting in his Dad's Dairy TV Commercials with his brother; so of course he would explore that aspect of his performance skills. Dale said that Ken also stayed at Dennis Hopper's house once.[55] This was all between 1954 and 1957, when Ken graduated from the U of O. "During his years in Eugene, he was a minor campus celebrity, an athlete, and an accomplished actor. In that time span, Kesey also came under the influence of the first of a series of prominent writer-teachers, James B. Hall. By 1958, when he entered Stanford University as a writing student, Kesey had completed a decent body of writing: short stories, one-act plays, poetry, and an unpublished novel about college athletics, *End of Autumn*."[56]

There is so much written about what happened next, from scholars more knowledge-able than I. However, as someone who had attended the U of O and knew him, his family, including his nephews, and his Grandmother Ophelia; there are a few things I would like to clarify. One was that James B. Hall, a prestigious professor at the U of O who taught Creative Writing, was the one who actually entered Ken's "creative" written work for consideration in the prestigious Woodrow Wilson Fellowship; but because Ken's degree was in Speech and Communications, he could not pursue a Master's degree in English Literature at Stanford. Instead, I heard that he only got to audit the writing program at first, but tried especially hard to get into it when Wallace Stegner was away on Sabbatical. As Steven Tanner seems to identify below, the goal here is to fill in the blanks of this great body of academic scholarship by perhaps contributing to the following: "...and it is likely that recent ecological approaches to literary criticism will further delineate relationships between the (*Cuckoo's Nest*) book's themes and methods and Kesey's *environmentally shaped values and frames of reference.*"[57] It is exactly this "environmentally shaped values and frames of reference" from where Kesey and I are from, a truly bicultural space; that makes us bicultural people. And what makes us bicultural is living on stolen Indian Land.

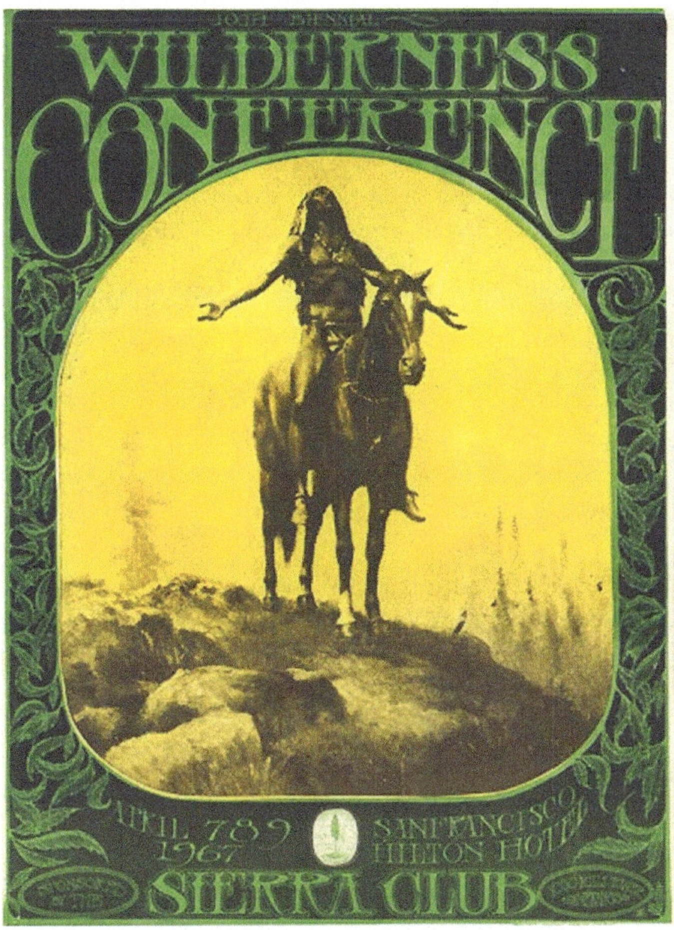

Courtesy of the Gary Westford Collection

I would also like to contribute to Tanner's idea by adding some anecdotal experiences I had with Ken over the 30+ years I knew him. When Tanner quotes Peter O. Whitmer in his *Saturday Review* article called "Ken Kesey's Search for the American Frontier," it rang a lot of bicultural bells: "Later in the same interview, when asked what interested him about himself, he said. "It's 'Why me?' What is it about me, my family, my father, this part of the country that caused it to be me who wrote *Cuckoo's Nest*? It is not something I set out to do. It's as though all the angels got together and said, 'Okay, here's the message that America desperately needs. Now, let's pick him to do it.'"[58]

Tanner's quote helps point us to those "ecological approaches to literary criticism," and especially Kesey's *environmentally shaped values and frames of reference* that I hope to illuminate. One approach is the new DNA memory research in Neuroscience, which is pointing to mine and Kesey's inherited gene pool, that for Kesey may have also included Cherokee DNA. Some tribes believe that *story* is sacred and choses whom it wants to tell the story. Ken sensed this in the quote. When he mentions his father, I think of his Grandfather, too. It also is fascinating that Jack Kerouac picked up on this as well in this quote from Tanner:

> What did Kerouac think of *Cuckoo's Nest*? In the Kesey Collection is a letter from Kerouac to Tom Ginsberg at Viking written October 19, 1961. Kerouac, who had read an advance copy of the novel, praises it highly but, perhaps because of his own autobiographical approach to writing, is convinced that the author must be the Columbia Gorge Indian himself, who used "Kesey," perhaps his wife's name, to avoid being identified with the "deafmute" hero. He says the author is certainly right about the Combine and praises the way he captures the American lingo. Kerouac even senses the flavor of "real western Indian talk" in the narration…[59]

Like Kesey, I am bicultural, a child with Grandparents from Oklahoma. However, I was living on an American Indian Reservation in Southern Oregon; not even knowing (except for vague hints from her) about my heritage until my Great Aunt died, the last keeper of the secret. My Grandmother was the Klamath Falls City Treasurer for 10 years, and would never have been hired if they knew she was even "part" Indian. We were not Klamath or Modoc, our heritage came from her family from Oklahoma. Turns out Kesey's heritage is last traced back to Oklahoma as well. Keeping mixed-race secret was a survival tactic whenever possible. There are truly a lot of us "lost children." But genetic DNA is like Blood

Quantum. It is not the definition of "belonging" to most tribes. However, DNA memory may be if it is tied to Landscape, because landscape is tied to language. And language is tied to culture, but it is only a beginning. The true bicultural is one who grew up with two cultures, sometimes as a minority in a dominant one; but no matter how minor the culture is, it still creates a liminality in the person. Biculturality is like the minority heritage being like the Gulf Stream in the dominant Atlantic Ocean of your dominant cultural heritage. The two don't mix, like oil and water. Here is a quote about it from Wikipedia. I will go into more depth about this concept later in the book, but here is a good place to start:

> In regards to bicultural identity, an individual may face conflict assimilating into both cultures or finding a balance between both. An individual may face challenges assimilating into the whole, collective culture. Similarly, an individual may face difficulty balancing their identity within themselves due to the influence of both of their cultures.
>
> Being an individual with identity plurality can be hard mentally and emotionally. The different levels of biculturalism can be defined though the way people are able to simultaneously manage their two selves. The more they alternate between them, the more cognitive complexity they face, since they avoid cultural duality and do not practice handling both cultures at the same time. It is through identity integration that they will be able to solve the problem and alleviate the tolls that come with identity plurality. Bicultural identity also may have positive effects on the individual, in terms of the additional knowledge they acquire from belonging to more than one culture. Furthermore, with the growing number of racial minorities in American society, individuals that identify with more than one culture may have more linguistic ability.[60]

According to Dale Kesey, their mutual Grandfather would be the father of Fred Kesey, Ken's father and Dale's father, Grandpa Paul. "Grandfather Kesey looked very, very Indian. My brother Jimmy is looking into our heritage."[55] This "looking into our heritage" is so common now, but because of the hegemony of white supremacy, so many of our ancestors hid their heritage to survive. There are millions of us who are bicultural without even knowing it. Wilma Mankiller, Principle chief of the Cherokee Tribe from 1985-1995 stated, "An Indian is an Indian even if they have only one drop of Indian blood;"[61] In response to this quote, the internet is alive with agreement:

> And I say to you, my Indo-mestizo brothers and sisters in North, Central, and South America: Recognize your other half. Embrace your Indian heritage. Explore your roots and never forget who came before you. Because we are more in number than what we think. We are 96 millions of federally recognized Indians in the Americas, but we are 500 millions of Indians of all mixed-back-grounds. We let labels wipe the Indian out of us. We let ignorance thrive and let discrimination surround us. We let white-mestizo and Euro society construct our identity and marginalize us in census boxes. We let media depict our Indian brothers and sisters as poor and illiterate when the truth is that some of us are talented and strong.[62]

This also applies to Steven Tanner's "ecological approaches to literary criticism," because the very ecology of our bicultural Oregon encodes and informs several things: One, our Oregon sense of humor is indigenous. I go into this in great detail in my last book: *Echoes From the Set: 50 Years of Filming on Location Hollywood and Oregon's Cinematic Literary Voices.*[63] The thing is, all of our native voices are also poetic and/or metaphoric, which is also present in our American Indian sense of humor. You may notice I rarely use "Native American." I am with Russell Means, a famous American Indian Movement leader and actor, who once told me that "everyone who is born on American soil is Native." The distinction he said, was that HE was an "American Indian," an Indios (In God) that the Creator placed on the earth to live where He wanted them to live and grow. I have given up on trying to explain this as well, that the Earth is our mother, like Oregon's own Chief Joseph tried. National Poet Laureate Joy Harjo even states her agreement with this in her introduction to *Reinventing the Enemy's Language.*[64] But Native Oregonians get it. We have learned from the First people here to be environmentalists. Oregon has led the way in Environmentalism because Oregon is very bicultural. Two, our understanding of the mythology about the Indigenous Coyote, the trickster, is that he really is a kind of prankster. Like the Merry Pranksters, from whom I've learned to laugh at myself. I even feel as if God is a Prankster sometimes with a great sense of humor, in dealing with me. Three, the landscape of Oregon invokes a religion close to pastoralism. My mother's side of the family came to Oregon in 1849, and our 1870 family farm is still out River Road. The ecology of Oregon that encodes and informs us is this: Pioneer stock learned from the local Indians that collaboration is key to survival. And I don't mean just Barn Raising. I mean the consciousness of collaboration is paramount in us everywhere we turn. When Kesey stepped into the Bay Area in the late 50s, he brought that bicultural ethic with him. I don't think it is a coincidence that the 60s were very tribal. And I don't think it's a coincidence that certain 60s literary theories in the New Criticism seem very psychedelic to me, in that Jacques Derrida, de Man and de Bolla also have a certain 60s ecology to their theories, nor a coincidence that bi-culturalism has become their hot topic since the 90s.

The first of these theories is what Hannah Arendt called Derrida's 'Marrano Metaphor'[65] idea of biculturality. Applied to similar situations, (the Jewish people forced to adhere to a Christian religion in the 1400s in Spain) such as The American Indian was forced to adhere to a Christian Religion in America, has created a bizarre after-effect, and that is called a "bicultural writing between the lines." These views on biculturality are from articles attained through the Knight Library, well cited, and published online; and edited by Agata Bielik-Robson as explained here:

> ...the Marrano strategy offers an alternative practice of universalization, conceived as an 'after-Babel project' to mend the broken whole from within, horizontally, without assuming the lofty abstract position of a general meta-language, but through the effort of bi- or multi-linguality, and also without overstressing the catastrophic nature of the Babelian dispersion of tongues.[66]

In my research on the "Marrano" I first found Derrida's and then Levinas' theories on it; but then I found Walter Benjamin's, and he made me feel at home with it. And it was here, with author Daniel Weiss, Faculty of Divinity at Cambridge, is where I found the same words I have always called my "duality of culture," but what my professors have called my "Between -the-lines" writing:[67] According to Leo Strauss, writers like Baruch Spinoza resorted to secrecy and concealed-ness primarily because of fear: they avoided the issue of "coming out" due to the anxiety of persecution, caused by the discrepancy between their radical views and the opinion of the masses, still entrenched in their fixed cultural identities. They were, therefore, forced to convey their messages "in between the lines" to connect with those in the similar position, capable of immediately recognizing the "secret message" (Strauss, 1988).[68]

And after all these years of feeling as if I was myself using subterfuge, I especially resonated with this:

> Claims have also been advanced to the effect that the question of Marranism was recently closed for good. I don't believe it for a second. There are still sons – and daughters – who, unbeknownst to

> themselves, incarnate or metem-psychosize the ventriloquist specters of their ancestors.[69]

That "ventriloquist specter" of the third quote was Ken Kesey. The quote in the second was my Grandmother and me: "due to the anxiety of persecution, caused by the discrepancy between their radical views and the opinion of the masses, still entrenched in their fixed cultural identities." We spoke the same language. He spoke in metaphor and I spoke in images, both are very cinematic. But what they are together is Poetic Cinema. And THAT is what this book is really about. But before we go there, just mention Derrida, and I think of de Man and de Bolla, all whom are relevant to Kesey's novel, for instance, de Man's use of the term *subversive* here:

> Mere reading, it turns out, prior to any theory, is able to transform critical discourse in a manner that would appear *deeply subversive* to those who think of the teaching of literature as a substitute for the teaching of theology, ethics, psychology, or intellectual history. Close reading accomplishes this often in spite of itself because it cannot fail to respond to *structures of language* which it is the more or less secret aim of literary teaching to keep hidden.[70]

It is precisely those "structures of language," and Raymond Williams' "... structure of feeling "[71] that spoke to me with regards to Ken. But especially this from Benveniste, who, "... essentially posits that the word, aka language, is not "*just the very definition of man*" but preceded man and preceded his thinking."[72] Essentially, "In the beginning was the WORD, and the Word was God."[73] If this isn't *psychedelic* literary theory, I don't know what is!

Which of course brings us to a related anecdotal story about Kesey, one that only those of us there at the farm that April day in 1983 would know. It was the funeral of not one but two of our closest filmmaker friends who had died within days of each other. Kesey asked Ken Babbs, his best friend since Stanford, to read Percy Blythe Shelley's *Ode to the West Wind*. Suddenly, as Babbs read it as only a brilliant poet himselfcould read Shelley, the beautiful Spring day sky turned dark as a grave, and a terrible West Wind blew up strong like a miniature hurricane. We all looked at Babbs and Kesey because we all knew that this was not a coincidence, that they had summoned the West Wind with Shelley's WORDS. The very second Babbs had finished reading the following stanza, the skies turned blue again and the wind died down:

Drive my dead thoughts over the universe
Like wither'd leaves to quicken a new birth!
And, by the incantation of this verse,
Scatter, as from an unextinguish'd hearth
Ashes and sparks, my words among mankind!
Be through my lips to unawaken'd earth
The trumpet of a prophecy! O Wind,
If Winter comes, can Spring be far behind?"[74]

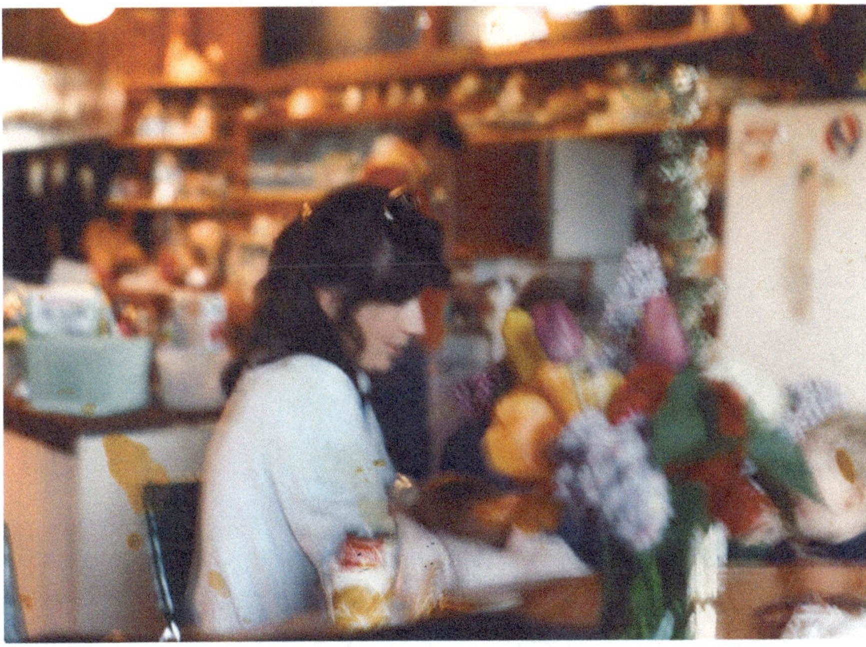

Photograph of Katherine after that mournful windy day in Ken and Faye Kesey's Kitchen, April 1983

All of these theories are very subversive, but so was Kesey. Does anyone think it is a coincidence that Kirk Douglas and Michael Douglas BOTH wanted the Director of *One Flew Over the Cuckoo's Nest* to be none other than Milos Forman, who had recently come to America and was one of the most subversive directors to ever come out of Russian-occupied Czechoslovakia? There is no such thing as coincidence. Just look at this text written by Kesey, in which he capitalizes the word WORD, and makes it sound as if Randle P. himself is God:

"Before Chief Bromden even sees the newcomer, (McMurtry) he hears the Word– a "loud, brassy voice" that "sounds like he's way above them, talking down, like he's sailing fifty yards overhead, hollering at those below on the ground. He sounds big."[75] For me, *One Flew Over the*

Cuckoo's Nest is not a Messianic Metaphor however; it's a bicultural "New Age Western," as Poetic Cinema filmmaker Kelly Reichardt calls her own film genre for her *Meek's Cutoff.* But Ken Kesey's was the very, very first; and John Barth, with *Sot Weed Factor* came very close. Dear Ladies and Gentlemen of the Jury, I present my literary theory defense herewith, starting with another quote from Kesey himself from his book, about the Hero, in *One Flew Over the Cuckoo's Nest* ('62); but remember that even though the description of McMurphy sounds John Wayne-ish, in the end the character is an Anti-Hero who treats everyone that is marginalized with respect, challenges authority, gets turned upon and murdered, and does NOT ride into the Sunset:

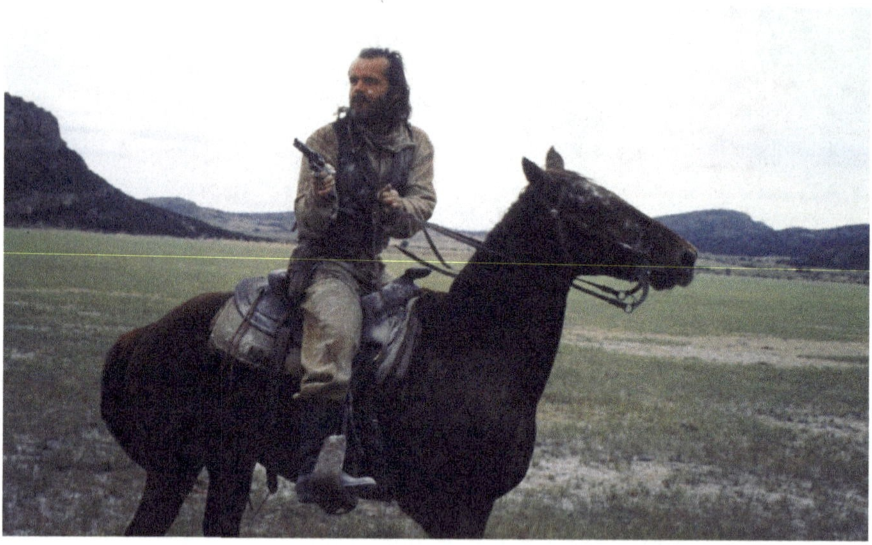

Photo of Jack Nicholson on one of his many Westerns

> Drawing upon popular culture, Kesey links McMurphy with the most familiar hero of the frontier – the cowboy. He smokes Marlboro cigarettes and is described as "the cowboy out of the TV set walking down the middle of the street to meet a dare" (CN, 172). He has a "drawling cowboy actor's voice" (CN, 232). Before his first meeting with Harding, he says, "this hospital ain't big enough for the two of us... Tell this Harding that he either meets me man to man or he's a yaller skunk and better be outta town by sunset" (CN, 24). He has a "cowboy bluster" and a "TV-cowboy stoicism" (CN, 62, 73). He sings cowboy songs in the latrine and has Wild Bill Hickok's "dead-man's hand" tattooed on his shoulder (CN, 83, 77). Just before he assaults Big Nurse he hitches up his shorts "like they

> were horsehide chaps, and pushe[s] his cap with one finger like it was a ten-gallon Stetson" Harding refers to him with an allusion to the Lone Ranger: "I'd like to stand there at the window with a silver bullet in my hand and ask 'who wawz that 'er masked man?'"[76]

Could it be the New Poetic Cinema/Existential Western? Could *Cuckoo's Nest* be the new mythology of the American Cowboy? Could that voice be bicultural *and the voice of the future,* in addition to being the Oregon Literary Cinematic Voice? As if in answer, I found this revelation of a quote as if it was a resounding *yes* in a Thesis by Matthew W. Driscoll, called *Ken Kesey and Literary Shamanism*:

> I have to add Oregon, Washington, and Alaska to the remaining American frontiers in the twentieth century, but even these frontier lands will be corrupted and exploited during Kesey's lifetime. According to Kesey though, hope remains. Frontier landscapes remind and inspire characters in his novels that there are alternatives to lifestyles based on materialism, consumerism, and cultural conformity. Integrating his personal experiences – his childhood in the Oregon wilderness and the model of manhood provided by his father – Kesey sees the independent and physically vital American Western man as the defender of a sense of individuality that is forfeited when man succumbs to the rule of "the inhuman part of American industrialism" (Kesey qtd. in Plimpton 224)[77]

He goes on later to quote Literary Critic Leslie Fiedler, who was, by the way, on the Woodrow Wilson scholarship committee; therefore also directly responsible for Kesey's getting a grant to Stanford Grad school; therefore even for his ability to write *One Flew Over the Cuckoo's Nest,* while there with Ken Babbs:

> As a young writer in the Sixties, facing the omnipotent influence of American capitalism and its many educational, financial, and cultural institutions, Kesey integrates the individuality of the cowboy into his recovery of shamanism through fiction. Thus, his homeland in Oregon, a place that Leslie Fiedler calls "one of our last actual Wests," (pg. 177) is integral in understanding what drives Kesey to design a number of his characters based upon the mythologized American cowboy. The cowboys that he incorporates into his fiction are not those of traditional American Western tales like Owen Wister's *The Virginian*. Kesey's cowboys pertain to a genre specific to the latter half of the twentieth century that Leslie Fiedler, a critic

> of literature from or about the American West defines as the "New Western" in *The Return of the Vanishing American.*[78]

I was fascinated by this book, and it made me wonder if Leslie Fiedler was a bicultural and how he can hear this "voice" in Ken. Recently, I learned he was adopted by the Blackfeet, so that makes sense. He is cited by an incredible academic writer named M. Elise Marubbio, who is the writer of the article: "The Emergence of the Indian Maiden" in her Journal titled *Killing the Indian Maiden: Images of Native Women in Film.* And speaking of Academic writers, there are rumors that the head of the Stanford Graduate Writing program, Wallace Stegner, was not a fan of Ken's writing. And neither was top literary critic, Harold Bloom. However, before he passed away in 2019, Bloom published many other literary critic's push-backs to his position, and they were fascinatingly adept. Perhaps that was because Fiedler had published *The Return of the Vanishing American* in the interim, amazingly enough published in 1968, and written during 1967 and The Summer of Love. Our source for this quote, Driscoll, continues:

> Fiedler's vanishing Frontier continues to be explored throughout the twentieth century, to the point that scarcely a Frontier or wilderness remains. According to Fiedler, rather than being nostalgic about the changing nature of the West, the New Western is psychedelic: "*But no other name fits as well as the New Western, which, like the Old Western at its most authentic, deals precisely with the alteration of consciousness.* Besides, many of the so-called 'psychedelics' themselves, those hallucinogenic drugs, at least, found in nature rather than synthesized in the laboratory (marijuana, peyote, the Mexican Mushroom, Ayahuasca, etc.) are our bridge to – even as they are gifts from – the world of the Indian: the world not of an historical past, but of an eternally archaic one.[79]

This novel, called *One Flew Over the Cuckoo's Nest,* created not just an "alteration of consciousness" like the "New Age Western" such as *Meeks Cutoff's* Director Reichardt said, but was a Shamanic "Psychedelic Western;" that revealed the first glimmerings of change in the New Age, period. Because of Kesey's book, in 1962, the world changed.

The world was waiting to change. We were listening for a voice, listening for The Word. And it came. As a bicultural word. It told us that Chief Bromden was just like us, a mixed-race, a bicultural man who was going to break out of the "Combine" of modernity and Colonialism under the stereotype of the Wooden Indian to return to his living, breathing, and the decolonized survivance of his contemporary people. We were all following him, too, then. We also heard, in a way that we could understand, that the world was an insane asylum. We were in Plato's Cave and we needed to see Truth and Beauty like Shelley and Yeats and Plato saw Beauty and Truth. We started to dress like these Romantic Poets. A few San Franciscans went to the Comstock to seek a better way with the Native American Church and Sacred Peyote. These San Franciscans were the ones that the Indians of "8th Hopi Prophesy" predicted.[80] They started to wear 18th Century Western Wear, or were already wearing headbands and beads and moccasins as a sign of solidarity and respect. They opened the Red Dog Saloon right straight across the California border in Nevada, and The Charlatans started to play there. They used psychedelics to tune in on this new consciousness, and started to play a signature Psychedelic Sound. Big Brother and the Holding Company (before Janis Joplin) came and took it to a new level. Then they took it all back to San Francisco and started holding dances in the Fillmore District while Kesey started Acid Trips with the Grateful Dead. At one point, instead of competing, they merged. The master voice joined in the symphony and soon millions of us joined them. This use of psychedelics ushered in a *Brave New World*: "Once they were back in San Francisco, the Family Dog couldn't wait to replicate the experience," as the founder of Family Dog, Luria Castell Dickson says "With LSD, we experienced what it took Tibetan monks 20 years to obtain, yet we got there in 20 minutes. We had to, to save the world."[81] Like the Old Western, the New Western brought with it "an Archaicness" including "'archaic values" to the New Mythology that guided the lights of my generation.

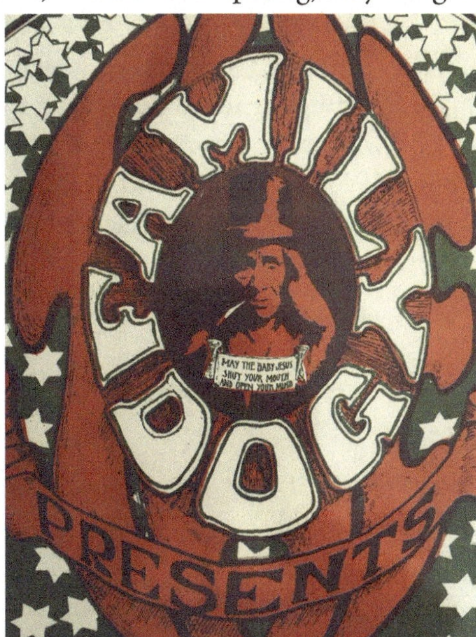

Just like Yeats' "Gyres of Time" based on Plato's Aeons, we saw the world on the brink of destruction, and we took it back; at first, 200 years, and in 2020 we are taking it back 2000 years, while we move it again forward to the New Age of Aquarius. But this time we are reclaiming the Divine Feminine that was thwarted 2000 years ago. And we are finally able to comprehend without dualism, because we are being led to a Unity that Einstein instinctively knew was there. Quantum Mechanics is our new religion, except it is not a religion, it is a spiritual emanation from the Universe. It is whole. We needed to get back to the garden, and we are.

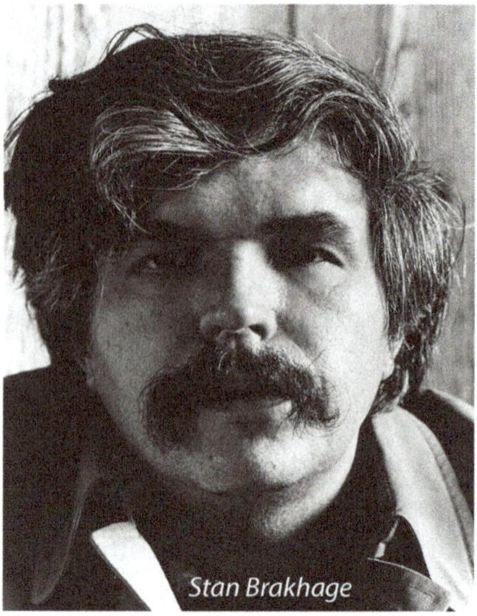
Stan Brakhage

These shadows of the underground were the foundation of the Sixties, and it is this author's hope to see with new eyes the Cinema of the following 10 years, the New Hollywood, beginning with Stan Brakhage, who called Eugene, Oregon "the Poetic Cinema Capitol of the World." Brakhage made this statement after Ron Finne screened *How Old Is the Water.* Brakhage was presenting one of his films at 150 Science at the UO. Campus film groups showed movies there, and my husband Philip's sister Marilyn used to invite him there with her. Philip says he will never forget seeing these films together. This was probably around 1967, as Marilyn and Philip went to Europe soon after. Coincidently, 1967 was the year Kesey returned to Oregon and became a filmmaker, and I had returned to the pastoral Danish farm of my ancestors,

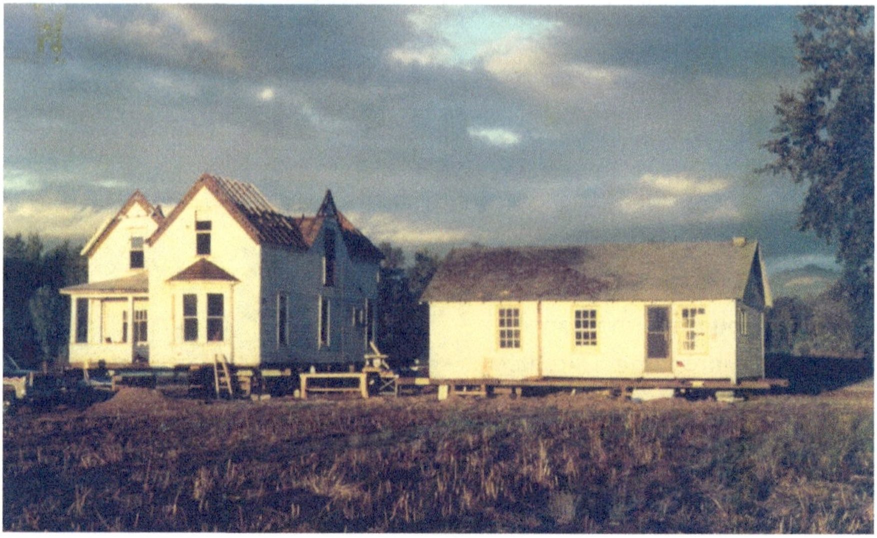

outside of Eugene, away from the violent Indian Reservation. It was to become the best of the beginning of times that are still finding its way to us through the "widening gyre" of both heaven and hell. People keep asking me: "Are our times now like the 60's? I answer, the 60's on LSD was not as psychedelic as these times we are living through right now in this pandemic ridden, polarized, racist and politically offensive election year. But yeah, it's similar.

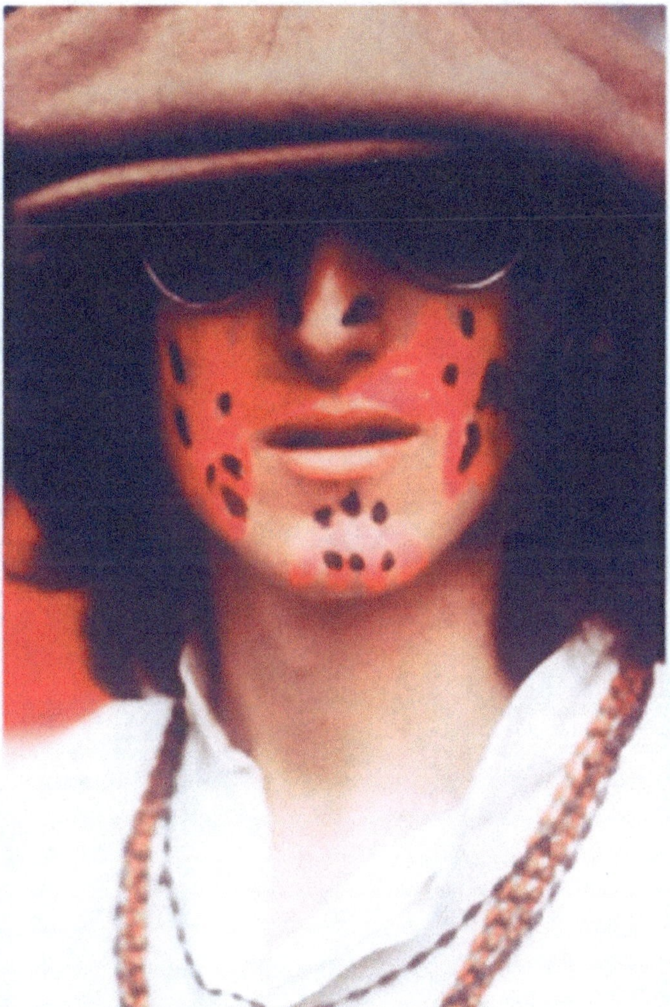

Bobby Steinbrecher, Kesey's and My Beloved Filmmaker Friend.
Photo by Jerry DeWilde, 1972

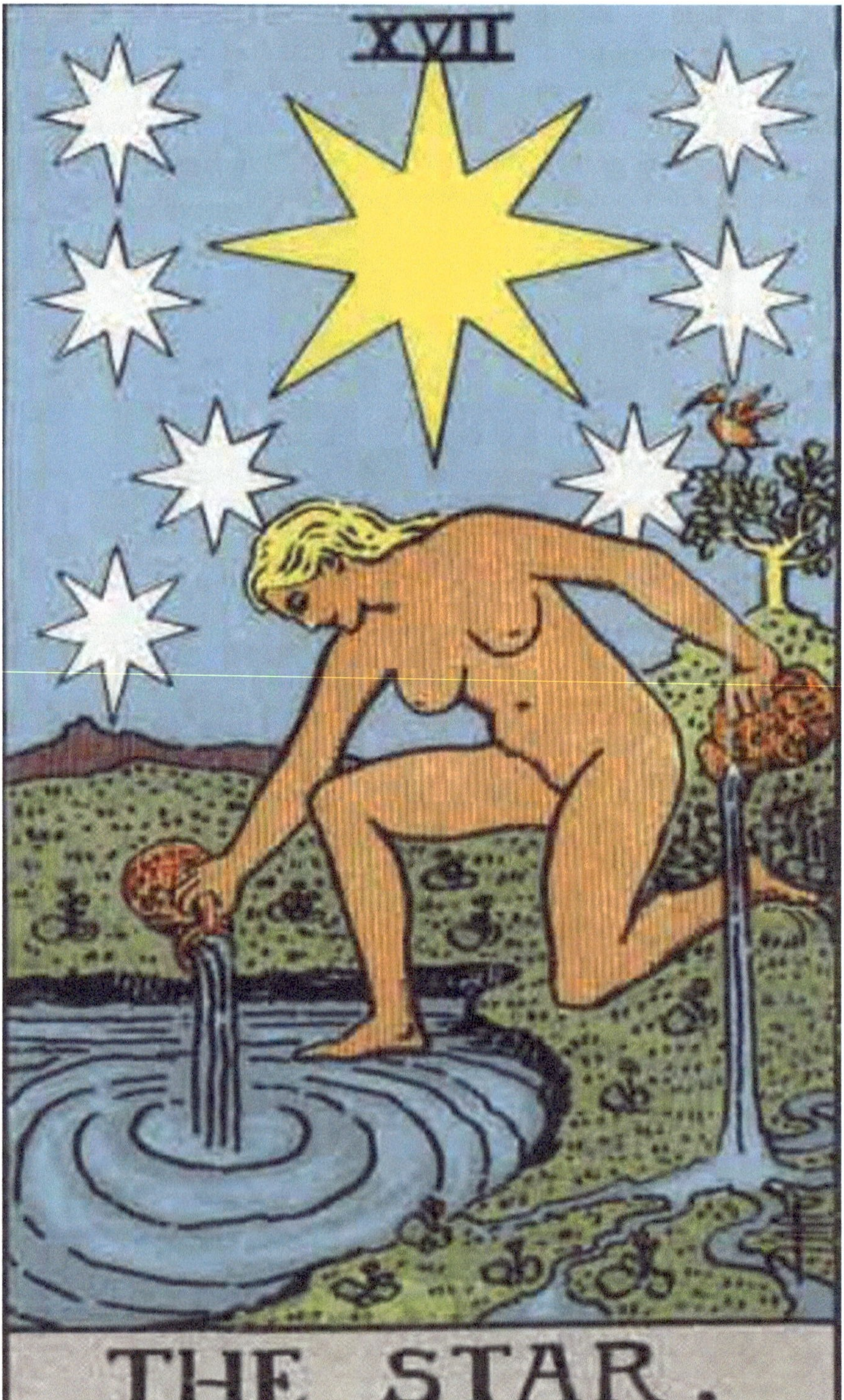
XVII
THE STAR.

Chapter 2

The Widening Gyre of Yeats & The Summer of Love 1967

Are you the leaf, the blossom or the bole?
O Body swayed to music, O brightening glance,
How Can We know the Dancer from the dance?
– William Butler Yeats,
Among School Children (1939)

What does Yeats have to do with the Summer of Love? He predicted something like this would happen in 1919 in his poem "Second Coming." Northrup Frye indicated it 50 years before the end of the "widening gyre" of the Age or Aeon Of Pisces, meaning around 1962.

According to his understanding of the Golden Dawn Hermetic theory, Yeats' Gyres are like a "Second Coming," and happen when the "Old Age" of history is in its death-throes, and the New Age gyre, usually a new age of Spirituality, is being born. *Sound Familiar?* The former Piscean Age, (Fisher of Men, Fisher King Mythology) is dying. The Age of Aquarius Constellation, an (androgynous?) woman pouring out blessings from an Alabaster jar, began as flashes of *revelations* some 50 years ago, and I believe that the advent of the 60s San Francisco tribe was the true herald of that new Aeon of Aquarius.

Yeats, however, in his poem was worried about the vision he saw as symbolic of the New Age, from "Spiritus Mundi" (The Universal Mind) ; one that he likened to the Sphinx, like a Dragon or a Thunderbird or other form of "rough beast" from the past. He foresaw this equivalent crawling "with slow thighs" to Bethlehem to birth the new age (like the old Piscean Age was 2000 years prior) but this time by the Sphinx.[82]

The Second Coming

Turning and turning in the widening gyre
The falcon cannot hear the falconer;
Things fall apart; the centre cannot hold;
Mere anarchy is loosed upon the world,
The blood-dimmed tide is loosed, and everywhere
The ceremony of innocence is drowned;
The best lack all conviction, while the worst
Are full of passionate intensity.

Surely some revelation is at hand;
Surely the Second Coming is at hand.
The Second Coming! Hardly are those words out
When a vast image out of Spiritus Mundi
Troubles my sight: somewhere in sands of the desert
A shape with lion body and the head of a man,
A gaze blank and pitiless as the sun,

Is moving its slow thighs, while all about it
Reel shadows of the indignant desert birds.
The darkness drops again; but now I know

That twenty centuries of stony sleep
Were vexed to nightmare by a rocking cradle,
And what rough beast, its hour come round at last,
Slouches towards Bethlehem to be born?[83]

He wrote this after he saw the world's first apocalyptic death by machine guns during World War I, and when he wrote the poem in 1919, he had also noticed that the same thing had happened some 2000 years before in Babylon, (which he addresses in his poems like "Byzantium") and 2000 years before that in Egypt and Sumeria. Ad infinitum. These Gyres are like Constellations that rule these 2000-year-long *Aeons*, which is what Plato called them, which are essentially intelligent emanations from the Universe. "In a note to the Cuala Press edition of *Michael Robartes and the Dancer*, Yeats describes in detail this historical process as it is symbolized in his double gyre:

> This ... is true also of history, for the end of an age, which always receives the revelation of the character of the next age, is represented by the coming of one gyre to its place of greatest expansion and

> of the other to that of its greatest contraction. At the present moment the life gyre is sweeping outward, unlike that before the birth of Christ which was narrowing, and has almost reached its greatest expansion. The revelation which approaches will however take its character from the contrary movement of the interior gyre. All our scientific, democratic, fact-accumulating heterogeneous civilization belongs to the outward gyre and prepares not the continuance of itself but the revelation as in a lightning flash, though in a flash that will not strike only in one place, and will for a time be constantly repeated, of the civilization that must slowly take its place. This is too simple a statement, for much detail is possible.[84]

Without Northrup Frye, we may never have known what it meant, either. Northrup Frye had "gained international fame with ... *Anatomy of Criticism* (1957), one of the most important works of literary theory published in the twentieth century. The American critic Harold Bloom commented at the time of its publication that *Anatomy* established Frye as "the foremost living student of Western literature."[85] He had also deciphered William Blakes's poems, and while embracing the "New Criticism" we discussed in Chapter 1, had also cautioned that we also needed a new "Archetypal Criticism" as a "New Poetics," which I also tried to address earlier in Chapter 1, in "The Archetype of the 60s." But why am I doing this? Because our world is truly in need of Archetypal criticism as "a new poetics." Here's one reason why:

> "... what criticism can do," according to Frye, "is awaken students to successive levels of awareness of the mythology that lies behind the ideology in which their society indoctrinates them" (Stingle 4).[86]

Frye was very interested in the Student Protests and the Counterculture according to the list of topics he was interviewed for. *Mythology: Timeless Tales of Gods and Heroes* by Edith Hamilton[87] was a huge influence on us in English Classes at the University of Oregon in the late sixties. I still have my copy.

Frye also goes on to explain how recurring structural patterns, like those he found in the poem "In Xanadu" by Samuel Coleridge, can elevate our critical thinking:

> That is, the study of recurring structural patterns grants students an emancipatory distance from their own society, and gives them

> a vision of a higher human state – the Longinian sublime – that is not accessible directly through their own experience, but ultimately transforms and expands their experience, so that the poetic model becomes a model to live by.[88]

This poetic model we came to live by was exactly from Coleridge's era, too, in his and the aesthetic works of William and Dorothy Wordsworth, Percy B. Shelley and Mary Wollstonecraft Godwin Shelley, Yeats and Keats.

Northrup Frye goes even *Furthur*:

> In what he terms a "kerygmatic mode," myths become "myths to live by" and "metaphors to live in," which "(...) not only work for us but constantly expand our horizons, [so that] we may enter the world of [kerygma or transformative power] and pass on to others what we have found to be true for ourselves."[89]

In his spirit of passing "on to others what we have found to be true for ourselves," I am passing on what I found to be true for myself, which is what I know from living in the 60s, being on the psychedelic bus, getting sober 35 years ago, being a filmmaker, studying under a Jungian Apprentice screenplay writer, working with quantum mechanics physicists, studying comparative religions; and throwing the *I Ching* and divining with The Golden Dawn Tarot Deck for 50 years. And what I know is this. Yeats' Sphinx was a woman, not a man, because Egyptologists discovered the beard was an add-on after Yeats' death. She is mentioned in 9500 B.C.E. so she is older than Yeats thought. She is aligned with the Constellation Leo, which supports the Aeon theory, because that was in 9500 B.C.E. (And the pyramids are aligned with Orion, the Lion Hunter.) The Star of Bethlehem's astrological configuration was predicted by three Wise (Astrologers) Men from Egypt and the East heralding the time of Christ's birth. Astrologers now are heralding the birth of Aquarius with the conjunction of Saturn and Jupiter on Dec. 21, 2021, with three *asteroids conjugating within the conjugation, named Isis Horus and Osiris*, as discovered by Alice Macdonald.[90]

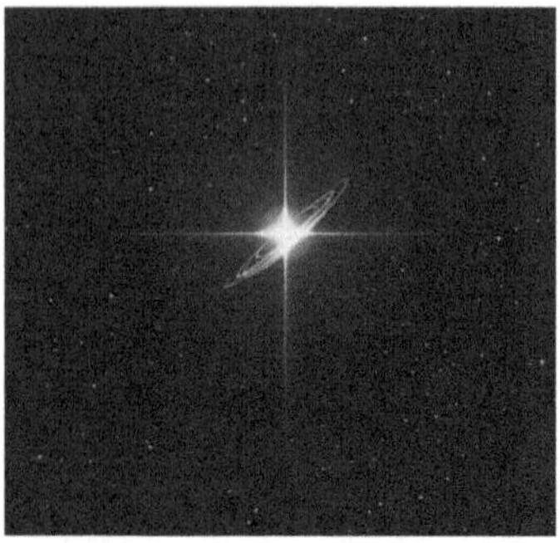

Her aspects are peace, love, and understanding. Carl Jung was the way-shower to this age. Synchronicity is a hallmark of it. But the Gyres are something else. Yeats was on to something. And boy, his poem rings so true for today. The 60s are just getting started. All of us see what is happening today as a direct correlation with our burgeoning Aeon. But it's going to be all right. No, it's going to be better than all right. It is going to be another Renaissance. Even better than the last. As the Gyres go full circle through space and time, there is a returning. And it is now.

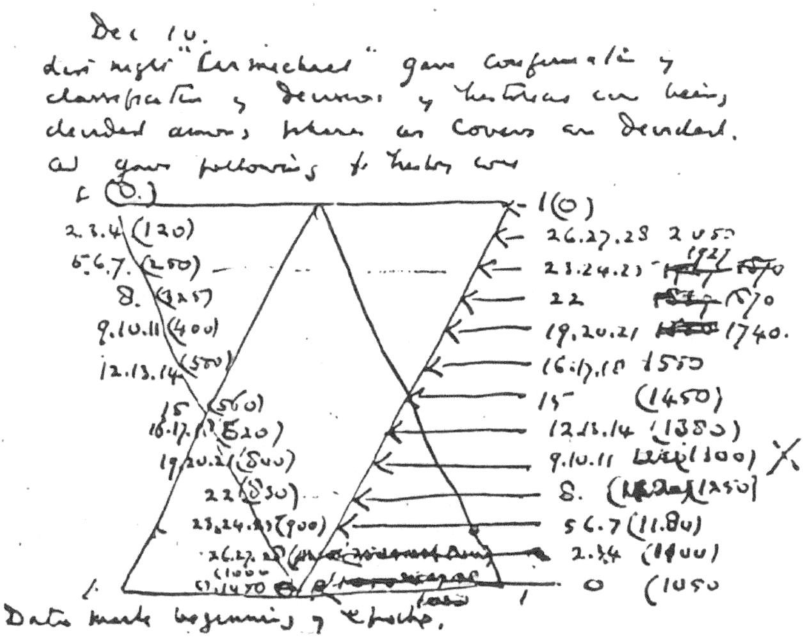

The Historical Cones given by 'Carmichael', 10 December 1920 (YVP 3 61)

In *An Honoured Guest: New Essays on W. B. Yeats*, published by Edward Arnold, Northrup Frye also discusses men as gyres, too, in an "as above, so is below" quantum way, before he talks about Yeats 'Widening Gyres":

> ...The human soul is always moving outward into the objective world or inward into itself; and this movement is double because the human soul would not be conscious were it not suspended between contraries, the greater the contrast the more intense the consciousness. The man, in whom the movement inward is stronger than the movement outward, the man who sees all reflected within himself, the subjective man, reaches the narrow end of a gyre at death, for death is always, they contend, even when it seems the result of accident, preceded by an intensification of the subjective life; and has a monument of revelation immediately after death, a revelation which they describe as his being carried

> into the presence of all his dead kindred, a moment whose objectivity is exactly equal to the subjectivity of death. The objective man on the other hand, whose gyre moves outward, receives at this moment the revelation, not of himself seen from within, for that is impossible to objective man, but of himself as if he were somebody else.[91]

I think it is important to include this because it also gives us understanding of the Gyre we are leaving, which in essence is Piscean consciousness. But like the objective man, The Age of Pisces created "scientific objectivity" during the Age of Reason, and that is exactly what Yeats is railing against. The Age of Aquarius and Northrop Frye encourages us to return inward to symbolism and mythology just like Jung and Yeats do. And with that, we might as well bring the Father of all of our (and theirs) Philosophy, Plato back into the mix; and remember the Aeon theory which Plotinus opens this last chapter with:

The "Intellectual-Principle ... *brings compulsion* not persuasion." Because this New Age of Consciousness, the subjective soul-searching Age of Aquarius, turned us into compulsive-like lemmings searching for that *vibration, that consciousness.* My favorite encapsulation of how this felt, and how that feeling was out-pictured in our lives, was also in the article by *New York Times* best seller and book reviewer Sheila Weller for *Vanity Fair,* called "Suddenly That Summer:"

> In a 25-square-block area of San Francisco, in the summer of 1967, an ecstatic, Dionysian mini-world sprang up like a mushroom, dividing American culture into a Before and After unparalleled since World War II. If you were between 15 and 30 that year, it was almost impossible to resist the lure of that transcendent, peer-driven season of glamour, ecstasy, and Utopianism. It was billed as the Summer of Love, and its creators did not employ a single publicist or craft a media plan. Yet the phenomenon washed over America like a tidal wave ... ushering in a series of liberations and awakenings that irreversibly changed our way of life.[92]

Except it really wasn't that sudden. It just hit critical mass, and it had been building for quite a long time. As Dave Getz, the guitarist from Big Brother and the Holding Company said at The Red Dog Saloon Reunion, "This whole scene essentially had a Medieval, a Classical and a Baroque Era, by 1969 it was the Baroque."[93]

"The Medieval" foundations were laid in the early 50s (1951) when Maya Deren, an experimental filmmaker, visited the U of O campus, The Beats hit San Francisco, and then Jack Kerouac wrote *On the Road* in 1957. In the late 50s another "experimental" filmmaker, Stan Brakhage, started making films in a whole new unorthodox way. My favorite quote about him is from film historians David Bordwell and Kristin Thompson: "Brakhage considered the artist as a visionary who perceives and feels more deeply than others. He sought to capture on film untutored vision, a sense of space and light unspoiled by knowledge and social training."[94]

I just find this quote so poetic, because he seems to be railing against the intellect, too, like Yeats. The artist's way of perceiving is aesthetic, based in the senses, but the tutored vision and ways of knowledge in society are scientific. Those ways got us to where we were, which was way out of balance. We needed to let the Poets and Visionaries have a voice to try to save us with a new way of seeing. And that meant stripping and undoing and starting over, by returning to where we first went wrong, and that was the Medieval Period, which is represented as between the end of the Roman Empire, and before the Renaissance. In some circles we wish we could go back and reclaim the period when Christ's teachings were usurped by the Church at the Council of Nicaea in 325 AD; and insist that the Gospels of Mary Magdalene and Philip had prevailed in keeping Mary as Christ's chosen Apostle, not her brother Peter, who started the Catholic church. The trajectory of that decision resulted in women being burned at the stake and the Inquisition. And then there was The Plague. The Renaissance and Age of Discovery came after the Plague, and the world started over with new visions of what humanity could really be like. But the Doctrine of Discovery Papal Bull in 1493 would eventually cause the genocide of hundreds of millions of Indigenous people. So much for the Rational that became rationalized thinking when not connected to the heart. And what came next, the Industrial Age didn't have one. Which in my mind is when people started going insane. Fritz Lang's film *Metropolis* tried to warn us.

And even our National Hero John Wayne couldn't save us. The Western died in 1962, and even had a funeral in Hollywood's *The Man Who Shot Liberty Valance*, just as a New Age hero was being born. But this hero wasn't larger than life, wasn't measured against doorways and Monument Valley; he was the Anti-hero, the everyman, a guy who treated insane asylum inmates as regular people; and who also caused the American Indian, relegated to the Wooden Cigar Store deaf and dumb trope, to speak and become visible. And that was in 1962, that seminal year, when *One Flew Over the Cuckoo's Nest* was published, Aquarius pierced the Veil, and now the world has not been the same since.

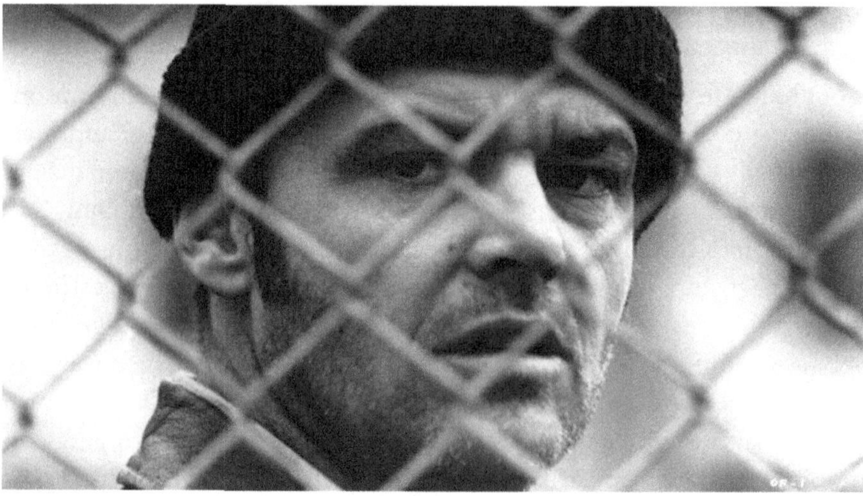

Jack Nicholson in *One Flew Over the Cuckoo's Nest.*
Given to Katherine Wilson by Producer Michael Douglas in 1975.

1962 was a seminal year for a lot of reasons: The Coffee House Folk Scene was incubating singers and players like Bob Dylan, Joan Baez, Jerry Garcia, Janis Joplin, Jorma Kaukonen, Milan Melvin and Hoyt Axton. And as a result of the Coffee Houses and Bars, other amazing things started, like a young Laguna Beach Boy, who was already following Hoyt Axton around on the East Coast Folk Circuit the day JFK was killed in 1963, and whom was so traumatized that he sold his guitar and caught the first boat that left the harbor, and ended up in India; looking, he said "for Camelot." He later took Richard Alpert, a close colleague with Timothy Leary in the Psychology department at Harvard on the Maharishi circuit, just like Hoyt had done with him on the folk circuit, earlier. And as a result, the Harvard Professor is now known as Ram Das, joining the Beat Poets including Allen Ginsberg, Gary Snyder, and even Jack Kerouac into Eastern Mysticism.

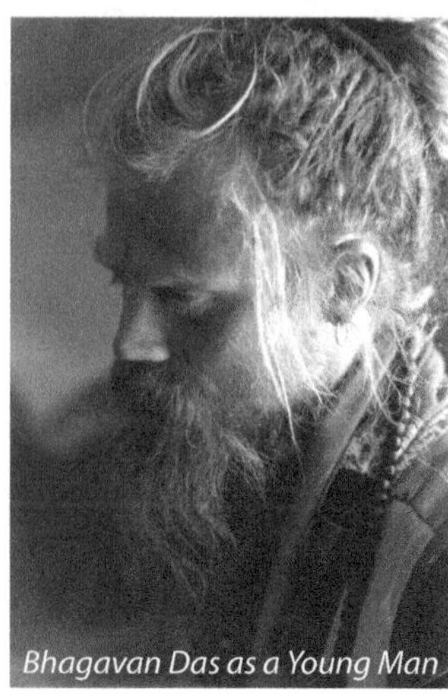

Bhagavan Das as a Young Man

His name is Bhagavan Das, and he told me this story one dark night at the Belknap Hot Springs, when my dear friend (and screenplay agent at the time) Susan Grant, brought him up to see if there was a screenplay in a book he wrote titled *It's Here Now (Are You?).*[95] Of course there was a screenplay there, especially after coaxing him into telling me what "the inciting incident" was that wasn't in his book. And that inciting incident was when he had heard Hoyt Axton first sing folk songs, possibly at a Huntington Beach, California venue called The Golden Bear, then went out and bought a guitar and followed Hoyt around in 1962. And speaking of 1962 (what some called "the last normal year in America" before Kennedy was killed) was not very "cinematic" at the time. But when a man named Zapruder filmed the actual assassination of Kennedy in 1963, suddenly everyone was buying a camera, and filming with 8 or 16mm. Some were already making amazing "home movies" like Stan Brakhage. Stan was an early experimental filmmaker with ties to Eugene.

And at home, in Eugene, Oregon – filmmakers were cropping up everywhere. Ron Finne met Cinematographer Haskell Wexler at the University of Oregon, and ended up as part of his film crew on a bus to film the *March on Washington* in 1963. South Eugene High alumni Loren Sears was filming the infamous "Diggers" in San Francisco and another famous South Eugene alumni Richard Brautigan, who was in San Francisco; and then filmed American Indians with his wife, Pat Ferraro; who later became a film instructor at San Francisco State for 30 years. Another South Eugene alumni, Mike Dilley owned his own audio recording company before he even graduated from high school, and was piping music into department stores and elevators over 100 dedicated phone lines. He recorded another South Eugene alum Tim Hardin, who performed at Woodstock. We will revisit these filmmakers in the subsequent chapters.

AUDIO RECORDING COMPANY

1247 WEST EIGHTH AVE. EUGENE, OREGON

ARCO BACKGROUND MUSIC SYSTEMS
COMPLETE STUDIO RECORDING FACILITIES
SOUND SYSTEMS & HI-FI EQUIPMENT

MICHAEL S. DILLEY RES. PHONE DI 4-2305
ROBERT F. SIEGENTHALER RES. PHONE DI 4-2089

Audio Recording Company Business Card courtesy of Mike Dilley

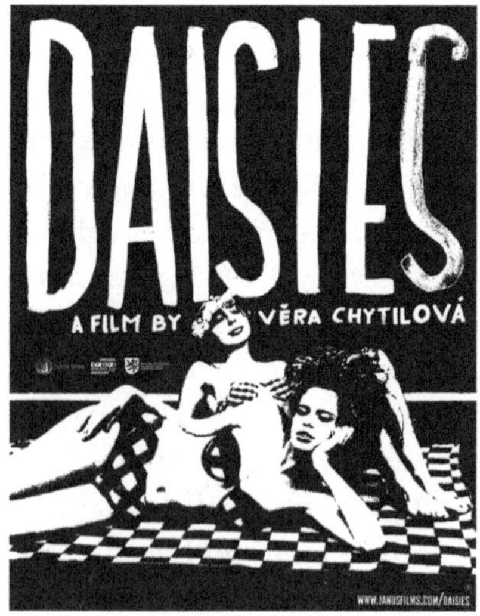

In 1964 Ken Kesey and the Merry Pranksters were following themselves around, too, with a 16mm Arriflex, but on a psychedelic bus, all the way from the West to the East Coast and back. Later, in 1966, one of my favorite films was made in Czechoslovakia, called *Daisies* which also seemed to just follow two young women around with a camera. By 1967, everybody was following anybody around with a camera, because the scene was so psychedelic. And what a scene that was filmed, with an incredible soundtrack. It would take a whole other book just to talk about the music that came out of my generation. It was if the Music of the spheres was singing and we were there catching it and downloading it.

> The Summer of Love also thrust a new kind of music – acid rock – across the airwaves, nearly put barbers out of business, traded clothes for costumes, turned psychedelic drugs into sacred door keys, and revived the outdoor gatherings of the Messianic Age, making everyone an acolyte *and* a priest. It turned sex with strangers into a mode of generosity, made "uptight" an epithet on a par with "racist," refashioned the notion of earnest Peace Corps idealism into a bacchanalian rhapsody, and set that favorite American adjective, "free," on a fresh altar.[96]

Our parents didn't know what hit us, we didn't even know what had hit us. But calling a sufficient measure of LSD for a "trip," a "hit', seemed appropriate, and a whole new language evolved. The energy of Creativity and LOVE was also very strong. It made us want to not just create a song, a poem or a painting, or a film, it made us want to create LIFE, but film was the only medium we knew that could capture ALL of that. Mountain Girl put it beautifully in Sheila Weller's article: "It was this magical moment ... this liberation movement, a time of sharing that was very special," with "a lot of trust going around," says Carolyn "Mountain Girl" Garcia, who had a baby with Ken Kesey, the man who helped kick off that season, and who then married Jerry Garcia, the man who epitomized its fruition."[97]

Mountain Girl and The Grateful Dead spent a lot of time in Oregon at Kesey's Farm, either on the road for concerts or performing in Eugene in Concert over the years. However, Oregon's Portland filmmakers like Harry Smith were contributing to the Tribal energy of San Francisco, too. He, Jack Smith, Stan Brakhage and Jonas Mekas were screening their Poetic Cinema films in the Haight in 1966. They must have felt the call, too.

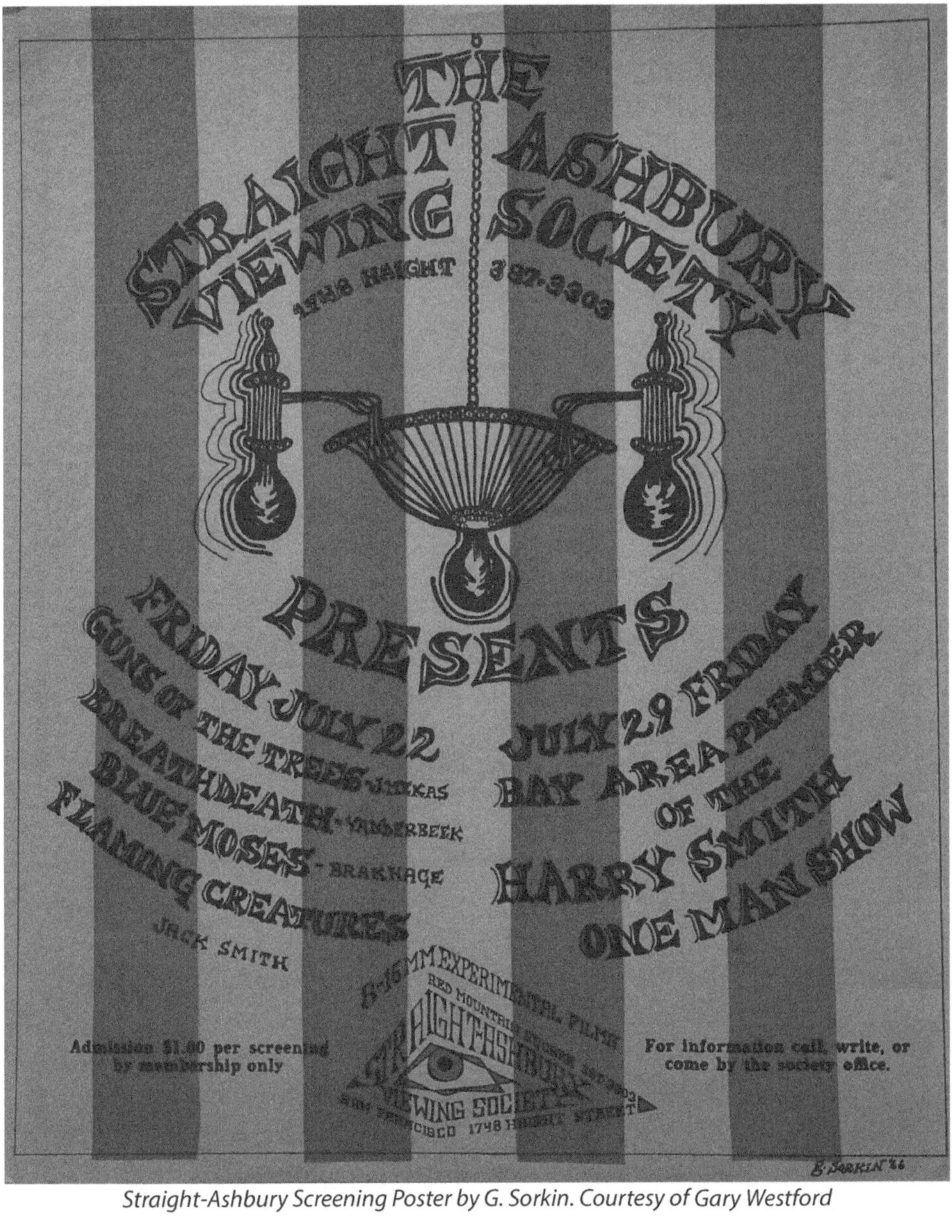

Straight-Ashbury Screening Poster by G. Sorkin. Courtesy of Gary Westford

Here is part of the Harry Smith Presentation that Anne Richardson made that Dr. Rust and I were a part of:

November 5th, 2014
Knight Library
Katherine Wilson, Dr. Stephen Rust
And OREGON CARTOON INSTITUTE PRESENTS:

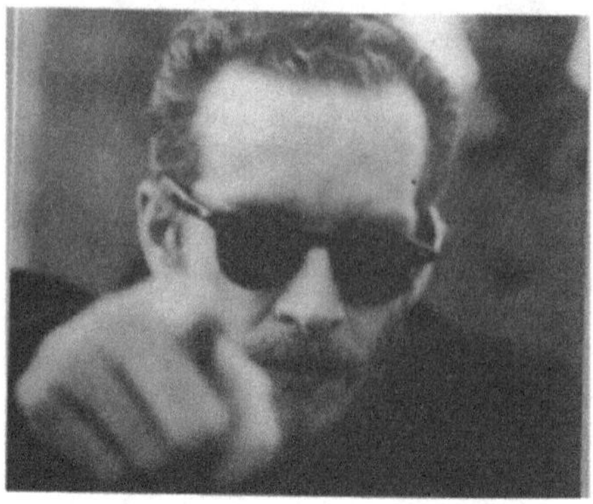

HEAVEN & EARTH MAGIC

Anne Richardson, the director of Oregon Cartoon Institute, will give a talk **"Harry Smith: Cross Culturality and Regional Identity in a Salmon Nation Beatnik"** on Nov. 5 at 5:00 PM in Room 41 of the Knight Library basement. The talk is free.

SCHNITZER CINEMA PRESENTS:
7:00 PM on Nov. 5, Dennis Nyback's "expanded cinema" version of Harry Smith's 1962 feature length stop motion masterpiece, **Heaven And Earth Magic**, and will screen in the Jordan Schnitzer Museum of Art. The screening is free.

http://jsma.uoregon.edu/experimental-media-theme-2014-15-season-schnitzer-cinema

This is also after Anne and I made our giant in-roads into naming Oregon's Literary Cinematic Voice. We named it cross-cultural, but after this event the Elders told Anne that Oregon was not Cross-Cultural, but Bicultural. Also, thanks to this presentation by Anne, the U of O also screened Oregon's own James Blue's films, who was the first American to win at Cannes for *Olive Trees of Justice* (1962) and the first Oregonian to be nominated for an Academy Award for his documentary *A Few Notes*

On Our Food Problem (1968). This was huge feat in 1968, not even our most famous Oregon-made director James Ivory was nominated for an Academy award until 1987, almost 20 years later. I also claim James Blue as a bicultural filmmaker, who like Hoyt Axton, Kesey, and I had heritage from Oklahoma, and all whom have a bicultural voice.

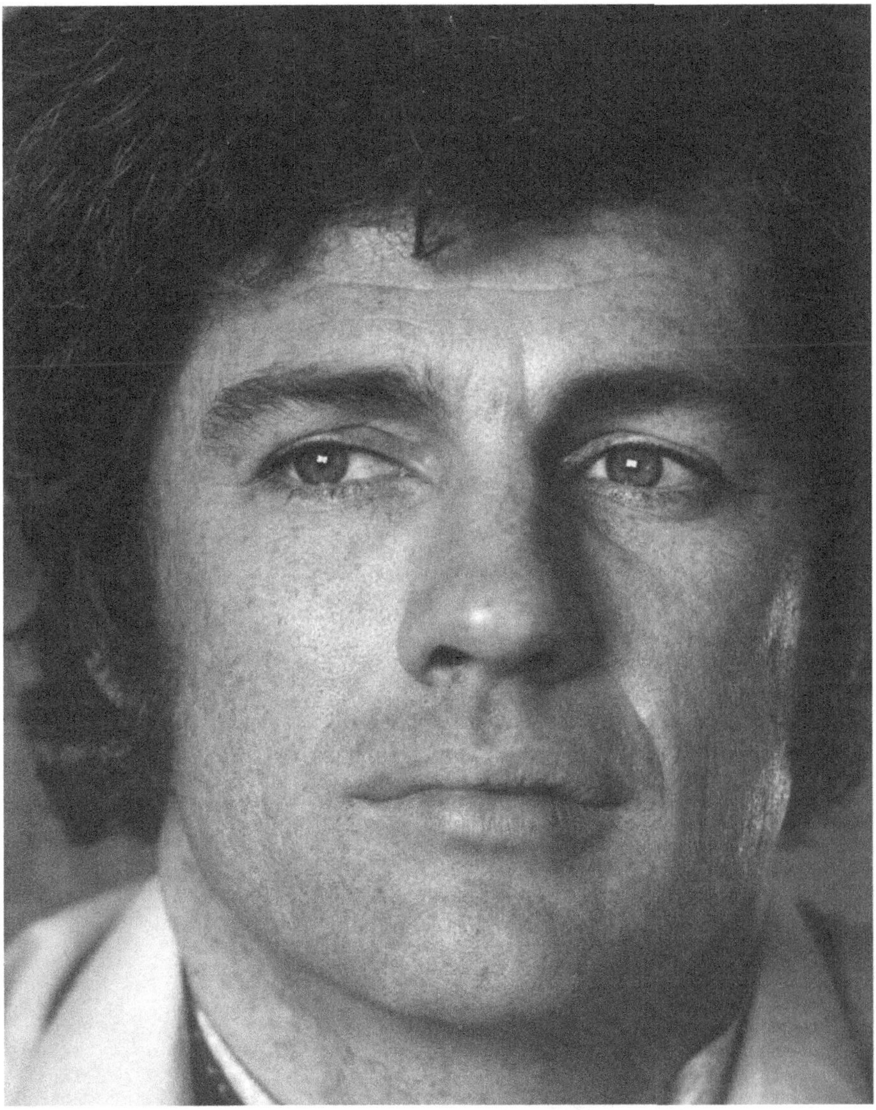

James Blue, Class of '53, University of Oregon. Photo courtesy of family archives.

Meanwhile, back at the ranch, in the second half of the 60s, Kesey had moved back to Oregon, and started editing the footage that would become *Magic Trip*; the Haight/Ashbury originals had moved to Marin,

Dan Hicks from the Charlatans had moved to Gate 5 in Sausalito, and they all continued to lead the way, from their houseboats and farms, especially Kesey with his bus footage gathering filmmakers together, that Jack Nicholson would benefit from later in 1969. And we followed them, everywhere they went. They were indeed the "Flower Power people" whom Poet Allen Ginsberg had called together in Berkeley in 1965. The truth is, the Hippies came later, around the time of the media frenzy we call the Summer of Love in '67.

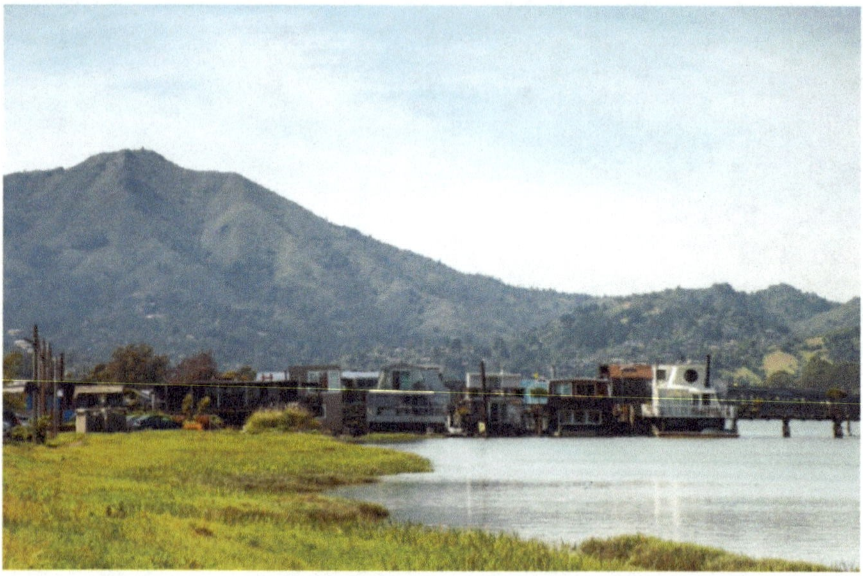

Houseboats at Gate 6, Sausalito

I know that the first of these "Flower Children" were biculturals, like the Red Dog Saloon Founders, and our own friend Kemo, who initiated us with an Indian ceremony before smoking our first joint. This was on Gate 6 on The Issaquah, an old 1914 Ferry Boat from Seattle, with a "Ballroom" in the hull, and a Bathroom.

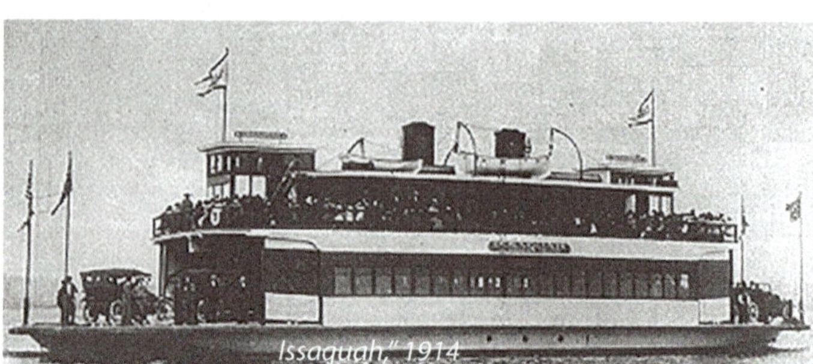

Issaquah," 1914

I had been out to Kesey's farm long before I made it to San Francisco, which was within weeks of my leaving home to go to college the Fall of 1969. But the father of my children had been working in San Francisco over the last four summers at Bally Lo, which was a "Hip" Boutique in Union Square.

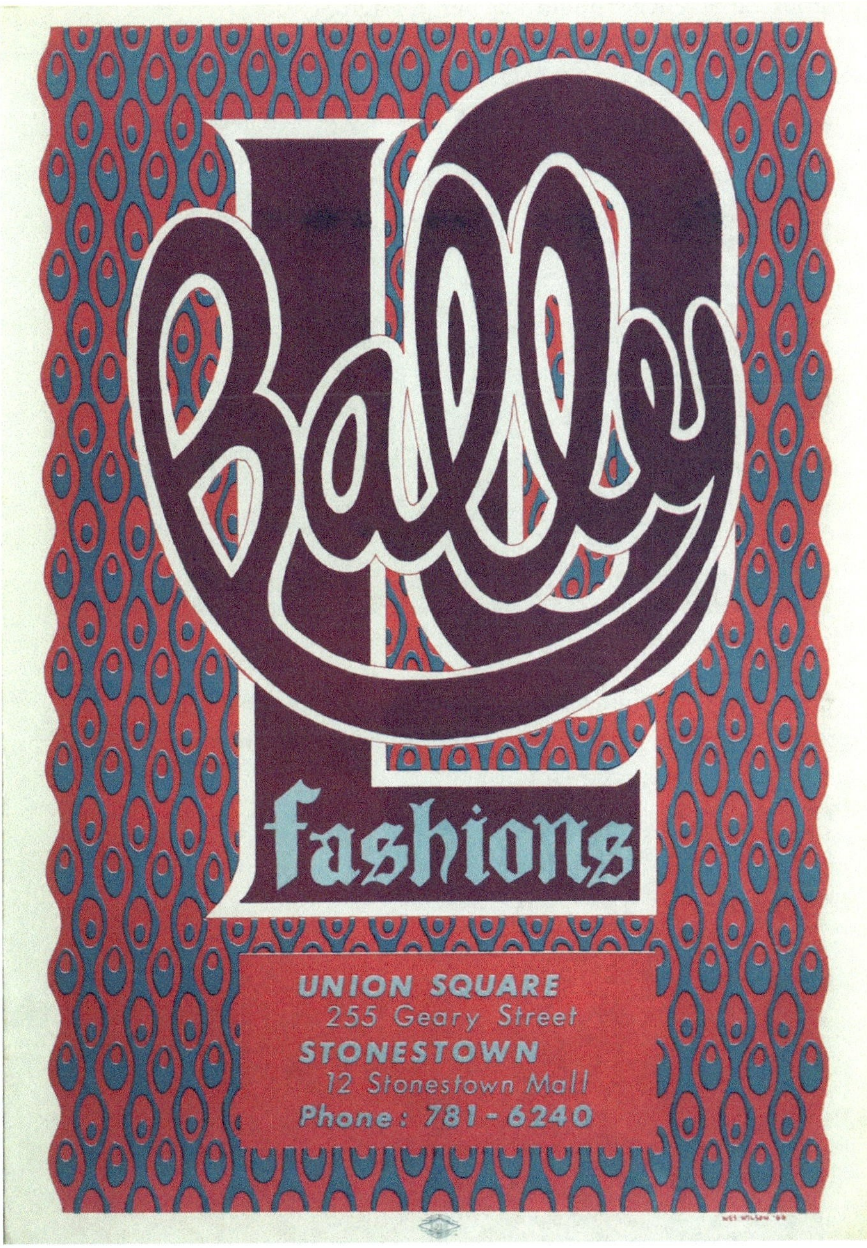

Bally Lo Boutique. Poster 14 x 20 inches by Wes Wilson 1966.
Courtesy of Gary Westford

Jay Wilson brought that *Flower Power* back to Eugene with a handful of Psychedelics, Psychedelic Posters, Vinyl Music and Bally Lo clothes (like the Beatles line) which he wears in this photograph of him in Eugene's very first Rock-n-Roll Band, The Hammond Typewriter. He was my Political Science student teacher in High School.

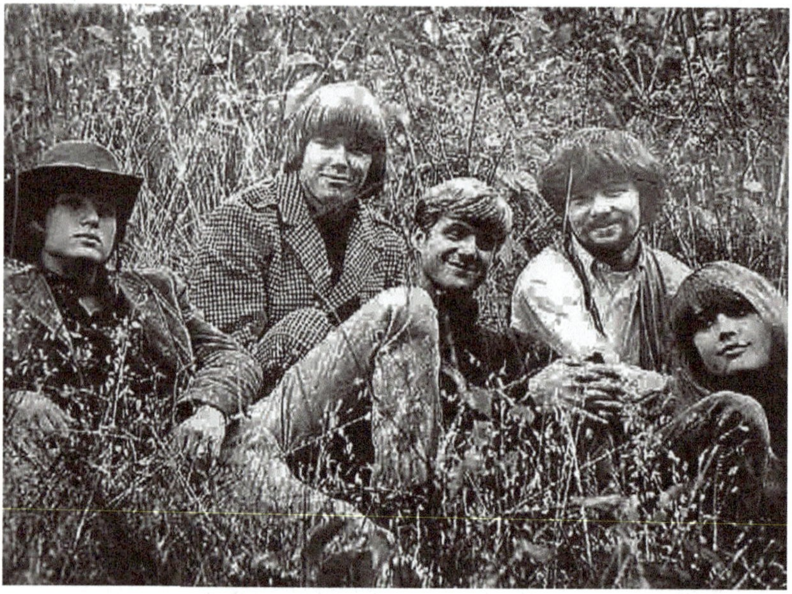

Wane Fuday, Jay Wilson, Ben Hall, Cliff "Bummer" Hunter and Debbie Gordon in Hammond Typewriter.

The band also had a dance hall called Billy Shears in Eugene OR. Here are 2 of their posters. The father of my children is Jay Wilson, from our 18-year marriage. Great Guy!

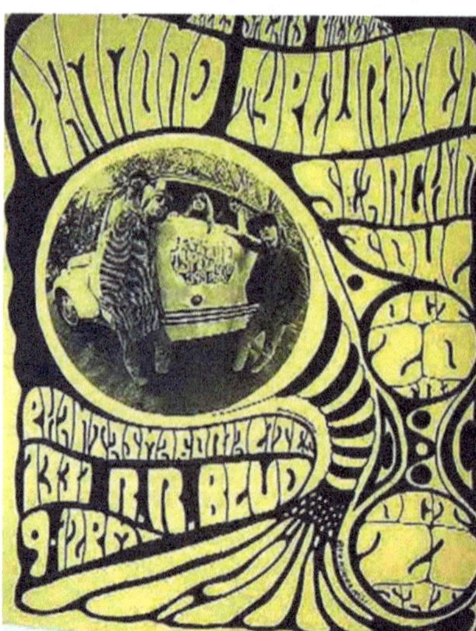

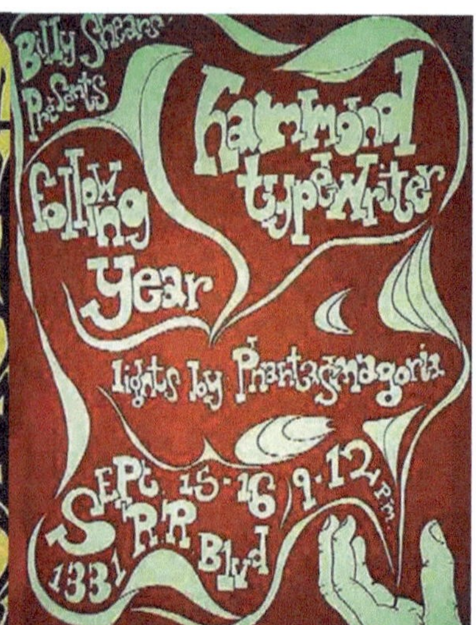

The Peace and Love generation actually created something to generate peace and love, and that was a counter-culture to what academic, Andrea Smith now calls, *Heteropatriarchy and The Three Pillars Of White Supremacy.*[98]

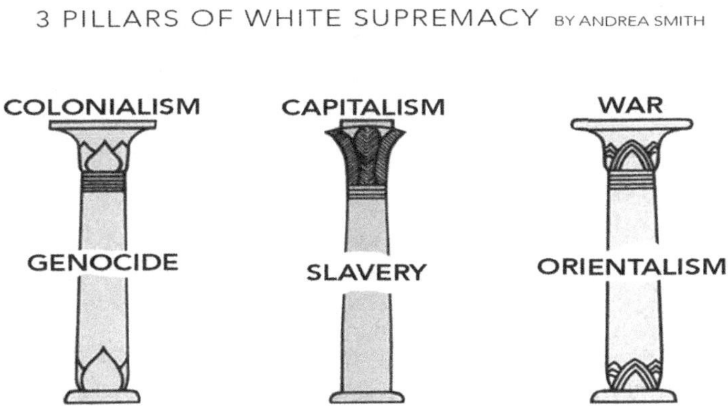

The Three Pillars of Racism by Andrea Smith, Feminist and Cherokee Intellectual

To counter war, we needed to counter Political Conservativism; which is why the father of my children, Jay Wilson, wanted to teach Political Science. To counter Colonialism we needed to counter its Cultural Genocide of Native American people, and honor and celebrate them and their culture. To counter Heteropatriarchy we needed Sexual Freedom, but to counter that we needed to counter Monotheism and Puritanical constructs that kept women prisoners; to counter that Monotheistic Patriarchy we needed Feminism; to counter war and genocide we needed to counter Capitalism; to counter earth exploitation we needed environmentalism. And last but not least, to counter racism we needed to counter White Supremacy, which were all tied together in supporting the three pillars of racism: Monotheism, Capitalism, Heteropatriarchy, War mongering, Genocide *et al.,* fed into each other and were intertwined.

It is important to me to relate this history before it is lost. If you read current Academic literature on the subject, such as Harvard Professor Philip Deloria's recent work titled *Counterculture Indians and the New Age*[99]; which he begins with an experience on a commune in 1971 as a boy; and which somehow gives him authority to essentially lump *counter-culturalists, communalists and New Agers* into a stereotype of cultural appropriating Hippies of Indian-ness. I counter this by trying to show in this book how the whole movement was most probably birthed in a Tribal Peyote ceremony of the Native American Church of the Comstock. I also countered this in a presentation with the simple fact that by 1971, the original Flower Child movement had been commodified by the Media.

In all fairness, he highlights crucial concepts like Postmodernism and uses critical terminology such as symbolic meanings, by which "we can also witness the continued unraveling of the connections between meanings and social realities," and "one can see the long shadows of certain strands of postmodernism: increasing reliance on texts and interpretations, runaway individualism within a rhetoric of community." But I hope in my book to disagree with the rest of the paragraph denoting, in Deloria's word: "the distancing of native people, and a gaping disjuncture between a cultural realm of serious play and the power dynamics of social conflict. New Age thinking tends to focus on ultimate individual liberation and engagement with a higher power, *having little interest in the social world that lies between self and spirit*."[100] Yeats would also counter with this: "Within this system it is pointless for the soul to seek to express itself with subjective intellectual sincerity when it is in an incarnation that requires it to explore worldly or spiritual objectivity, and similarly a soul whose purpose is to explore imaginative creativity should not attempt to lead the life of a social reformer or saint."[101]

And with great respect to his father, Vine Deloria, Jr; I do agree with Philip Deloria's brilliant and nuanced claims that are true when he unpacks what it means to be "Playing Indian."[102] The weaknesses of his project, however, is in a generalized stereotyping of the 60s generation, which should really be named as "Hippies." I wonder why he never used that word. Perhaps he didn't know, like Wikipedia, that "The Flower Children" were NOT Hippies.

What he was too young to know was the true founders of communalism, the counterculture and the New Age in the very early 60s were truly the "Flower-Children" of San Francisco, who were very involved in creating the social programs of their counter-culture, like this one for the American Indian Well-Baby Clinic in 1967.

The Well-Baby Clinic was just one social effort, there were many more. Haight/Ashbury Free Medical Clinic according to David Smith, the founder began in 1967 as a social program, inspired by The Diggers, who provided free food:

> The hippies flowing into San Francisco in 1967 weren't embraced by everyone with open arms, and city health officials at the time thought that a clinic in the Haight would only encourage them to stay. Smith, who had never been involved in activism before, saw the suffering in his neighborhood, and inspired by other free movements like the Diggers (who served free meals) and a bit of drug experimentation of his own, decided he had to do something.[103]

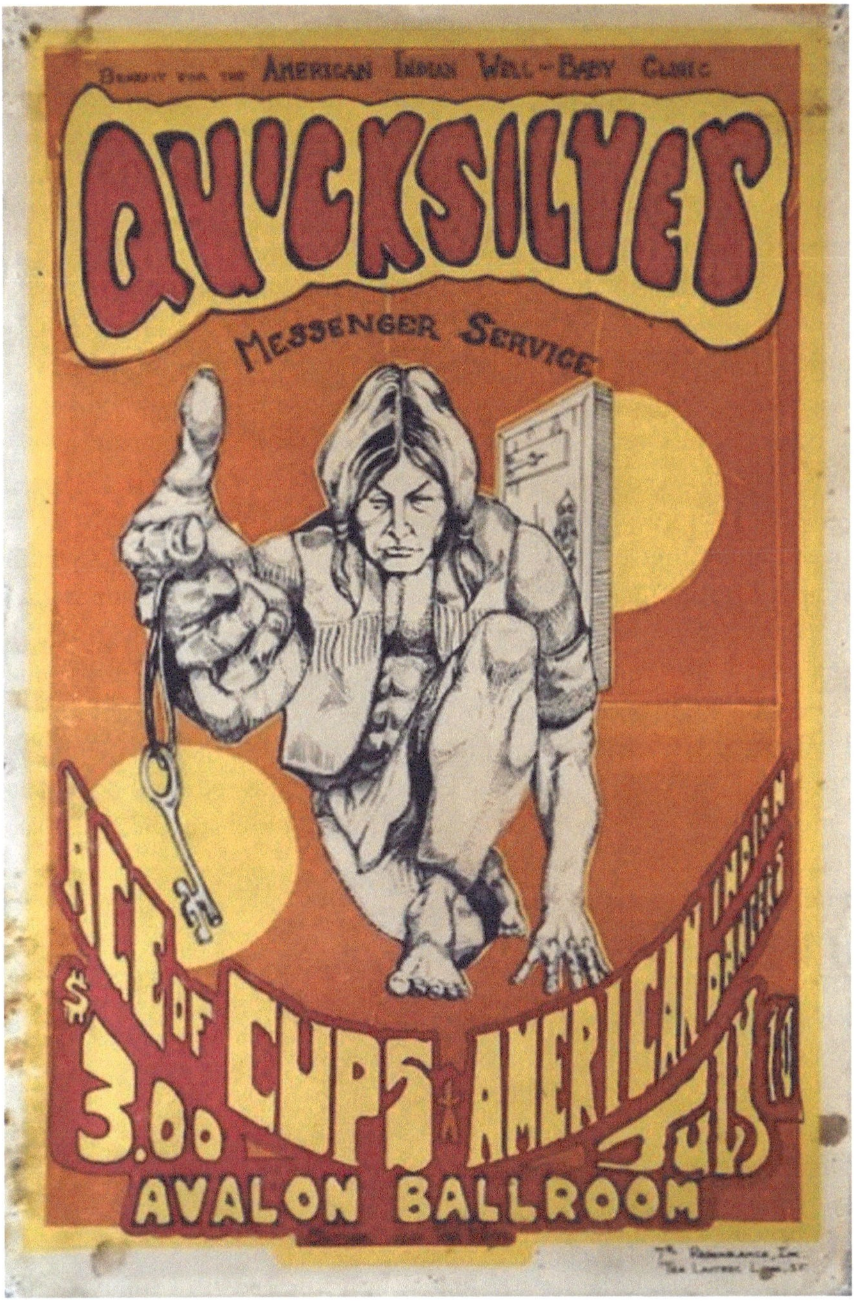

Benefit for the American Indian Well-Baby Clinic Poster, 1967. Courtesy of Gary Westford

The truth is, this generation created the greatest social changes ever known to Western Civilization since the French and American Revolutions. The postmodern crisis in America caused them to join together to embrace a new kind of multiculturalism. After all, it was this generation who went on to create solutions: "The Third World Strike at San Francisco State from November 6, 1968 until March 21, 1969 demanding that the university included histories of communities of color in their curricula to be taught by people of color. It united white students, community members and students from the Afro-American Students Union, the Asian American Political Alliance, the Mexican-American Student Confederation, and the Native American Student Organization."[104]

And so it is no accident that *Little Big Man* started production on July 14, 1969. Hollywood wanted in on the action. That is until they were called on the red carpet by an actual Indian in the most hallowed of Hollywood Halls, the Oscars. In *Making of the White Man's Indian: Native Americans and Hollywood Movies* by Angela Aleiss, the author begins her article by stating that in spite of the claims of some about her authenticity, Sasheen Littlefeather, by proxy for Marlon Brando at the Academy Awards in (March 27th) 1973, *had "foisted" the country's sins against the Native American people on their shoulders.*[105] It was incredible timing given the rise of the American Indian Movement's efforts to counter colonialism in Wounded Knee at the same time, (February 27 – May 8, 1973); in addition to their Bureau of Indian Affairs occupation in D.C. just a few months before. The Occupation of Alcatraz in the San Francisco Bay was "November 20, 1969 -June 11, 1971, a 19-month long protest led by Richard Oakes, LaNada Means, and others, while John Trudell served as spokesman."[106] All these dates give us context around the time *Little Big Man* was made all the way through the Oscars of 1973. There were 50 occupations at the time, including the BIA in Portland that my friend Ed Edmo was a part of, as well as my best friend Etta Conner, who was a secretary at Portland State.

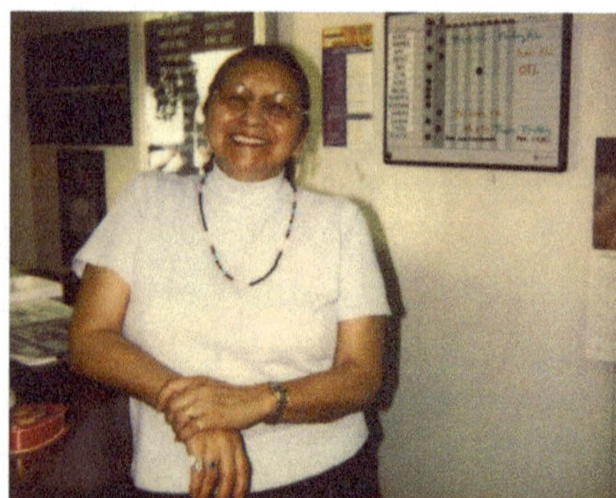

Etta Conner Scott at Portland State University

Regarding Deloria, it's ironic that even the Flower Children called the 75,000 mediated Hippies "tourists" when they descended there in San Francisco in 1967, and promptly left town for Marin County, until that too became overtaken; and then many of them moved to Oregon, to follow Ken Kesey. Additionally, let's take a look at Deloria's' "counter communalists." Michael Douglas was one, living on a Commune in Santa

Barbara when he talked his Dad Kirk Douglas into letting him produce *One Flew Over the Cuckoo's Nest* (1975). On the production he still had a dent in the back of his car because he had used the insurance money for groceries to keep going and not give up on the film. Another communalist, David Skinner, who lived in one in Oregon, went on to finance the making of *Smoke Signals*, the very first American Indian film to get a domestic distribution deal. It was directed by my friend Chris Eyre, and it was a huge hit. According to Cree director Neil Diamond in *Reel Injuns*[107] both *Cuckoo's Nest* and *Smoke Signals* represented a sea change in the depiction of the American Indian from the former Vanishing American ideology to ones who have broken out of that particular insane asylum and are reconstructing, embracing and celebrating their own culture. This evolution in the consciousness of popular culture and the American Psyche would never have happened on a grand scale if it stayed in the liminal spaces of "The Western" and *The Searchers*, without the powerful culture and intervention of the Hollywood Renaissance which was started and created by the 60s Flower Children.

In turn, the success of these films were built on the backs of a long line of Westerns that challenged the Colonialist paradigm and stereotype of Indian people as savages, beginning with colonialist manifest destiny film Director John Ford. In his film *The Searchers (1956)* however, his aperture shots of doorways and caves created a liminal space to beg the questions of colonizer definitions of blood quantum, family and Indianness. There, the Anti-western was born. And the John Ford cave became the very place that John Wayne, the representative of the American cowboy as symbolic of The US foreign policy in Europe, wrestled with his own hegemonic racism in both *The Searchers* and *Cheyenne Autumn* about Indigenous people; and in Howard Hawks' *Rio Lobo* about women. Director Arthur Penn then took up the Anti-western (read Anti-Hegemonic-Hero) with *Little Big Man*, and blew apart the liminal spaces of blood quantum and family hegemonic conversations and resulting definitions of what is Indian and what is white; when the protagonist Dustin Hoffman bounces back and forth between the cultures and ends up blending them in himself and therefore the family of man. Talk about bicultural!

It occurs to me that these liminal spaces may have been places of consciousness, and if ancient psychotropic drugs were a way to access that consciousness, then the advent of the psychedelic 60s may have had a hand in changing the consciousness of a critical mass of Americans. And is it possible it also accessed ancient DNA memory? Ken Kesey wrote the first chapter to *One Flew Over the Cuckoo's Nest* on Peyote, and was thought by his cousin Dale to possibly be Cherokee on his Grandfather Kesey's side, who was also from Oklahoma. Kesey's other cousin, Jimmy, is looking into it, he said. There are hundreds of thousands of people on the West Coast with Indigenous DNA. And yes, a great many families I personally know are from Oklahoma, like Hoyt Axton, James Blue, and my Grandmother. Remember that American Indian Activist John Trudell believed in DNA memory. He stated in the film *Reel Injuns* that these "hippies" may just be remembering: "They were, in a way, trying to imitate us, but in another way they were trying to remember who they were. Every human being is a descendant of a tribe. So these white people, they are a descendent of tribes. There was a time in their ancestry when they wore feathers all right, and they wore beads, and they wore shells. There was a time in their ancestry, all right, before this colonizing mentality did to them, to turn them into the white people they are, and then it came and did it to us. That very same thing that happened to us, happened to them."[108] This is what Yeats would say about what we now call DNA memory:

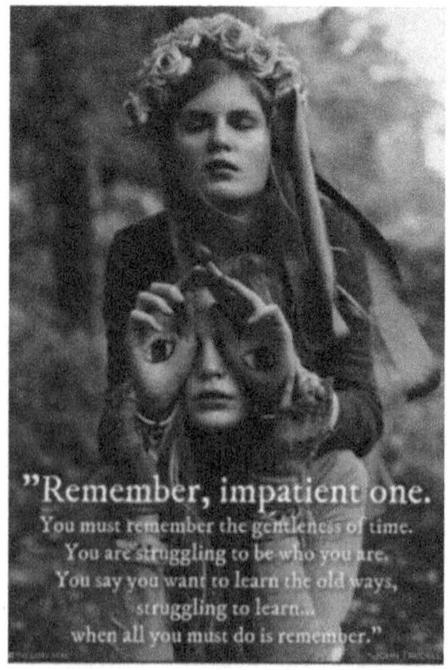

"One of the objectives of this technologic reality has to do with erasing the memories of the human beings, because we have a common collective experience. We are all the descendants of tribes. Because we have ancestral memory. It's encoded in the DNA – it's a genetic memory." ~John Trudell The Lion's Roar

> Before the mind's eye, whether in sleep or walking, came images that one was to discover presently in some book one had never read, and after looking in vain for explanation to the current theory of forgotten personal memory, I came to believe in a Great Memory passing from generation to generation. But that was not enough, for these images showed intention and choice (...). The thought was again and again before me that this study had created a contact or mingling with minds who had followed a like study in some other age (...). Our daily thought was certainly but the line of foam at the shallow edge of a vast luminous sea.[109]

The mother of my Grandson, Dr. Sara Waters is a neuroscientist and is constructing research right now with Indigenous people to help their children with transgenerational trauma. Could it be that all of us have transgenerational trauma, and are looking for answers back in time before it all went wrong? That seems to be a logical place to start, to me.

Here is a census from 2010. If you look closely at this diagram of it from Wikipedia, you will see, that of the nearly 5 MM Indigenous people and mixed-race people in America are on the West Coast of North America, alone.[110] The largest concentration. Even if I feel my generation was generalized, I am grateful to Dr. Deloria, however, for defining Post-modernism so well, because he was one of the first to be so articulate about that paradigm:

Native Americans

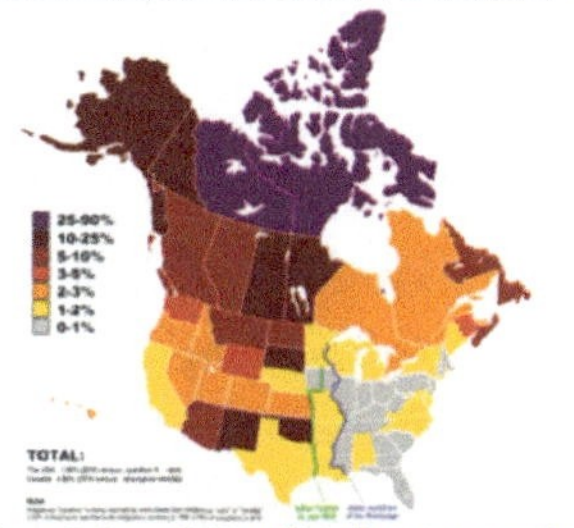

Percent of population with indigenous ancestry by U.S. state and Canadian province/territory

Total population
American Indian and Alaska Native (2010 Census Bureau)[1]
One race: 2,932,248 are registered
In combination with one or more of the other races listed: 2,288,331
Total: 5,220,579 ~ 1.6% of the total U.S. population.
Regions with significant populations
Predominantly in the Western United States; small communities also exist in the Eastern United States

> But Indianness has always been about contradictions, and its uses were hardly confined to this creative, confusing world of free meanings. Indeed, in such a decentered world, many people found themselves searching for something fixed, real, and authentic. *Paul Goodman concluded that what really drove the counterculture was a crisis of meaning that was spiritual at base and that "in the end it is religion that constitutes the strength of this generation and not, as I used to think, their morality, political will, and common sense."*[111]

And really loved it when he said:

> ... Indianness could also be a sign of something unchanging, a first principle. This other kind of Indianness also had a powerful, if often half-conscious, history.[112]

Which brings me to the fact that many, many people of my generation were accessing this consciousness of "something unchanging, a first principle" through the use of psychotropic drugs like peyote. No wonder they craved wearing symbolic clothing that expressed their inner consciousness. I believe it was this, in addition to an ever-increasing amount of biculturals like myself in the population, that helped this generation's ideals reach critical mass. By pushing back on Deloria's article, I was forced to research even more into my own truth (and consequently the Truth of

Yeats' theories through Literary critic Northrup Frye) where I found Deloria's Postmodern symptoms were identical to those that Yeats and Frye stipulated as indicating the end of one aeon and the beginning of the next. *Just where we are now*. For instance, Literary Critic Northrup Frye said, when talking about Yeats' Gyres of Time: "...prepares not the continuance of itself but the revelation as in a lightning flash, though in a flash that will not strike only in one place, and will for a time be constantly repeated, of the civilization that must slowly take its place."[113]

The "revelation as in a lightening flash" was hitting the towers of the new age which were like hotspots all over the country: The Civil Rights struggles in the South with Martin Luther King; Women's Rights on the East Coast with Gloria Steinem; Environmental Rights on the West Coast with the Sierra Club, and the Anti-war Movement, both in San Francisco; and the American Indian Movement in the Midwest, and from the Southwest came the Hopi Prophesies. Remember, the Hopi had predicted our long hair generation long before 1967.

"This is the Eighth Sign: You will see many youth, who wear their hair long like my people, come and join the tribal nations, to learn their ways and wisdom.[114] The 8th Prophecy about "many youth who wear their hair long" came true ... because I was one of them. The very first very long hair people came from San Francisco, went to San Francisco State, like George Hunter, who became involved in the Red Dog Saloon through the Charlatans. The Red Dog Saloon Cowboy and Indian people became the Family Dog people who started the infamous concerts at the Fillmore, the Avalon, and Winterland. Although we were popping up everywhere, but when the American Indian Movement took over Alcatraz Island in the San Francisco Bay, the center of all of the Countercultural Movement was there.

And the Countercultural Movement had indeed, as Deloria has written, called to ask what was God, now that God was Dead, (and his Dad Vine Deloria had answered, God is Red!;) was taking to task notions of objective Truth, such as what was Democracy, what was Altruistic, which, according to Northrup Frye, by unpacking Yeats' Gyre's of Time theory, and his poem Second Coming, began "the counter-active movement" towards another Troy; towards being "strongly individualized" with an antithetical and different birth of a Messianic entity; then to another Charlemagne; another fall again of another Byzantium; back to where we were just at the beginning of the century: objective Truths, Altruistic, and Democratic, in 2000 years, the full cycle of an Aeon. Frye also explains Yeats' Gyre theories which are also tied in with his Lunar Phases of the Moon:

> There are two great rhythmical movements in all living beings, a movement towards unity and a movement towards individuality. These are opposed and contrasting movements, and are symbolized in Yeats by a double gyre; a movement in one directions which, as it grows more pervasive, develops the counteracting movement within itself, so that the apex of the next gyre appears in the middle of the base of the preceding one and moves back through it.... Of course it is in history that these cycles are easiest to see. The conception is similar to ... Spengler's *Decline of the West.* [115]

Yeats' theory about the cosmos was designed similarly, "in that as above, so below" kind of way, as we shall see here in this quote from Northrup Frye about them:

> In Yeats this communal consciousness is part of the drive toward unity. It is the primitive mentality in which all historical cycles begin, and the decadent mentality in which they end, hence it is the 'primary' rhythm of existence. Over against it is an 'antithetical' development of individuality, which reaches its greatest height in the hero. In primitive society the communal consciousness is so strong that there hardly seems to be any real individuality, as we know it, at all.[116]

However the sentence I resonated with so much was when Frye showed us how Yeats was likening this cycle to the 28 days in the cycle of the Moon, where we were, prior to the turn-of-the-century, in Phase 8 to 15:

> ... Individuality begins in the unhappy and tormented souls who are aware of a double pull within them around Phase 8. As we cross the quadrant of Phase 8 we begin to move into the antithetical area, beginning with intense and withdrawn figures like Parnell (Phase 10) or Nietzsche (Phase 12). Individuality then advances to heroic proportions, and we have 'sensualists' so complete that they represent a kind of antithesis to sanctity (Phase 13), artists of tempestuous passion, women of fully ripened physical beauty, and heroes of arrogant pride like the heroes of Shakespeare's tragedies. [117]

Charles Stewart Parnell (27 June 1846 – 6 October 1891) was an Irish nationalist politician who served as a Member of Parliament (MP) from 1875 to 1891, also acting as Leader of the Home Rule League from

1880 to 1882 and then Leader of the Irish Parliamentary Party from 1882 to 1891.[118] Nietzsche was a contemporary, he lived from 15 October 1844 – 25 August 1900. Then comes the WWI, The Victorian Era of Art; The Roaring 20s; and the Great Depression.

> At the point of highest development represented by Phase 15 *the counter-movement back to communal consciousness begins.* Artists become less embodiments of passion and more intellectualized (Phase 21), or technicians (Phase 23); heroes come to think of themselves as servants of impersonal force, like Napoleon (Phase 20), or the money obsessed characters in Balzac; women come to be guardians of a generally accepted morality like Queen Victoria (Phase 24). The 'personality', which is the fully developed individuality, becomes the 'character', a *subjective conception implying that something objective to it is greater…* [119]

And then WWII and our generation is born:

> At later primary stages personality becomes more fragmented, this fragmentation being represented by the physical deformity of the hunchback (Phase 26), and the mental deformity of the fool (Phase 28). What Spengler calls the 'second religiousness' comes into society in the forms of spiritualism, theosophy, and various forms of revived occultism, *seeking the same kind of kinship with the invisible world, at the other end of the social cycle, that primitive societies show in their myths and folk-tales and so-called superstitions.*[120]

Suddenly, everything makes sense. The Critical Literary Deconstructionists theories born in the 60s like Roland Barthes' "The Death of the Author," Derrida's "Double Liminality"[121] and Raymond Williams' cry for an academic "Structure of Feeling," are very psychedelic. There is also a new Spiritual Quantum Mechanics Religion emerging within Ernest Holmes' church of "New Thought" (1926) making room in Christianity for a new understanding of "The Holy Spirit":

> The passing of old orders of thought is but a proclamation of the inauguration of new and higher orders. Modern psychology, metaphysics, and philosophy all announce a new birth of the Mind, a new discovery of the self, a new consciousness of the intimacy of the Mind with the subtle Spirit within each of us. There appears to be one persistent purpose behind the great forward movement of

> evolution, namely, the expression of Intelligence, through creation, into higher, finer, and more complex forms. An insistent and intelligent Urge in the Life-Principle impels it to express. Spirit IS forever clothing itself in form. If we were to ask our imagination why this is so, the answer might be that God Himself would remain a nonentity unless (S)He were expressed.[122]

This non-denomination religion's largest church is in Los Angeles, California led by the Dr. Rev. Michael Bernard Beckwith. It's called *Agape,* and it celebrates all religions and races. For example, one week a relative of Black Elk may lead, another week Martin Luther King, Jr. may lead. Musicians, Artists and Filmmakers have belonged to it since the late 80s. "Since its doors opened in 1986, Agape's active teaching and practice of the New Thought-Ancient Wisdom tradition of spirituality has expanded into a trans-denominational movement and community; Over 10,000 local members and 1,000,000 friends (streaming) worldwide. Through Dr. Beckwith's weekly services, Agape's University of Transformational Studies and Leadership classes, ministries and other outreach programs, the heart of Agape reaches deep into local and global communities teaching individuals about the transforming, healing power of prayer, meditation, and selfless service."[123] I guess you could say that Dr. Rev. Michael Beckwith was just one of the people I know who experienced Frye's "flash that will not strike only in one place."

In remembering this, I also saw the residual effect of the "lightening striking" people like him, even up here in Oregon. Though they have passed away, they were two of the most important American Indian people to the University of Oregon; and my friends. One of them, Gordon Bettles, was the Steward for the U of O Longhouse from 2003 to 2018. The other was George Wasson, who worked in The Office of Academic Advising and Student Services, and a friend of Kesey's and mine whom I met in 1969 at The American Indian Student Union. They, too, were very active in the New Age of service, and welcomed us all.

Bicultural people have an amazing ability to know each other as "skins" (as Etta Conner called it); and it happened with Gordon the first time I went to the U of O Longhouse in 2004. I was hurting, and needed sacred space. Instinct led me there, and I found it in Gordon's care. As we are wont to do, he asked me where I was from and I told him Klamath Falls. He nodded his head downward as if he already knew. He asked me my last name. I told him, and he seemed to know even that, too. He softly said with a fond smile, "Your Mother was my 3rd grade teacher in Chiloquin." And I was home.

Thinking of Gordon brings up memories from Chiloquin. Not the murders, not the racism and grief and drunkenness, but the good memories. While writing this Chapter, I called my Dad, who knew of Gordon and his family to break the news. My Dad was a Special Education teacher for the 7th and 8th graders there, trying to get them so they could at least pass Jr. High and then try to get their diploma from Klamath Union High School. My Dad was bicultural, too. He really didn't like school all that much, either. He wanted to be a professional Boy Scout, or a Forester in the woods. But Carroll Howe, the Superintendent of Schools of Klamath County talked him into teaching. Carroll was very sympathetic to the Klamath/ Modoc Tribe and their deplorable situation of being terminated in the early 50s by the U. S. Government. Hiring my Dad, an Eagle Scout, and my Mom, an artist, were something he thought might help, as they both had training in helping non-traditional students. Before long, my Dad was taking these kids to Doak Mountain where he would get Park and Forestry people to share knowledge with them and they would share their knowledge back. One of my favorite memories was learning the names of Pipsissewa and Chinquapin, magical medicine plants. My Dad would go on to create the early Outdoor Schools in the 60s, and by the 70s were in such high demand he did them full time at various schools.

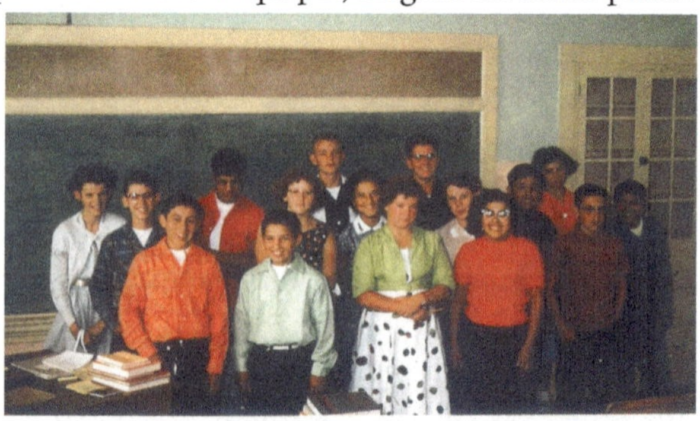

My Dad's Class in Chiloquin, Courtesy of John Heilbronner

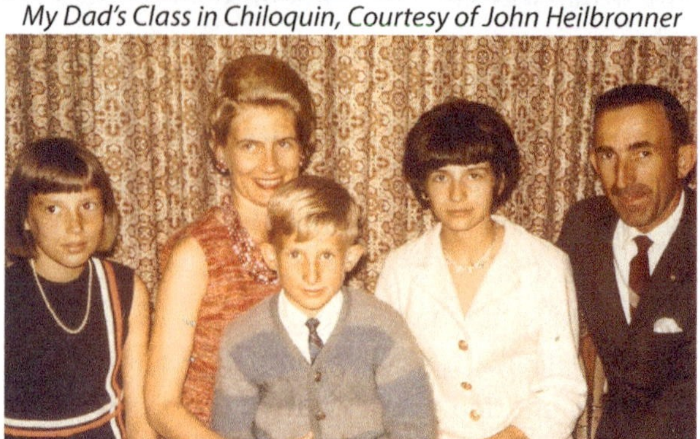

My sister, brother and I with Mother and Dad in the early 60s.

In the early 60s, I remember my mother, a Dane who looked like Marilyn Monroe, participated as an elementary teacher with the Kingsley Field Airforce Base in giving "special education" children LSD-25 to see if it helped them, just like Kesey's MKULTRA program. Our very own government was putting LSD into the Kool Aid. By the late 60s it had become a common quantum mechanics-like spiritual experience.

> This side of the LSD experience – the feeling! – tied in with Jung's theory of synchronicity. Jung tried to explain the meaningful coincidences that occur in life and cannot be explained by cause-and-effect reasoning, such as ESP phenomena. He put forth the hypothesis that the unconscious perceives certain archetypical patterns that elude the conscious mind. These patterns, he suggested, are what unite subjective or psychic events with objective phenomena, the Ego with the Non-Ego, as in psychosomatic medicine or in the *microphysical events of modern physics in which the eye of the beholder becomes an integral part of the experiment.*[124]

And back in the 60s, when it all began, just as Northrup Frye stated, these "white lightning" episodes of consciousness were cropping up everywhere. Us "round thinkers in a square world" had suffered in schools created by business leaders to make good office workers who would do what they were told, sit still at a desk and use small motor skills. We were gazing out the windows daydreaming in 3D. Suddenly, by the 60s the daydreamers got a chance. There were teachers at the U of O who cared more about your creativity than your grammar.

Kesey benefitted, Stephen J. Cannell benefited, and I benefitted in the later 60s.

And just like in this quote, it was because this revelation also became a template:

> "The Summer of Love became the template..." says Joe McDonald, the creator and lead singer of Country Joe and the Fish and a boyfriend of one of that summer's two queens, Janis Joplin. "And it became the new status quo," he continues. "The Aquarian Age! They all want sex. They all want to have fun. Everyone wants hope. We opened the (LSD consciousness) door, and everybody went through it, and everything changed after that."[125]

In those early days of the 60s, even kids who were being abused could be taken home by their teacher. We had a few of them living with us now and then. My favorite was a boy named Deter. What my Mom may have known, but I didn't know myself, until I, a failing student, started smoking tobacco and drinking coffee to medicate my ADD; was that I was a Special Education child myself. Remedial and Brilliant can be two sides of the same coin. The cigarettes and caffeine helped me get a 4.00 my senior year. I took my SAT's then too, and scored so high the U of O's head of the English Department called my Mom requesting I go to college. But it was not possible until I survived moving to Eugene the early summer of 1967 with my family, failing English at South Eugene, learning how to drive, and being so totally off the reservation that I didn't know what to think. That's when I started to smoke tobacco. When I met my current husband in Art Class, met Actor Ed Ragazzino in Drama Class, started hanging out with these long-haired boys in Errol Flynn dueling blouses tucked in their jeans, and rings on all of their fingers, something clicked. I found my tribe.

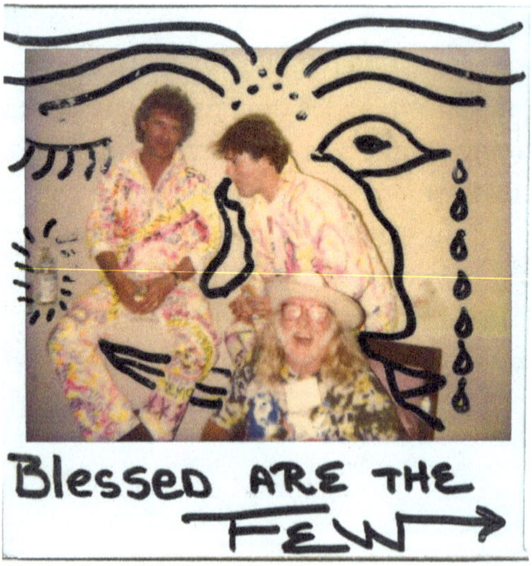

My husband Philip, with John Swan wearing Bus Uniforms and w/friend in Vegas with Kesey '90. Art by John Swan.

That's when my Mom asked me to participate in an 'in-service' Educational Sensitivity Seminar sponsored by Eugene's 4-J school district, with her and a bunch of older teachers. Turns out my super-sensitivity was now in fashion. And "suddenly that summer of 1967" I, like Dorothy in the *Wizard of Oz*, knew I was not in Kansas anymore. And I followed the yellow brick road which led me to Ken Kesey. My new tribal leader:

> From an early age, he was fascinated by fantasy, by any hint of exciting and mysterious things just beyond the reach of ordinary experience. He read a good deal as a boy, but until high school that reading was mostly comic books, Westerns, and science fiction – comic books

> such as Superman, Batman, and Captain Marvel; authors like Zane Grey, Edgar Rice Burroughs, and Jules Verne. This reading was the beginning of a quest, a manifestation of that perennial appetite for transcendent consciousness, a yearning instinctive in most everyone but especially acute in Kesey. It was this desire that enticed him, after he had written two novels, to seek beyond writing – through experiments with electronic media and further experiments with drugs – new forms of consciousness and artistic expression.[126]

And like Ken, I was soon to realize that writing was not enough, either; that I was a visual artist, sometimes a poet, but not really English Major material. But because of an almost-famous Drama teacher, Ed Ragazzino, and his soft words encouraging me, by telling me I was a natural actress; I joined the long list of the sort-of-famous-in-their-own-way South Eugene High's "Fame" School Kids; kids that danced to a different beat of the 60s; which included Richard Brautigan, (the voice of the 60s) Tim Hardin, (Woodstock) Julia Anne Robinson, (*King of Marvin Gardens*) Sue Pack (Holy Modal Rounders) Charlie Milhaupt (*Agnes of God*) my husband Philip Krysl (*Twilight*) and Oscar-nominated E. Max Frye. We all had that Oregon Bicultural Cinematic Voice, but by standing on the shoulders of these giants, and looking through their looking glass, I soon became a filmmaker because of them, and because of the Pranksters and Ken Kesey.

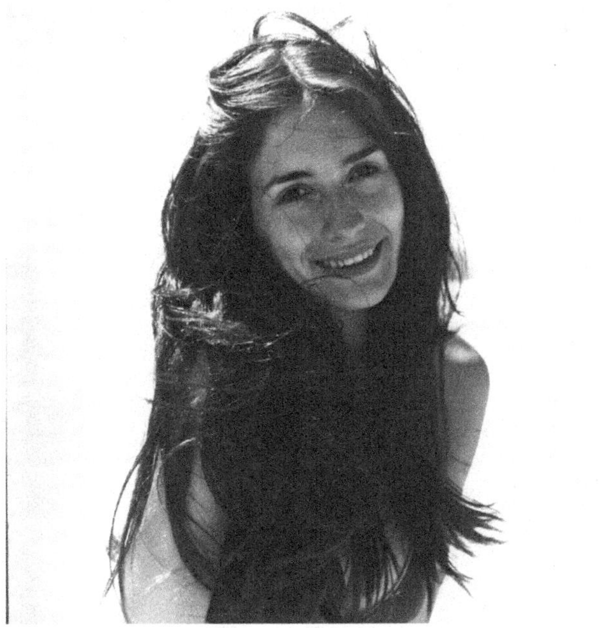

Photo of Katherine by Jay Wilson

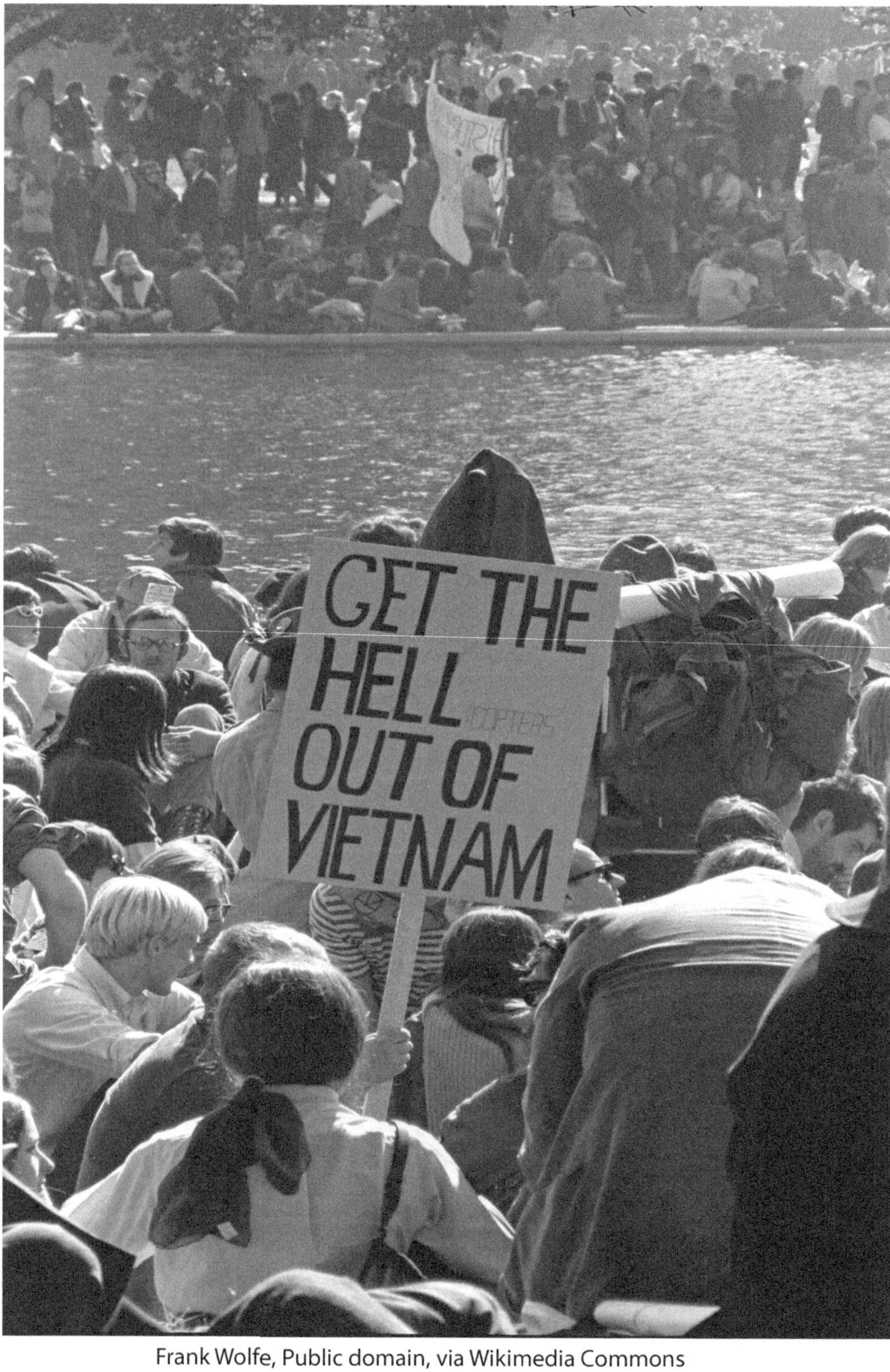

Frank Wolfe, Public domain, via Wikimedia Commons

Chapter 3

The Year of Revolt World-wide ~1968

> The United States is not at war; the United States *is war.* For the system of white supremacy to stay in place, the United States must always be at war.[127]
>
> –Sora Han, *Bonds of Representation*

The Year of Revolt was like Yeats' revolt against the intellect on a world-wide scale; the intellect as best represented by patriarchy. Patriarchy as Colonialism. Patriarchy as Puritanism. Patriarchy as Capitalism. Patriarchy as Cronyism. Patriarchy as rational, ordered, and linear. And ensued "the struggle between cold Apollonian categorization and Dionysiac lust and chaos"[128] as The Divine Archetype of Aquarius was now becoming the Universe's New Age, and was "claiming it's kin and bringing all into accord with the divine imprint on it."[129]

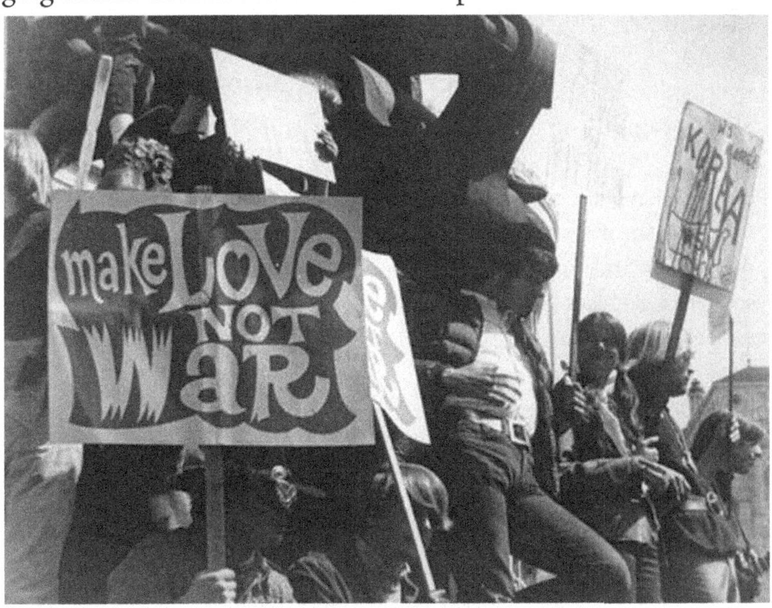

Make Love Not War Student Protests

And it was also about sex. The Patriarchal view about sex was that men controlled the bodies of women, so that they could ensure that their progeny was really theirs.

If you follow that logic, underneath it was the fear of being cuckolded and the fear of spending money raising some other man's child. But essentially to the reptilian mind, it was what was needed to guarantee the male progeny's seed of immortality.

> Everything was patriarchal, starting in the family, where you couldn't speak at the dinner table unless spoken to," says Josette Preud'homme, who took part in the 1968 protests as a 20-year-old and says it changed her life. "You couldn't go out with friends, and never with boys. Everything was forbidden everywhere. You had to obey orders in the factories, in the schools. We were suffocating. There was this enormous need to talk and share. Everyone was fed up.[130]

From what I have learned about from Russel Means and others about alternatives to patriarchy, American Indian tribes were mostly matriarchal, in that the seat of power was with women, and their lineage, of course, was never questioned because they birthed it. They decided who they wanted to sleep with. And suddenly with the advent of "THE pill." women everywhere started doing just that, upsetting the equilibrium between the sexes where men once tried to control women's sexuality through marriage and other legal means. But that was a one-way street in men's favor.

> Events that led directly to the revolt of May 1968 began in March on the campus of the University of Paris at Nanterre, on the far western edge of the city. The children of mostly bourgeois Parisians did not have sophisticated political demands. Their spontaneous occupation of some of the administration buildings was partly a demonstration against the Vietnam War, and partly to demand something closer to home: to be able to spend the night in each other's dorm rooms. Several students were arrested, and the university was temporarily closed.[131]

So essentially, students in Paris started protesting because they could not sleep with each other in sexually segregated dorms. And were soon joined by a general strike eventually involving some 10 million workers.

> Today in France, the events of May 1968 have taken on romantic, mythic proportions. On the 50th anniversary this month, mag-

azines and exhibitions are devoted to it, and documentaries and conferences are analyzing and re-analyzing it. May 1968 encompassed a cultural revolution, even a sexual revolution, before a political one. And in no other country did a student rebellion lead to a workers' revolt that nearly brought down a government.[132]

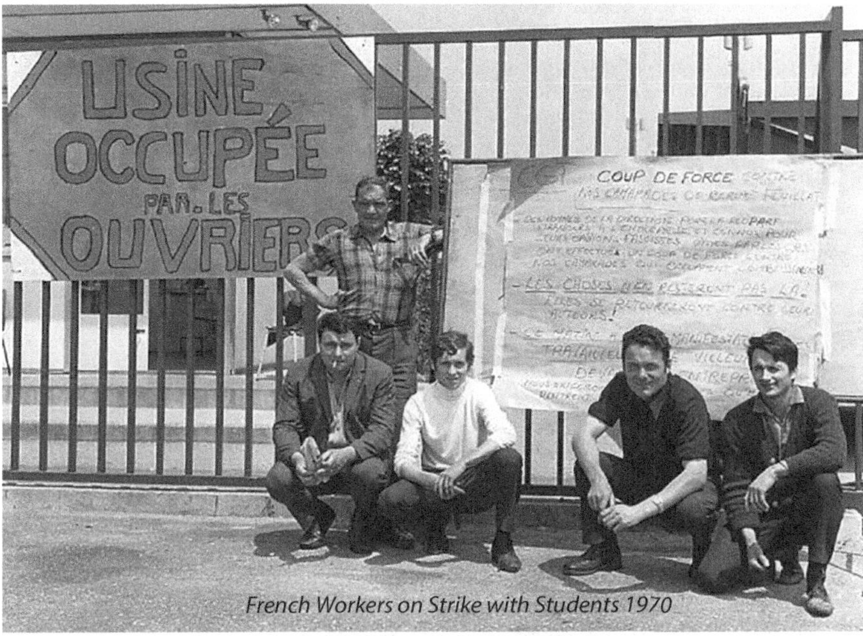

French Workers on Strike with Students 1970

BeenAroundAWhile via Wikimedia Common

Why would workers go on strike and support students who wanted to have sex? First of all, it was Paris, which has always been less prudish about sex, but sexual freedom also represented freedoms of personhood that the average worker felt had been compromised by the government. We have talked about the Cultural Revolution in the prior chapters, but what created the Sexual Revolution and this open attitude about sex, now, coming up above from the underground? Sex had always been treated with "kid gloves" in the past, from the Bible's Song of Solomon to D.H. Lawrence and James Bond movies. But we were in a Sexual Revolution now. And the revolution WAS being televised! It all began with the influences of First Wave feminists like Gloria Steinem and even Beat Poetry like Allen Ginsberg's *HOWL* in 1956, and then by artists and filmmakers, and consequently engendered lawsuits.

> It is not true that "Howl" was written as a performance piece and later published by poet Lawrence Ferlinghetti of City Lights Books.

(in San Francisco) This myth was perpetuated by Ferlinghetti as part of the defense's case during the poem's obscenity trial.[3] Upon the poem's release, Ferlinghetti and the bookstore's manager, Shigeyoshi Murao, were charged with disseminating obscene literature, and both were arrested. On October 3, 1957, Judge Clayton W. Horn ruled that the poem *was not obscene.*[4][133]

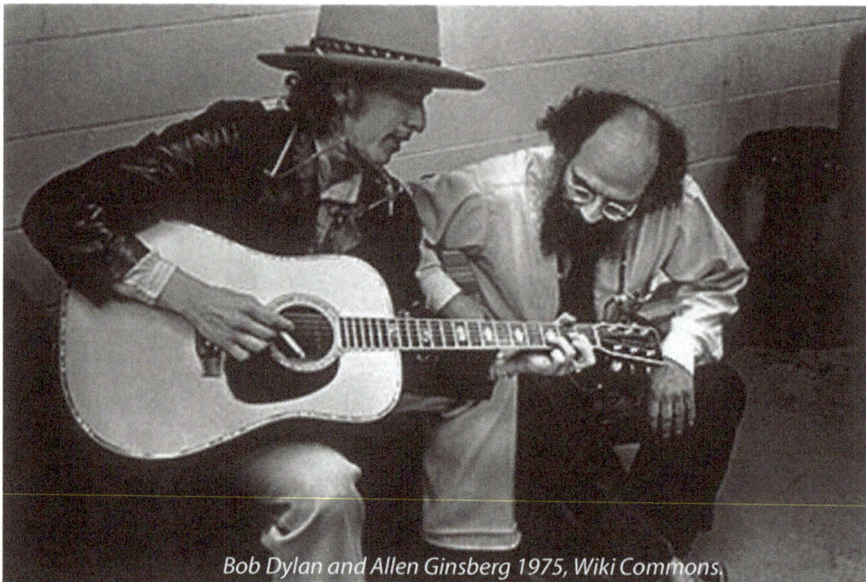

Bob Dylan and Allen Ginsberg 1975, Wiki Commons.

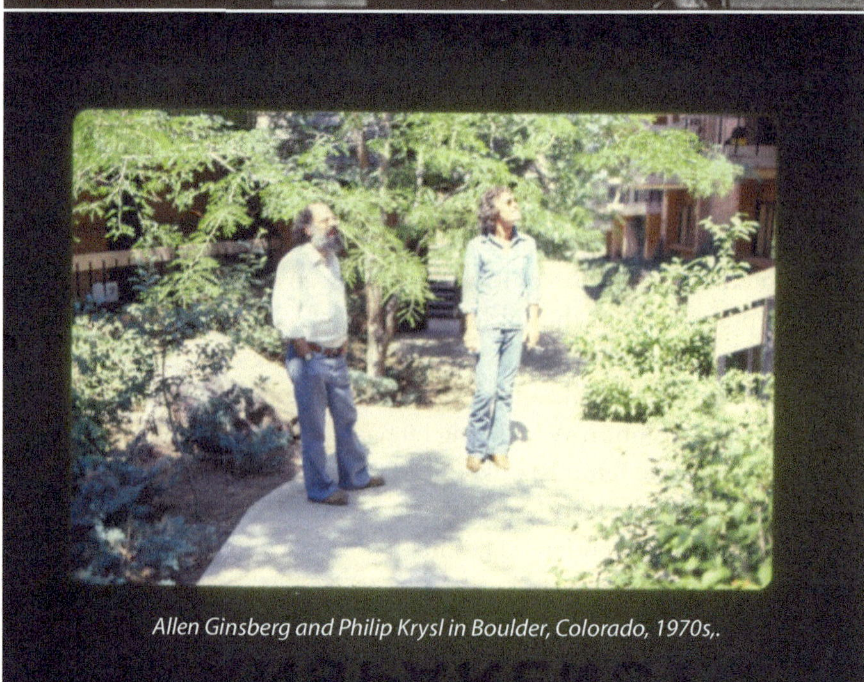

Allen Ginsberg and Philip Krysl in Boulder, Colorado, 1970s,.

My husband Philip Krysl's brother-in-law, Peter Michaelson, was friends with Allen Ginsberg, and with Avant Garde Filmmaker Stan Brakhage. They all were living in Boulder, Colorado in the late 60s and early 70s. Peter was a Professor of English at the University of Colorado at Boulder, and was married to Marilyn Krysl, Philip's sister. She was the head of the Creative Writing Dept. Ginsberg was there, however, because of the Naropa Institute, a Buddhist Enclave surrounding the "Holy Man" Trungpa Rinpoche, who in 1960 had escaped the Chinese Occupation of Tibet by climbing 19,000 feet and walking across the Himalayan Mountains on foot. Trungpa was funded to attend Oxford University and then came to America. His teachings were centered around crushing the ego body/spirit with alcohol, drugs and sex so that the authentic Dharma spirit could emerge; coining the phrase "Crazy Wisdom."[134]

"Naropa was founded by Chogyam Trungpa Rinpoche and the Poets Allen Ginsberg and Anne Waldman ... and was the largest Buddhist center in the U.S. because of Trungpa, who was a renowned Buddhist Luminary. Ginsberg and Anne Waldman started the writing program there named The Jack Kerouac School of Disembodied Poetics. Guest writers included William S. Burroughs, John Steinbeck IV, Gregory Corso, Gary Snyder, Ken Kesey."[135]

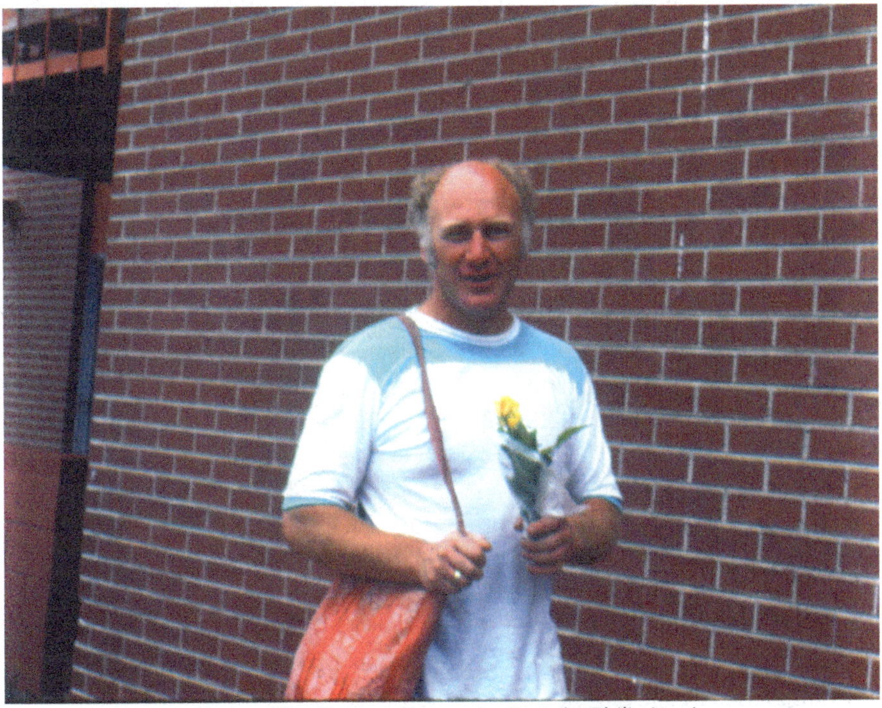

Photo of Ken Kesey @ Naropa Institute by Philip Krysl

Philip first went to Boulder to work as an artist and worked for an academic publisher. One day Peter took him up to Stan Brakhage's cabin in Lump Gulch near Nederland, Colorado for lunch. Somehow the conversation turned to where Philip and his sister Marilyn were from: Eugene, Oregon. That was when Brakhage told Philip he thought "Eugene was the Poetic Cinema Capitol of the World."[136]

Stan ended up teaching at CU Boulder with Marilyn and Peter, and helped jumpstart the Telluride Film Festival.

What this has to do with the "The Year of Revolt" and the Sexual Revolution, is that Stan's Poetic Cinema was revolutionary and very sexual: Brakhage even turned down a Hollywood Career because he "discovered the power of eroticism."[137]

"Only the subject of sex," Brakhage says, "would have had the power to get me to not only make a completely private film, but to also turn my career away from Hollywood."[138] And here is where Stan's poetic vision and Peter's academic work merge; and with Beatnik Allen Ginsberg, all come together, in a book written by Peter:

> Brakhage was among the first of the post-war filmmakers to challenge cultural duplicity about the role of sex in life and art by demonstrating that pornography imagery had aesthetic viability... the film's erotic vision has archetypal as well as persona.... If its erotic yearning is intensely personal, so does it reveal the human spirit's yearning to articulate the sexual nature.[139]

As you can maybe tell by now, Peter Michaelson is a great resource about Brakhage; but he also is a great resource for Avant Garde Film, which also ties the New Art of the 60s Beat Poets to film:

> ...the Avant Garde film has had an aesthetic impact far beyond either the volume of its production or its the limits of its distribution. Underground though it may have been, its spirit continues to pervade the study and practice of cinema. This ephemeral state makes documentation of its influence speculative at best. Nonetheless, it is there. And when one sees how television advertisements have, after polishing them up, co-opted the techniques of avant-garde films, one recognizes how pervasive their influence has been.[140]

Peter ended up writing two major books on the subject; the first, *A Poetics of Obscenity* was written from articles printed in well-known literary magazines in the early 60s, as shown here:

Portions of this book have appeared in somewhat different form in *Another Chicago Magazine, Continuum, The New Republic,* and *TriQuarterly* magazines, now published by State University of New York Press, Albany (SUNY). Rev. ed. of: The aesthetics of pornography. 1971.

The second book, *The Aesthetics of Pornography* was published in 1971, by Herder & Herder, New York. Peter is also a published poet and writer, and is revered by the counterculture for his work in unmasking the stigmatism of sexuality. The first book delves into Cinema as well as consciousness. It is in an article aptly called "Consciousness And Love's Body:"

> Complex or artistic pornography differs from hard-core or simple pornography in not being exclusively committed to the myth of animality and its explicit sexual imagery. And, while soft-core pornography offers ethical encouragement to the sentiments of the status quo, complex pornography, like most artistic modes, explores the moral recognition that necessarily precedes and informs true ethical perception. In the sense then that art is moral rather than ethical, artistic pornography is moral. It is generally distinguishable, however, by its matrix of consciousness, obscenity and the myth of love.[141]

Peter taught Literary Criticism and the Modern Novel at Notre Dame from 1965 to 1969. In an interview with a former student, they discuss his controversial 1969 academic Pornography and Censorship Conference, with Allen Ginsberg; that the Police raided and shut down. Peter and Ginsberg went way back to the days of the obscenity trials of Ginsberg's *Howl,* which Allen also wrote from a peyote-induced vision. As a result, others fought "A series of Supreme Court decisions (which) eased restrictions of movie obscenity, and the MPAA's liberalized Code and Rating Administration of 1968 replaced the stringent Production Code of 1934."[142] This was because Hollywood was afraid that the

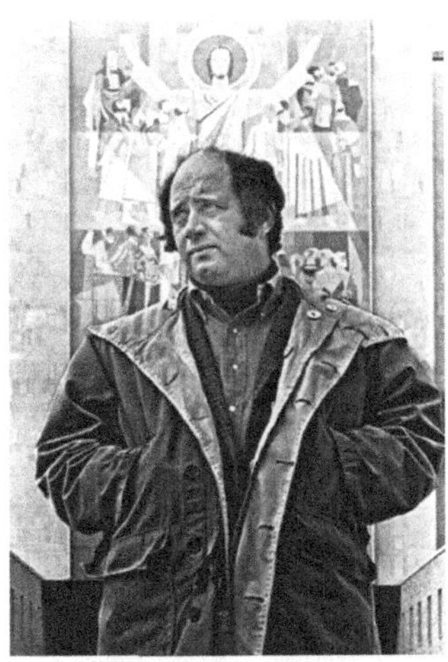

Peter Michaelson at Notre Dame

government would also start censoring and interfering in the motion picture industry, so Jack Valenti and other Studio Heads agreed to self-censure their own films under a new system when the 1934 Hays "Moral" Code began to become challenged by filmmakers. Their system put moral judgment in the hands of the parents when it came to questionable content. But Jack Nicholson famously derided the Motion Picture Association of America rating system when it formed in 1968. He said that it was ludicrous, that "if you kissed a woman's breast in a film, it was an X-rated movie, but if you sliced it off, it was only rated R."

But with those new movie rating "guidelines" in place, we were now able to jump off the cliff into the "New Consciousness" of the "New Hollywood" which was indeed a grand exploration of the "matrix of consciousness, obscenity and the myth of love." For instance, 1967's *The Graduate* was a good example of why the Hays Code was challenged. By exploring the character of Mrs. Robinson in the context of her generation, and the 50s obsession with sex as a well-known reaction to the threat of extinction; (read Nuclear Annihilation) this story brings out of the closest a well-known syndrome known as MILF. (Look it up in the Urban Dictionary.) It's "obscenity" is *poetic* in *The Graduate.*

Robert Evans then created an even more eclectic New Hollywood at Paramount a few years later by taking something like *The Graduate,* and making it even more poetic, aka "obscene" with an 18-year-old boy sleeping with an 80-year-old Grandmother. The Poetics of *Harold & Maude* was even stronger, however, because it truly was a *Love Story*. But it would never have been made if Robert Evans hadn't gambled everything for this new voice in film: "What do you think most studios would have said to me if I went to them and said 'I want to make the story of 18-year-old boy who falls in love with an 80-year-old woman, to be directed by an acid head (Hal Ashby) and written by a guy who cleans swimming pools (Colin Higgins)? They'd throw it out the window! (laughs) And that's how we touched magic."[143]

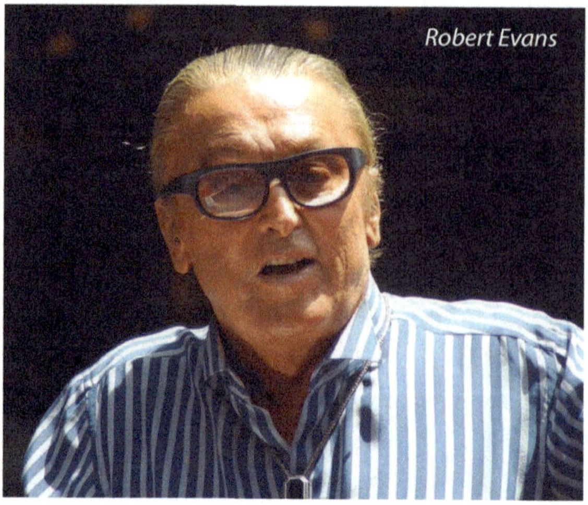
Robert Evans

Evans' "magic" saved Paramount by finding stories for and by our generation (Polanski, Coppola, Rafelson) and made history in the late 60s and 70s by exploring truths of this consciousness, obscenity and the myth of love: in *Godfather,* the gangster family code of honor, archaic in its consciousness and rigid in its love. And, I might add, expressing both with a violence that was obscene. Just like *Bonnie & Clyde,* which is a love story, too.

> When Evans was first hired, Gulf+Western regarded the Paramount lot as merely a piece of real estate. It was ready to sell. Evans, outmaneuvering them, dragged the studio, kicking and screaming, into a cultural revolution, and turned Paramount into the top studio of its day. He saved the lot. He saved the studio. The only studio that is still in Hollywood.[144]

That cultural revolution is exactly what Yeats was talking about, what Shelley, Walt Whitman and John Keats were getting at with their Apostrophes and The Sublime and its symbolism. Around that time, the Golden Dawn opened a chapter in San Francisco, when 1967's Love and Peace still echoed from the Flower Children. Robert Evans could feel the vibration. He saved the studio by gambling his severance package of $300,000 (due him in a bet because the Studio was in danger of folding) that he could turn the studio's finances around in a year against his 300k. He then began pitching them his idea to turn it around with Romance and Love Stories "that would bring people together" during that violent year of 1968. He also sold them on creating "a trend" in stories that were about "How it feels, rather than where it's at."[145] And true to his word, the first was aptly called *Love Story* under his reign. He also made Shakespeare's *Romeo and Juliet,* and went on to win 44 (Academy Award and other) nominations during his tenure. However, as Robert Evans is quoted in his documentary *The Kid Stays In the Picture;* the new age love "is unrequited."[146] There are no happy endings. Even Ken Kesey once said: "There are no more guarantees of "Happy Endings" in films since Kennedy died."

Now, in the "Age of Anxiety" the best we can hope for is an "existential" ending, where we, the audience get to decide if the film has a happy ending or not, because the filmmaker refuses to, like the ending in *The Graduate.* And I agree, Kennedy's assassination ended our belief in the power of Good to prevail. It ended our belief in Good, period, and God. In the past, the good guys always won. But God was dead. If anything, we decided to take things in our own hands. And it was like we HAD to! We had come out of

Plato's cave, the new vision in our eyes that saw the truth about so many things; about racism and war and equality and sex and we could not unsee them. However, at the end of 1968, after the "Year of Revolt," as *Time* magazine called it, there were glimmerings that a new hope or a new Spirituality was on its way, and somehow tied to Synchronicity and Love. A kind of Unified Field Theory, but not dialectic and including gravity. It felt like a Quantum Mechanics' kind of "Downward Causation" of the Music of the Spheres.[147] And speaking of Music, it would take me a whole book to talk about the music from my generation. But it was the soundtrack of our lives, and absolutely inimitable, because it was from the Universe.

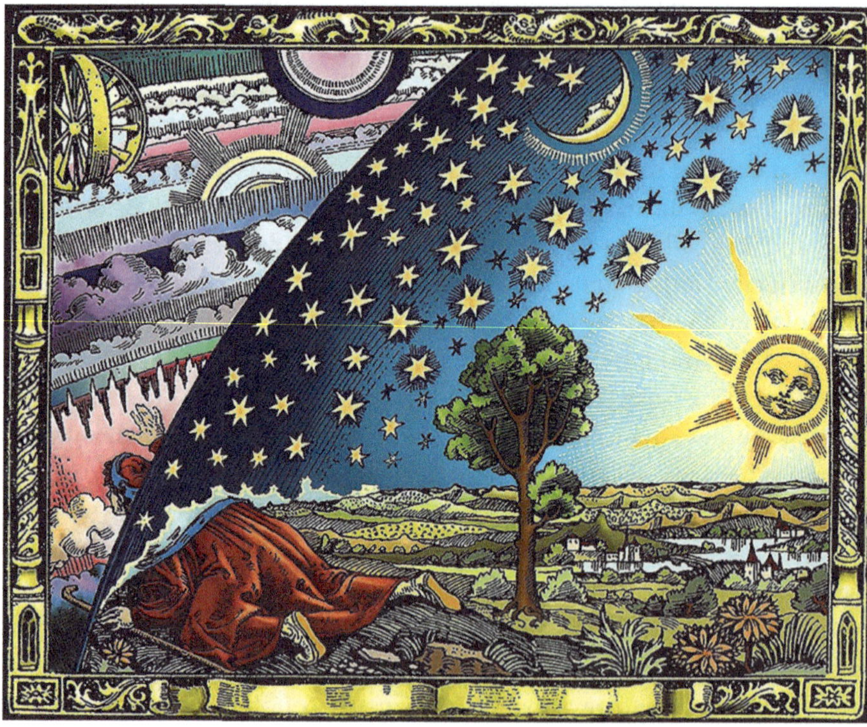

Furthermore, existentialism seemed to be the common genre of the 60s and early 70s Cinema, even in Westerns. Jack Nicholson wrote and produced a few under Roger Corman when he joined forces with Director Monte Hellman, another poetic cinema filmmaker in the early 60s.

> In 1964, he wrote the screenplay for, and starred in, *Flight to Fury,* directed by Monte Hellman. In 1965, he co-produced *The Shooting* and *Ride the Whirlwind* with Hellman, also co-authoring the script of *Ride the Whirlwind.* Both of these films are brooding, mystical,

> psychological Westerns which have enjoyed considerable success in Europe but never got off the ground in the United States.[148]

Monte is known for *Two Lane Blacktop (1970)* a film which ended abruptly in a metaphor for speed, depicted with film melting and burning in the camera; just like the cars seemed to be doing in the end of the movie. A proven poetic cinema director with his films, even the Roger Corman ones; Monte still wears to this day a belt buckle given to him by Slim Pickens, an ex-rodeo clown and actor, in tribute to his and Jack's glory days of making Existential Westerns.

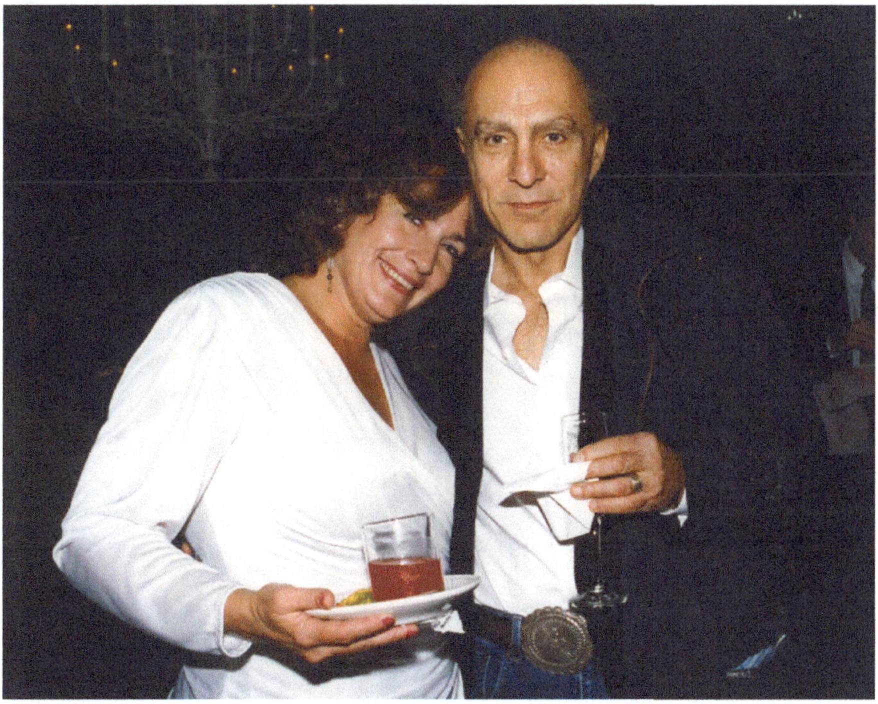

Monte Hellman with his Belt Buckle, at an AFM party with Katherine (1991)

But unlike the Westerns made as "American Cowboy Archetype" films, which follow the old worn out tale of the "Silver Bullet theory"[149]; wherein an American Cowboy, a stranger, comes into a community that has a problem, and with quick violence solves the problem and leaves again. That tale of happy endings died when a stranger with a gun came into our communities and murdered our President John F. Kennedy in 1963, and then murdered Rev. Dr. Martin Luther King in March of 1968, and Senator Robert Kennedy in June of 1968. If we, as youth, were not revolting before that, we surely started now. Suddenly groups of students formed the SDS, the Students for a Democratic Society; the Chicago 7; the Weather Underground; the Black Panthers; the American Indian Movement; all which all erupted world-wide along with the Czechoslovakian "Prague Spring." In the US, we realized we were on our own, because the Lone Ranger was out of Silver Bullets and his sidekick Kemosabe was unmasked as a Hollywood Indian. There was no going back, anyway, because our mythology of the Old Western had already died in 1962. James Stewart gave a funeral for it in the John Ford directed epic *The Man Who Shot Liberty Valance.* It was released the same year Kesey's New Western *One Flew Over the Cuckoo's Nest* came out with the bicultural, poetic, and cinematic literary voice. And by the time it came out, Ken was already writing another one of these new mythologies in *Sometimes a Great Notion.* And it was a New Western, too. It was metaphoric, it was symbolic in Yeatsian ways that are so many layers deep, we are still uncovering them. They truly inspired Directors Milos Forman and Paul Newman when they made these films. I discuss this symbolism in my Chapters on *One Flew Over the Cuckoo's Nest (1975)* and *Sometimes a Great Notion (1972).*

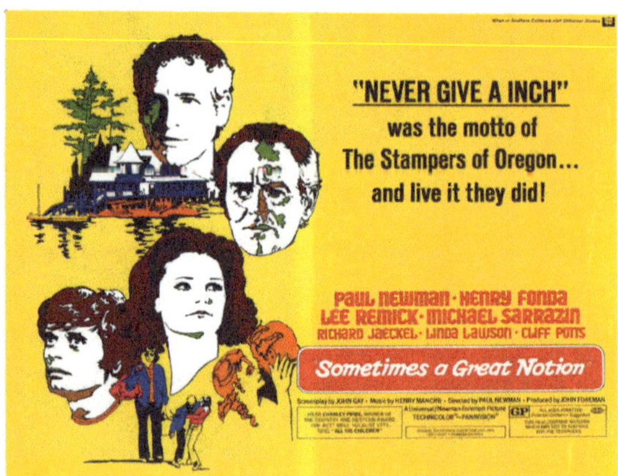

I wanted to learn more about the power of such symbology, discourse and ideology while taking Dr. Alilunas' History of Film II class in 2020, so I chose Howard Hawks' *Red River* as my research term paper. That's when I found, in the Knight Library, Dr. Stanley Corkin's incredible work in his essay "Cowboys and Free Markets: Post World War II Westerns and US Hegemony":120

> This essay looks at the historical phenomenon of the western as a focal genre in post war America. Through discussions of Howard

> Hawks' *Red River* and John Ford's *My Darling Clementine,* it shows how the western was well suited to convey important ideological rationales for postwar U.S. foreign policy, including the inevitability of American expansion and the strategies for hegemony that guided the Truman administration's foreign policy.[150]

I had already unpacked *Cuckoo's Nest* and *Sometimes a Great Notion* (121) as Poetic Westerns in my first book, *Echoes Vol. I* before I read this. Turns out that Professor Corkin and I have a lot in common. He had started his scholarly career around Westerns when he wrote his very first paper: "I wrote my first paper in college, at Bard in 1971, about *Sometimes a Great Notion,* which had its own John Wayne character."[151] In an interview of Professor Corkin, I shared Leslie Fiedler's theory with him about *Cuckoo's Nest,* and he said:

> I can see John Wayne-type shadows on Randle McMurphy. I like your discussion and think that connecting the radical individualism of Kesey and his books to the western hero, or anti-hero makes sense. Did you ever see Lonely are the Brave, which can be a kind of Douglas companion piece to *Cuckoo's Nest,* or read novels by Wallace Stegner – a Kesey connection or Edward (A)bbey, and then Ivan Doig later. All were trying to reimagine the Western as a vehicle for the any-establishment antihero. Paul Newman was a Hollywood leading man closely connected to this vision of character.[152]

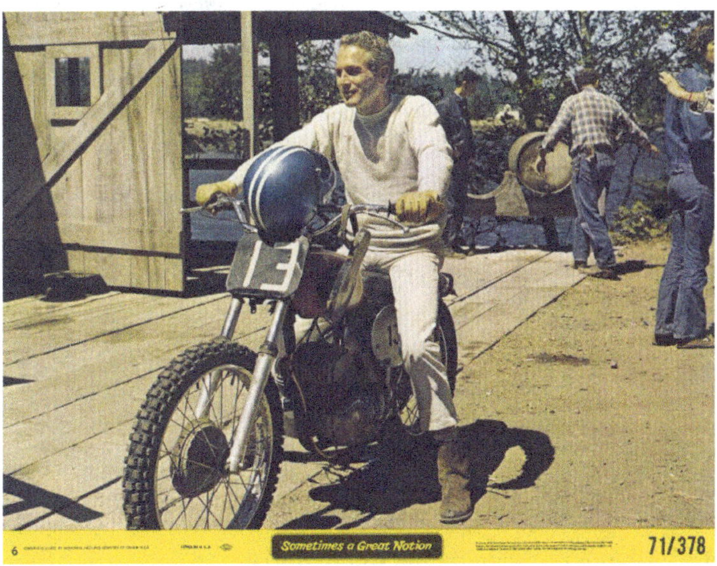

Paul Newman wearing white (even in a dirt-bike race) instead of a white cowboy hat in Sometimes a Great Notion

And when I say Poetic Cinema or Existential Western, it is just another way of using Aesthetics and Poetics in Filmmaking, much like Brakhage did in his films, or Kesey did metaphorically in his books. We are still coming to terms with what to call it … but Poetic Cinema denotes Art House Cinema which is a 60s global phenomenon from filmmakers like Akira Kurosawa to Francois Truffaut; and the Existential Western is certainly not just a Western, or an Anti-western; it too is something born of an Art House cinematic nature, and can embrace people of color as its hero or anti-hero. And speaking of the archetypal Anti-hero, if there was one for my generation on the screen and off, it was Jack Nicholson.

In Vol I of *Echoes From the Set* (2019) I write about the times I stayed at Jack Nicholson's house, and I quote Jack and Monte from the American Film Institute's program honoring Jack in a Lifetime Achievement Award. The quote I love from Jack is about the low budget existential westerns that he wrote, co-produced and acted in, made in the early 60s with Director Monte Hellman for Roger Corman: "Roger wanted some good Tomahawk numbers with plenty of Ketchup, but Monte and I were into these films on another level."[153] That "other level" was influenced by 1962's *One Flew Over the Cuckoo's Nest* in its respectful depiction of the American Indian, and the poetics of the New Age Existential Western. Together they redefine the Poetic Cinematic Literary Voice as a bicultural one. I was working on packaging both Jack and Monte in 1991 while producing Ken Kesey's *Last Go 'Round*. Especially fitting since Jack had been up here in Oregon trying to option *Cuckoo's Nest* in 1962, when he and Don Devlin were trying to write and option screenplays like *Thunder Island* to express this new biculturality we had become aware of. He also bought the rights to Don Berry's exquisitely bicultural epic *Moontrap*, while Dennis Hopper had optioned the rights to another one as equally exquisite called *Trask* by the same author. Paul Newman had bought the rights to *Sometimes a Great Notion*. There is no mistake that all of these Existential Westerns were being snapped up by Hollywood's most enlightened filmmakers.

> This was a beginning of the independent movies and, more than that, a kind of celebration of anti-establishment movie subjects," producer-director Bob Rafelson, who was one of Schneider's partners in the company that produced *Easy Rider* and six other films, said in an interview Tuesday.[154]

Dennis Hopper was living in Hollywood in the late fifties when Kesey stayed with him,[155] and then lived in an Ashram East of Los Angeles in

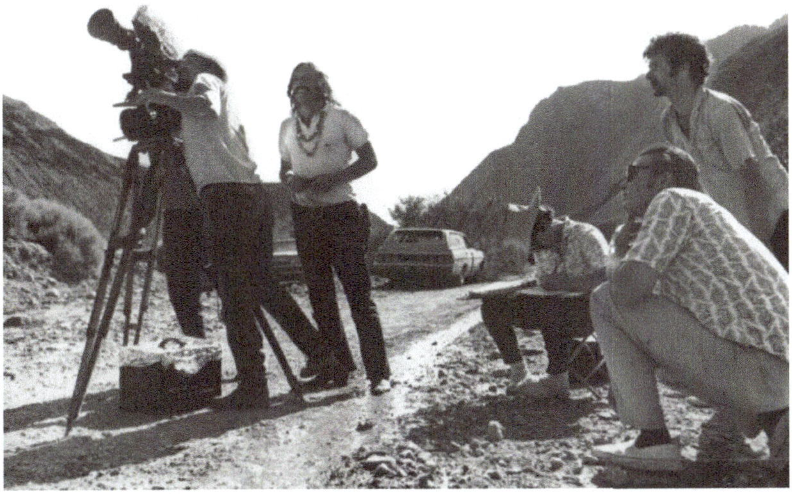

Dennis Hopper directing Easy Rider circa 1968.

Taos, New Mexico after that.[156] But in 1968, his and Peter Fonda's *Easy Rider* was being filmed with Jack, a film Peter Fonda was quoted as saying that he wrote as an "Existential Western" in the BluRay DVD release copy by Criterion Collections. You can see it in Dennis Hopper's wardrobe, who is wearing a fringed leather jacket, like the bicultural Oregon mountain man of Don Berry's *Trask*.

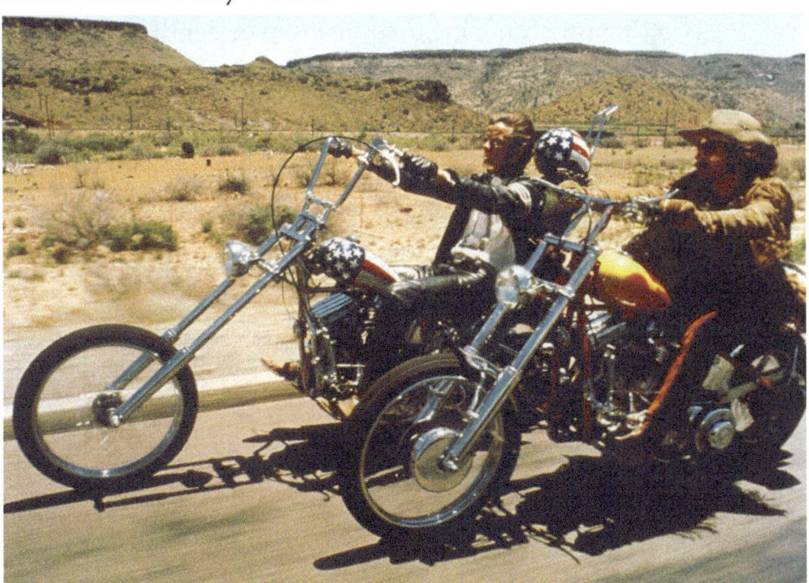

Peter Fonda as the future Captain America and Dennis Hopper as Johnson Monday from Trask

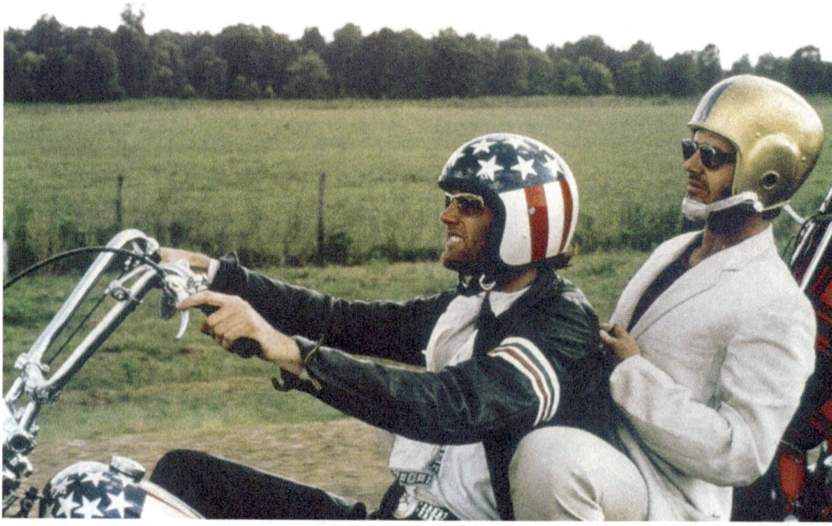

Fonda and Nicholson in Easy Rider. Even the Anti-western Hero Jack Nicholson is wearing White.

Peter Fonda seemed to embody Kesey's comic book hero Captain America; representing the *new* Cowboy, as in the superheroes. Both of them together are representing the archaic and new bicultural and therefore the existential ethic and the symbolic future of freedom.

As it turns out, Dennis and Peter only hired Jack after Rip Torn quit: then Poetic Cinema's darlings Bert Schneider and Bob Rafelson sent Jack to not only replace him, but to keep an eye on the production. They were all working together on producing their first film under their new banner, BBS productions, called *Drive, He Said* which was to be filmed entirely in Kesey Country, Oregon, the next year. There are many reasons for that, which we will go into in the next chapter.

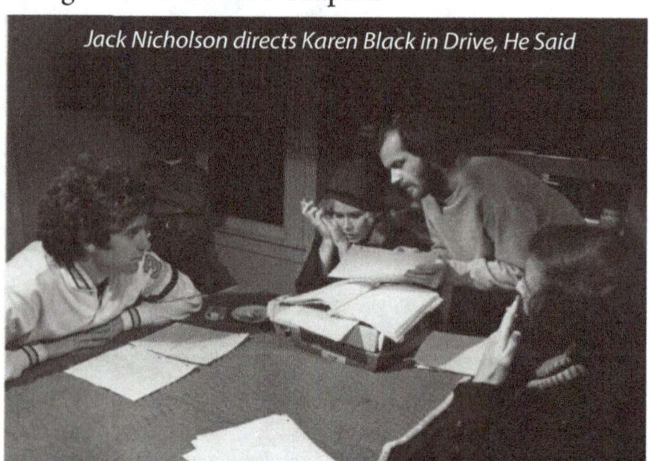

Jack Nicholson directs Karen Black in Drive, He Said

But his role in *Easy Rider* would not be the only time Jack would play an anti-heroic character sacrificed on the Alter of Truth. The same Alter that Jack Kennedy, Martin Luther King and Bobby Kennedy were sacrificed on was the alter we worshipped, the Alter of Freedom.

And while Nicholson and Newman were in Oregon, looking for this voice, Ken Kesey had moved on and was returning to his earlier fascinations with filmmaking. As I understand it now, it has always been his favorite medium. By 1968 Kesey had 9000 feet (almost two miles!) of 16mm footage from the psychedelic bus trip to New York and back, he had tons of audio tape, he had footage of the Acid Trips, and he had captured a time that by 1968, we were afraid would never come again, but they were just getting started, as I am hoping this book will show us…

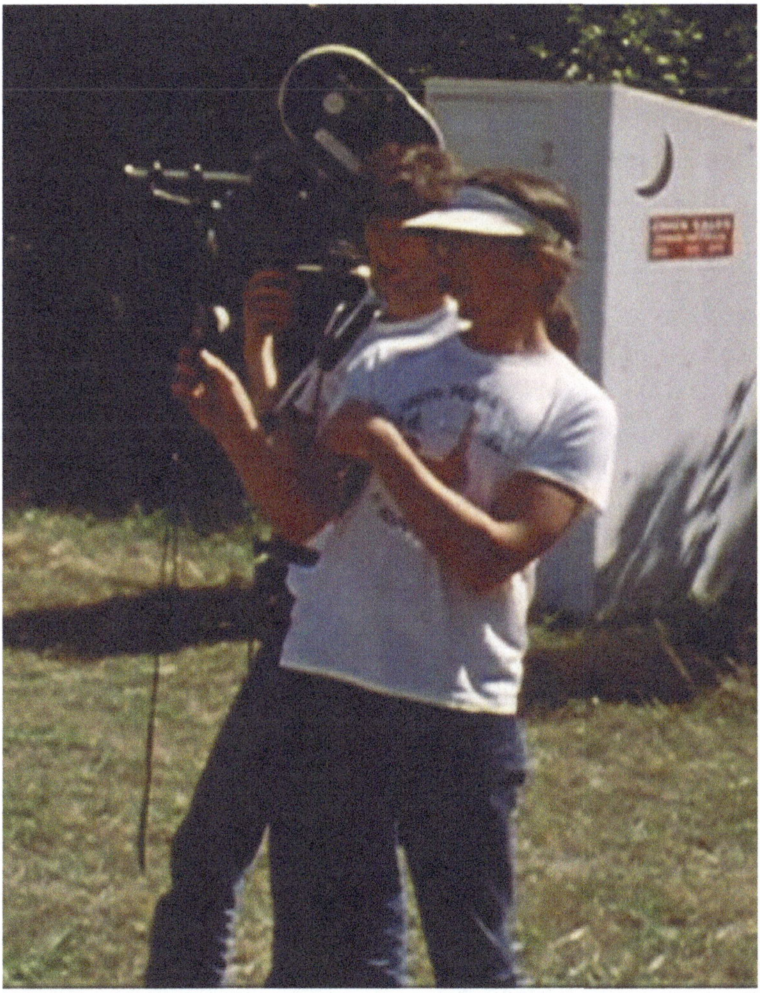

Flash and Sky filming the Grateful Dead in Oregon

Two gentlemen Kesey had met in New York in 1964, filmmakers who had got on the bus, came to help him with the footage. One was the son of a famous writer, Arthur Miller, named Bobby Miller. Marilyn Monroe was his stepmother for a while. The other was Bobby Steinbrecher. In typical Kesey style, he nick-named them as Pranksters. Steinbrecher was named Sky, probably for his luminescent blue eyes. Miller was named Flash. Probably for his eyes, too, which were dark but full of fire. Mike Hagen's was "Malfunction' because he was always the one who loved new technology and would puzzle over it until it stopped malfunctioning, like the new 16mm Arriflex that was impossible to figure out. Ken Babbs was "Sky Pilot"; Steve Lambrect was "Zonker," Dale Kesey was "Highly Charged" and the Bus Chaplain.

All of these Pranksters were involved in creative problem solving with regards to Kesey's footage, and eventually were all involved in film one way or another. Looking for a job once, Dale Kesey randomly called up a Hawaiian TV station, and asked them if they needed a camera man. They said yes. Zonker was always coming up with ideas for commercials like filming Timex watches that accidently were submerged in acid baths, but that still kept ticking. He inspired the character Zonker in the Doonesbury comic-strips. Ken Babbs had a beautiful voice and was so charming and good looking that he belonged on the screen. And I put him there, when he would let me. According to Dale Kesey and Mike Hagen[127], they first worked at Bobby Flash's new house up on Lorane Highway, a bit from Eugene in the South Hills, where his wife Erica and daughter Jessica lived with him. Then Joey Valentine and Bob Laird joined in the editing, and it got so crowded, that Kesey found a house to rent on 10th and Jefferson in Eugene, and they called it the "Film House." Zodiac and Roy Seburn lived there, as well as Kesey's parrot Rubiako. The amount of equipment he was buying was becoming quite impressive. And they needed a larger place, so first they rented an empty airplane hangar out by Joey's place, on Marcola Road, and then the empty KEED station on Day Island Road. The production company was called *Far West Action Picture Service.*

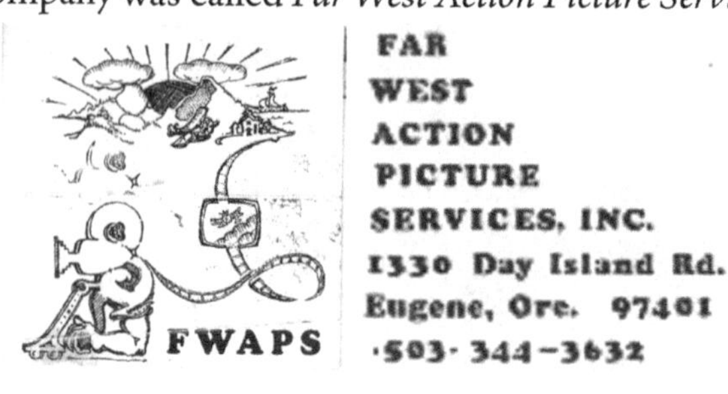

This band of Merry Prankster filmmakers would eventually launch the esteemed Oregon Film Industry, as well as becoming part of what Brakhage called the Poetic Cinema Capitol of the World. Filmmakers like Ron Finne, Loren Sears, Sharon Genasci, Lew Melsen, Gary Neustader, Ulysses Cheng, and Don Cato (who won a Silver at Cannes) had all gravitated to Eugene, merrily making poetic cinema movies. Kesey was the cultural magnet for all of us when he returned to Oregon. We had the Army-Navy surplus store at 666 Willamette Street to buy cheap ends of 16mm film. We had Evergreen Photo to process it. And we had the University of Oregon to support training these filmmakers. "What began as a simple code receiver for the University Newspaper by the Physics Department in 1922, morphed into a full-scale studio for educational broadcasting in 1932, when the 'Eugene studio on the University of Oregon campus (was) involving journalism, music and speech students. Grant Feikert designed and installed a program control console in a practice room in the UO Music building and telephone lines (speech only) were leased over which to send direct live broadcasts for KOAC.'"[157] This became Oregon Public Broadcasting, and attracted filmmakers like Ron West, who worked at its Classical Radio Station KWAX. By 1963, Oregon poetic cinema filmmaker Ron Finne had gone with Haskell Wexler as two of the Cinematographers on a bus with an inter-racial couple to film *The March on Washington* for the famous James Blue project. He had met Haskell at the University of Oregon where Blue had been a student. And if there was one film I would nominate for making Eugene the Poetic Cinema Capitol of the world I would say it was Finne's bicultural *Tamanawis Illahee: Rituals and Acts in a Landscape*, which was "A poetic environmental and cultural history of Oregon. Includes readings by William Stafford, Don Berry and others. Producer, writer, and director, Ron Finne; consultant in history, Edwin Bingham; consultant in literature, Glen A. Love. 700 ft.; color, sound; 16mm film."[158]

We were proud to show Finne's films at our arthouse called Cinema 7 in the early 70s. Loren Sears, another filmophile, graduating from the U of O in 1963; began making avant-garde films and video in San Francisco; became a founding member of Canyon Cinema Coop; and manager of Canyon Cinematheque. He produced numerous artistic /documentary films and videos of alternative and Native American cultures; was an artist-in-residence and guest director, KQED-TV. He taught filmmaking at the San Francisco Art Institute and University of California SF; video at Evergreen State College, Olympia, WA.[159] His wife, Pat Ferrero, a paint-

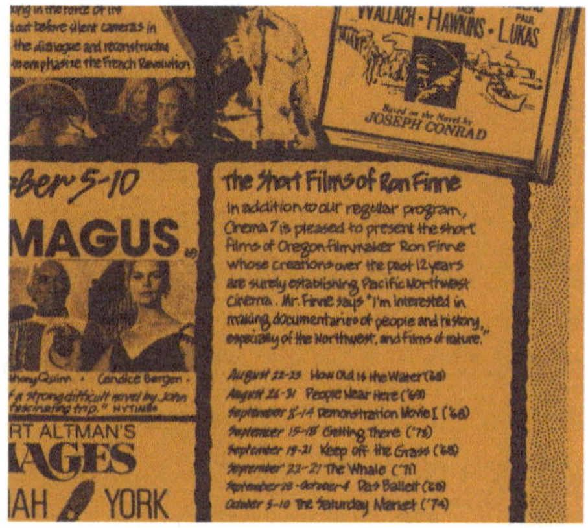

er, also became a filmmaker and taught filmmaking at San Francisco State for 30 years becoming the head of the Department. Loren also invented the Optical Printer for Canyon Cinema Corp and had gone to the first Acid Test that Kesey held at Ken Babbs' house.[160] So now you can see how these Eugene innovators all were tied together in an ever-expanding network, tied together by the bicultural thread of politics, music, filmmaking and especially the University of Oregon and its Alumni. But there were even more. U of O Architecture student Don Preston Cato "was an experimental and feature film maker with a strong academic background, a BS and BLA in Landscape Architecture from Michigan State and an MLA from the University of Oregon where he also studied extensively in the department of Motion Graphics. He was the Director of the Eugene Filmmakers Cinematique and his films have screened at an international and eclectic group of venues and festivals: Anthology Film Archives, National Academy of Television Arts & Sciences, Lincoln Center, and the Dylan Thomas Center in Wales."[161]

In 1986 he and I joined forces to produce *Dixie Lanes* with Hoyt Axton, Ruth Buzzi, Tina Louise and Karen Black. We were also proud to show Don Cato's films at Cinema 7. All of these filmmakers, except for those who have passed away, still stay in touch with each other, including me, Dale Kesey, Bob Laird, Joey Valentine, Ron Finne, Loren Sears, Ron West, Mike Hagen, Ken Babbs, and Bobby Miller. It was members of this conclave of filmmakers that impressed Jack Nicholson so much when he met them in 1969 on *Five Easy Pieces* that he returned to Eugene to film *Drive, He Said* in 1970. His friend Robert Towne not only played a role

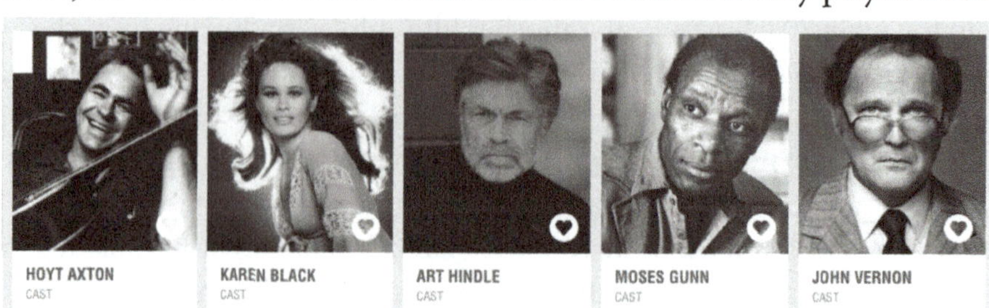

Katherine Wilson's Cast for Dixie Lanes. Not shown Ruth Buzzi, Tina Louise and John Freeman

in the film, but started a screenplay from an article his wife found in the Eugene Public Library on shortages of water in the world, which became *Chinatown* (1974;) and then wrote two other films for Eugene called *Personal Best* (1981) and *Without Limits* (1997). The producer of *Drive, He Said*, Richard Rush, returned here for *Getting Straight* (1970) with Elliott Gould, and the screenplay writer, Robert Kaufman, returned to Eugene in 1979 to film *How to Beat the High Cost of Living*. We also think Jack had something to do with *One Flew Over the Cuckoo's Nest* filming in Salem in 1975; and just like that, a lot of these filmmakers were also involved in getting *National Lampoon's Animal House* and *Stand By Me* here. But it all began in 1969, which is also when Kesey's Psychedelic Bus came by and I got on, and I made my first film with Mike Hagen, Ulysses Cheng and Ken Kesey's Arriflex.

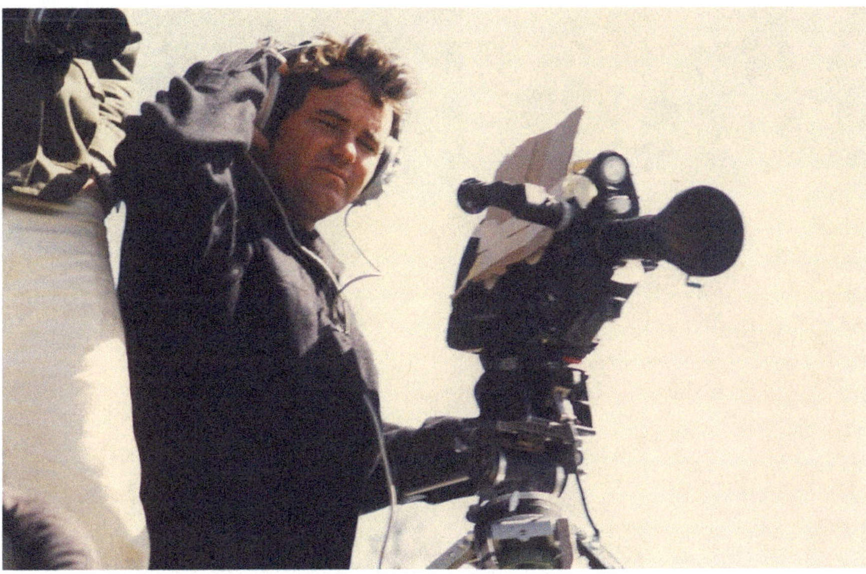

Oregon's First Cinematographer Mike Hagen

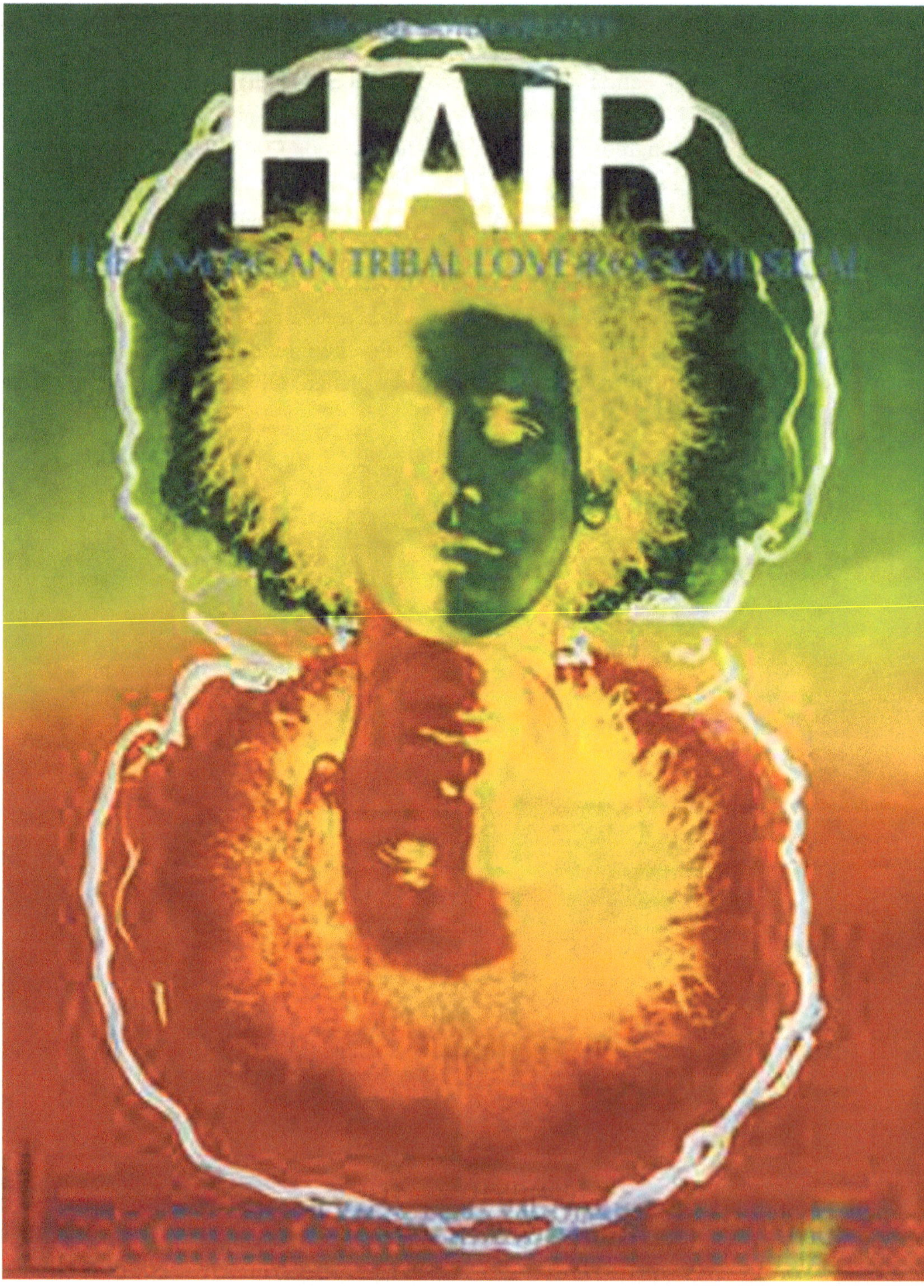
HAIR

Chapter 4

A Vortex and a Matrix of the "Sphere of Influence" 1969

"... we had vision because we drew all into unity – for the thinker in us was the Intellectual-Principle telling us of itself – and the soul or mind was motionless, assenting to that act of its prior. But now that we are once more here – living in the secondary, the soul – we seek for persuasive probabilities: *it is through the image we desire to know the archetype.*"

– Plotinus, *6th Ennead*

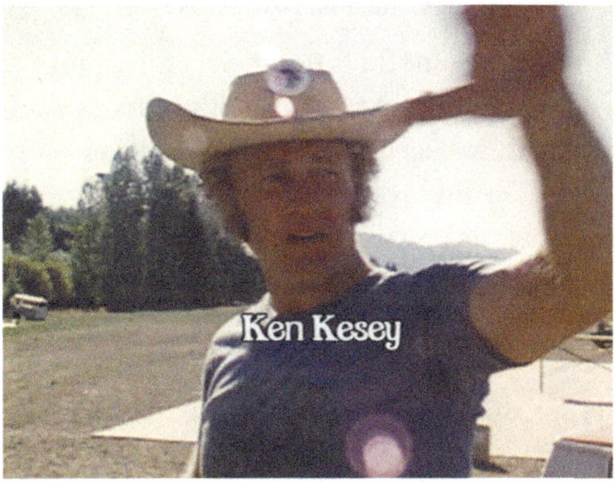

When Burton Wolfe asked him why ... (Kesey) had abandoned writing, he replied. "There are too many things to be done. Until the final earthquake, the big zap when we're all one again, we've got to play a dual role. But it's coming, *things are changing*. We've already moved out of the Age of Pisces into the Aquarian Age. The millennium started some months ago.[162]

– Mark Christianson, *Acid Christ*

And Kesey was right, in 1969, things were really changing. I finally finished high school, was going to college, but only because I found a reason to live: Poetry. It was a visual, metaphoric language I could understand. And the radio was playing visual, metaphoric song-poems about this archetype we called "the calling" for years, not knowing what it was, until the songs came out, *everywhere,* like this one: "Age of Aquarius":

When the moon is in the Seventh House
And Jupiter aligns with Mars
Then peace will guide the planets
And love will steer the stars
This is the dawning of the age of Aquarius
Age of Aquarius
Aquarius, Aquarius
Harmony and understanding
Sympathy and trust abounding
No more falsehoods or derisions
Golden living dreams of visions
Mystic crystal revelation
And the mind's true liberation
Aquarius, Aquarius

When the moon is in the Seventh House
And Jupiter aligns with Mars
Then peace will guide the planets
And love will steer the stars
This is the dawning of the age of Aquarius,
Age of Aquarius
Aquarius, Aquarius,
Aquarius, Aquarius
Let the sunshine, let the sunshine in, the sunshine in.[163]

This song was from a theatrical play, called *Hair*; first emerging from an East Village Public Playhouse; debuting on Broadway in April of 1968. In 1975, Director Milos Forman told me on the set of *Cuckoo's Nest* that he wanted to make it into a movie. Four years later he did. For me, this cemented my belief, that this whole theory was indeed valid; if Milos Forman, the subterfuge king of film wanted to direct it, it must have been worthy of his underground genius. When I knew him, he seemed very pragmatic. This was huge news. But at the time, in early 1969, I didn't know anything about Broadway or the Underground, but I was soon to find out. And so much I learned came through the lyrics of poetry and music, like this song from 1969, by Crosby Stills, Nash & Young. By the end of the year, I would have seen them live in San Francisco at Winterland:

Turn, turn any corner
Hear, you must hear, what the people say
You know there's something that's goin' on around here
That surely, surely, surely won't stand the light of day, no (it)
Appears to be a long time
Such a long, long time before the dawn
Speak out, you got to speak out against the madness
You got to speak your mind if you dare
But don't, no don't, no, try to get yourself elected
If you do you had better cut your hair
And it appears to be a long
Appears to be a long
Appears to be a long time
Such a long, long, long, long time before the dawn
It's been a long time comin' (Long time comin')
It's goin' to be a long time gone (Long time gone)
But you know
The darkest hour
Is always, always just before the dawn
And it appears to be a long
Appears to be a long
Appears to be a long time
Such a long, long, long, long time before the dawn."[164]
– David Crosby, "Long Time Coming"

What we knew that could not stand the light of day, was the War in Vietnam; because that was really about profit. That particular racism, misogyny, and hate were so deep in Plato's cave, that we would have to enter the cavern and fight the good fight in the dark, and would then need to bring all of these soul-sicknesses up to the light to heal them. All I could do then was to be a young feminist, throwing pots in art class and adoring my English teacher Jane Middlehurst, who would cry when she read Robert Frost. I wanted to emulate her and teach poetry, and change the world as she had changed mine.

I also had a student teacher in Political Science courting me, even though I didn't know it yet. He waited until the day after school was out. And sent me a hand-drawn card with a little poem. He was in a band called *The Hammond Typewriter* and worked in North Beach during the summers that he was attending the U of O in '65, '66, '67, and '68. He was *there*. You could tell. North Beach, where he worked, was the part of San Francisco that the Beats hung out in, and was part of the Barbary

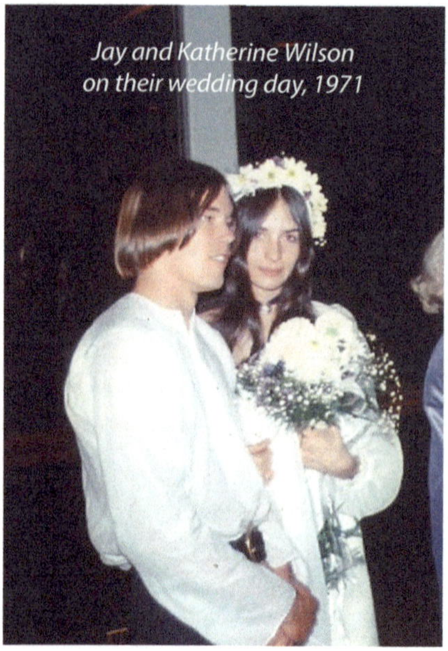
Jay and Katherine Wilson on their wedding day, 1971

Coast. He worked at a place called Bally-Lo. The shop imported Beatle Suits and other hipster paraphernalia. It also posted all the Avalon, Fillmore, Matrix and Winterland show posters in the windows. He had quite a collection in the room he had at the "Band's House" in Eugene when I met him. Right after completing his student teaching requirement at my high school, he graduated from the U of O in 1969. That summer he got a job at the Crystalship Record Store downtown. And I went to see him there after he sent me the card. He also had an incredible collection of vinyl albums, that he then loaned to me. He was a wonderful guy that I later married and spent 18 years with, and also had two children with.

But something happened a few weeks after I met him that became a point of contention for the rest of our relationship; and in all fairness, he tried hard to navigate the rocky road that I stubbornly clung to, but there was no turning me away from it. Because on July 8th, 1969, the psychedelic bus came by and I got on. And once you are on, you never get off. As a direct result of that, I became a filmmaker, instead of the high school English teacher like he and my parents wanted me to be. This is my story of how that all happened, and how it is still happening after 50 years.

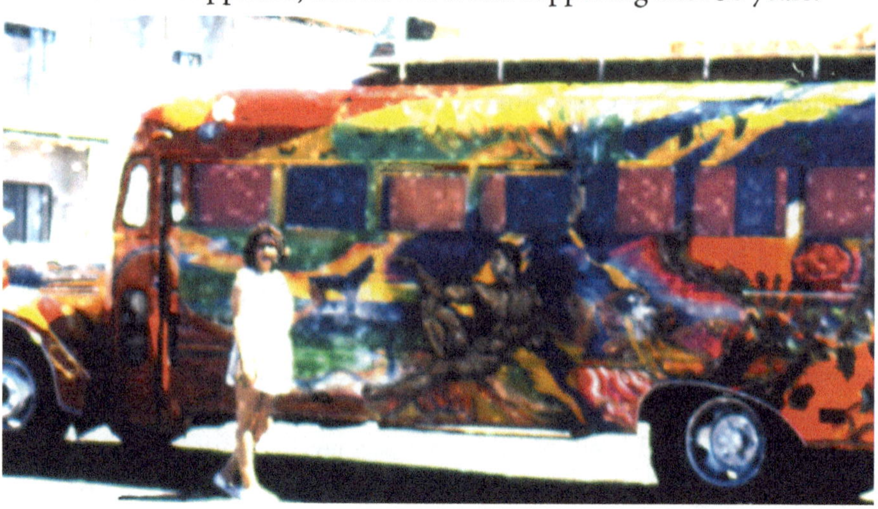

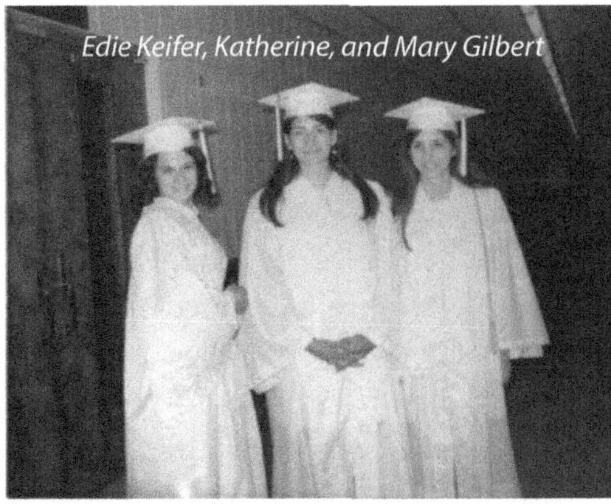
Edie Keifer, Katherine, and Mary Gilbert

By June in 1969, my high school girlfriends were all lined out to attend college. Mary was accepted at Mills, but Edie was going to attend the U of O, after she went to Woodstock in August. My grades were not the best in early high school, so I never really entertained the idea of applying to either.

But evidently my SAT scores were high enough to get the attention of Dr. Edwin Coleman III, the Head of the English Department at the U of O, and he enrolled me. I didn't know any of this until 40 years later, that he had called my Mom and asked her why I wasn't enrolled. My Mom was attending the U of O's summer school then, getting her Masters. All I knew was that suddenly I was going to go to College, and just as suddenly had enough money to live in the dorms, like my girlfriend Edie was. So on July 8th, 1969, my Mom wanted me to come with her to campus so I could walk around and get to know it a little, while she was in class. She was teaching me to drive a stick shift on our old '47 GMC pick-up, and I know I probably ground the gears a lot that day driving to campus. Not trusting myself to parallel park, I took the first parking place I could find, so I could drive straight into it on the corner. It was right across from the ERB Memorial Union, by the Collier House. There was a crowd outside of the EMU's front door surrounding two men, whom I found out later were debating each other about Communism, on the EMU Free Speech Platform. The older one was Floyd Ramp, a 90-year old communist, and the younger one was the University of Oregon's ASUO Student Body President. His name was Kip Morgan. With him was Mike Hagen, one of Ken Kesey's original Merry Pranksters. Both of them were clean cut, with short hair.

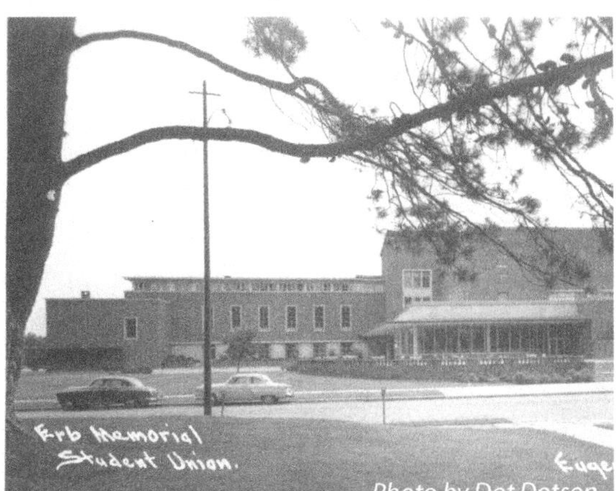

Photo by Dot Dotson.

I was scared of talking to strange men after the last time I had been to the EMU, about a month before for "Seniors Night;" when we graduating seniors from the local high schools were invited to a party there, hosted by the University. To make a long story short, we were then invited to a Frat house party, and I was sexually assaulted by one of the Athletic Department's finest, after leaving; and walking in the dark to where my girlfriends had gone to, a Motel we rented on Franklin Boulevard. I was trained as a South Eugene Gymnast (State Champions) and the manager of the Track team at Sheldon High School at the time, and was stronger and faster than him, but I carried scissors with me from then on. You can take the girl out of Klamath Falls, but you can't take Klamath Falls out of the girl.

However on this particular day, I felt a kinship with these guys at The EMU, and Mike Hagen seemed more interested in my '47 Ford pick-up truck than me, and wanted to borrow it to help a friend move. Evidently Kip Morgan saw my hesitation, and offered to wait there at the EMU with me for my Mom, while Hagen borrowed my truck. As it turned out, Hagen was moving furniture into Kip's house, not far from there. Now, with happiness in my heart, I can say that Kip and I have had a long-term relationship like Mike and I, that has lasted more than 50 years. And as I attended school the Fall of 1969, the EMU became an incredible Vortex of energy for all of us; whether working, teaching, or studying at the University of Oregon. It was a Vortex of Socializing, of Activism, of being with other Cultures and learning from them. In the basement we created the Black Student Union, along with the American Indian Student Union. It had a grand piano in a rehearsal room where Scott the Lion (Bartlett) held reign while he played. It had a bowling alley, and a barber shop. On the main floor it had a Post Office, a giant Cafeteria (where we filmed the food fight scene from *Animal House* 8 years later) the EMU Cultural Forum, a long hall where you could sit in window seats and study. Up the grand stairway was the Ballroom, where we saw so many incredibly great shows from George Benson to the Grateful Dead and Bob Dylan. Down the hall from the Ballroom were more window seats and a music listening room. At the end was the Oregon Daily Emerald newspaper, that

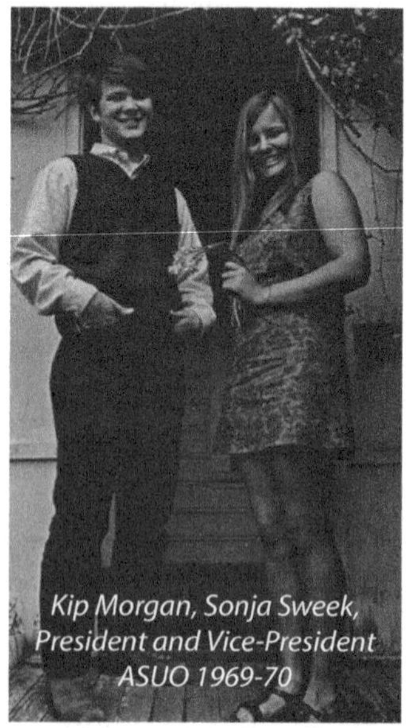

Kip Morgan, Sonja Sweek, President and Vice-President ASUO 1969-70

was on the floor above the Post Office. And I practically lived there. Here was a place I felt at home in. There were Indian people and Black people and they seemed to understand me better than white people did. I was in heaven.

While moving into the Dorms, my first roommate and I made a promise to each other that we would not start smoking cigarettes, have sex, or smoke pot just because we were away from our parents. That lasted about a week. She brought home a boy on the basketball team, and I had to sleep in the hallway with my quilt and alarm clock. And after a week of *that*, of course I started smoking full time, my own packs; instead of "borrowing" from my Mom, as I had done in High School. Then something happened with her boyfriend that involved dialing O for Operator and reporting an emergency; and I moved down the hall. From then on, all of my dormmates were soulmates. Somehow all of us on the 4th floor of both the women's and the men's sections of the Earl Dorms were "radicals." My friend Terry O'Conner and I would hang out in the "Listening Room" at the EMU together. We would build a fort out of the furniture and put Holst's "The Planets" on their excellent record player. In an interview for this book with Terry, 50-some years since I last talked to him, I asked him if he felt "called" in the 60s. He said yes, especially when growing up in Marin county across the Golden Gate Bridge from San Francisco, but he said attending the U of O created a "Sphere of Influence." We will be talking more about how much of an influence this "Sphere" had on him by early 1970, when Hollywood actor Jack Nicholson paid his bail for protesting the Vietnam war. But that fall, we just had fun being 18-year-old innocents going to college for the first time. We had both seen *2001 A Space Odyssey* and loved the soundtrack, which we also played in the Music Room. I had dropped mescaline with Kip Morgan earlier that summer when we went to see it at a drive-in movie theater, and when we saw that in places the night sky and the movie screen would become one universe, we threw a blanket on the grass and watched it without anything between us and the image. Speaking of image, the im-

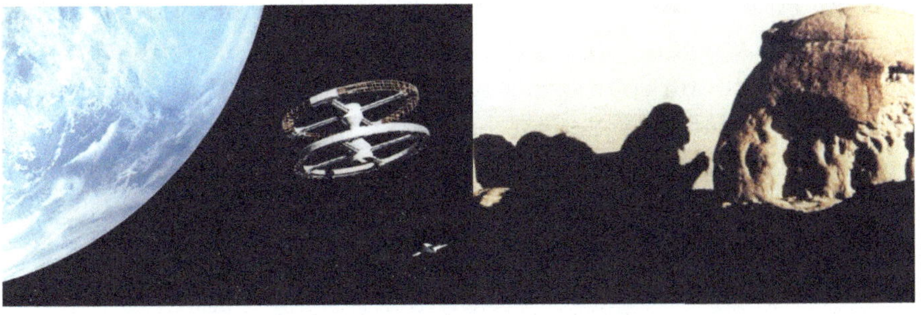

age of director Stanley Kubrick's monolith, which in the film represented the evolutionary download of what was later touted as the "100th Monkey Theory" or "evolutionary knowledge" was, to us, addressing the Archetype of an ancient Aeon that implicated our own age's technology in what would become the defining principle of Darwin's " survival of the fittest." That scene was also so powerful because we knew deep inside that we had been there aeons ago. And that technology itself was birthed from early man picking up a bone and using it as a weapon. That technology was what had now created everything we were against, as Lynn Hughes said in the documentary, *The Life and Times of the Red Dog Saloon*:

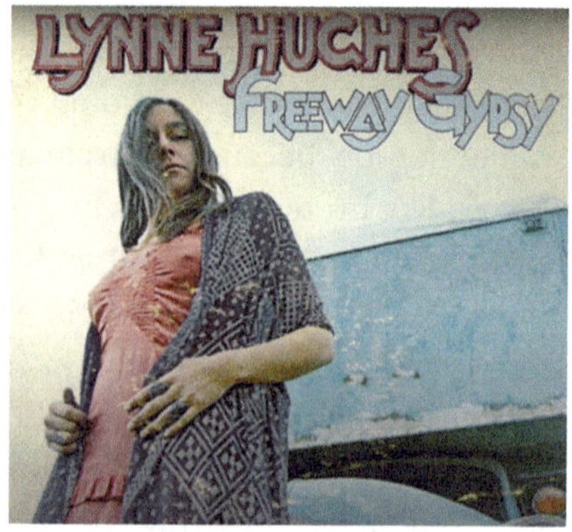

> The future appeared to be uncertain in many respects, based on a materialistic culture that emphasized a uniformity of dress and success.
>
> After World War II, all of us were presented with something that artificially separated us from the human spirit and the rest of the world. Technology became king. Intuitively we knew that all of this served to isolate us from our surroundings (environment) and our communities.[165]

In the same film, Chan Laughlin answered her statement with: (When you drop acid) "...you get the whole world disassembled before you so you can examine the component parts seriously..."[166] That was how we could see so clearly what wasn't working, because it did not contribute to the whole. Listening to the soundtrack while living in the dorms kept me anchored in my new-found reality of cosmic consciousness. And if the EMU was the Vortex of this Sphere of Influence at the University of Oregon, Villard Hall was The Matrix. What started in 1922 as just a receptor for code signals became, by the time Kesey majored in Speech and Communications at the U of O a full-fledged Oregon Public Broadcast Studio housed at the top of Villard Hall. In 1956 the U of O even sponsored a "U of O Campus Film Group formed by the Dept. of Speech and Drama, the Art Museum Desk and the School of Architecture and Allied Arts."[167]

Those of us who knew Ken, and attended films with him, have no doubt he was part of that effort. Especially since he was spending the summers in LA between attending classes for four years at the U of O, trying to break into the Film Industry.

Mike Dilley, U of O '61, became a Filmmaker after participating in the activities on the top of Villard Hall. His story is that as a child in Eugene, when local radio station KORE would broadcast live a children's show (before the Saturday matinees) from the McDonald Theater stage Saturday mornings; the host would choose randomly from the audience and interview the kids and record them on a disk-cutting lathe. He would then give the record to the kids in return for participating.[168] The process fascinated Mike, and he ended up ordering a kit from EICO to build his own amplifier. By the time he was a Junior at South Eugene High School, he and Bob Seigenthaler, another student, purchased the bankrupt Audio Recording business on the second floor of the Smeed Sound Service building.

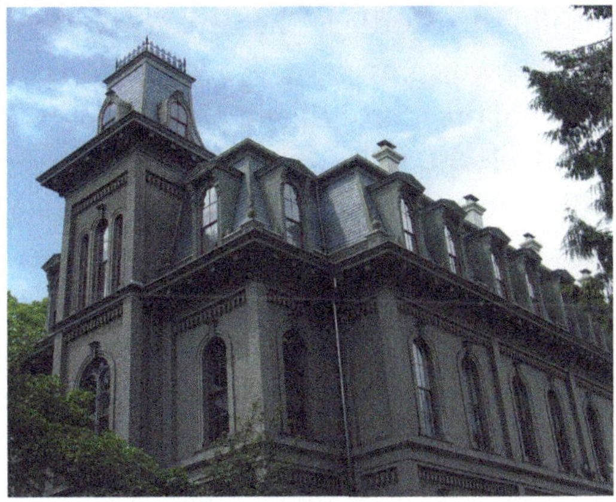

Photo of Villard Hall by Katherine Wilson

This service provided "... about 50 dedicated back-line phone lines of "Muzak" to different Department Stores, Elevators, etc."[169] He also performed in a Folk Trio for these early OPB video and audio programming at the top of Villard Hall in the early sixties, and as a result of the Trio performing at Tino's Italian Restaurant at 15th and Willamette streets on weekends, ended up getting discovered by Hollywood Producer Harold Hecht, who was in town filming *The Way West* in 1967. Mike went on to work as a Stunt Man on Elliott Gould's *Getting Straight,* also shot in Eugene in 1969. The early 70s found him creating and designing recording studios and providing his services for films over the next several decades, when he created the Eugene International Film Festival.

Ron West, U of O '69 BA. remembers attending the University of Oregon's first film class in the Spring of 1969.[170] When he first attended the U of O in 1963, as a freshman, he answered an ad in the Oregon Daily Emerald for a job at KWAX as an announcer. He soon moved up to Program Director for a Friday night music show, and was consequently hired by several other radio stations in Eugene as a DJ. Like Ken Kesey and Mike Dilley before him, he also attended the University of Oregon in Speech and Communications, and ended up becoming a filmmaker. By this time, however, the U of O had a professor who had experience in Broadcasting. His name was Ed "Fast Eddie" Halle, and was one of two professors teaching "a film class;" even though they were listed as Speech and Communication classes in the Spring of 1969 called Seminar on TV and Film 407 and 507. Ron went on to get his Masters at Brigantine U '84; and in '94 his PhD. in Seattle at the University of Washington. He currently works for his own company called Work Print Productions in Portland. And he is one of the most brilliant people I know.

By 1969, full programs for OPB were being created at the top of Villard Hall, and my partner in film on and off for the last 50 years, Bob Laird, (UO '70) was finally getting closer to graduating. He had an Athletic scholarship to the U of O for the 1962-63 and 63-64 school year (Swim Team) but then worked in the Haight/Ashbury for a few years and returned to the U of O for the 69-70 school year, like me. He graduated in 1970, in Speech and Communications, like Kesey and Mike Dilley had a few years before. While at the U of O in the early 60s, he was legendary Producer Don Simpson's roommate in the Phi Delta Theta Fraternity (U of O '67) a Duck who would become the infamous producer of *Top Gun, Flashdance* and *Beverly Hills Cop,* etc.. One day, while watching TV in the fraternity, they looked at each other and went "We can do that, we should get into this."[171] From then on, Don Simpson kept in touch, as they both ended up in San Francisco during the Summer of Love. Don had found a job promoting films in the Bay Area, but in the Fall of 1969, he followed Laird back to Oregon to "feel the pulse" of the film-going Baby Boomers. He invited Kesey, Bob and Babbs to a special Premiere of *Woodstock* at the Baghdad Theater in Portland, and Ken took them and others in the Psychedelic Bus.

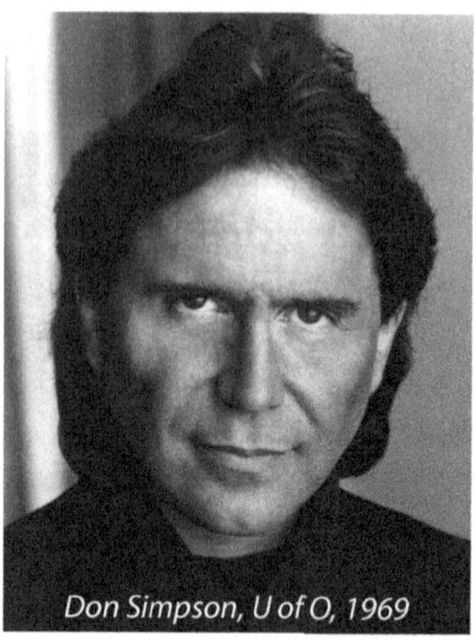
Don Simpson, U of O, 1969

Laird was learning his future job with Public Broadcasting up at the top of Villard Hall; where they had a small stage, two giant cameras, and a sound-switcher. First, he said, "You would take a beginning TV Class, and learn how to use the camera. They had a first sound taping machine, about six feet high. After the basic class, you could learn how to work the control booth. And then learn how to "Ready Camera, Switch, and Dissolve."[172]

While 1969 was still young, The Beatles had even formed a new content company, called Zapple. They invited Ken Kesey in January to walk around London and record his impressions, much like Ken and Babbs and the Pranksters did, in some 100 hours of *audio tape* in the early 60s. They also invited Ron Finne. The day I called him about an interview, he said he had just found his recently deceased wife's, (Mary-Lou) notes on that event. He said "... in Feb 1969, he showed his film *How Old Is Water* to George Harrison at Apple."[173]

I heard the Beatles had also recorded Richard Brautigan, but their business manager closed it down and not much, if anything, was ever done with the tapes.

> From late 1968 to February 1969, Brautigan recorded a spoken-word album for The Beatles' short-lived record-label, Zapple. The label was shut down by Allen Klein before the recording could be released, but it was eventually released in 1970 on Harvest Records as "Listening to Richard Brautigan."[174]

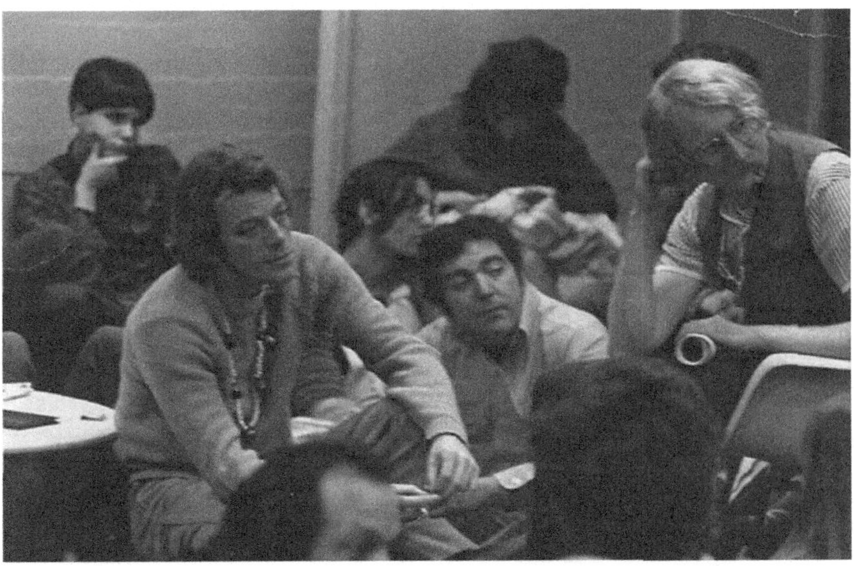

The Diggers with Richard Brautigan, (far right) courtesy of Loren Sears.

> Literary critics labeled him the writer most representative of the emerging countercultural youth movement of the late 1960s, even though he was said to be contemptuous of hippies. *Trout Fishing in America* has sold over 4 million copies worldwide.[175]

It amazes me how many Oregonians the Beatles wanted to record. But then again, Brautigan, like Kesey, had that Bicultural Voice:

> Critics have interpreted Brautigan as experimentally hippie/beat, and neurotic. The author of this essay constructs him as narrative aesthetician, whose Zen-based strategies let him balance extreme emotional tensions with simple form and encourage an unusual kind of reader response.[176]

And that particular voice has special powers for the coming age:

> The only way to reach universality is horizontally, never pre-tending to abandon the realm of particularity; the way leading through a completing translation, making various languages "clash," "marry," and "weave into" one other. This openness towards "translatability" (Tradierbarkeit) reveals the heterogeneous element present in all languages: their wishful gesturing towards universal communication. In this manner, the Marrano strategy offers an alternative practice of universalization, conceived as an "after-Babel project" to mend the broken whole from within, horizontally, without assuming the lofty abstract position of a general meta-language, but through the effort of bi- or multi-linguality, and also without over-stressing the catastrophic nature of the Babelian dispersion of tongues.[177]

It took me 50 years to find out what this voice was, and I owe it in part to my friend and scholar Anne Richardson, (who discussed with me thinking out-loud of Oregon as "cross-cultural," and then schooled me that it was "bi-cultural") and there is a huge difference. I owe the rest of it to my Professors at the U of O, from 1969 until now.

But in that first year, 1969, everything seemed idyllic on the surface. During the summer I loved hanging out with Kip Morgan and his friends at the 1010 High Street Commune. It was an incredible group of people. Connie Epstein managed the New World Coffee House, and she was the Den Mother. Ron Eachus was the Editor of the *Oregon Daily Emerald*; and had a girlfriend named Louise living there; David Gwyther was there, as was Lew Melsen, who would later become a fellow filmmaker, and once brought a Venison roast over and asked me to cook it. Having grown up in Indian Country with avid duck, geese, and deer hunters I knew my way around the kitchen. But the truth is I am a vegetarian at heart who has an O blood type, so it makes me a problem eater because I have to eat meat.

LOCAL DRAFT BOARDS ON TRIAL

They Face Real Court

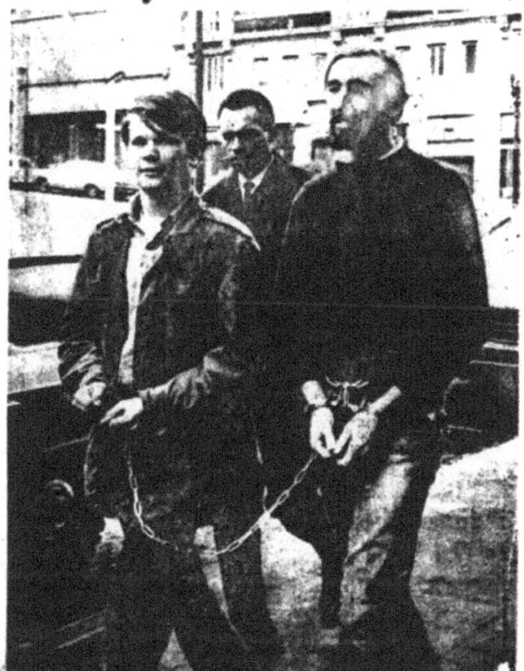

DRAFT OPPONENTS Kip Dallen Morgan, 21, Roseburg, left, and David George Gwyther, 21, Creswell, enter U.S. Court House here to face charges they interfered with Selective Service.

MORGAN AND GWYTHER DEFENSE COMMITTEE

Oregon Journal Article. From the David Gwyther Collection.

But not long after I met all of them, Kip and David's political activities regarding the Vietnam War in 1967 came surging up from the Underground. Evidently, they had conducted street theater with their Draft Boards and served them very adept Indictments for War Crimes. Street theater was a great way to critique politics. And a very serious way.

It is important to me to include these actual indictments, because these men were persecuted and labeled dangerous and dark forces of the underground; when in fact, it was they who had left Plato's cave, and gently and articulately told The Truth about what was happening in Vietnam, hoping to bring it into the light. The other force that was contributing to their dilemma was the Media. Just like David Getz, the drummer for

Big Brother and the Holding Company said, when the media twisted the truth about the psychedelic scene in 1967, they never knew "what the Spirit was about,"[178] just the sensationalism of the New Journalism. Kip and David had trumped up charges against them that eventually put them in jail. But I have known them for 50 years, and I can attest to the fact that they were and still are about Truth, Peace and Love. But in the summer of 1969, they were hauled back into court, and Kip was put into jail, and I had to leave 1010 High Street to concentrate on my studies.

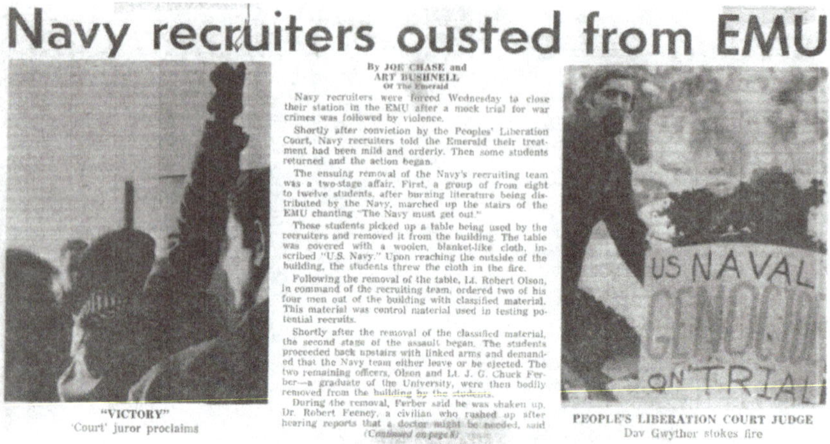

Navy recruiters ousted from EMU

By JOE CHASE and ART BUSHNELL Of The Emerald

Navy recruiters were forced Wednesday to close their station in the EMU after a mock trial for war crimes was followed by violence.

Shortly after conviction by the Peoples' Liberation Court, Navy recruiters told the Emerald their treatment had been mild and orderly. Then some students returned and the action began.

The ensuing removal of the Navy's recruiting team was a two-stage affair. First, a group of from eight to twelve students, after burning literature being distributed by the Navy, marched up the stairs of the EMU chanting "The Navy must get out."

Those students picked up a table being used by the recruiters and removed it from the building. The table was covered with a woolen, blanket-like cloth, inscribed "U.S. Navy." Upon reaching the outside of the building, the students threw the cloth in the fire.

Following the removal of the table, Lt. Robert Olson, in command of the recruiting team, ordered two of his four men out of the building with classified material. This material was control material used in testing potential recruits.

Shortly after the removal of the classified material, the second stage of the assault began. The students proceeded back upstairs with linked arms and demanded that the Navy team either leave or be ejected. The two remaining officers, Olson and Lt. J. G. Chuck Ferber—a graduate of the University, were then bodily removed from the building by the students.

During the removal, Ferber said he was shaken up. Dr. Robert Feeney, a civilian who rushed up after hearing reports that a doctor might be needed, said

(Continued on page 8)

"VICTORY"
'Court' juror proclaims

PEOPLE'S LIBERATION COURT JUDGE
Dav Gwyther stokes fire

The Emerald. Article. From the David Gwyther Collection.

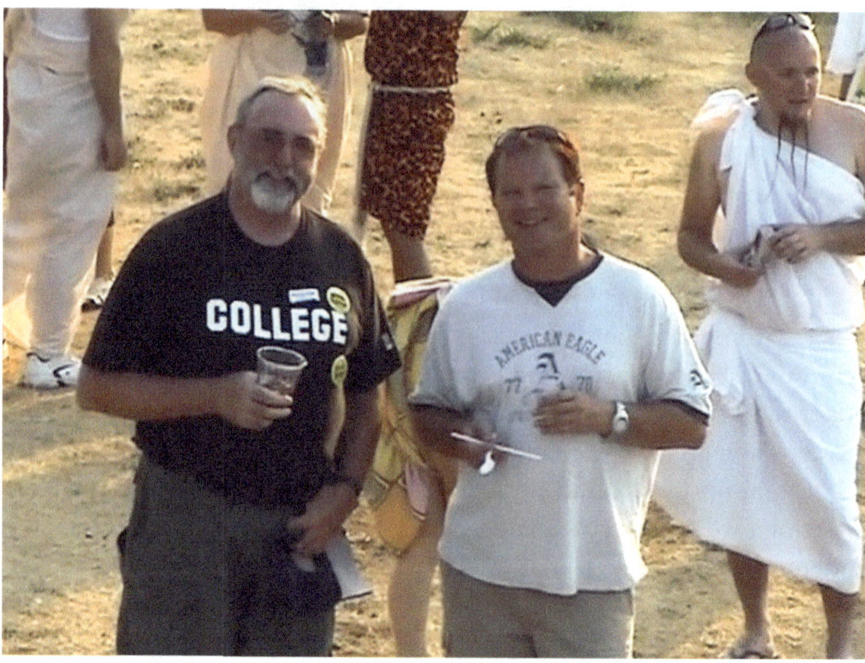

David Gwyther and Kip Morgan consistently show up to support Katherine's events.

That was when I met Ken Kesey one night, when he dropped by Kip's house, who was being interviewed by *Life* magazine about fighting the draft. Ken took us all to Dairy Queen afterward for ice cream, and of course I wanted the most expensive item on the menu, a banana split; but he smiled and graciously paid for it. That's when I was officially on the bus, the very bus that was now wired "to seek beyond writing – through experiments with electronic media and further experiments with drugs – new forms of consciousness and artistic expression.[179]

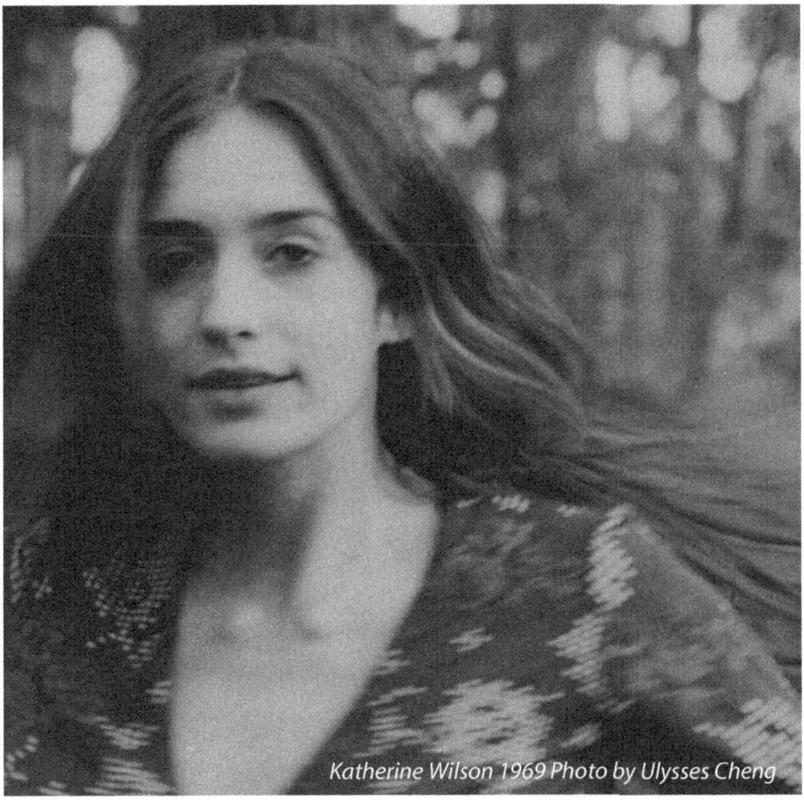

Katherine Wilson 1969 Photo by Ulysses Cheng

In the late fall, something happened. My Dad called me and told me they really couldn't afford for me to go to school Winter term, or any term. I was devastated. But the Universe provided. I found a job in the *Oregon Daily Emerald*, as a model, for $25 an hour. Initially I was very suspect about the high fee, like a hooker's! Back then, minimum wage was $1.95 an hour. You could rent a place for $25 for a whole month! I met with him anyway.

His name was Dan Webb and he had Cerebral Palsy. And he never laid a hand on me. Over the years he taught me how to adjust f-stops in order to film with a camera, and how to process it; he taught me to study at the Knight Library anatomy and art, in order to be a better film subject.

His fee paid for some of my books for several years at the U of O. He later took me to LA; introduced me to filmmakers in Portland, and then by his going to the Seattle Film Conference, was how I got my first job on a Hollywood film in Seattle.

Prankster Mike Hagen also helped me pay for my books when he hired me to be in a Poetic Cinema Short. Ulysses Cheng was there and had Kesey's Arriflex, Hagen ran the Nagra for ambient sound. I was the sad-eyed lady of the lowlands, worried about my future, the world, Vietnam, and our Earth. That is what they wanted to film. And they had me walk to the U of O Pioneer Cemetery. Little did I know what the Universe held in store for me. At the time, I wanted to be a Poet. I didn't want to be a model or actress really. I thought film was frivolous. How wrong I was. Because the world needed us poets to interpret our culture *in all mediums.* Just like Hagen and Uly and Kesey and Brakhage were doing in the Poetic Cinema way. So, I have no doubt that what happened next was because the Gods of Film wanted Jack Nicholson to meet them too, in a great-minds-think-alike-way. He had already been up here wanting to option *Cuckoo's Nest* in 1962, and had bought film rights to Don Berry's *Moontrap* outright. But what he needed was a place to film his own *Drive, He Said* later in the year, and he needed experienced filmmakers as long-haired protesters taking over a College with Police arresting them, and in Eugene he found them. No wonder the lunch at Denny's for *Five Easy Pieces* lasted a week. He was in filmmaker heaven.

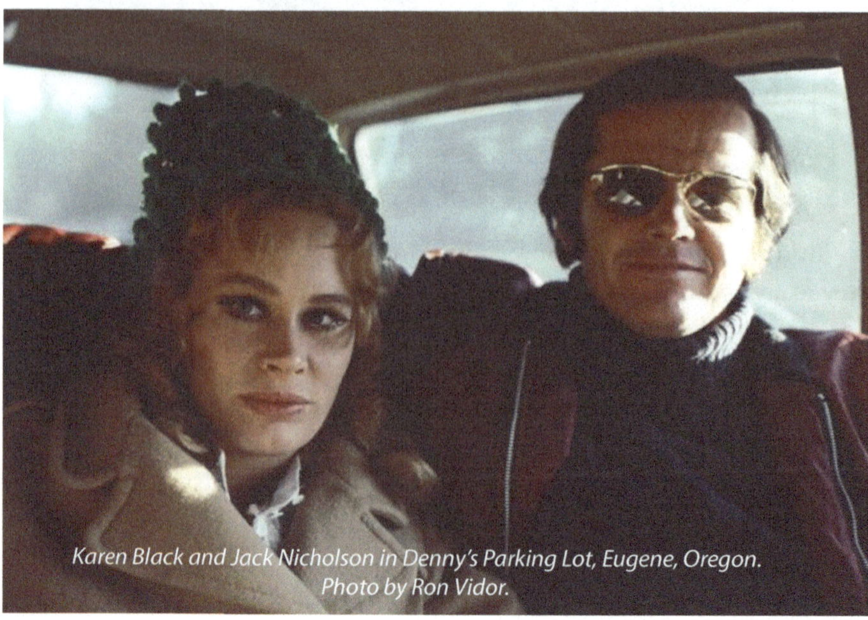

Karen Black and Jack Nicholson in Denny's Parking Lot, Eugene, Oregon. Photo by Ron Vidor.

This is how it happened, to the best of my ability to piece it together:

On Thanksgiving Day, 1969; I was on my way with my family to my Grandmother's house in Klamath Falls. Right before you leave I-5 Freeway south to exit onto Highway 58 to Klamath, is a Denny's restaurant. I drove right by it. Little did I know that on the same day, not finding anything open for lunch, a rag tag group of filmmakers had seen the sign "Always Open" and stopped for lunch while caravanning up to Puget Sound.

They filmed the infamous "Chicken Salad Scene" there, and then courted by Oregon's Film Commissioner Warren Merrill to stay the night at the Eugene Hotel, and have the only Thanksgiving Dinner around on him. They ultimately spent 5 days filming from Lowell to Florence in Lane County. The film was called *Five Easy Pieces* and would be nominated for 4 Academy Awards. It was pure Poetic Cinema. And I KNOW that Jack and Cinematographer Laszlo Kovacs and Bob Rafelson fell in love with the Eugene Hotel crowd, an eclectic group of artists and filmmakers like Mike and Uly; because not only would Jack and Bob Rafelson, with their BBS Productions, bring Jack's next film, *Drive, He Said* to Eugene a few months later, but Producer Richard Rush brought *Getting Straight,* his film with Elliott Gould to Eugene too, in July. And DP Laszlo Kovacs was the link. There they made history, because Jack Nicholson, Karen Black and Sally Strothers would act in the first real poetic cinema commercial success, *Five Easy Pieces,* under the direction of Bob Rafelson. And yes, it's true: "Bob was regarded as one of the founders of the New Hollywood movement in the 1970s."[180]

One could say that *Five Easy Pieces* was pure Yeatsian in its portrayal of a man, (Jack Nicholson) who came from a wealthy family and was trained

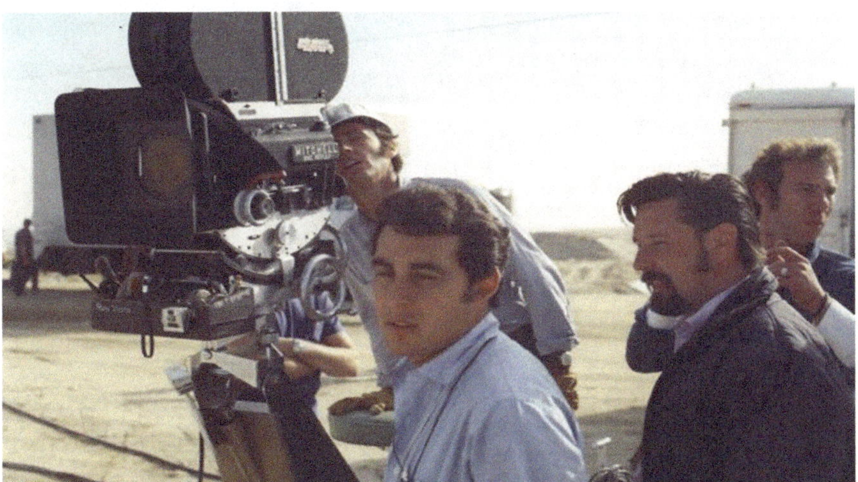

Five Easy Pieces, far left, Ron Vidor foreground, Laszlo Kovac DP & Director Bob Rafelson

as a concert pianist, only to abandon his heritage and work as a foreman on oil derricks near Bakersfield, California. As the prodigal son, he then returned to his family upon news from his sister that his father had had a stroke. His girlfriend (Karen Black, a waitress) returns with him, only to be ridiculed by the family's intellectual snobbery in a scene involving the family dynamics that he had run away from. In an incredibly powerful scene, he then goes to spend time with his stroke-ridden deaf and mute father, who is in a wheelchair (and metaphorically placed on the edge of a cliff by his son) trying to talk to him. Jack instead is the one who then steps off the metaphorical cliff, when he leaves his family, his car and his pregnant girlfriend at a truck stop, by getting a ride with a trucker, that is bound for Canada. "Just get out the back Jack."

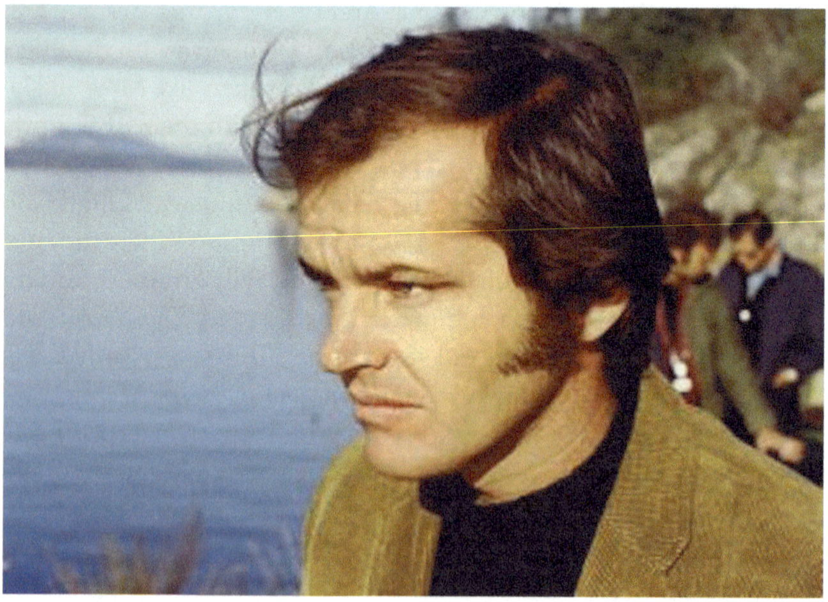

Five Easy Pieces Photos courtesy of Ron Vidor. Used By Permission.

Like Jack's standing up for Karen against the intellectual snobbery of his family's milieu; over and over again, Kesey also pitches heart against intellect. Little did Jack know that someday he would win an Academy Award for portraying the Anti-hero in Kesey's *Cuckoo's Nest.* And he would go on to have a full career portraying these Kesey-ian characters over and over again.

So, I tried to turn to academia to unpack this Anti-hero. Besides the letter from Professor Stanley Corkin from the University of Connecticut, while discussing Kesey's use of the New Western, remember he said this about the anti-hero:

> I like your discussion and think that connecting the radical individualism of Kesey and his books to the western hero, or anti-hero makes sense. Did you even see *Lonely are the Brave,* which can be a kind of Douglas companion piece to *Cuckoo's Nest,* or read novels by Wallace Stegner – a Kesey connection or Edward Abbey, and then Ivan Doig later. All were trying to reimagine the Western as a vehicle for the anti-establishment antihero. Paul Newman was a Hollywood leading man closely connected to this vision of character.[181]

"This vision of character" is what we will be exploring, by these Poetic Cinematic & Bicultural Voices that created these Anti-heroes, including Nicholson and Newman's, in the next chapters.

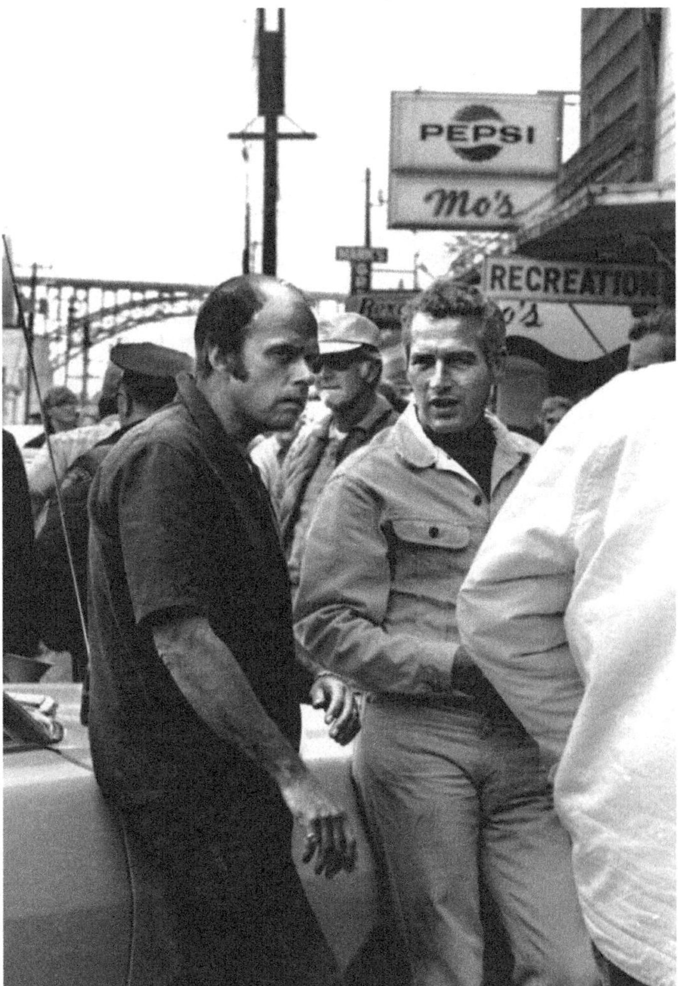

Paul Newman on the set of Sometimes a Great Notion. Photo by Gerald Manly. Used by Permission.

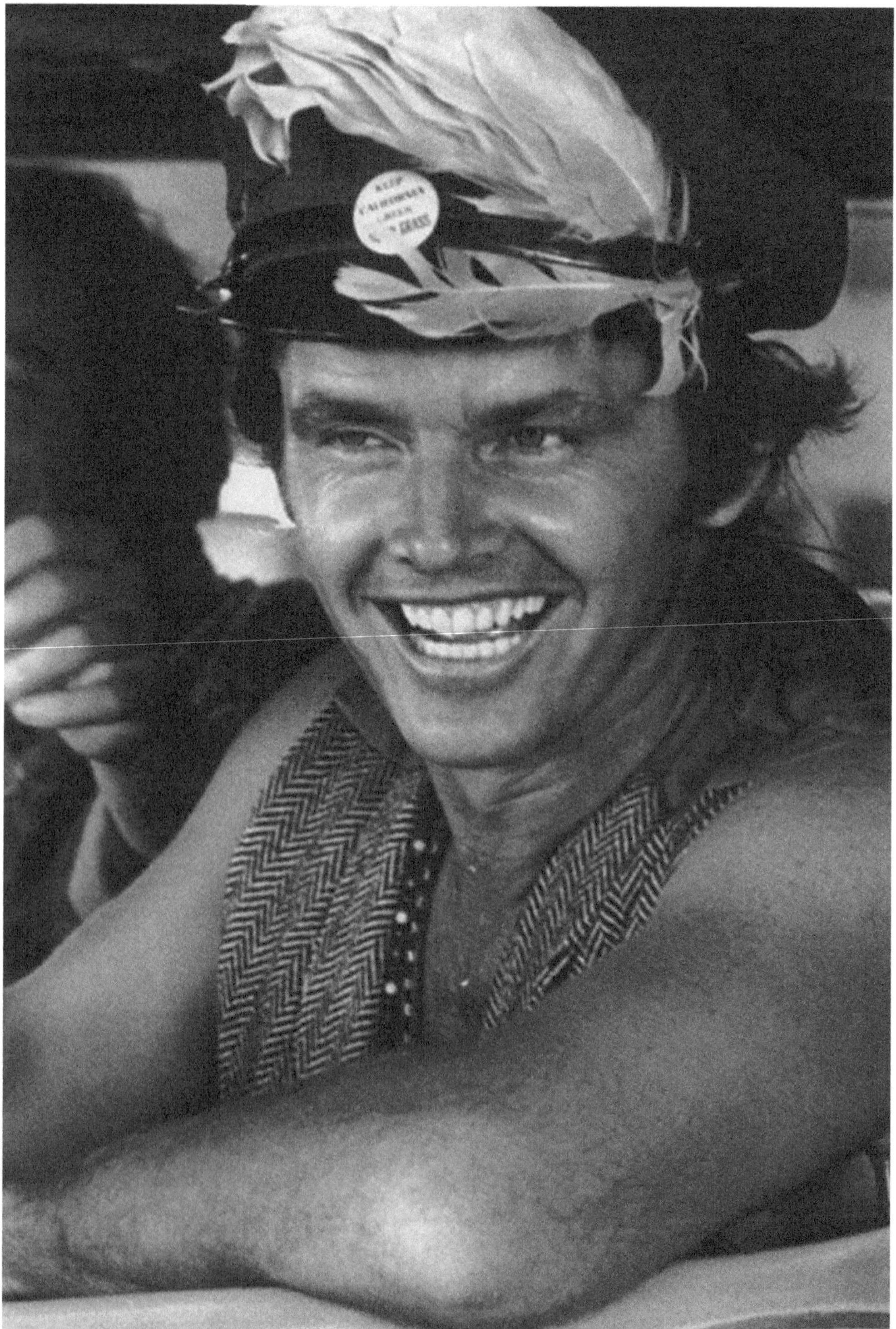

Photo of Jack Nicholson courtesy of AIP

Chapter 5

The New Western's "John Wayne" is Jack Nicholson 1970

> ... (S)elf-creation- it can take many forms. It can be the long and difficult remaking of an inherited (determined) practical consciousness: a process often described as development but in practice a struggle at the roots of the mind- not casting off an ideology, or learning phrases about it, *but confronting a hegemony in the fibres of the self* and in the hard, practical substance of effective and continuing relationships. It can be more evident practice: *the reproduction and illustration of hitherto excluded and subordinated models;* the embodiment and performance of known but excluded and subordinated experiences and relationships; the articulation and formation of latent, momentary, and newly possible consciousness.
>
> – Raymond Williams, *Marxism and Literature*

Director Milos Forman is quoted as saying about Jack Nicholson: "I see his extraordinary acting brilliance in every film he does, even the bad ones."[182]

Other major film makers agree, all noting with wonderment Nicholson's almost unprecedented capacity for range in his performances – from the bespectacled introvert of *The King of Marvin Gardens* to the bawdy iconoclast of *The Last Detail* to the pseudo-suave idealist of *Chinatown* to the frizzy-haired boob of *The Fortune*. Bob Rafelson theorizes that Nicholson can enact a full spectrum of characterizations because, like a director, he studies each role as if it were for a total stranger, not Jack Nicholson."[158] Sound familiar? The stranger who comes into a community to risk his life to solve their problem, but leaves again without marrying the girl or joining the community? That's the Jack I know and love. Jack the writer of existential westerns with Monte Hellman in the early sixties, now studying his role as a way of depicting "the total stranger," just like the lone gunman who is the definitive American Cowboy Archetype; is now "*confronting a hegemony in the fibres of the self*" in the New Age. We find that particular hegemony of the American cowboy was not only representative of "the bad guy" of white supremacy and patriarchal dominance, and what used to be known as the Good Guys; but is now, out of necessity, being confronted by the Anti-hero. Just like we can see in Jack's films:

> Within real pressures and limits, such practice is always difficult and often uneven. It is the special function of theory, in exploring and defining the nature and the variation of practice, to develop a general consciousness within what is repeatedly experienced as a special and often relatively isolated consciousness. For creativity and social self-creation are both known and unknown events, and it is still from grasping the known that the unknown-the next step, the next work-is conceived."[183]

I used to stay at Jack's house, off and on for years; in his daughter Jennifer's room. He liked having company, and was an incredibly gracious host. He loved women, smart women, beautiful women, talented women, and married women, like me. I was safe, I think. And I didn't want anyone's baby, and he knew that. With the advent of the sexual revolution, especially coinciding with or as a direct result of readily available birth control, a refreshing honesty about sex developed between men and women. And even in 1969, when babies were conceived accidently, we knew where to go for an abortion. Of course this was not ideal, but it was a step in the right direction of freeing men and women from an age-old *mores'* of shame and blame, and when people are freed from outdated constructs, they are then free to come back into balance. And for the most part, men are truly coming back into balance about sharing responsibility for the consequences of sex, like Jack. He was a wonderful

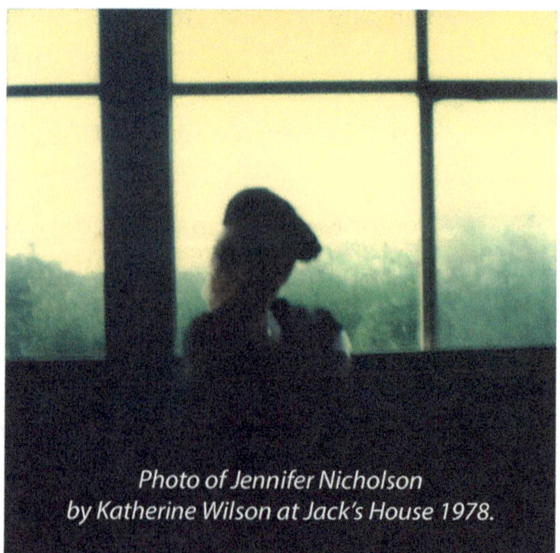

Photo of Jennifer Nicholson by Katherine Wilson at Jack's House 1978.

father, too, if how he was with Jennifer, whom I used to play with, is any indication. And I know he took responsibility for the children he sired. He had a refreshing if not unusual morality.

The Anti-hero that Jack played is a more humane version of the hero, even if he is a downright outlaw, especially when society has become rigid in its outdated rules. In both cases, the Outlaw becomes a hero when he thinks for himself, and when society decides he is right. For instance, here is an example in one of Jack's very first films: *The Broken Land* (1962) as found on IMDBPro: "A cowboy rides into a small town that is ruled with an iron fist by a *corrupt Sheriff*. He becomes involved with a pretty young town girl and some residents who are trying to oust the Sheriff, resulting in a robbery, a murder, and his being pursued by a vengeful posse."[184] Our Jack works within the community to help the girl and doesn't leave her alone. And like Jack, in the film, our generation didn't feel that we had just a corrupt Sheriff, we felt the whole system was corrupt. Because the old heroes of the Piscean AEON of the Fisher King Mythology were dead. And Merlin was dead. But the "Literary Shaman" Ken Kesey had created a New Mythology with a New Hero, who was depicted as an Anti-hero, but went through the same Heroes Journey to find redemption, and as a consequence, even sometimes died for the greater good. I agree with the first part of this quote: "An antihero or antiheroine is a main character in a story who lacks conventional heroic qualities and attributes such as idealism..." but I disagree that he or she lacks "courage and morality."[161] The New Sheriff in town of the New Westerns of the 60s may be full of existential hubris, but they were even more courageous and moral, especially without the belief in a punishing and/or rewarding God.

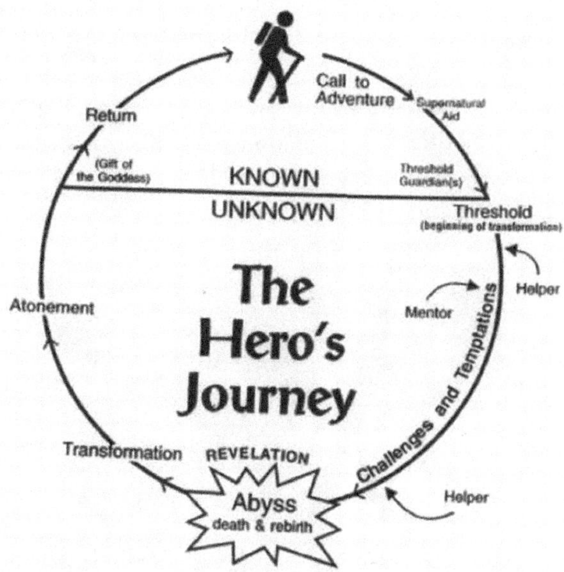

This process, for both the Anti-hero and The Hero, is actually built into every story, from Beowulf on, and is represented as a circular journey. Just look at his character in this quote from *Five Easy Pieces:* written by his Existential Western collaborator Carole Eastman:

> "I move around a lot because things tend to get bad when I stay..." Nicholson's character, an often-loutish guy identified in the closing credits with the grandiose handle "Bobby Eroica Dupea," says to his comatose father, by way of confession.
>
> When we meet Dupea he's just plain ol' "Bobby," working as a hand in the California oil fields, but when his father's illness draws him back to the family compound on an island in Washington State, we learn that Bobby was trained from the cradle to be a piano prodigy, before he dropped the concert hall for the honky-tonk.
>
> Forced to return home to confront his cozy past, Dupea unexpectantly finds love with a concert pianist. The 'five easy pieces' of the title refer to piano works; along with Mozart's Piano Concerto No. 9 in E-flat major and his Fantasy in D minor we hear pieces by Chopin and Bach.[185]

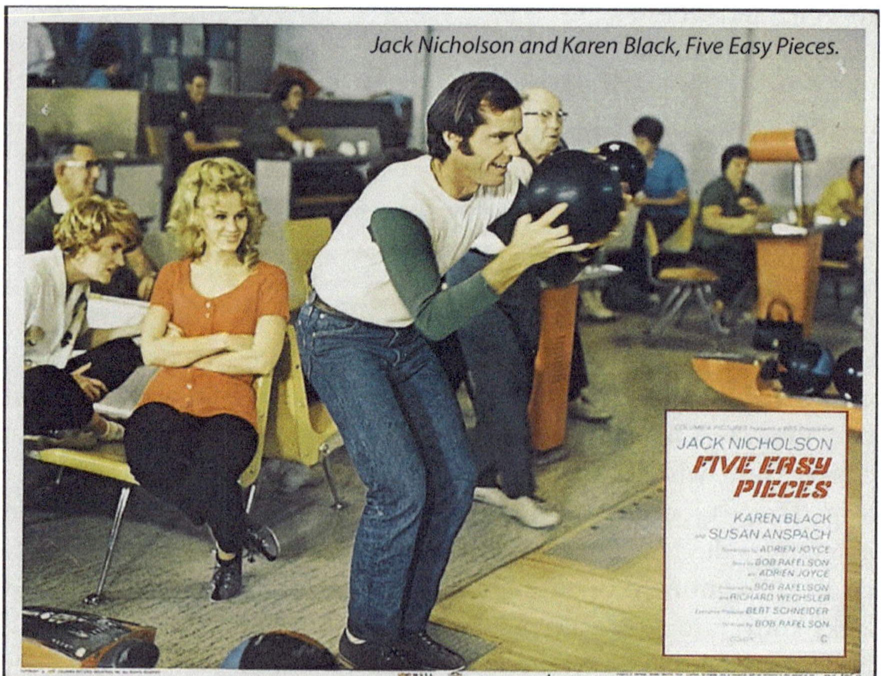

Jack Nicholson and Karen Black, Five Easy Pieces.

I can't help but think the *Five Easy Pieces* uses the same metaphors for Jack and the women in his life, as David Getz mentioned in *The Life and*

Times of the Red Dog Saloon[164] when he said, using musical terms, that the 60s in San Francisco went from Medieval (Gregorian Chants) to Classical (Mozart) to Baroque (Bach) in three short years (1965-66-67). Wikipedia tells us the "The 'five easy pieces' of the title refer to piano works; along with Mozart's *Piano Concerto No. 9 in E-flat major* and in his *Fantasy in D minor* we hear pieces by Chopin and Bach."[186] In *Five Easy Pieces,* his sister represents his Medieval, the family "love"; Susan Anspach is the classical "love he finds," and is playing Mozart. As the New York Times states " In "Five Easy Pieces" (1970) ... she is a "New Age intellectual who sleeps with Jack Nicholson's character, even though she's engaged to his brother."[187]

Susan Anspach and Jack Nicholson Photo by Ron Vidor

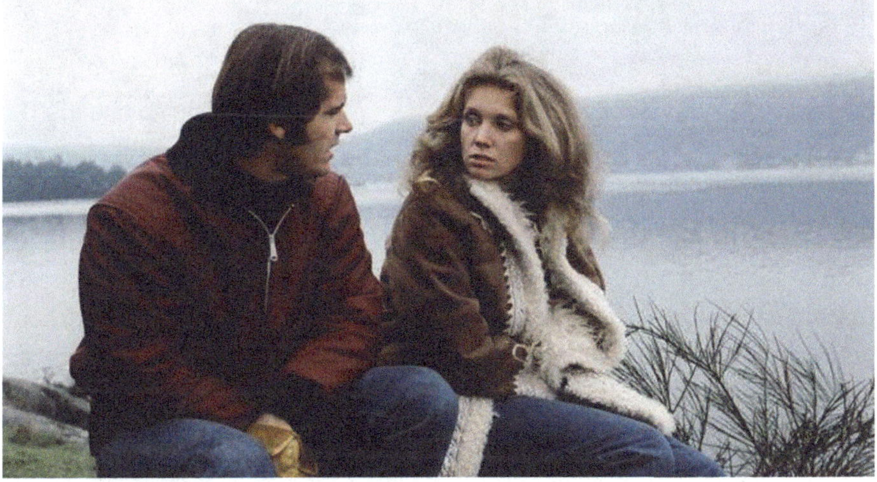

The table has been turned on him. Karen Black represents his Baroque, period, especially after turning his back on his family and living the life of the songs in the Honky-Tonk. Yet he defends her against the intellectuals at his family's house; giving us a clue as to why he may have left in the first place. But even Karen Black, called a "hash-slinger" from also working in a Diner, is confronted with her own shadow too, in the scene with the waitress who tries to exert control over Jack in the Chicken Salad Scene, and where he explodes.

This is what I was talking about as the New Age behavioral role-reversal upsetting the equilibrium between the sexes in the New Age. The Anti-hero that Jack plays is confronted with his own hegemony. Black also sings "Stand By Your Man," a Baroque Country-Western Contemporary song. But when Susan Anspach's character plays Mozart, Jack is confronted with his own deep-rooted DNA memory of family, and disappears into the mystery to find himself again, And I was always hoping, to reinvent

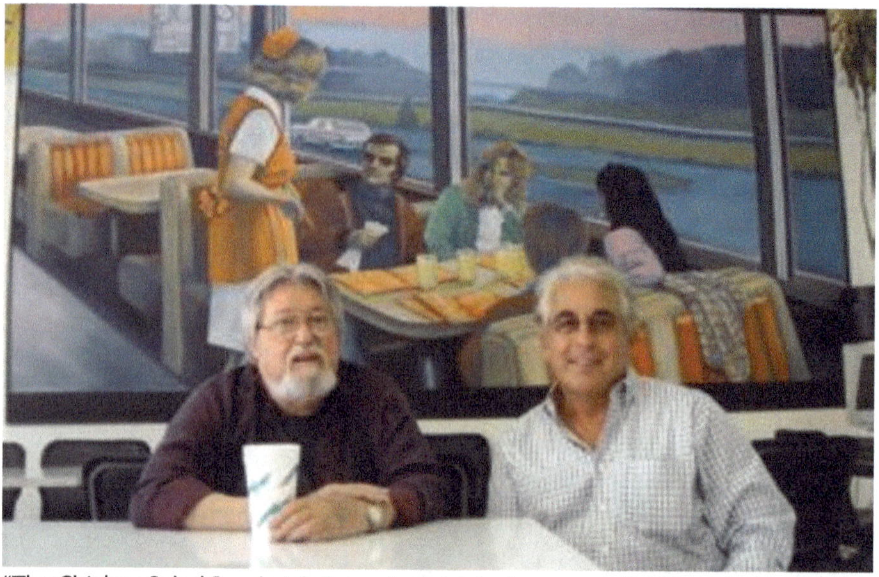

"The Chicken Salad Sandwich Scene" celebrated on a mural at Panavision with *Five Easy Pieces* Cinematographers Laszlo Kovacs and Ron Vidor. Used by permission.

himself again. But in order to do that, he leaves his pregnant girlfriend (Karen Black) at a truck stop with his wallet and car, when he disappears to Canada with a truckdriver. Writer Carole Eastman's brilliant indictment of the double standard and the evolutionary forces of what was happening in our generation, was cutting it really close to home with the Jack I knew. Come to think of it, all of his roles were an exploration of himself and the place he found himself in. Ironically, he fathered a child with Susan, a boy. I remember his business manager, Bob Colbert, who was trying to help me with Kesey's *Last Go 'Round*, let me know it was going to be a while before he could talk to him about the role we created for him, because he was in a bad mood. This was in the early 90s because he and Susan were in court, hashing out the ownership of a house Jack had provided for the child. As a casting director, I would say he represented a perfectly chameleon-like actor, who could play "everyman, the anti-hero" and he did. I think he must have wondered about his absent father a lot. His imagination about his situation may have created the fantasy of an iconic representative of the new male in the new age. When asked to support a women's movement, he is said to have replied: "I have my own favorite downtrodden minority, and it's not woman. It's the bastard, the illegitimately born."[188] And weren't the 60s James Bond characters always orphans? Could it be that our nation's Archetype of the Lone Cowboy, who has no history, no family, and who comes into a community to solve its problems with the bad guys, who brings the problem to a head with the courage of confronting it; uses sudden quick violence to solve it, and then sadly leaves again, alone, without bonding with the community; even though he may have fallen in love, may have even made love, and left the seed of a child within her, but still, he leaves her; could this be the shadowland of his "bastard, the illegitimately born"??? Isn't that what he does in *Five Easy Pieces* with Karen Black? With "Candy" in *One Flew Over the Cuckoo's Nest* and symbolically with Chief Bromden, the bastardized, bicultural child of miscegenation? Don't forget the whores in *Easy Rider*; nor Tepper and Karen Black in his own *Drive, He Said*. And don't even get me started with *Chinatown*!

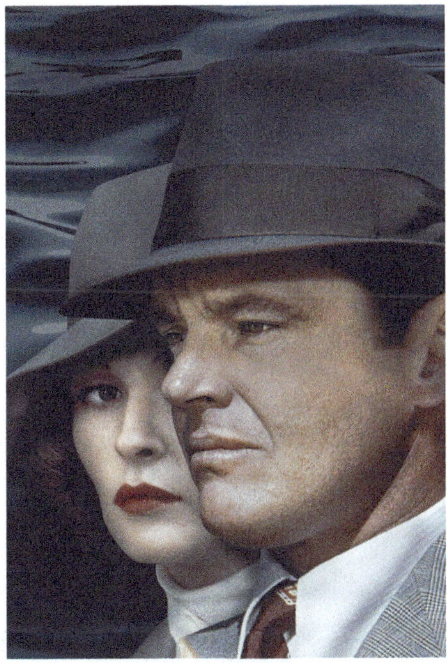

Faye Dunaway and Jack Nicholson in *Chinatown*

I love how the New Western boldly explores this mythology within its Hero-Anti-hero dialectic. And how, as we discussed in the last chapter, *Five Easy Pieces* was Yeatsian in how the protagonist "revolts against the intellect;" especially in the scene that Carole wrote with "the character of a highbrow party guest (Irene Dailey) at the Dupea estate, who goes into ecstasies over Ray's (Karen Black) lower-class patois ("The choice of words, 'squashed flat,' juxtaposed against the image of a fluffy kitten ..." she coos); right before Bobby (Jack Nicholson) jumps in and cuts her off at the knees."[189]

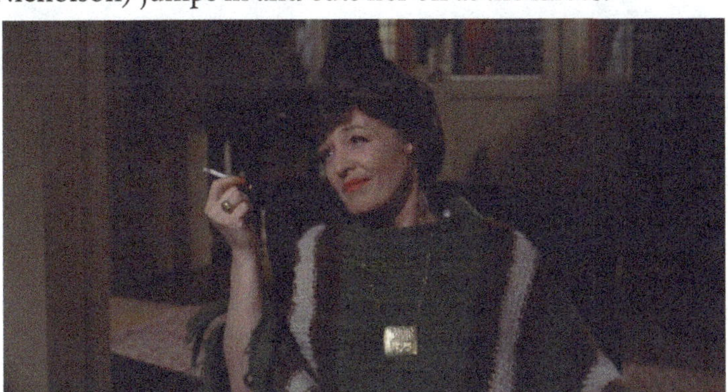

The rumors that Jack was trying to put together his own repertoire film company back then ... were true. Like me, who wanted to work with the same people, he was a Taurus, and very loyal. He was loyal to Robert Evans for life, he was loyal to Director Monte Hellman from his Roger Corman days, he was loyal to the film company he was now a part of that was called BBS, one that we discussed during the last Chapter around *Easy Rider*.

> Like the rest of America, Hollywood was ripe for revolution in the late sixties. Cinema attendance was down; what had once worked seemed broken. Enter Bob Rafelson, Bert Schneider, and Steve Blauner, who knew that what Hollywood needed was new audiences – namely, young people – and that meant cultivating new talent and new ideas. Fueled by money from their invention of the superstar TV pop group the Monkees, they set off on a film-industry journey that would lead them to form BBS Productions, a company that was also a community. The innovative films produced by this team between 1968 and 1972 are... – works that now range from the iconic (*Easy Rider, Five Easy Pieces, The Last Picture Show*) to the acclaimed (*The King of Marvin Gardens*) to the obscure (*Head; Drive, He Said; A Safe Place*), all created within the studio system *but lifted right out of the countercultural id.*[190]

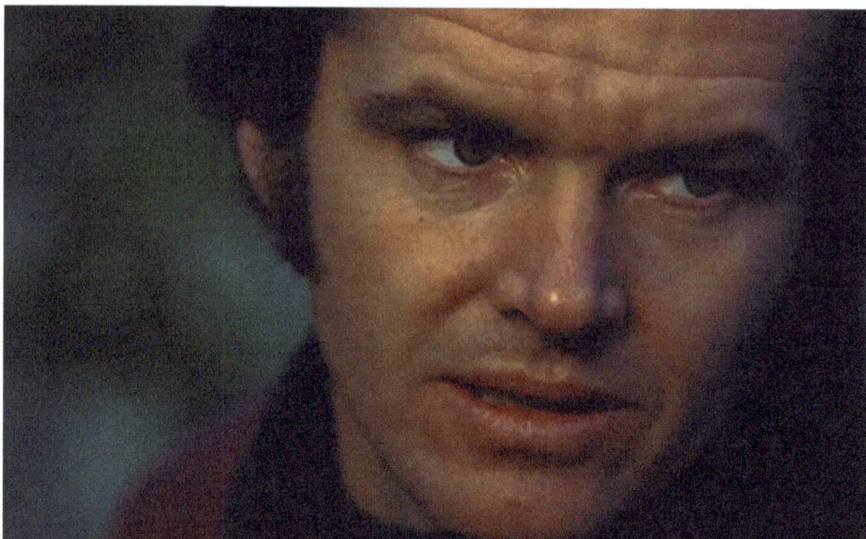

Jack in *Five Easy Pieces*. Courtesy Ron Vidor

Jack, to me, was the absolute symbol of that id. I have mixed feelings about writing about him in this way, because of my love for him. But in trying to talk about the archetype emerging in the 60s and early 70s in film, the New Age of sexuality, etc. and the New Cinema trying to express it, it is because it is through these *images that we know the archetype*. And these quotes have been such a wonderful guide for me, a bicultural poet who receives words as images that have to have time to be unpacked; kind of like what Kesey's Merry Prankster Mountain Girl had to say about Jerry Garcia: "I think he had synesthesia, which is the professional word for when you [hear a sound and it causes you to] see color and sculpture."[191] Except what happens to me is, when I hear a word I see color and images.

So with that, I'd like to share one more quote from Literary Critic Raymond Williams, that I find pertains to how we navigated the New Archetype, which is hard to talk about, *but easy to see*, with the New Anti-hero and the New Cinema:

> Within real pressures and limits, such practice is always difficult and often uneven. It is the special function of theory, in exploring and defining the nature and the variation of practice, to develop a general consciousness within what is repeatedly experienced as a special and often relatively isolated consciousness. For creativity and social self-creation are both known and unknown events, and it is still from grasping the known that the unknown-the next step, the next work-is conceived."[192]

When I used to stay with Jack, he had a separate room off of the living room just for watching sports. At the time, I was a sports widow, and knew what to do. DO NOTHING. I remember so clearly, so vividly, that from the Dining room, he looked like he was in this ad, except he was in PJ's, a bathrobe and slippers, and watching the world's finest TV set.

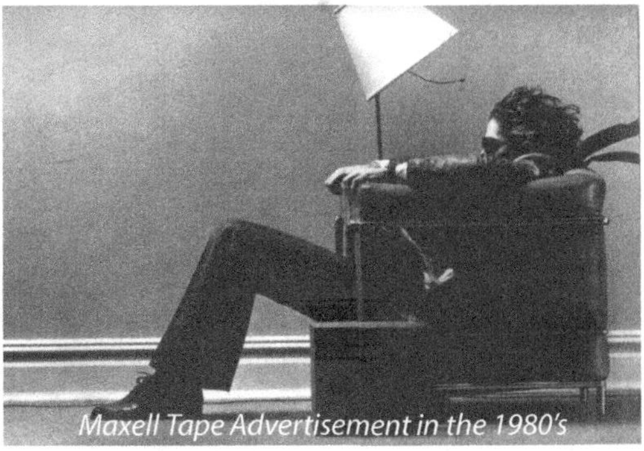

Maxell Tape Advertisement in the 1980's

So no wonder he loved the story of *Drive, He Said*: "The star player of a college basketball team starts to go off the rails with an illicit love affair and his roommate going crazy to avoid the military draft." First of all, the star basketball players he loved were the U of O Oregon Ducks. And he hired a lot of them for the film. Somewhere I once read that he even dragged Anjelica along for the games up here. He also loved the Country

Inn Restaurant out Coburg Road, and would fly in just for dinner. I once called there to see how much it might cost, and they actually told me if I asked, I couldn't afford it. The basketball players I knew then were Nick Jones, and another named Walt, who was dating my dormmate. I'll never forget that Nick would sit at the Student Union's (EMU) "King of the Hill" Booth and take our adulations in good humor and stride. Walt was always mortified to see me, because I had to call the operator to report an emergency one night while he was making love to my roommate, three feet away from me, and he got stuck in her "diaphragm." So Jack loved Eugene's premiere basketball team. We all did, back then.

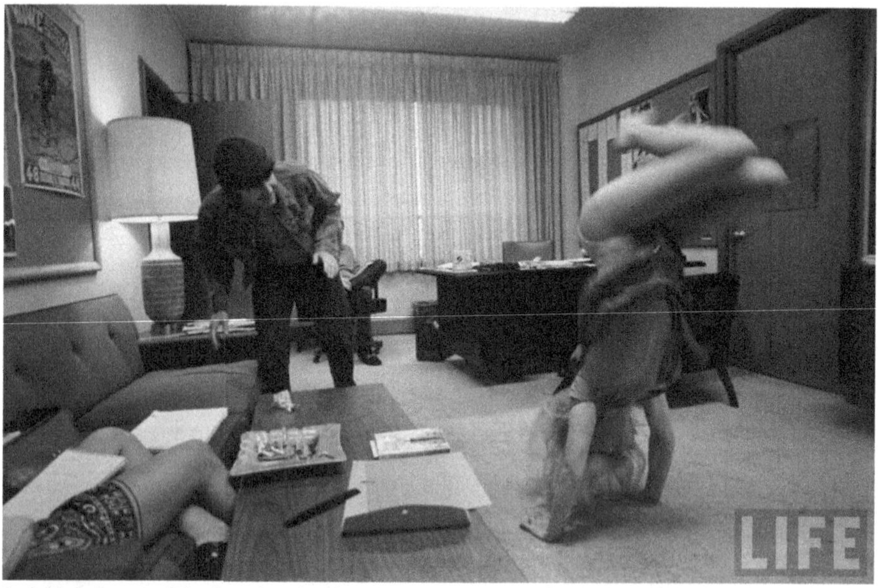

Jack Nicholson auditioning cheerleaders in Eugene, Oregon for *Drive, He Said;* (in a Logger Cap!)

The second thing Jack loved was that the story involved another MILF situation, where the illicit affair was with Olive, (Karen Black) who was married to the basketball player/student/protagonist's favorite professor. The third thing was that professor was played by Robert Towne (whose wife found an article at the Eugene Public Library that became the fodder for *Chinatown*). And the fourth thing was that Jack must have loved was my radical dormmates, because he had hired all of them for the student protest scenes. And because they were in his sphere of influence, they kept him updated on our campus' student unrest activities. I heard a lot about the filming in the dorm cafeteria, where we would all eat together. Several of them were really involved in the political scene, like my dear friend Rick Johnson, who was the head of the Bail Fund Committee for protestors in Jail.[193]

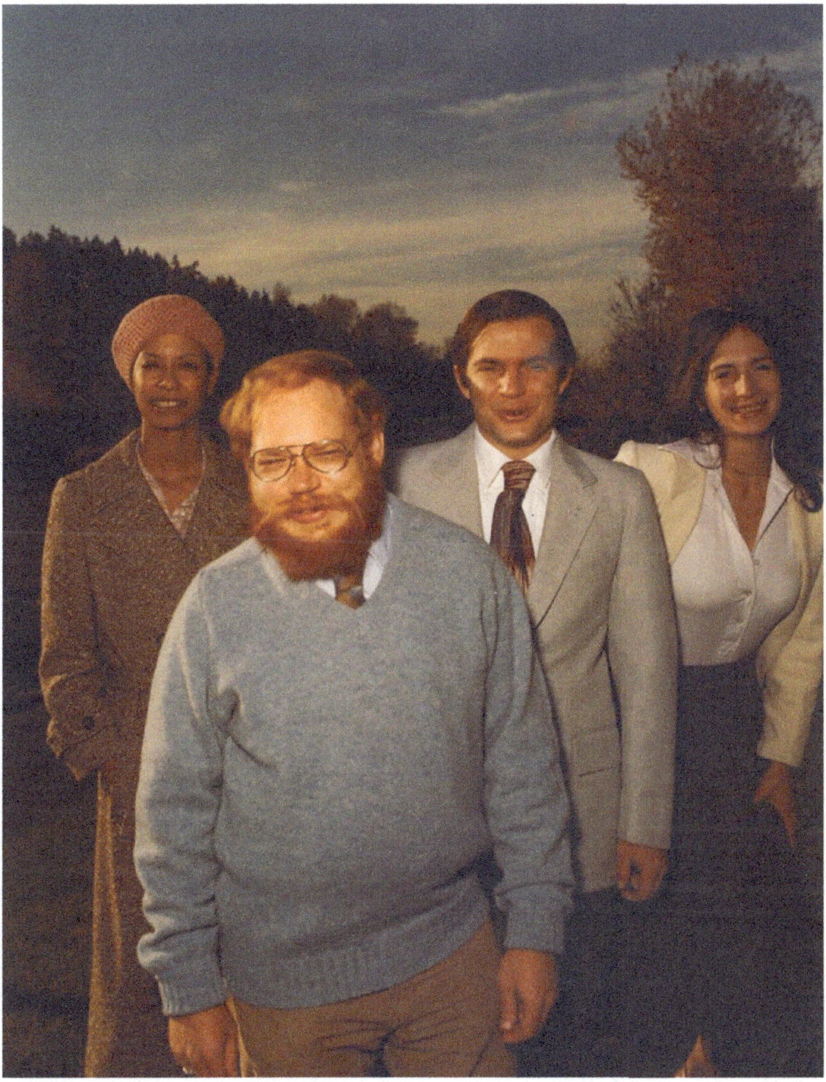

From left, Beverly Cadbury, wife of Film Professor Bill Cadbury; Dormmates H.J. Langtry, Rick Johnson, Katherine Wilson

And I was there that fateful day, April 24th, 1970; the day that Jack not only filmed the protests, but as promised, put up their bail money, although I didn't know it at the time. Terry O'Conner told me that it took an extra day to release "the out of state kids" because of "flight risk."[194] And I knew Jack had promised to put up bail if they were arrested, because our other dormmate H.J. Langtry told me that as he chased after me as I was leaving that day, telling me to please stay, because Jack wanted me in this scene. But I said "No. I can't. I am failing biology."

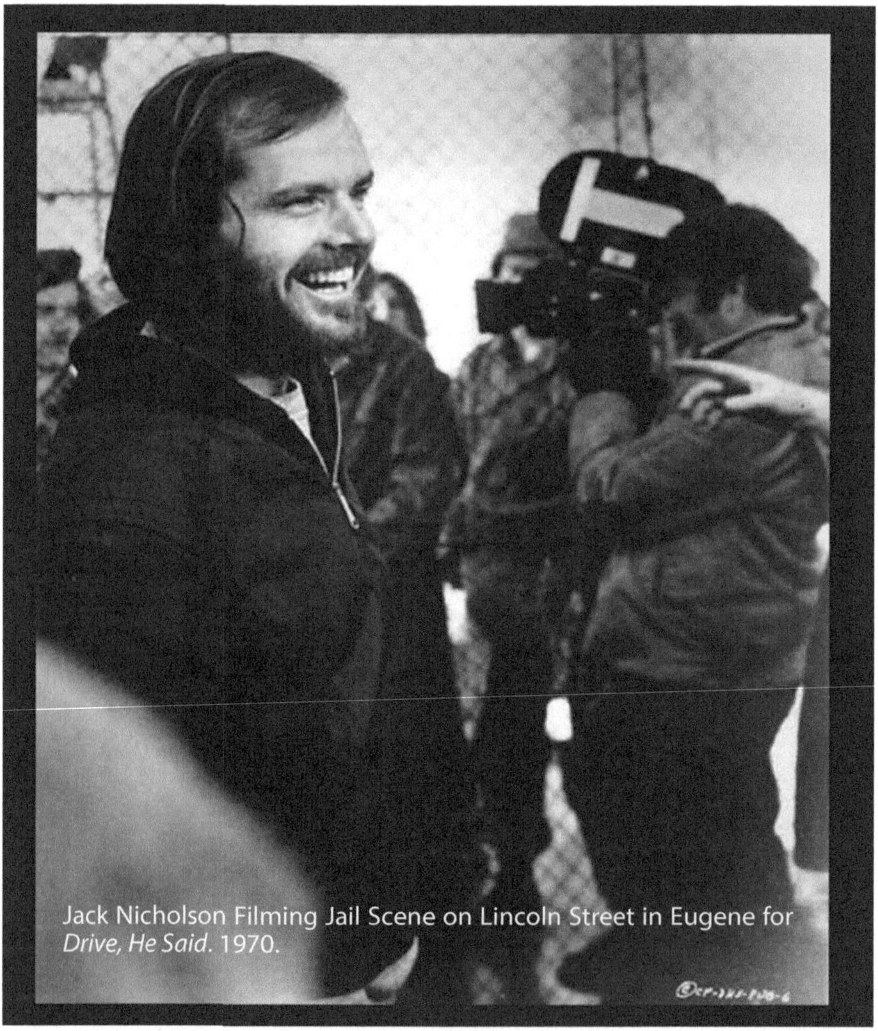

Jack Nicholson Filming Jail Scene on Lincoln Street in Eugene for *Drive, He Said.* 1970.

I really was failing biology, I just confirmed that with my transcripts. From a 3.79 GPA fall term and being on the Dean's list; to failing my Biology Midterm and having to pull off a "C" for Winter term. When this happened, early Spring term, I was determined to not let my political activities interfere again, like they did in January and February. Of course I did not believe Jack would put up their bail money for some reason. By then I had been pranked enough to be skeptical. Imagine my shock all these years later learning that he had!

I also heard that Jack said he had secreted the footage away in the trunk of the Producer's car (Bert Schneider) to California. When the Eugene Police came to his door at the Eugene Hotel to try to find it, he answered the door naked. And said: "Search me."

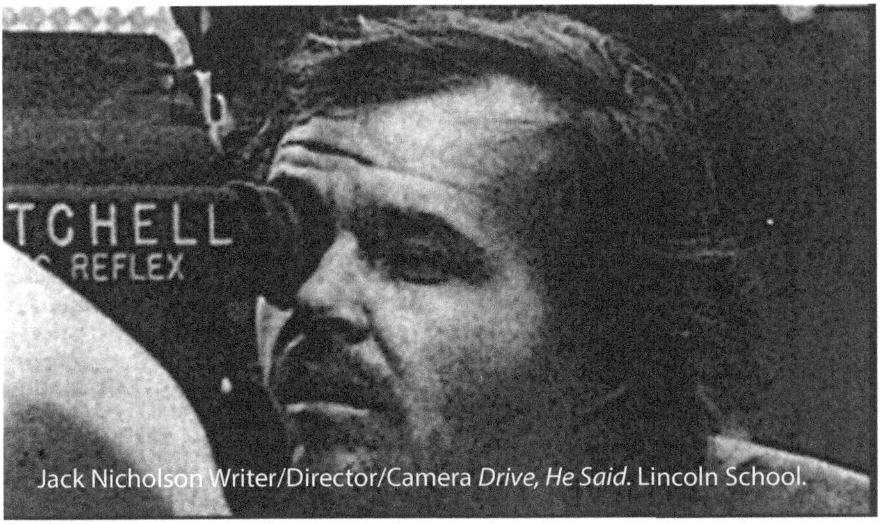

Jack Nicholson Writer/Director/Camera *Drive, He Said*. Lincoln School.

That day, according to Lynn Peterson, who is one of my oldest, dearest friends and was an extra, "We were filming with Jack over by Deady Hall, when suddenly we heard that someone had called the National Guard on the Protestors at Johnson Hall. I think Jack had even let it be known that if it escalated to that level, he was going to film it. Jack started to run over to Johnson Hall, and the rest of the cast and crew followed as quickly as we could, carrying equipment."[195] The War that was tearing our country apart, brought us together. And Film brought even more of us together that year. Because of *Drive, He Said,* we now had a larger film crew base, and the following photographs are of two other people who worked on *Drive, He Said,* that are still part of the community of the Prankster Filmmakers. A photograph that Uly took of me that year is in the middle. James and Uly feel like family to me.

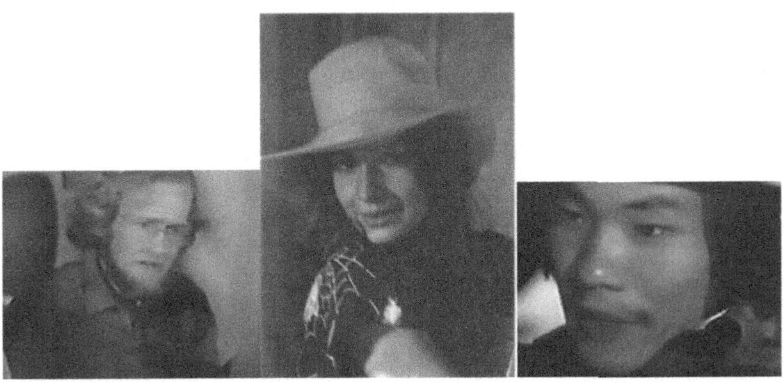
James Aday, Actor, *Drive, He Said*. Katherine Wilson 1970. Uly Cheng, Cinematographer, Actor, *Drive, He Said*

Back then, my dormies and I did everything together. Trips to San Francisco, Salem, concerts, you name it. 10 years later a few of us were even partners in a Film Production company called Associated Film Producers' Services, Inc.

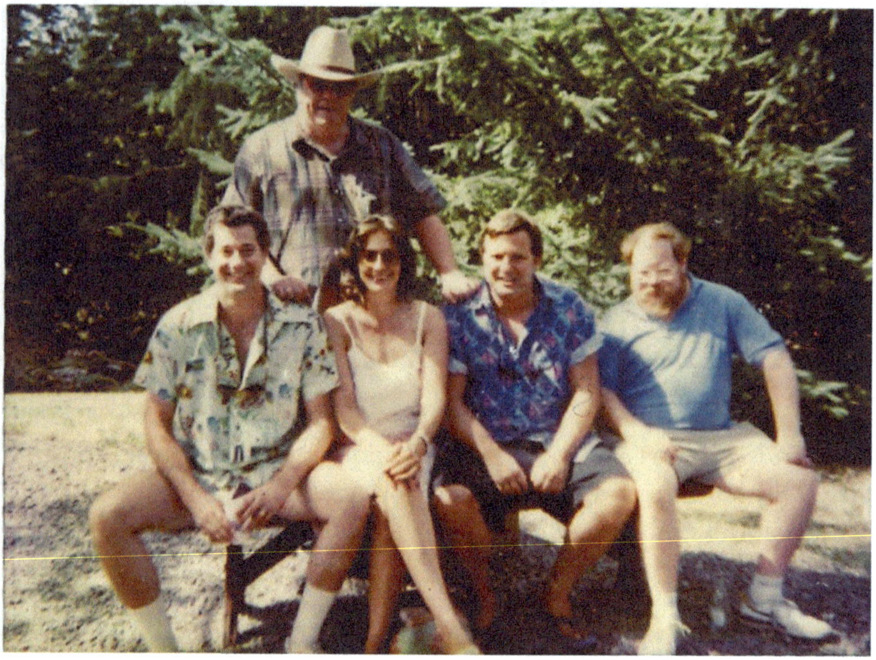

Dormmates Graham Marden, Katherine Wilson, Rick Johnson, HJ Langtry. W/ Hoyt Axton, rear.

20 years later we had a reunion with my friend Hoyt Axton at Graham Marden's house; and 30 years later we got together again at Horton's Hideaway in Portland. 40 years later we met at a party I held with Chris Miller, the first writer on *Animal House*. It's now our 50th Anniversary, but because of COVID, we have been talking by phone. According to Terry O'Conner, another close dormmate, it was very clear about what brought us all together. He called it a "sphere of influence" that was generated right next to our dorms: The Erb Memorial Student Union. He was one of my favorite people, ever, and still is. He said what keeps our group together is that "We carry on, speaking our Truth."[196]

> *Drive, He Said* opened in New York on June 13. 1971. Starring Karen Black and William Tepper, the film was about sex and radicalism on the campus, a theme which was about two years out of date. Most of the critics were kind to Nicholson the director, finding in-

> teresting tidbits of staging here and there in the picture. On the whole, though, the film bombed. Disappointed but not wholly dissatisfied ("The kids on my college campus said a lot of things about society that I wanted to say"), he returned to full-time acting with a vengeance. "But acting," he told me, "is only one part of my four-part development as film maker." Next June, Nicholson will direct a film called *Moontrap,* a Western for which he has co-authored the script and which he also will produce."[197]

According to Bob Colbert, Jack's Business Manager, *Moontrap* is still Jack's favorite story ever, as it is mine. It "is still in the vault." Written as a book by Oregonian Don Berry and published in 1962, the same year as *Cuckoo's Nest,* it is as bicultural a tale as you can get. The Governor's Office of Film and Television's Executive Director, David Woolson and I met with Bob Colbert at La Scala in Beverly Hills, to try to see if we could help Jack make his dream come true, to get it filmed. There is a saying in LA, "half a dollar," coined by a Bank of America film loan officer. If you can raise 1/2 Million, you can make any movie you want. Guess what number Bob came up with? I am still working on it. But now I just call Jack to wish him a Happy Birthday almost every April 22nd since 1975. That's 45 years he has had the same phone number. And every summer I send him a case of my homemade raspberry jam. It's our tradition. One jar for each month of the year. A piece of Oregon that he relishes.

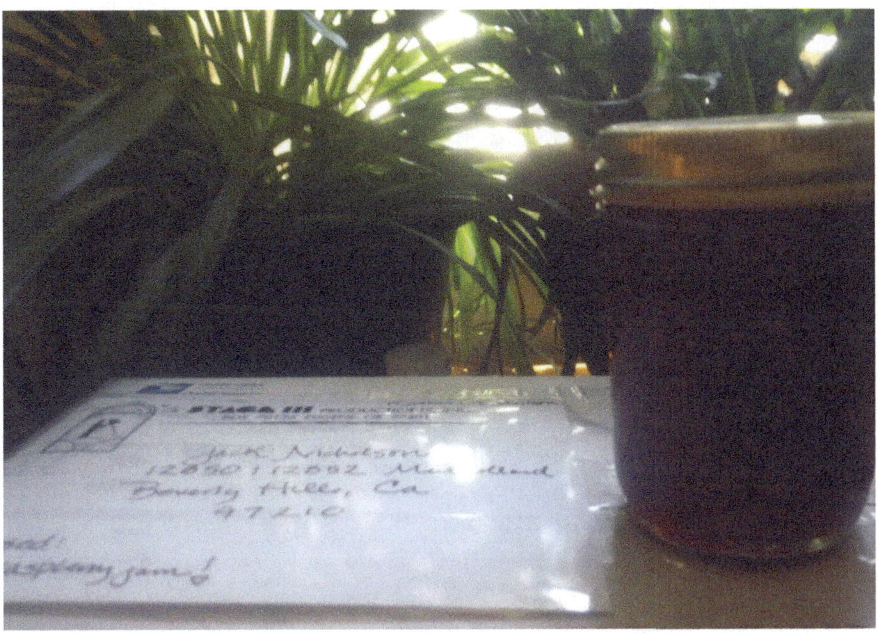

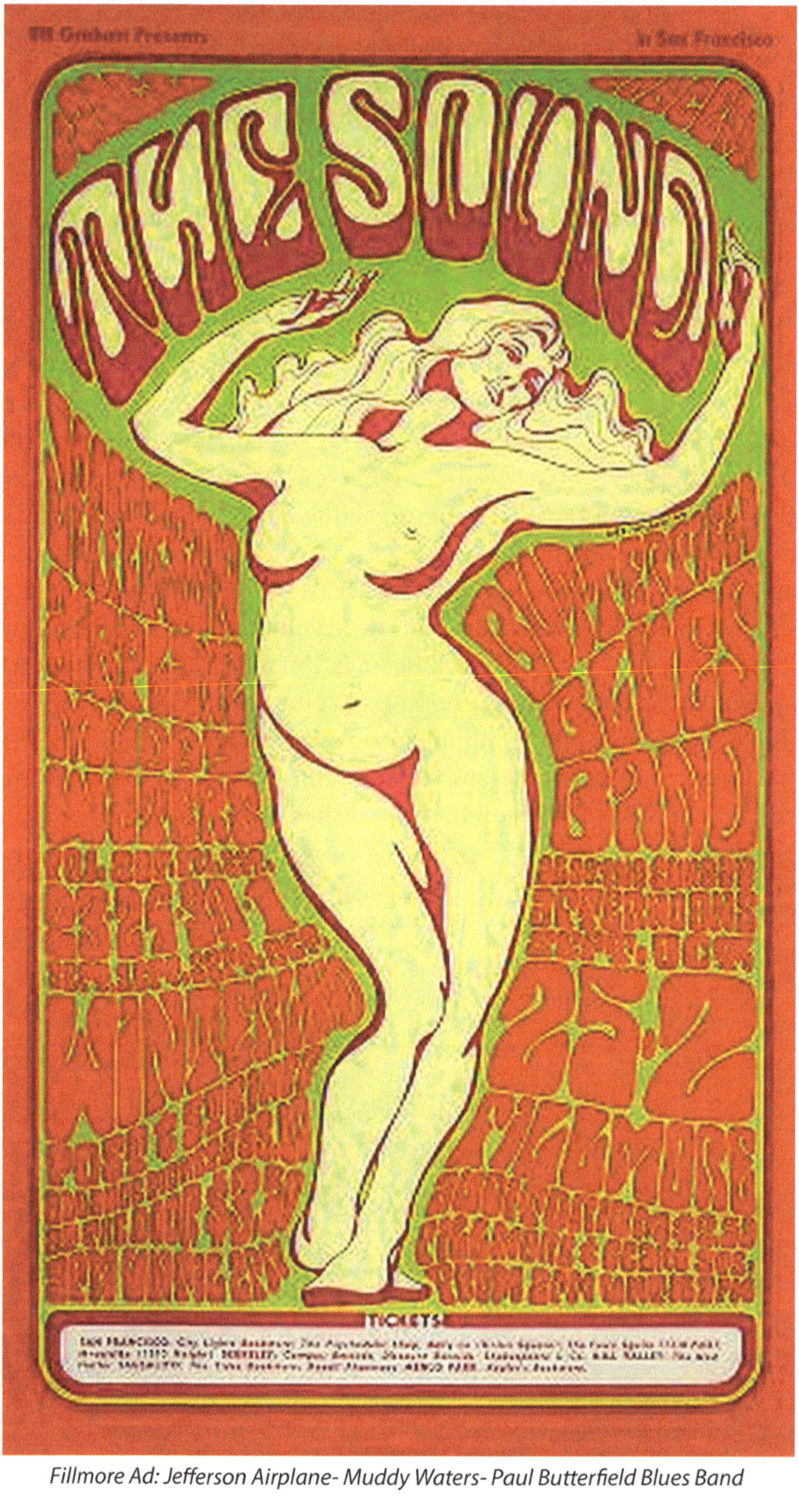

Fillmore Ad: Jefferson Airplane- Muddy Waters- Paul Butterfield Blues Band

Chapter 6

Speaking Archetype into Moving Images
1971

According to Strauss, writers like Spinoza resorted to secrecy and concealedness primarily because of fear: they avoided the issue of 'coming out' due to the anxiety of persecution, caused by the discrepancy between their radical views and the opinion of the masses, still entrenched in their fixed cultural identities. They were, therefore, forced to convey their messages *"in between the lines"* to connect with those in the similar position, capable of immediately recognizing the "secret message."

– *The Marrano Phenomenon* edited by Agata Bielik-Robson[198]

And YES, we created a lot of "Slang" words, that were secret messages; *but mostly we were metaphoric, we were poetic, we were Onomatopoeic, we were "La Nouvelle Vague,"* (the new vague) we were "*The New Wave," we were the "Miracle Subterfuge Artists."* And by 1971, we were just not "half a million"[199] but "millions strong." and like the Marranos of the Middle East, who were Jewish, but captured in the dominant and conquering culture of Christianity; we found a way to survive as "bicultural." And like other biculturals, like the American Indians colonialized by Christian Europeans, especially in their Boarding Schools; we were careful and talked "between the lines."[200]

Nietzsche was right. Modernity had killed God: "The feeling that God himself is dead is the sentiment on which the religion of modern times rests.' G.W.F. Hegel."[201201] And it was *not* cool to talk about it. But by 1971, our belief systems had also become Paganistic, similar in the celebration of Pastoral Religions; but what it was, even more important than that, was our spirituality was more like Archaic Quantum Mechanics. This can best be summed up by a man named Ernest Holmes, who wrote a book in 1926 called *The Science of Mind*. And unlike the cult of Scientology, which gave

Science of Mind a bad name by its similarity in name only, this belief system was not religion, but closer to an Quantum Science spirituality, an amalgamation of all faiths' truths throughout the world. It was shocking because it was not dualistic. Imagine after nearly 33 years of believing this way, then finding a "Spiritual Center" in Los Angeles based on this same idea, and founded by Black Man who in the 60s was jailed for dealing dope, but was "schooled" there by his grandmother with this book. And Michael Bernard Beckwith's Agape movement evolved from there, including studying at the same Seminary that Martin Luther King did.

Today, a lot of musicians and celebrities are counted in the 10,000 members, and who study and practice New Thought-Ancient Wisdom.[202] Because it is not dialectic, I myself joined in 1993.

> Good is at the root of everything, regardless of its seeming absence. But this good must be recognized. Since there is but one Spirit, and this Spirit is you and everything, then everywhere you will go you will meet this Spirit in all people and in all places, and in all things. This one Spirit, which manifests Itself in and through all, including you, *automatically adjusts parts to the whole*. Therefore you may accept with positive certainty, that the Spirit within you goes before you and prepares your way. Your faith is placed in something as positive and certain as the laws of life, *exact as the principal of mathematics, something ever present as the ethers of space, ever operating like the laws of nature.*[203]

"Muslims, Jews, Christians, Buddhists, young, old, rich, poor – we cut across all lines to reach what is true..." Beckwith says.[204]

> How then to think – within the limits of reason alone – a religion which, without again becoming 'natural religion', would today be effectively universal? And which, for that matter, would no longer be restricted to a paradigm that was Christian or even Abrahamic?
>
> –Jacques Derrida, "Faith and Knowledge"[205]

"...a Marrano whose main motivation is *not fear, resentment, and revenge*, but a 'magnanimous' (Arendt 2007, p. 275) wish to become universal – without, at the same time, giving up on the cultural difference and heterogeneity."[206] Furthermore, it allowed us to be free thinkers, and to *just step off of the cliffs, trusting*. Just read Quantum Physicist Amit Goswami's *The Self-Aware Universe*.

> And if "free thinking" needs a space, it is delivered precisely by this very void or the radical emptying of all identitarian logic, which paves way to truly liberated – i.e., uprooted – philosophical reflection. It is, however, possible to combine these two views which seem contradictory only on the surface: in fact, the Marrano sub-identity (where the prefix sub-suggests another and more complex level of identification and simultaneously a subversion of simpler models of belonging) uses both strategies, conjunctive and disjunctive, in order to combine heterogeneous influences and, at the same time, gain distance to the cultural totalities from which they derive.[207]

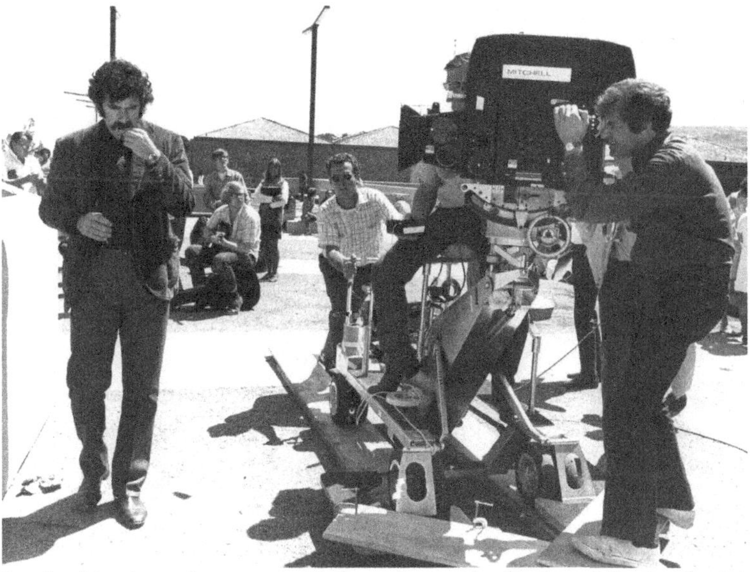

Eliot Gould at Lane Community College during the filming of *Getting Straight*

The thing about film, like any art, is that it filled that void. And allowed us to speak archetype in images, in metaphor, *and* in song, because they became the best languages for our generation. Speaking of moving archetype into images; the film *Getting Straight* was made here at Lane Community College just a few months before *Five Easy Pieces* arrived in Eugene in November. The film starred Elliott Gould, who had just been nominated for an Oscar for *Bob & Carol, Ted & Alice* and *MASH*. And the residual energies of both of those previous films lent a deep subtext to his new role, wherein he is celebrated by anti-war radicals as a returning military man, but who tries to be the voice of reason and the Peacekeeper between the radicals and the college administration that he is trying to finish his Masters' Degree for, and the pressure creates a third persona outburst that is shocking to see, during his masters dissertation reading. It's as if this character and the alter ego of his other character, Bob (from *Bob & Carol, Ted & Alice*) who "insists that everyone "feel" rather than intellectualize their emotions"[208] had been to the Red Dog Saloon to learn how.

Starting in July of 1969, the filmmakers of *Getting Straight* took advantage of Lane Community College's almost-open new school to film it in. My friend Mike Dilley was hired as a stunt man, and starred during the "protester's riot scene." And my South Eugene High fellow thespian Julie Anne Robinson was cast as a girl driving a VW Bug. How would an uncredited lowly extra like Julie Ann, in this film, get cast as Jack's Nicholson's co-star just a few years later in *King of Marvin Gardens*? It probably had to do with Richard Rush, a long-time collaborator with Jack as director on *Thunder Alley* and *Hell On Wheels* for AIP, as Director/Producer on *Getting Straight*. It's really not what you know, it's *who* you know.

And I always wondered what had changed Rafelson and Nicholson's minds about "just stopping for lunch" at Denny's for *Five Easy Pieces* and instead shooting here for 5 whole days. And I am pretty sure it was because of Laszlo, the Cinematographer on *Five Easy Pieces,* who had also just filmed *Getting Straight*. I think he knew Eugene by then and wanted to show Jack around, because Jack was location scouting for *Drive, He Said*.

The production *Getting Straight* lived and breathed at LCC. Most of the community didn't even know they were there. Except Warren Merrill, the Oregon Governor's Film Commissioner, because he got them their permits and had a scene in the movie. So now we also know who had his home phone number and why Warren Merrill was "conveniently available" on a Thanksgiving Dinner Night when Jack was in town for *Five Easy Pieces*. No doubt Laszlo called him, to give him a head's up about another production in town needing some government perks like dinner and rooms at the Eugene Hotel. Laszlo was no fool. He had been here with director Richard Rush on *Getting Straight* and knew Warren quite well. And knew he had a fat wallet for filmmakers.

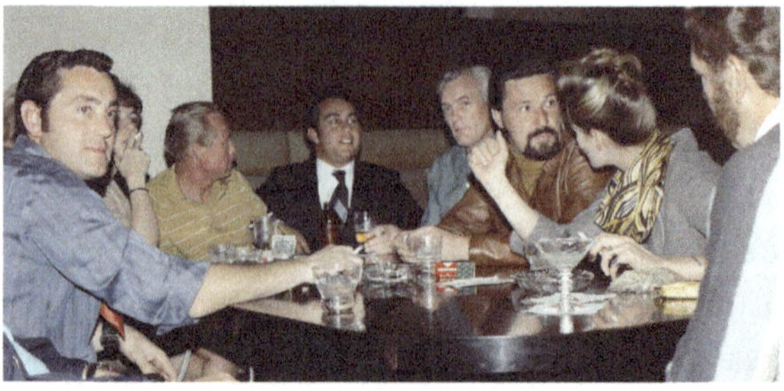

From Center, left, my dear friend Ron Vidor, 1st Camera in the dark suit with tie; Center right Warren Merrill, Oregon Film Commissioner; next to him Laszlo Kovacs, Cinematographer.

This Chapter on 1971, actually began in 1970 (kind of like an Academic Year) but it philosophically belongs here; in that my political life at the U of O with my dormmates soon ended after the protests at Johnson Hall; but my cultural life at The EMU was just really beginning. I wanted to do more than just protest, and so I made a commitment to help the struggling Black and American Indian Student Unions. One other way I had hoped to help was by volunteering to be on the UO Student Court. After I saw how Kip Morgan and David Gwyther were railroaded, I thought this might be a positive thing I could do. For instance, the *Emerald* published a photograph of David Gwyther cleaning up a mess that protestors made on the EMU Free Speech Platform, and they instead captioned it "Dav (sic) Stokes Fire." In a campus newspaper article, the photograph below is captioned "Court Juror Proclaims Victory." That is Tommy Anderson, of the Black Panthers. Dr. Ed Coleman asked me to mentor him, because he was having trouble with poetry in his English classes, that might endanger his affirmative action grant. Evidently, Dr. Ed felt I could help Tommy, because I could speak in a Bicultural way. I was raised both on and near an American Indian Reservation, which had a major train switchyard, with a large Black community that worked there. I had a best friend, Brenda Moore, a beautiful Black girl in Junior High, until she moved away. And my long-time "babysitters" were Hispanic and Black as a child. Eugene was much different. But I was clueless to that, as I had never paid much attention to someone's race. That's what happens when you come from an integrated multiracial town on an Indian Reservation where everyone is poor. The poor have to pull together to survive. Poverty is a great equalizer.

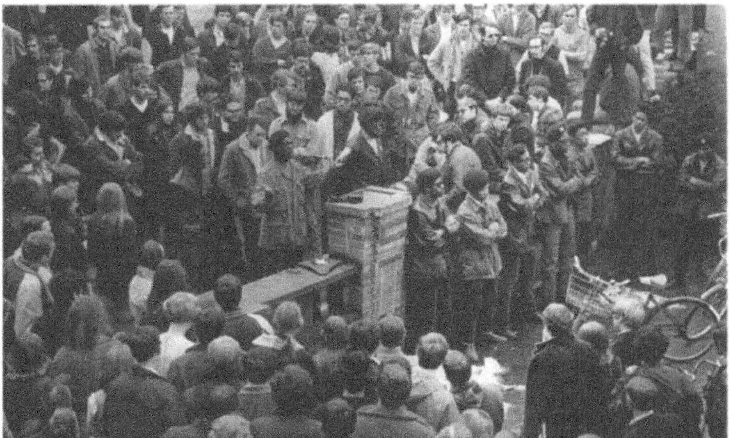

Tommy and Howard Anderson at Black Panther Rally Free Speech Platform EMU

> "Claims have also been advanced to the effect that the question of Marranism was recently closed for good. I don't believe it for a second. There are still sons – and daughters – who, *unbeknownst to themselves, incarnate or metem-psychosize the ventriloquist specters of their ancestors."*[209]

In an interview with Lyllye Reynolds-Parker, for whom the new University of Oregon Black Cultural Center is named; and whom, for years, was part of our Chief Joseph 7 Drum Circle; revealed she is also "bi-cultural." Her father told her they were not only Black, "but Blackfoot-Choctaw." My dear friend Dewayne Jessie, who played "Otis Day" in *Animal House* is American Indian as well as Black. I too, am "mixed race," and I use that term because there is no other, except bicultural, and because my Elders say, "You are not part Indian. What part? You are either Indian or you are not." I identified as an Indian since I was 5 years old, when I lived in Chiloquin; and I identified with those at the EMU, people like Lyllye, Dewayne, Ed Edmo and last but not least Gordon Bettles, who was in my Mom's 3rd grade class at Chiloquin. It just occurred to me that Lyllye and I have both found our way to Dr. Reverend Michael Beckwith's and Chief Joseph's teachings. What are the odds?

I always felt so different, because while other kids were buying the Beatles' 45's; I was buying The Temptations. While other kids were going to see The Wailers, I was going to see Buddy Guy with my girlfriend Edie Keifer, who was also a big fan like me, of the Blues. And somehow, we were invited on the "Chitlin" tour with Buddy, which back then meant that the promoters found you a place to stay that was centrally located, (like Eugene) and then you would venture out in many directions to other gigs each day for a week or so. I remember us riding with him and A.C. Reed, Fred Below and others in a white van, drinking Lemon-Hart Rum, going with them to the concert at Reed College in Portland, and being treated like Queens, because they knew we both loved the music so much.

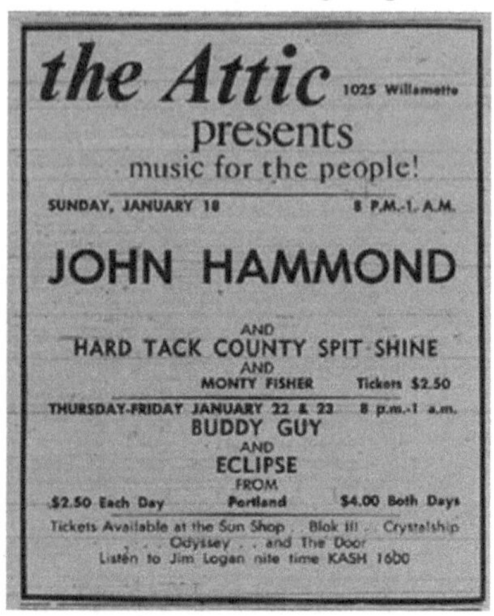

Edie, Mary and I then traveled to San Francisco to see Albert Collins at the Glide Gospel Church and Sonny Terry and Brownie McGee at the

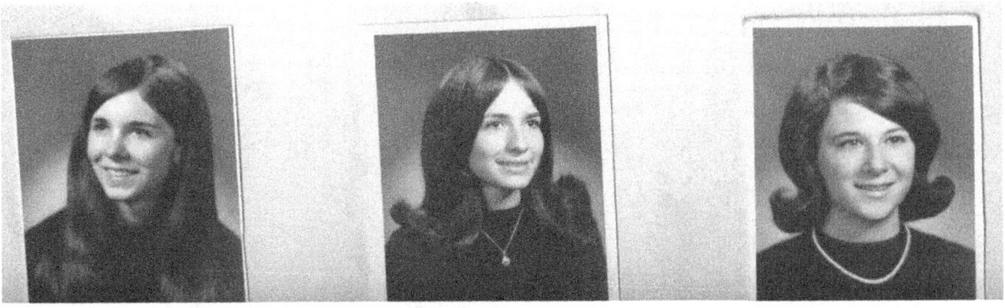

Mary, Katherine, and Edie; The 3 Musketeers for Life. Circa 1969.

Matrix in San Francisco. We also went to Albertine's in Berkeley for lunch. When the three of us white girls walked in, the whole place went quiet. Now I know where that scene from *Animal House* came from; just like when the Delta Tau Chi "Animals" walked into the Dexter Lake Club, and Otis pretends he doesn't see nor hear them.

The Klamath's and the Modoc's did the same thing in Chiloquin. One day I was walking down the sidewalk from school, and two 7th grade girls who were in my Dad's class pretended they didn't see me, a mixed breed, and knocked me off the sidewalk. The 1000-yard stare is part of it. They won't even recognize you with a flick of their eyes. It's as if you never existed, which fits with their belief system that what they focus their minds on becomes reality. You aren't there, you never were there. This particular behavior is also what I have seen regarding other instances of my tribes' practice of Quantum Mechanics. My best friend Etta, a Wallowa Band Nez Perce, had a mother named Elsie *who could make the weather change* with this practice, on laundry day. Etta said sometimes she had to "shoo them, the clouds, away." And she did it every time she needed to, like clockwork, every week, the clouds would move so her laundry would dry. Just try those odds in Oregon.

Etta Conner and President Ike Eisenhower

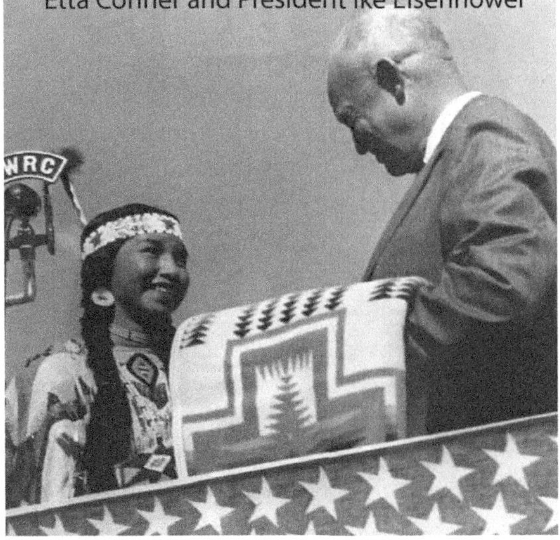

This photo is of my friend Etta, Pendleton Roundup Princess and delegate from the Tribe to the President of the United States when she was young, gifting him a Pendleton Chief Joseph Blanket. A High Honor.

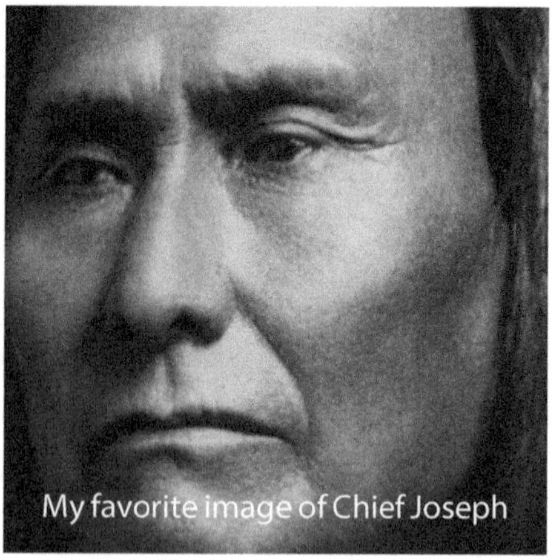

Etta's tribe, under her Great Uncle Chief Joseph, and Etta's great grandfather Alikut, the War Chief; were also known as the Dreamer Society. They did not want to go onto a reservation in Idaho, nor to go to war with the whites for not complying with General Oliver Otis Howard's order to do so in 1877; so instead they embarked on a 1700-mile trek to find political asylum with Sitting Bull in Canada. Allegedly they are documented by the US Calvary being able to create fog banks on hot July summer days to hide behind, and when surrounded by the Army, escaped from their tipis by shapeshifting themselves into horses, which they knew the Army would never shoot, as they were prized Appaloosas, that the US Army wanted badly as war booty. And that is how they escaped to fight another day.

The biggest reason they refused to go on the reservation was because they knew that they would have to abandon their culture and religion and "assimilate" the white man's culture. They felt they needed to keep their religion hidden away. This is why I have adapted the term "Marrano" to apply to this syndrome of the American Indian and the Black man, and any other people of color who have had their own religions overtaken by Christianity as discussed below:

> Having learned from Scholem's studies that there is an elective affinity between Lurianism and Marranism, Derrida – obliquely and allusively – calls this heterodox lineage "Marrano" after the experience of the Spanish and Portuguese conversos, forced to convert to Christianity but keeping their Judaic faith undercover or, in the secret imitation of the Lurianic God, "in retreat."[210]
>
> It is precisely the Marrano "secret" – almost forgotten, bordering on a theology or even atheism, yet at the same time, not without its own irregular form of piety and memory – that offers the aptest model for the "religion of modern times."[211] Just as the Marrano encrypts the Jewish *deus absconditus* in the inner crypt of his seemingly impious self, so does the modern faith hide behind the façade of knowledge and develops further (FK, p. 53),[212] undercover and in secrecy.

> Knowledge, therefore, not only represses faith in the (once) Living God, but it also protects faith in the second source of the messianic retreat. This alternative, fides abscondita, is not to be dragged out from the shadow of the crypt into the light of presence: if it develops and becomes a new "religion of the new times" (der neuzen Zeiten), it is only thanks to the darkness of the "desert in the desert," which is its hiding place. *The hiddenness is the necessary condition of its survival.*[213]

Today we have a Longhouse at the University of Oregon, and one also at LCC. It was the one at LCC, where our Elder Roy Hayes had led the 7 drum Washat Ceremony when it started to outgrow Betsy and Dave's house in Cottage Grove. I'll never forget the first time I met him, at a Root Feast down near the Rodeo Grounds. I was lost, trying to find it, and saw a Tibetan woman with her scarlet Buddhist Robes carrying a potluck dish marching down the street. Spirit told me to stop and talk to her, and sure enough, she was heading to the Root Feast, too, which turned out to be a long walk. I gave her a ride even though I did not speak her language, nor her mine; but somehow we knew what each other was saying. She was Tibetan in a White Community, and we both spoke a bicultural metalanguage. Evidently she loved the Drums and the Bells which spoke a universal one. Could this be because each of the 7 drum songs come from each of the 7 stars of the Big Dipper? Music has always been a Universal Language. And in the 60s it became paramount, because it not only had minor pentomics and healed us, but it expressed our feelings and gave us names for them. Names for feelings that had been lost for over 100 years in the Age of Reason.

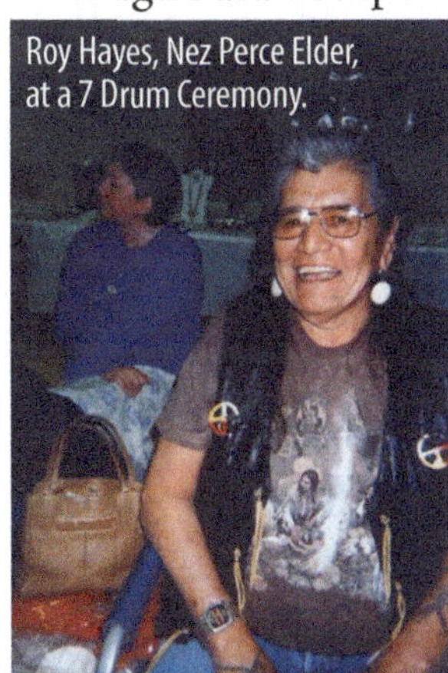

Roy Hayes, Nez Perce Elder, at a 7 Drum Ceremony.

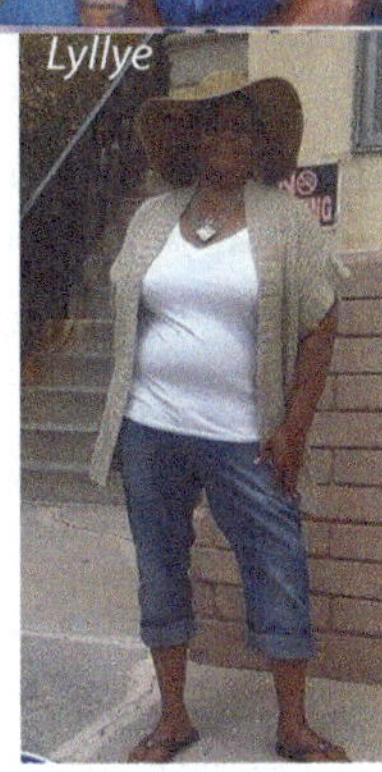

Lyllye

So, I ended up there that day because a mutual friend wondered why I was driving 8 hours one way to attend the Washat Ceremony in the Wallowas; when there was one she knew of in Cottage Grove. And that is how I met my new tribe, and where I met Lyllye. She and I would sit together at Powwows and harmonize in Minor Pentomic with the songs. Recently, I asked to interview her about her experience in the EMU, because I knew she knew Tommy Anderson; and it was Lyllye who told me that Tommy had become a professor after he left the U of O and the Black Panthers. And that he had passed away. Lyllye also said that her brother, Sam, returned to college after he had been in the service, and after he was placement tested they enrolled him as a second term Junior at the U of O! "He also heard the call from the Bay Area." she said. But it was the call to join the Civil Rights Movement. One day Sam invited her to go with him to Oakland, California, for a Civil Rights Conference in the early sixties. They rode with our Poetic Cinema Hero Ron Finne, who was driving. Lyllye said they were run out of Medford in a racially motivated attack. That didn't stop Finne, who would later join Haskell Wexler and eleven other Cinematographers for a *March on Washington* documentary, riding on a bus with an inter-racial couple. That was very likely because of Sam. Sam had also been the first to encourage Tommy and Howard Anderson to return to Eugene with him to help integrate the community.

Lyllye had gone to Sheldon High School and graduated in 1964, five years before me in the first graduating class. She returned to the U of O at 40 years of age, as her children were preparing to graduate from high school. "I wanted to be their role model, she said."[214] But back in the early 60s, as she debated in a High School debate contest at the U of O, she said there were not a lot of inter-mingling of races. However, she said, it was a start, a beginning of "the Demographics of Diversity." And because they all shared the same space at the EMU, it was "a hub-bub of socializing." It was then, in the 60s, that the EMU Cultural Forum started putting on amazing music shows in the EMU Ballroom, which rivaled even the incredible Foreign, Experimental and Avant Garde Film showings at 150 Science, that I believe had been growing in popularity since 1951, when the famous Maya Deren, an experimental filmmaker, visited campus. I can't help but wonder if my father's childhood friend, James Ivory attended any of these, the same year he graduated from the U of O in 1951. And sure enough, by 1956, the U of O Campus Film Group was officially formed by the Depts. of Speech and Drama, the Art Museum Desk and the School of Architecture and Allied Arts, also known as the "UO Film Society (which) is organized to present 'unusual' foreign, classic, documentary and experimental films on campus."[215]

Here is a U of O timeline:

In 1956, a group of faculty and students organized the University Film Society (1956-1973) with the goal of presenting films that would rarely be seen in mainstream movie theaters. Their diverse programs included foreign, classic, documentary, and experimental films.

> The UO Film Society printed programs to advertise the upcoming season.
>
> Film required projectors in good working order. There is a flyer for the 16mm projector the UO Film Society purchased in the late 1960s.
>
> Film Society members composed "Film Notes" to audience members to provide background and context about the films and filmmakers on the program. The issue of "Film Notes" about Maya Deren was written by English professor Bill Cadbury.
>
> English professor Bill Cadbury was a passionate force for film culture on campus.
>
> Attendance at Film Society screenings was impressive, averaging several hundred people for each film.
>
> Notable filmmakers frequently visited campus to screen their films and talk about their work with students.[216]

Professor Bill Cadbury showed his film classes at the U of O in 180 PLC starting in 1970. The community was invited to attend, and did we ever. Lynn Peterson remembers her husband, Gregg Thurlow Weed and her selling tickets at the door for Professor Cadbury.[217] Little did we know that one day soon, Gregg, Lynn and I would soon form our own showings. More about that in the Chapter on 1974.

In the meantime, in my own life, the Spring of 1970 had come, and I was worried how I would be able to stay in school without financial aid. I couldn't go home again. It's true you can never go home again after you have seen the world. And while Philip, my future husband and his sister traveled the world, literally; I had traveled the interior-world on a Psychedelic Bus, in the foreign films of 150 Science, and by road trips (even hitch-hiking!) to San Francisco to the world of music found there. And that is when my former student teacher from High School, Jay Wilson, re-entered my life in a big way. First it was a trip to San Francisco to see Crosby Stills, Nash & Young in the late Fall of 1969, then I brought him home to meet my Mom at Christmas. He started working at the Sun Shop Record Store on Campus, and I started hanging out there. Summer was coming and he invited me to live with him on a Commune out Dillard Road, on a back road to Kesey's (in Pleasant Hill) from South Eugene, where the U of O was. And I got a job, thanks to my best friend in High

School, Mary Gilbert, at the U of O Biology Department; of counting Copepods under a microscope, and befriending the pet Tarantula.

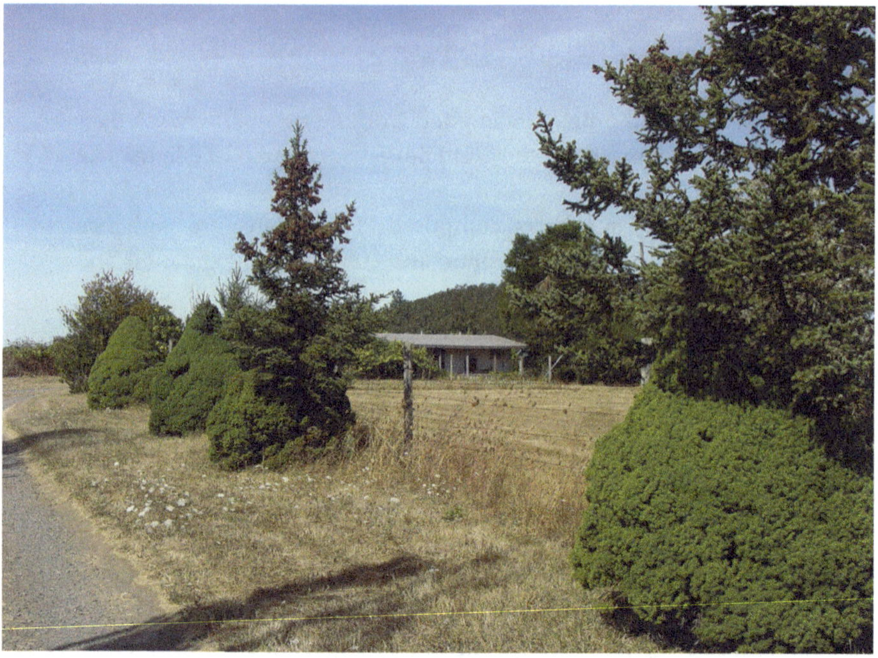

The commune had 16 people living in a 2-bedroom shack with one bathroom. The owner was one of Jay's best friends from High School, with his wife, Ginger, who had just graduated from Northwestern University with their Masters degrees in Political Science. Tom was an intellectual, and invited his friends from New York, as well as their "gang," including Jay and Tom Evans from high school. I spent a lot of time in the barn, weaving hangings and firing up a welding torch and sculpturing sheet metal on Purple Haze from Owsley. When I ran out of sheet metal, we started using the torch on giant candles, that we had poured multi-colored wax into. The mold was made from giant bulk Ice Cream containers. So we would let it cool, strip the waxy container off, and then torched the sides of the candles like sculpturing until some colors were revealed. I wasn't doing very well in school, needless to say. No one had a job, but me. And the partying and music and day trips to Fall Creek took their toll.

We had a car we had hidden LSD in, and forgot. One day it started spitting out Orange Sunshine LSD tabs from the air vents. But besides this manna from heaven, we were not doing well financially; so we decided to open a record store called Sherwood Forest, in one of the two storefronts of the Mayflower theatre, of course, right next to Stage I women's clothing store, and around the corner from Block III men's store. The theater had been catering to the College Crowd since 1950 evidently, when I found that the "Foreign Movie Club sponsor(ed) film screenings at the downtown Mayflower Theater, and boast(ed) a membership of 1,150."[218]

Both of the clothing stores were showcasing very high-end fashion styles from the big cities; and The Black Panthers and their girlfriends loved them. They would also come into the record store, and order obscure, (to us) music. We soon got a reputation for being really great at that (The Jazz distributor was in Berkley) and were honored one day when one of our customers brought in a Shrine to Rashad Roland Kirk. It was an elaborate Victorian electric chair with wires and Rashad's dedication on a Brass Plaque at the top.

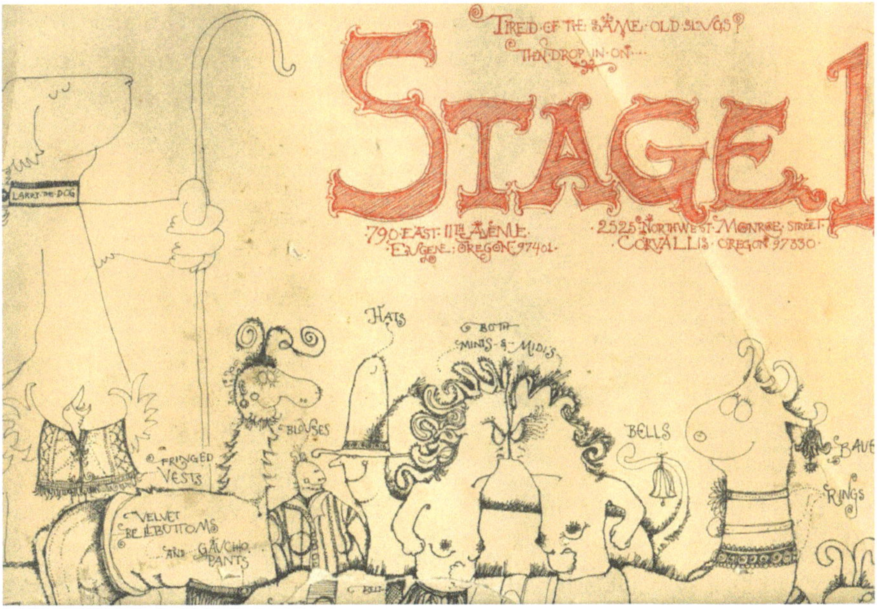

Stage I had fringed vests, velvet bellbottoms, hats, bells, baubles and mini and maxi skirts.

If you look at the left of the poster, made by artist Paul Ollswang, you can see a dog that has a name tag. Larry the Dog kept peeing on the racks when customers came in, so the owner, Mona gave him to me when he was about 2 years old. That meant that I needed to live away from the commune and Ginger's cats, so we moved into a Victorian House on 11th and Jefferson. I was still going to school. And away from the madding crowd I did better at school, for just that term. However, later we kept being lured to San Francisco for shows, and would stop and get the records for our store on our return. We had also found a great cold-water dye place in Berkley, and I would stock up on earring supplies for the weekends, when

I sat behind the counter at the record store and made earrings. The candle making was by then delegated to Fast Eddie, from the commune; but I would drop acid and listen to Debussy in the basement, while I painted cold water dye onto elaborate lace tablecloths we found from the Victorian era, at the Goodwill shop just 3 blocks away. The Motley Hotz Band, that played at Jay's and my Wedding party in April of 1971, practiced in the basement.

In the meantime, Kesey had rented a house just 2 blocks away, on 10th and Jefferson and called it "The Film House."[219] Rumiako the Parrot lived there, as well as Zodiac, and Roy Seburn. Ken was writing and financing a film called *Atlantis Rising* at the time with the Merry Pranksters Bobby Miller and Bobby Steinbrecher. If you take even just a cursory look at the UO Knight Library's itemization of the Ken Kesey Collection, you will see that he made more attempts to create films than he did novels. From 1954 to the day he died, he was a true filmmaker.

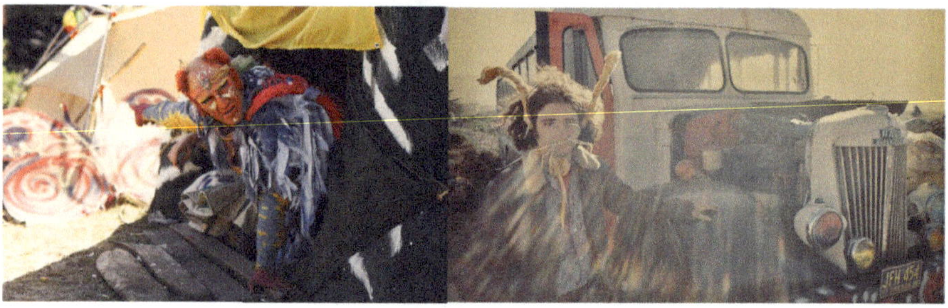

Ken Kesey and Zodiac on set of *Atlantis Rising*. Photos by Jerry Dewilde.

I only saw *Atlantis Rising* once, years later. And it was the most incredible poetic film I have *ever* seen. Zodiac on the right plays the Joker, the Fool, and as a symbol, still rides on the bus as a hood ornament. Kesey was playing a Merlin-esque character. Here is a link to what remains to be seen. https://vimeo.com/82658257.

However, at the time, the Film House was off limits for visitors and was a place for him to work. Yet once in a while we would go out to the farm for a special gathering such as watching Kesey's latest edit of the bus footage, but the bus footage made me seasick. So I would go out on the deck outside the barn for some fresh air, and Ken would follow me out. He just sat next to me for a long time. He did that almost every time I would see him. Then one particular time he quietly said : "I have a feeling we are going to be friends for a very long time." And he was right. We were, over 32 years.

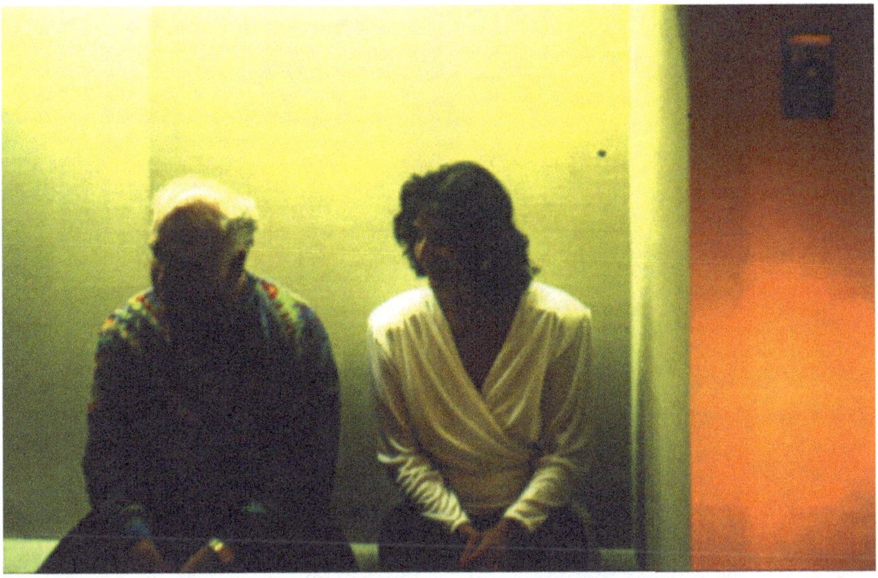

Kesey and Katherine at the Las Vegas Publishing Convention June 1990

While Kesey was making *Atlantis Rising,* our record store was failing in the Fall of 1971. And I was nearly failing school, too, at the U of O. I spent too many days missing class to go to Berkeley with Jay to get records for the store, timed around incredible concerts in the Bay Area, like the Jefferson Airplane, and The Who; in addition to the Rolling Stones in Seattle. During that year at the U of O, I got three Incompletes and two No Passes. I can still tell you which concert I attended for each one of those grades, and they were all missed finals scheduled at the same time as the Concerts. But it was time to change our bad habits. So Jay negotiated a deal to merge with the Sun Shop on Campus. And I buckled down and brought my grades way up in the Spring of 1972. The record store had provided us with a silver lining, and that was that our friend Steve Bove from Sheldon High School, whom had been living at the record store, was listening to the Mayflower's movies through the walls at night; and had begun to make friends with the manager. Before we knew it, he was booking films there, and so we let him move into our basement, where we could all continue to work on realizing a dream of having our own movie theater someday. While Jay was at work, Steve and I would listen to Debussy as we painted old Victorian tablecloths with cold-water tie-dye; and talked about film.

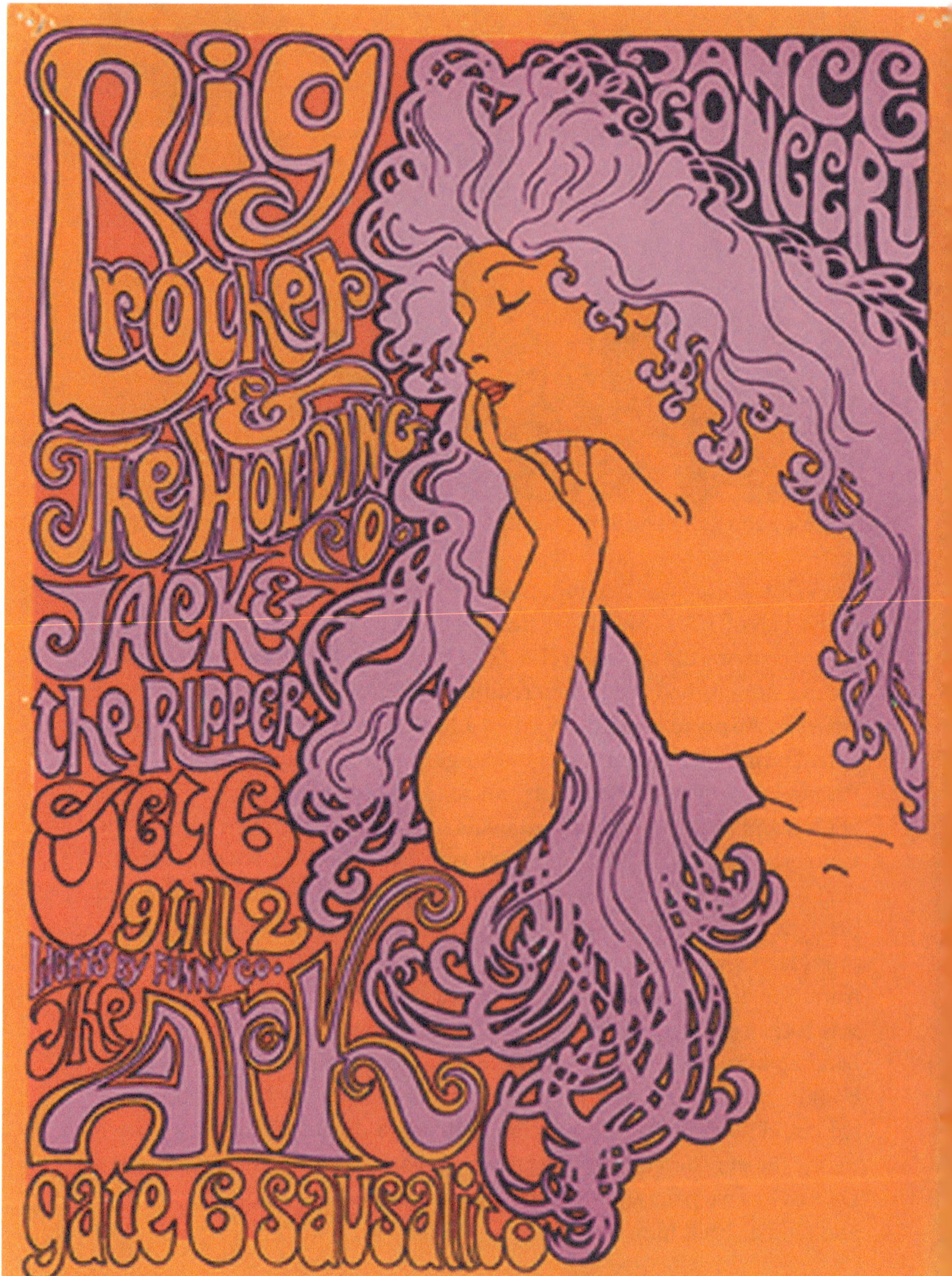

Dance at the Ark. Gate 6, next to the Issaquah. Sausalito

Chapter 7

Stripped Down Moral Universe
~ 1972

The object of this study therefore is to demonstrate that obscenity is not simply a cultural aberration but that it is a complex expression of human imagination, humanistically vital enough to have its own poetics.
– Professor Peter Michaelson, *The Aesthetics of Pornography*

It is said that Erica Jong's book, *Fear of Flying* started the second wave of Feminism: "*Fear of Flying* is a 1973 novel by Erica Jong which became controversial for its portrayal of female sexuality and figured in the development of second-wave feminism."[220] But I say it started first in the film industry, not in publishing. Famous Film Critic Roger Ebert, (who even worked with XXX Russ Meyers) would tell you that our generation was very sophisticated when it came to film, and it is why we created such great art. We had our finger on the pulse of sex, too. Just ask Stan Brakhage. Or check out Maya Deren. And, for us second or third generation "liberated women;" (whom like our Grandmothers, that worked during World War II, like Rosie the Riveter; or our Mom's, who were their daughters, whom *chose* to work) we were really unsatisfied with the Post World War II movies that weaponized women in Noir films, where the femme fatal is sexually alluring but dangerous;[221] or the movies that were constantly depicting John Wayne riding into town as the Archetypal American Cowboy, solving the community problem, finding the town girl, loving and leaving her, and riding off into the sunset. The bigger the male hero in the doorways of film, the smaller the women's presence seemed to become. We were just shadows now, kept in the cave, reminiscent of *The Searchers,* like Natalie Wood. Hollywood didn't seem to know what to do with us. The Madonna/Whore complex needed to be reconciled. In the Noir film genre mentioned above, women were wearing giant shoulder pads and pants, and the gun was symbolic of a phallic heterogeneity.

Some of us multi-generational liberated women were, as Helen Reddy stated "[W]omen who had been initially turned off by some of the more strident feminist voices; or women who believed they were already liberated."[222] I was one of the latter. My mother, who looked like Marilyn Monroe, and dressed just like her, had a Master's Degree in Special Education. She raised me to believe women were very powerful. And to understand sexuality as a healthy way to express desire. As for the John Wayne movies, that Archetype was DEAD, along with the Patronymic GOD. Besides, by then, that Male archetype had gone Baroque in order to rationalize the U.S.'s hegemonic Foreign Policy.[223]

Where did all the smart, hip, and chic women go? Like Lauren Bacall and Ingrid Bergman? Where was the romance? One reason was that women weren't writing anymore.

> As televisions invaded American living rooms and audiences were less apt to go out to the movies, movie ticket sales plummeted; it was only one of many factors that threatened the film industry. The decline in the number of female screenwriters was stark during this period, with one author commenting that Hollywood had essentially "shutout" female writers and that only a "handful" actually found work.[224]

Or at least it appeared to be so, until screenplay writer Leigh Brackett was discovered to be a woman, not a man. "Hollywood director Howard Hawks was so impressed by one of her novels that he had his secretary call in 'this guy Brackett' to help William Faulkner write the script for *The Big Sleep* (1946). As a screenwriter, she is best known for her work in *The Big Sleep* (1946), *Rio Bravo* (1959), and *Star Wars: Episode V - The Empire Strikes Back* (1980).[225] Later, after he met her, Hawks thought Leigh Brackett was a good writer because, according to him, she wrote "like a man."[226]

Well, this "man" wrote Hawk's trilogy of the New Westerns so beloved by Cineastes: *Rio Bravo, El Dorado,* and *Rio Lobo*. And there were always lots of women. But it was *Rio Lobo* that she wrote, that created the first "New Age Western Film" with real women protagonists.[227] Howard Hawks is my favorite director. Some of his classic films, *Scarface, Twentieth Century, Bringing Up Baby, Only Angels Have Wings, His Girl Friday, Sergeant York, To Have and Have Not, The Big Sleep, Red River, Gentlemen Prefer Blondes* and *Rio Bravo* span five decades; telling the stories of the disenfranchised so well that the national consciousness was ready for *Rio Lobo* in the early 70s. From sympathetically portraying the disenfranchised gangster, detective, show girl and drunk; his favorite screenplay writer then provides him with a major issue of the day, how to depict the disenfranchised woman as an archetypal western hero. Leigh Brackett was known as the "Story Queen of Space Opera." I don't even think our heroine of Princess Leia would have even been born in *Star Wars,* without her. And don't tell me that George Lucas didn't know what he was doing by taking Leigh's somewhat masculine name, and created Leia, a more feminine homage to her.[228]

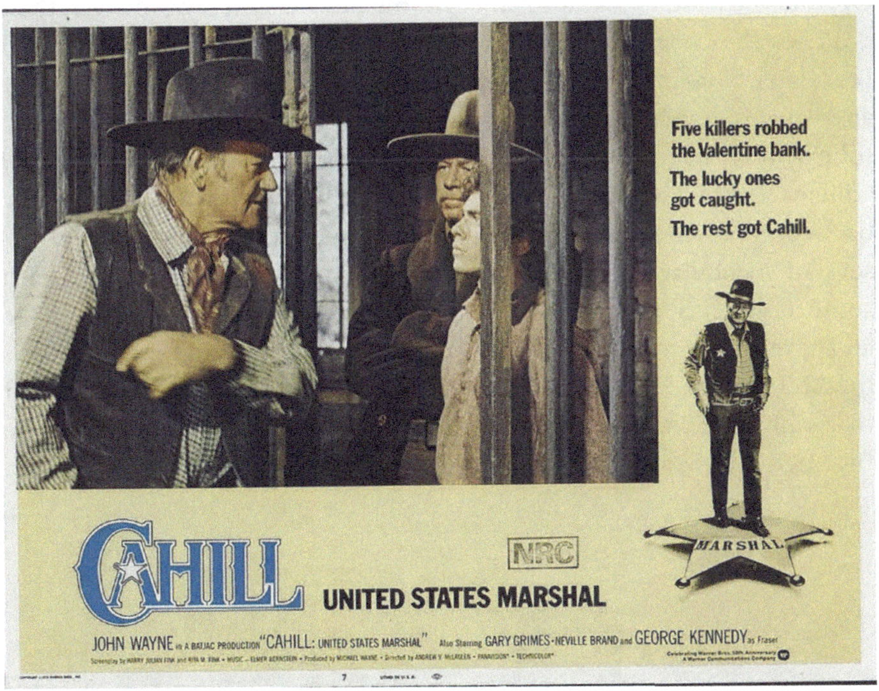

Not long after this film was made, I met John Wayne at a Premiere for *Cahill, U.S. Marshall* in Seattle. He had just been in a fistfight with some Indians who were protesting the portrayal of their people in his movies. It really was right after the American Indian Movement took over Alcatraz. And it wasn't pretty. His toupee was ruffled. But he won my heart anyway, (albeit an Indian heart, which was, truthfully, on *their* side) after complementing me on my dress. "I like the way you look in that dress, little lady." he drawled. Actually, I don't think it was the dress; it was what wasn't on *underneath* the dress. It *was* the 70s. Or maybe because, from across the room, we were heads above most people there, and I was 23 years old and

6'4" in my stacked heels. But by then film snobbishness had already kept me from seeing *Rio Lobo*, and it wasn't until I was attempting to write an existential screenplay in the early 90s that I ever took John Ford seriously. And John Ford led me to landscape films, and landscape films led me to Yakima Canutt, who was in dozens of films from the Lone Star Studio in Texas with John Wayne as his nemesis; a bad guy in a black hat on screen, but then, with a white hat, he also doubled for Wayne as a stuntman. I once heard that Yakima was so much a personal inspiration to Wayne that the star adapted his swagger. Yakima later became a second unit director and was also from the Northwest, a cowboy hero of the Pendleton Round-Up, the heart and landscape subject of my best screenplay. Not even then did I see *Rio Lobo*, however. It wasn't until I went back to film school 20 years later, a dream of mine, (even after being in the business for decades) and was re-introduced to Director Howard Hawks' *Rio Bravo* that I saw John Wayne again. I was a fan of Hawk's work, he had been a staple at Cinema 7, a film art-house I was a part of in the mid to late 70s, but our back-room discussions were limited by Pauline Kael's reviews, and my on-set film vocabulary. Attending film school in my late 50s armed me with some tools of critical analysis. And studying *Rio Bravo* with them gave me an appreciation for two actors I felt (as a casting director) were just cultural celebrities: Dean Martin and John Wayne. Urban legend even has it that John Ford was rumored to say to Howard Hawks: "I didn't know the Big Lug (John Wayne) could act," meaning Hawks was the better director.

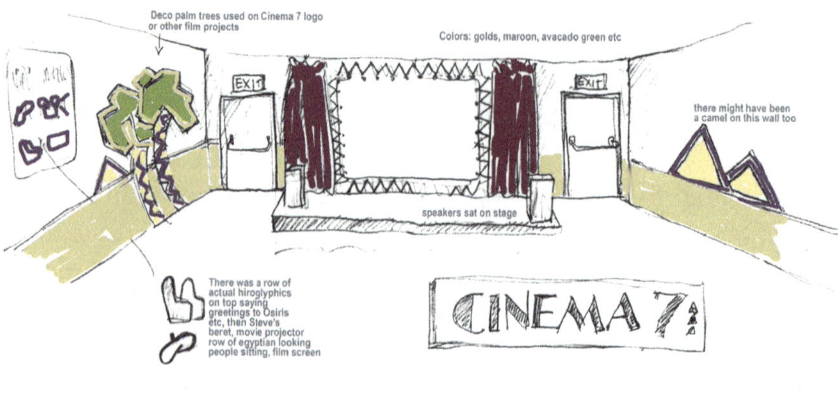

After reuniting with film bloggers Sean Axmaker and Dennis Cozzalio recently, and prior acquaintances from our old Cinema 7 days, I was inspired by them and embarked on a quest for great films from the past that

I hadn't seen. And there it was, finally, at a Goodwill store, a real film copy of *Rio Lobo*. I had read the reviews, I wasn't expecting much, but to my surprise and delight, it held me spellbound, and at the double-barreled second act turning point, it snared me. I was going, "No, no, this can't be the answer to the existential questions I had been asking my whole life!" My angst had been underscored years ago by a short story written by film academic and writer Bill Kittredge in his book *Owning It All*; and the story was aptly called "Silver Bullets":

> It's an old, smoked, and seasoned American scenario: rescue by heroes come from our wilderness, cowboys and mountain men, Shane and George S. Patton, Big John Wayne from the Monument Valley, Deerslayer after Deerslayer defending us from dark tides, bad dreams, savages, and bankers. Our sweet farmstead family-centered life will last forever, so the implications go, if we simply trust such horsemen to defend our property and our virtue. Heroes are an ancient problem. There is the cutting quickness of violence, the warfare so elementally ended, and then what? The good hero, Shane, rides away into the mystical Tetons and is never heard from again. Who was that masked man, why did he leave this silver bullet?[229]

I told Director Monte Hellman about this interesting existential film theory called the "Silver Bullet theory" one day while discussing Walter Hill's quote: "All my movies are Westerns. Even *Aliens*."[230] It was electrifying to read these words that challenged my beliefs in the sacred mythology of the western, because, Indian or not, my heroes had always been cowboys.

Kittredge goes on to say: "Our society had grown up believing in heroes who would come riding in to save us, and now we found ourselves in a society that wasn't worth saving. Our mythological story was a horseshit excuse for bad conduct…"[231] I grew up in the rugged west, not far from where Kittredge grew up, and our Grandfathers were friends. Dennis Cozzalio is also from that High Desert landscape near Klamath Falls, Oregon, the former Cowboy and Indian murder capital of the world. And we grew up on Westerns: *The Lone Ranger, Have Gun Will Travel* and *The Rifleman*. All which told a similar archetypal story, the sexy lone gunman coming into a community and solving its problems, then leaving again, never marrying, unsuccessful at joining the community, breaking young women's hearts, aloof, above the law; but before riding off, creating a new fertile Spring in a dark land, almost like the mythical Fisher King.

For me, it was James Fennimore Cooper's character "Hawkeye" that first epitomized this archetype of American Literature. Half civilized American colonial/British subject, half Indian, he came from civilization but embraced the wilderness. An early Jeremiah Johnson, he was the Poster Child for rugged individualism, the precursor to Daniel Boone and Davy Crockett, a man who thought for himself, and we loved him for it. He was an ethical anti-establishment pioneer, a hybrid of cultures that were necessary to tame the West. As a 1970's filmmaker, I was amazed to learn a new language in film school. I was able to articulate why I was drawn to John Ford's films, the sensibilities I resonated with but wasn't conscious of until I had the language to express 70s ideals such as his exquisite eye for composition, but especially the relationship of humans to the landscape, which were in proportion to their importance to Mother Nature, and that was not so terribly important in the scheme of things. Like an Andrew Wyeth painting, humans were rarely in the foreground of the drama. Desert heat, lack of water, thunder and lightning causing stampede's, floods, barns on fire, smallpox, threatening Indians appearing high on a cliff, all were more powerful than the average citizen, who needed a larger than life savior. Technology has not only changed that proportion, but the technological advent of the Television made it nigh impossible to portray. Give me Cinemascope any day!

Now we watch films on Smart-phones, and it is comical for me to hear a set designer say, 'I know you can't see any of my set, but darn it, you can feel it on the screen!" I like to think it is something that Director Howard Hawks would say to me, now that I have, perhaps foolishly, turned down financing from locations with the wrong landscape, for a screenplay about Chief Joseph's people, the Nez Perce. I'll never forget financiers trying to convince me that Luxemburg's Black Forest could stand in for the Big Empty Steeps and the Glacial Moraines of the Wallowa Mountains, also called the "Alps" of America.

Never-the-less, in *Rio Lobo* (1970) Howard Hawks has left us with a new kind of film and in its Joseph Campbell way is a True Hero(ine)'s Journey; a film that has not only saved me from my existential sadness for the emerging culture, but has re-invented the archetype for the new age, to survive the new age. And he did it by doing what he always did best in his films, which was to explore the hidden story of the disenfranchised. From *Scarface*, to *Diamonds Are a Girl's Best Friend* to *Rio Bravo* Hawks would take the stereotypical gangster, dumb blonde, drunk, etc. and by exploring their reality with the camera, would turn the stereotypes in on themselves and hit us unsuspectingly with them, making them humane, brilliant, gallant and heroic, all at the same time, our anti-heros.

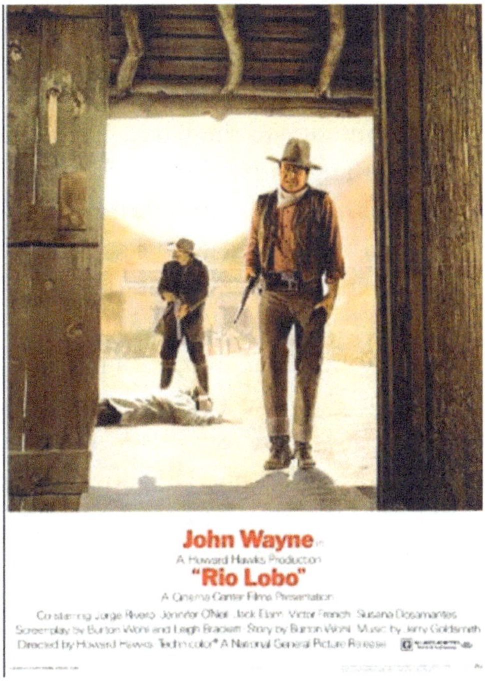

He does this in *Rio Lobo,* his last film, but this time he tackles the whole genre and archetype of our white-hatted Westerns and their heroes. And creates "The New Age Western" in its place. Let's see how this could possibly be true by unpacking it: *Rio Lobo* (River of the Wolf) and I am begging to say, "Lone Wolf', because, sure enough, there is a Lone Wolf bad guy. The credits open with a man playing a Flamenco guitar, and we see different perspectives of his hands as he plays. When we see his fingers playing from the perspective of the inside of the guitar looking out of the hole, subliminal patterns of John Ford's Monument cave in *The Searchers* tickles our subconscious, and the Hawksian point of view of looking from the inside out foreshadows certain plot points in this opening palette of the film.

We then see Yankee soldiers in brand new serge suits. A kind of Corporate Armani of Wall Street look in a dirt floor town. A horse drawn wagon pulls up in front of a building with exquisite stone arches and at the same time we see a train pull up through these arches. Here we have the old uncivilized west symbolized by the old wagon, and the new civilized west symbolized by the train, like a visible double entendre. The soldiers carry a very heavy chest (we are told it is full of gold) from the wagon to the train. We see arches throughout the film, almost as if the mise-en-scene is trying to emulate church windows, so we have some indication we are seeing through them a spiritual or morality play.

John Wayne's stature was frequently measured by doorways in Ford's films, and Hawks also measured him from the tips of his boots, up, in a long camera tilt in *Rio Bravo*. But here, he is standing next to another soldier who is his same height. The camera angles shooting down on him also continue to make him look short in comparison!

The premise of the film is set up. Confederate rebels have been stealing gold from the Yankees. In the classic shot from the inside of the telegraph office looking out on the train, we are privy to the guarded telegraph communications. The next thing we see in a cut are drab and dingily costumed good old boys with a southern drawl listening in on some kind of homespun technology to the wires. The old-ear-to-the-rail trick tells them the train is coming, and they pull off a simple but ingenuous heist using hornets and rope. In the hold-up, a favorite soldier of John Wayne's is hurt, but we don't stop to dwell on it as we are led on the chase. And the chase leads to Wayne being knocked out and he comes to in a cave. Guess which cave? That's right, and it wasn't the cave so much as what shadow of memory had previously happened in it, because we are conditioned by this western objective correlative to witness redemption; and sure enough, the enemies spar with humor and the Prisoner Wayne good-naturedly tests their intelligence, revealing the good old boys as smart, articulate, and good-humored. And one of them is an Irish/Mexican from New Orleans, talk about being disenfranchised! But wait! Not only are they breaking stereotype, but they have switched clothing, as if the ghost of Natalie Woods had stripped her Indian clothes for a Pinafore, to make her Uncle see who she really was underneath all of his stereotypical Injun-hating judgments.

By using these same sets as *The Searchers, Rio Bravo*, and *El Dorado* Hawks is juxtaposing the old archetype with the new one, creating a conflict between the old story trajectory and the new unknown one. He also creates a depth of character in Wayne by having him wisely seeking the person behind the robberies, an informer from his own troops, instead of punishing the men beneath him for carrying out the bad guy's orders. "What you did was war, what he did was Treason." Wayne goes so far as give them a chance to escape, but they remain there out of a sense of duty, and there is honor among thieves.

Hawks also turns the table on our expectations, by using a storm as a positive elliptical device, and when the storm clears, the Civil War is over, and we watch the Rebels as they are given clothes and food and money. Wayne also buys them a drink, tells them he is still looking for the man who hired them, and asks where they are going. When one of them says Rio Lobo, Wayne gives him extra money, and tells him he needs it to get there. He also tells them he is from "those-near-abouts" and if they ever run into the traitor, to find him here.

Returning home, he runs into another generalization challenge in the form of a bright, out-spoken young woman who is seeking justice for the killing of her mentor in Rio Lobo. A tip of the hat to liberated women, she is very modern in her portrayal, breaking the pioneer woman mold. The

Irish Mexican falls for her, exacerbating the conflict between the romanticism of the Old West and the self-reliant sexiness of a Gloria Steinem in Tombstone circa turn of the century. But wait, there's even more! Once in *Rio Lobo* we find a whole town governed by a bad man, a "rabid wolf." The Mexican women there, too, are liberated, however; and a really brave and smart one has a Spanish accent, while her two good friends, pretty Jennifer O'Neill and Sherry Lansing, have good old masculine-American true grit!

By now, the bad guy's gunman has discovered they are all in town, and issues the proverbial "gone by sunset" ultimatum, but by that time they are way ahead of him, and are out to get the deeds to the ranches back from his boss. To do that, they have to outwit a crazy Southerner who shoots first and asks questions later, unless of course the object to be shot at has nice ankles. Proving their worth, Jack Elam then takes them in because his rebel boy who's being held in jail as a hostage had told his pa about the nice Yankee. Elam then leads them to the long-wanted Yankee traitor. Knowing they can't out-gun all the henchmen, they take him at gunpoint to the jail, where Elam reprises the Walter Brennen role in *Rio Bravo*. They had taken this traitor bloodied and bruised to the jail, in order to also protect one of their own, a rebel, and to await justice in the form of the Yankee Military out-post near there. But the Irish American wouldn't wait, and is caught by the bad guys riding hell-bent for leather to notify the Military Fort, so now they have a hostage trade-off instead.

What also surprises us is that the women have been abused, but instead of relying on the Lone Ranger to avenge them, they avenge themselves. And they don't even have to do it all alone like their hero counterpart, because not only do they help each other, but a regular Joe, a dentist, bravely brings them food and beer in the jail, and smuggles away the deeds to the ranch, which the Bad guy had been forced to sign back over to them.

All of this has led us to the third act climax turning point, where the set-up was true to form, in that the good guys were alone against the bad guys, and like every other Western, the town's people were hiding, taking no risk or responsibility, except for a town hero or two, who always seemed to get shot. But this time, we see saloon doors beneath an arch, and instead of just John Wayne, we see him side-by-side with the community of the town. And it is shocking to see that the townspeople do stand next to him, and overcome the Bad Guy by working together, trusting each other, and not setting one apart to be the responsible one. A truly democratic and wise maneuver, it is not even Wayne who shoots the bad guy at a pivotal moment, but a woman. All's she wants to know is that if

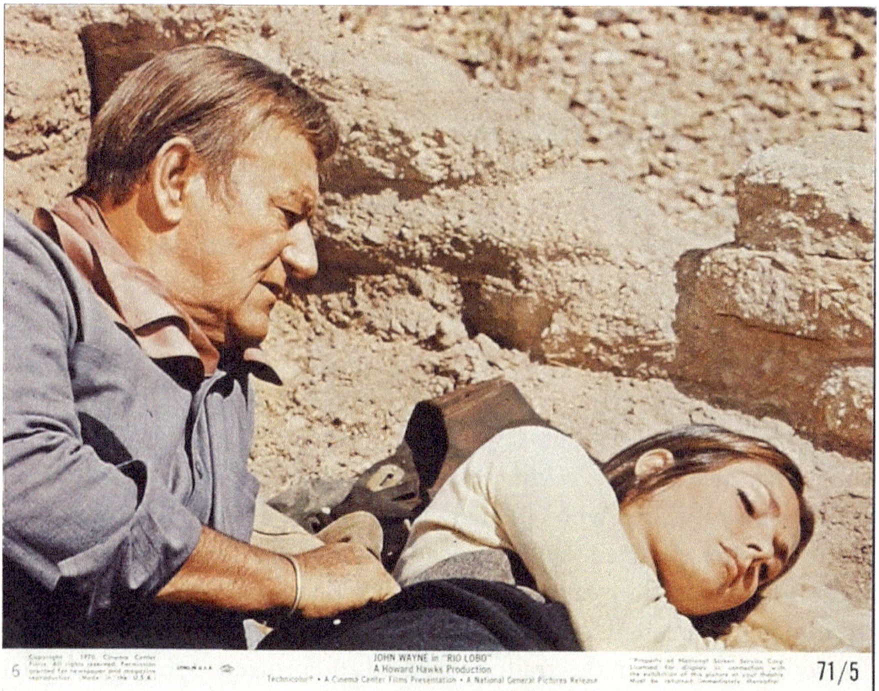

Jennifer O'Neil is comforted by John Wayne

every time she looks in the mirror (and would see his knife slice, a scar, like the ubiquitous x in *Scarface* on her face) she would know she did the right thing by killing the bad guy in the end.

And the women's relationship to the good guy is different too; Wayne is not seen as a potential sexual partner, a wild man, or a saver of virtue. He is called "comfortable" and is seen as safer than the romantic and handsome Irish/Mexican to these women. But when they do exact their revenge, it is Wayne who comforts them when they kill, and they do react dramatically. Wait! Was someone emotional? *And* with Intellect? Holy Cowgirl.

And instead of being threatened by the woman stepping into the role of the hero, Wayne tells her if it wasn't her, it would have been "somebody else," telling her that she is not alone, has acted not as a lone representative, a lone wolf, but as a member of the pack, a member of society. There is no need for silver bullets, there are no Lone Wolfs or Were wolves here where there is community solving problems together.

What I find so ironic, is that Sherry Lansing went on to be the head of Paramount Studios, and made strong movies about women's sexuality in *Fatal Attraction* and *Indecent Proposal*. "The Chicago native had gone from

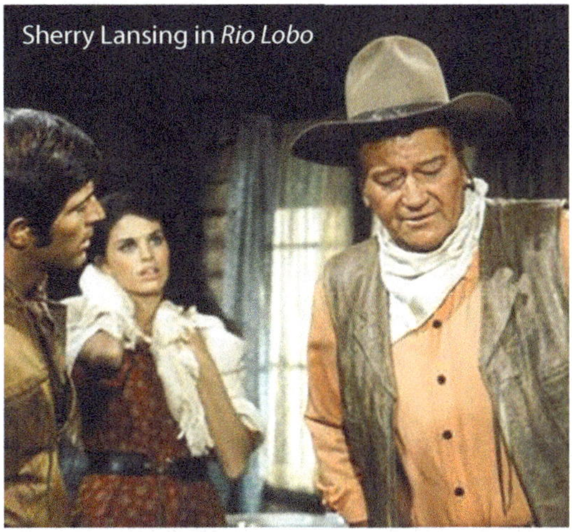
Sherry Lansing in *Rio Lobo*

being ... a teacher in South Central L.A., to an aspiring actress who landed a lead role opposite John Wayne in 1970's *Rio Lobo*, to a young woman who hated acting so much it made her physically sick. Changing careers, she became a script reader at $5 an hour and rose to become the first female head of a studio when she was named president of 20th Century Fox in 1980."[232] I agree that she was driven to explore the consequences of men exploiting women sexually in the above-mentioned films. Like Otter said to Boon in *Animal House*, when Niedermeyer was taking liberties with a new ROTC pledge and was debriding him: "He can't do that to our pledges ... only WE can do that to our pledges!!!"[233] Only Sharry Lansing could get away with that. But it was up to us women to find our voices and to interpret this New Age of Sexual Liberation.

> "*Fear of Flying* was written in the throes of the Sexual Revolution of the 1970s, as associated with second-wave feminism. Finally it was acknowledged that desire and fantasy are a good thing and not entirely condemnable in women, and Jong wanted to harness that newfound respect for desire into a piece of art that brought the intersections of sexual and nonsexual life together, something she felt was missing in literature. "*At the time I wrote Fear of Flying, there was not a book that said women are romantic, women are intellectual, women are sexual – and brought all those things together.*"[4] "What [Isadora is] looking for is how to be a whole human being, a body and a mind, and that is what women were newly aware they needed in 1973."[5] But she also points out the drawbacks of a sexually liberated life, acknowledging that sexuality "is not the cure for every restlessness." Male critics who interpreted Isadora as being "promiscuous," were actually misinterpreting her acts - she has an active fantasy life but doesn't in reality sleep with many men."[234]

And in 1972, I couldn't agree more with Erica about the fact: "At the time I wrote *Fear of Flying*, there was not a book that said women are romantic, women are intellectual, women are sexual – and brought all those things together...”

And I had a very rare opportunity to start in experimenting with this voice in fourteen films, in changing the role of women in movies about sex. Once again, synchronicity was at hand. But first I had to step off the proverbial cliff.

By Spring term at the U of O in 1972 college was excruciating. I was having to read postmodernist writers and I hated them. Samuel Beckett’s *Molloy* and *Malone Dies* plus H.P. Lovecraft’s *The Unnamable* seemed so existentially dreadful, but when I got to Harlan Ellison’s *I Have No Mouth But I Must Scream*; I lost it. Things in our home were not too good, either, paying back the loan for the record store that failed, had left us on food stamps, and we had to move, again, in with other people to be able to afford to live. I needed to get a job.

The only bright spot was that actor Paul Newman was coming to the Oregon Coast to film *Sometimes a Great Notion* (which btw, only took *six years* to get funded as a film) and a Grateful Dead concert was coming in August. By this time Kesey and the boys had formed Far West Action Picture Service, and had rented an old airplane hangar to house all of their equipment. They ended up being invited to the set in Newport by Newman. There is a great “home video” of one of their visits. https://www.youtube.com/watch?v=xVNG3IcUprY217[235]

I think that’s me with Mike Hagen. But as Wavy Gravy said: “If you remember the 70s you weren’t there.”[236] The partying there became legendary.

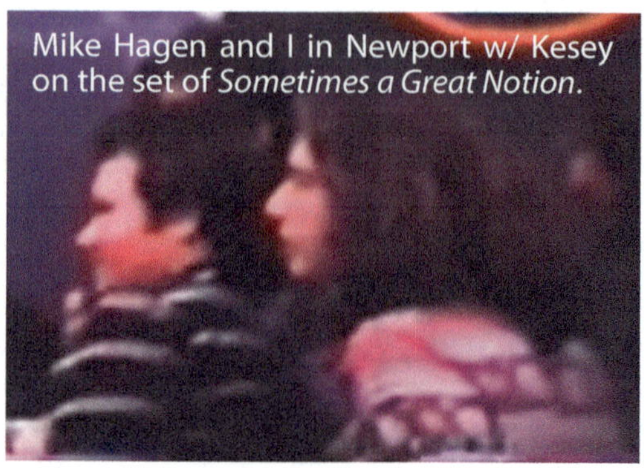
Mike Hagen and I in Newport w/ Kesey on the set of *Sometimes a Great Notion.*

For the first time, one of Kesey’s novels became a Western Film, with Paul Newman as the “swaggering gambler... the cowboy out of the TV set walking down the middle of the street to meet a dare” (*Cuckoo’s Nest* 189). I discuss this film in great detail in Vol. I, which this book is a sequel to. However, since then I have found several other wonderful quotes, the first I have mentioned by Director Walter Hill, when he said: “... every film I’ve done has been a Western;” and was elaborated on in another quote that “The Western is ultimately a stripped-down moral universe, that is whatever the dramatic problems are, beyond the normal avenues of social control and social alleviation of the problem, and I like to do that even within contemporary stories."[237]

The other quote I found, one I mentioned by Dr. Corkin, may also illuminate thinking about Kesey writing the New Western. "(... writers) were trying to reimagine the Western as a vehicle for the any-establishment antihero. Paul Newman was a Hollywood leading man closely connected to this vision of character." He was spot on as an Oregon Logger, too. But famous costume designer Edith Head would not let him wear a logger cap. If you remember, I pointed out that Jack Nicholson wore one for directing auditions in *Drive, He Said*; and he wore one in *Cuckoo's Nest*. Over 30 years later, even the *Twilight* film cast wore them. What's up with that??? What does this vision of the Oregon Anti-hero character entail? I think it is the modern version of the archetype of men making their way and surviving in the woods, but now as an Anti-hero for the New Age.

Early on in the filming, Paul Newman got hurt. So while he was waiting to get the cast off of his foot to resume filming, Kesey and the boys got a job working with Sam Cutler, the Grateful Dead's manager on filming the Springfield Creamery Benefit Concert. The Creamery was another Kesey family contribution to the counterculture. Nancy's Yogurt made

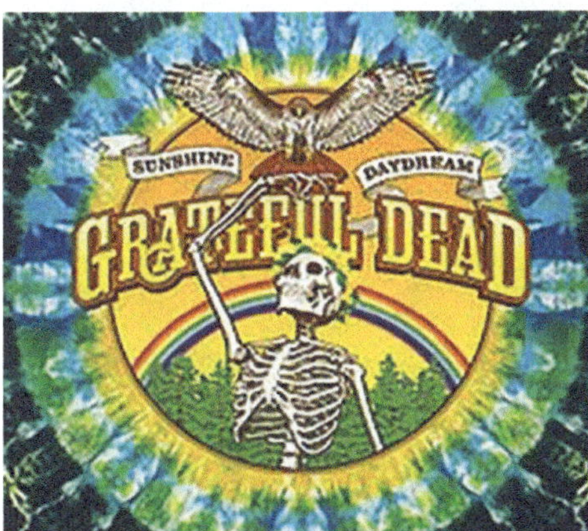

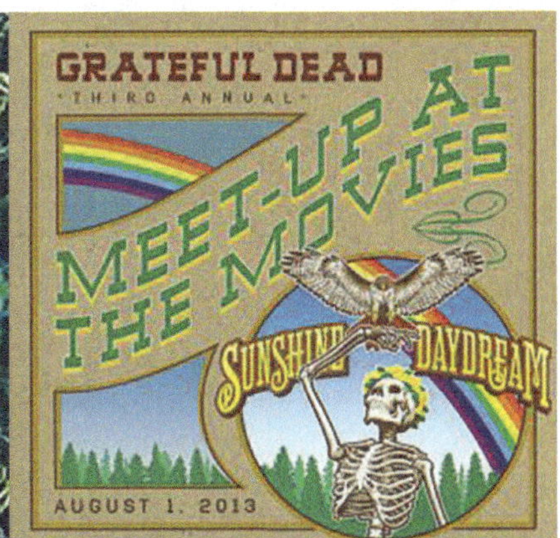

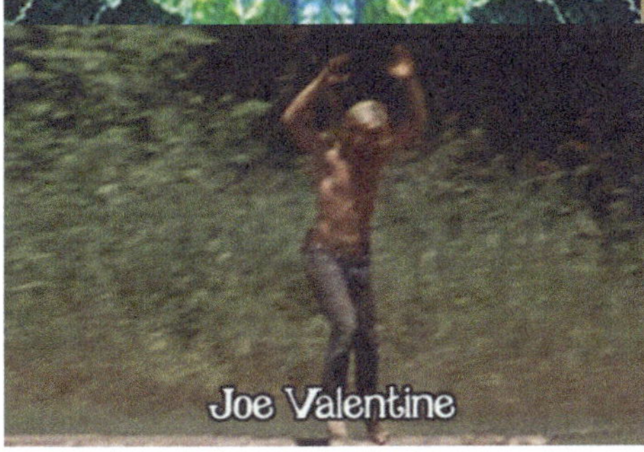

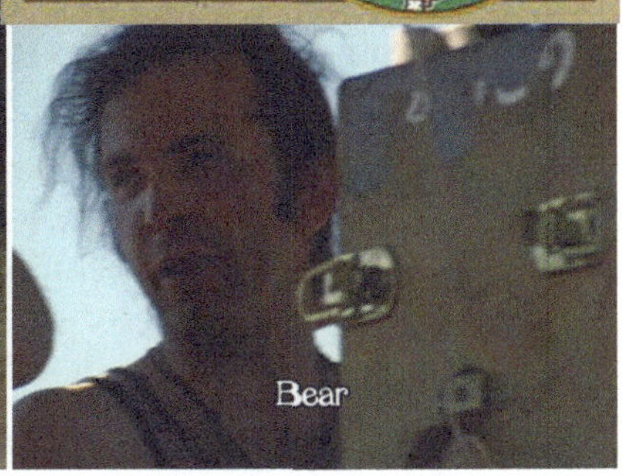

them famous all up and down the West Coast. But because there was a threat from the IRS because back taxes were overdue, The Dead came to help. 10,000 people showed up to create what I call the Magnum Opus of all Grateful Dead Shows, and with the help of Kesey and his film crew, my friends Bob Laird; (Assistant Director) Lew Melsen; (Camera) Bobby Steinbrecher; (Camera) Bobby Miller; (Camera) Joey Valentine; (Production Assistant) Karen Price (Child Care) and me as an extra; this timeless event was captured on 16mm film. Not only that, but Producer Sam Field would fall in love with Kay Erskine, (a production assistant) who had just purchased the Flatbed Movieola for FWAPS; would eventually be married to her for 41 years while he tried to get this movie edited and distributed. Finally it came out in 2013. The Producer, Adrien Marin, of the incredible documentary about us back then in the opening of the film, would even escort me to the Premiere.

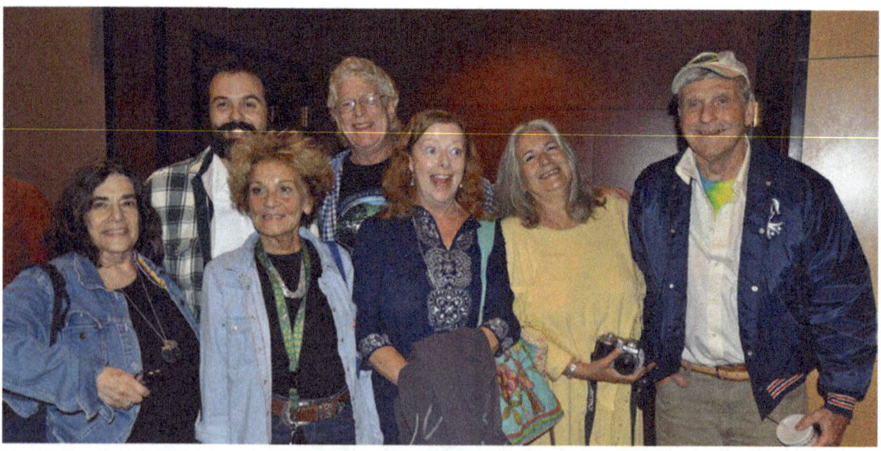

From back row, Adrien (dark mustache far left) Bill Goodpasture next to him, Sara Hammer in front of them; then myself and Ken Babbs, far right. Photo by Paul Petock.

In the same summer of 1972, our living situation with a friend was coming to an end. We found a place cheap enough about 45 minutes away on fire road, off of Siuslaw River Road, way past the tiny town of Lorane. The distance didn't matter anymore, because I could not afford going back to school, anyway. But we were still showing films around town under Screen Gems, with Steve Bove at the helm; Jay was working at the Sun Shop; and Bobby Steinbrecher had called me, wanting me to do location scouting for him and the FWAPS gang for a Williams Bread Commercial. He needed a kitchen large enough for lights, a Panavision camera, and crew, but none could be found. I cast Ken Babbs to star in it, and a woman

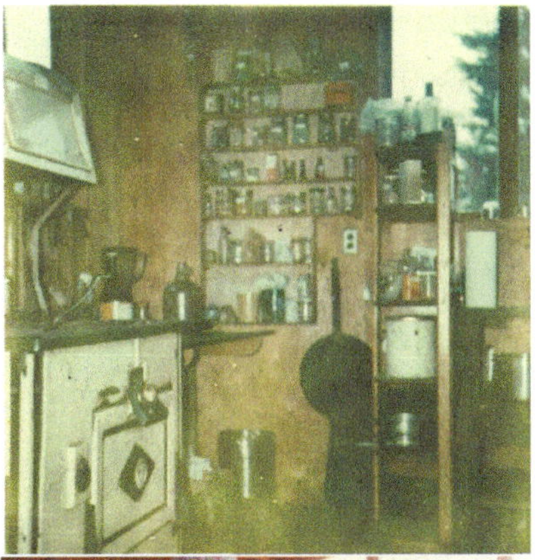

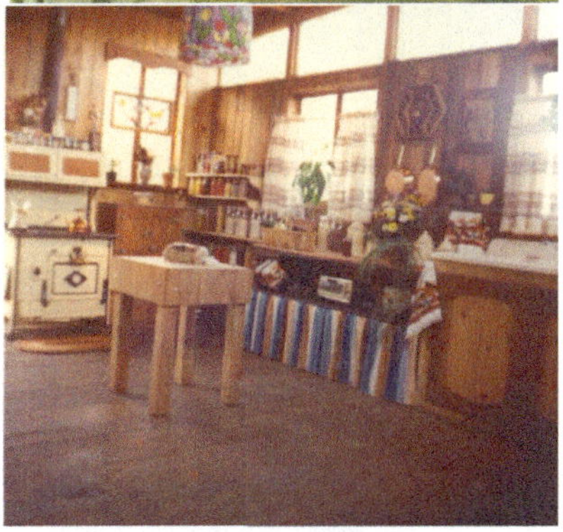

named Sharon Brown. Finally, I talked Bobby into allowing me to clean and set design an old Hippie Commune kitchen I found. It was beautiful, and I was so proud. That's when Kesey told me his favorite thing ever was to ride around in his El Dorado Cadillac, with the top down, location scouting. Here are the before and after photos.

Right after that, Hagen called me. He said a film was looking for people to work on it, and to meet him at the Eugene Hotel later that afternoon. While I was meeting with them, the phone rang and it was Warren Merrill, the Oregon Film Commissioner, welcoming them to Oregon. I remember thinking, well that's good, they must be legitimate. But then they asked me if I would take my top off for them. And I said absolutely not. But I would be a great gofer, and I could do hair, and makeup, set design and location scouting. I was hired, but they kept thinking I would relent and take my top off, but Hagen and the Pranksters knew better. I was a prude and had

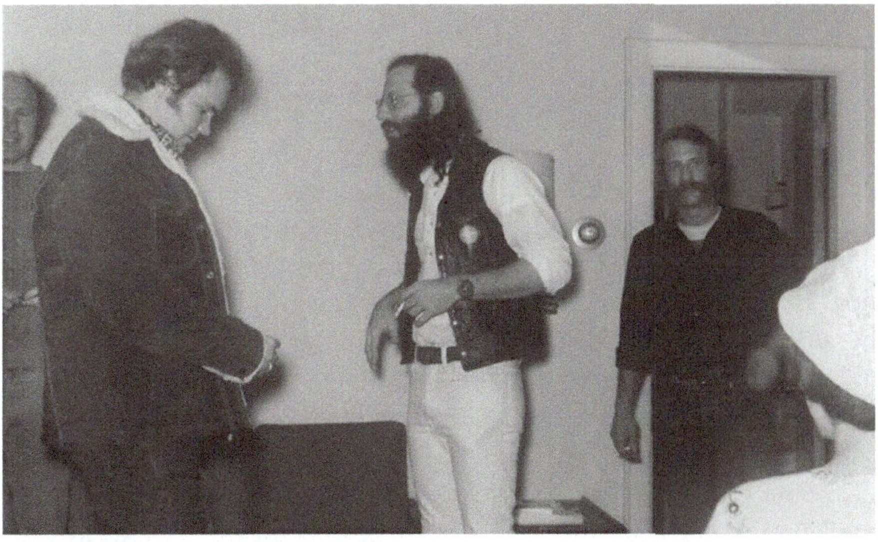

Kesey, Hagen, Andy Romanoff, Butch the Hog Farm driver. (Courtesy Andy Romanoff)

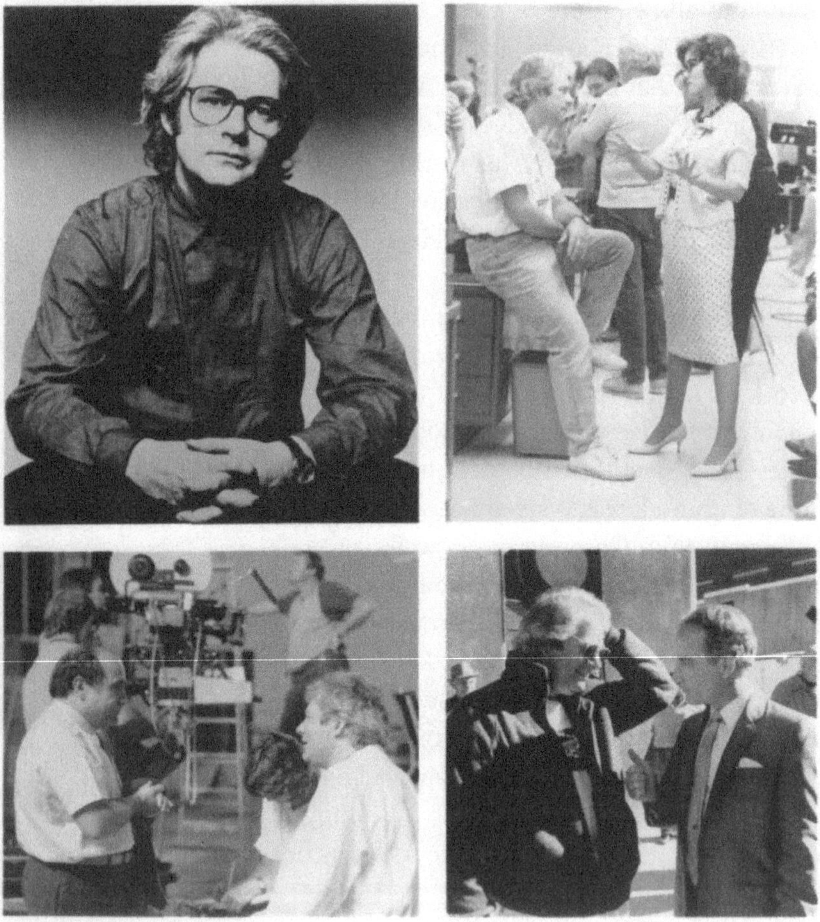

Barry Levinson ("Diner," "The Natural") is the director of "Tin Men," a comedy starring Richard Dreyfuss and Danny DeVito as feuding aluminum siding salesmen in Baltimore. Barbara Hershey (pictured above with Levinson) stars as DeVito's wife, who becomes an unsuspecting pawn in the pair's feud. Lower left, Danny DeVito rehearses with Levinson. Lower right, Richard Dreyfuss discusses a scene with Levinson. A Touchstone Pictures presentation in association with Silver Screen Partners II, the movie was written by Barry Levinson and produced by Mark Johnson. Buena Vista distributes. (TMBB-2)

never done that before, no matter how much money they offered me. The film was called *Street Girls,* and it was written by *the* Barry Levinson, his first. He also was a cameraman. It was directed by Mike Miller, whom I became friends with. The story was set in LaMar's, a topless go-go dancer club in the basement of the Tiffany Building two blocks from the Eugene Hotel. And that is when I started living there, because the worst ice storm inversion in Oregon History hit early that winter, and we couldn't get home because of downed trees. And consequently our house froze. Luckily Jay could live with his Mom, and he took the dog; while I lived in the giant Ladies Room in the Basement of the Hotel. The film starred Jimmy Smith, the semi-famous musician, and some local girls. One night, I think it was the Martini shot, (the last shot of the film) there was a topless contest at LaMars. So I took my top off, and won the $25 for a 5-minute schtick. That's when I realized why Hagen and Dan Webb and all these guys were paying me $25 an hour. If I had known better, I would have had "my girls" insured like Betty Grable did with her legs, even though I never showed them to anyone until now. But hey! It was the 70s and I was a liberated woman who wanted to be a filmmaker. And now I realized, I really was.

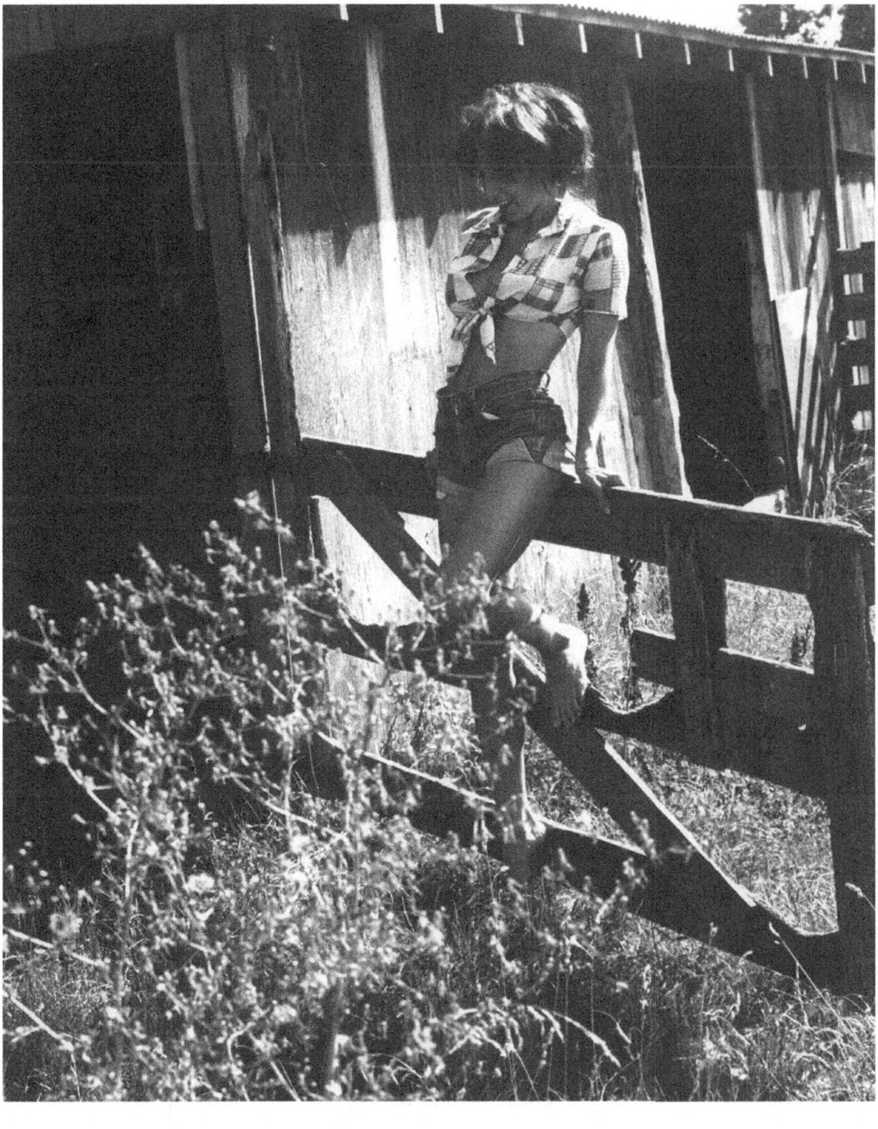

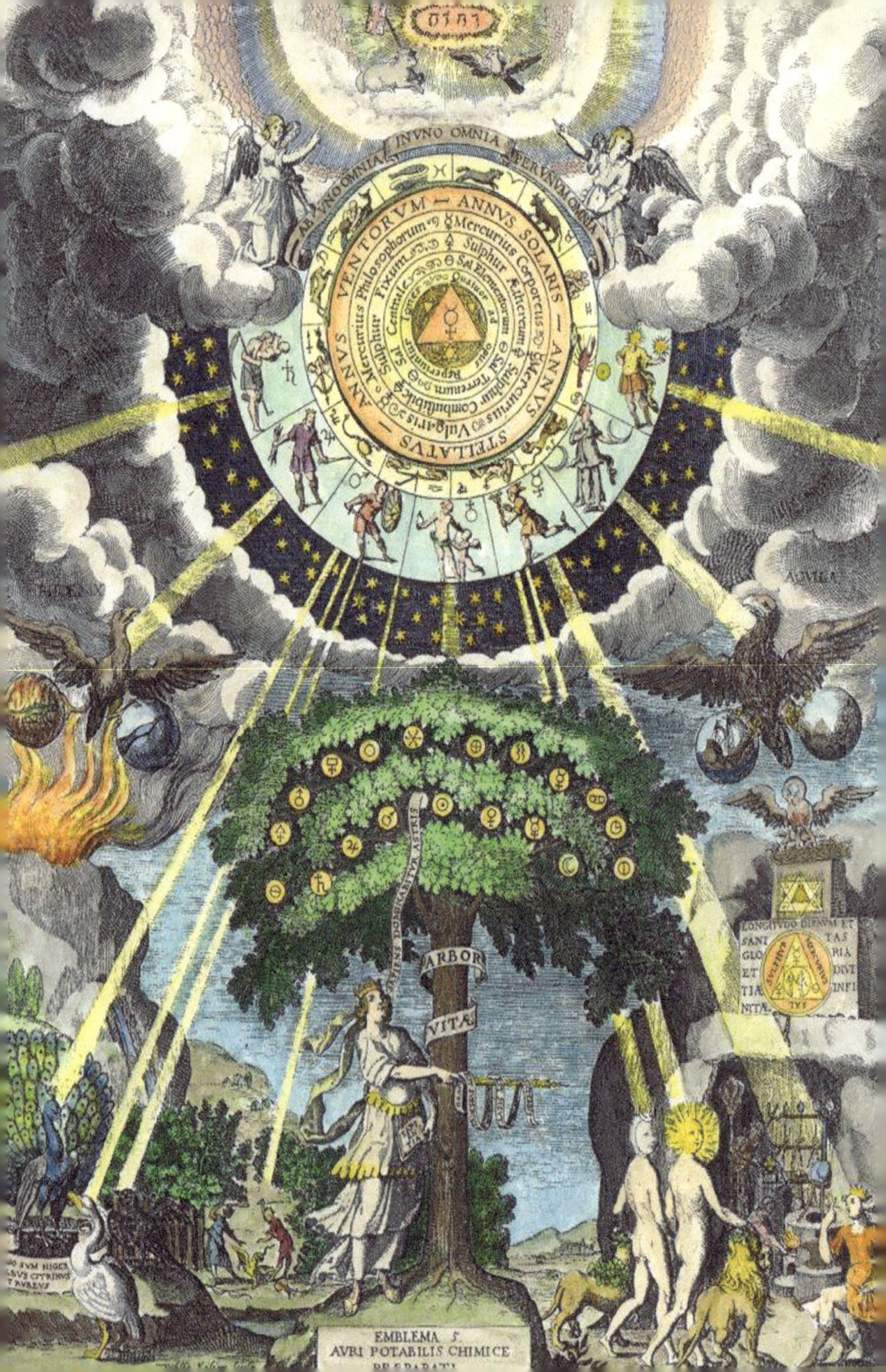
IN VNO OMNIA
VENTORVM — ANNVS SOLARIS — ANNVS STELLATVS — ANNVS
ARBOR
VITÆ
EMBLEMA 5.
AVRI POTABILIS CHIMICE

Chapter 8.

Bearer of Meaning ~1973

> In *The Marrano Phenomenon:* (re: Jacques Derrida's Essay "Faith and Knowledge)" Agata Bielik-Robson writes: "In Timeus, Plato talks about khôra as a passive, indifferent and infinitely susceptible 'receiving vessel' capable of accommodating all forms (pandechos), and, by calling her a 'nurse of generation', he denies her/it even the slightest activity that is implied by such Derridean terms as 'retreat', 'withdrawal' or 'making-place'. This residual activity imposed on khôra, in which khôrein consists in receding for the sake of all things to appear, seems to derive from a different tradition: the one of tsimtsum which, in 'Faith and Knowledge,' will secretly shimmer under the guise of messianicity."[238]
>
> – Agata Bielik-Robson, *The Marrano Phenomenon*

The above almost sounds like the definition of the Aeon emanation, yes? "There are two offshoots from all the Aeons.... One of them ... who rules all things and is a male; the other below is a great Thought, a female giving birth to all things." From Hippolytus. See the first page of the Introduction for the full image.

For as long as I can remember, Ken Kesey threw The *I Ching* every day. And my ex-husband Jay and I threw it, too. For instance, Jay threw it before deciding to go to the infamous Altamont concert. It said, "*armies in the night.*" and we didn't go. Thank God. This is why we consulted it. However, the language about The Receptive, Hexagram #2 is very, very similar to the above quotes regarding the "nurse of generation." Carl Jung wrote the forward to the English translation of the *I Ching* by Richard Wilhelm that Kesey and I used. In it, he talks about how the I Ching works, and says it is simply a matter of synchronicity. Synchronicity is the Hallmark of the Age of Aquarius. If Quantum Mechanics ever finds how Gravity fits into Einstein's Unified Field Theory, they will find how synchronicity works. For me, it is simple. If a butterfly winging in Taipei can create a Typhoon in the Gulf of Mexico; then truly everything is connected in a giant web governed by intelligence and cause and effect. The Word is Hexagram

#1, (Masculine) the Creative and cause; and the Receptive #2 (Feminine) is the effect. What this means to me, is the simple fact I was in the right place at the right time when I met the Pranksters, and ended up in film, which had set into motion a train of circumstances that I was receptive to, and in some degree, fated for, because it was Karmic:

> In the silent era, films were made mostly for women, and often by women. However, early female film directors are misrepresented by a 'scarcity myth. From the contemporary movie magazines to respectable film history books, early female directors are regularly referred to as rarities – even when that was not the case. A woman directed what was probably the world's first scripted narrative fiction film; in the mid-to-late teens the Universal studio was bursting with female directors.

I would like to add Doris Wishman as well, to this list, albeit in the 60s.

> Women such as Lois Weber, Alice Guy-Blaché, Germaine Dulac, Lotte Reiniger and Mabel Normand were leaders in their respective fields, and they were supported by an industry filled with female screenwriters, and some hugely important female producers producing movies for a majority female audience. But you wouldn't know that from textbooks that relegate "women in film" to a sidebar.[239]

I was paying my dues, yet not having to work from the ground up, literally, like I first did for the Pranksters; but by putting in 12 and 15 hours a day on *Street Girls*. It was originally called *Angel Goes to Town,* and I loved its writer, Barry Levinson. I should have known he was both a Writer and the Cameraman, because I remember how comfortable I was around him. He had a deep sensibility. I was terribly nervous in the first scene, shot at a dining room table, until he said, "just talk about anything, it will be great."

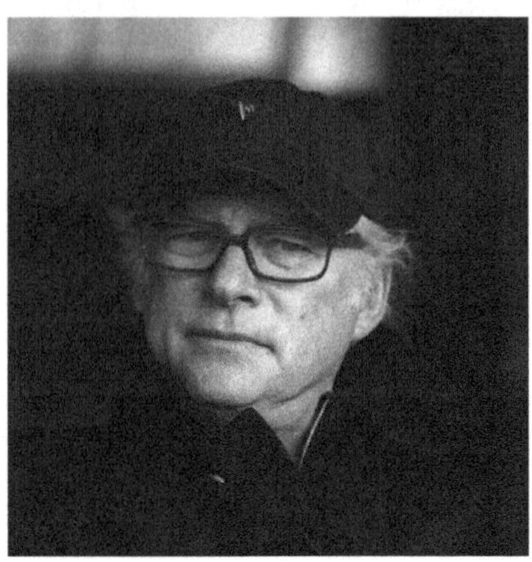

What I didn't know was that he was to become "*the* Barry Levinson" until just recently. Hagen wanted me to find a photo of his back then, and he remembered. We knew this guy. We worked with him for six weeks. Just goes to show you who you can meet in the oddest of places.

This acting job was far from the scripted plays I had done in high school, or filming with the non-synched ambient sound that I didn't have to worry about with the Pranksters. For them, my whole career, I only had to say one line. "Hey, Joe, way to go…" for a Joe Romania commercial about Minivans. The commercial showed for years, evidently they sold a lot of vans. But Barry was so much like them, including being a bit frumpy, and with that 16mm camera on his shoulder, that I soon forgot he was even there. And I just acted naturally, like my drama teacher Ed Ragazzino at South Eugene had taught me. But before I knew it, they were gone, and suddenly there was another one starting called *Swinging Sorority Girls*. This one, however, did not credit anyone with their real name. And I am SO glad! I was offered $300 a day to just do make-up and hair, and a little acting to set up the scene (because there were no pros, except one guy from LA) and I soon found out why. All the local guys evidently had a hard time "performing" on- camera.

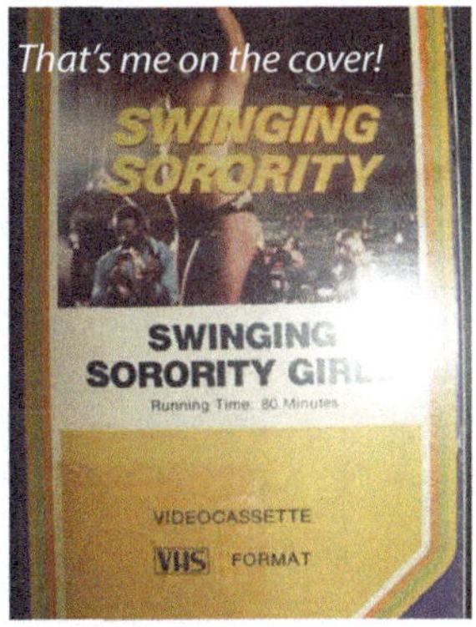

Like Gus Van Sant, I was just learning new skills on these films, but I made it clear that when it came to performing sex, forget it. Sex was a very complicated issue for me. At the time I did not know why, but around 5 years of sobriety in the early 90s, the memories came up. The subconscious memories I had drank and used over. Incest issues. And it contributed to why I couldn't handle all the attention I was getting in High School. By College I finally figured out that I just needed to get married, to hopefully stave off the advances. However, I was just going through the motions. A part of me was still very detached. I felt like I was watching myself from the upper corner of the room. And this detached logic in me shrugged and said: Your professors didn't really believe that a girl with your body could have a mind like the one they found in your papers, because they kept asking in-

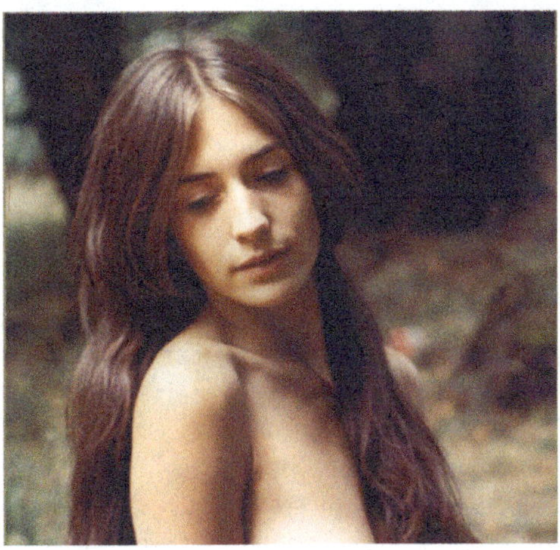

credulously, "Did you write this???" as if the size of your breasts shrunk your brain; so screw it, you might as well make some money off of them. And your body. The one you inherited from your Marilyn Monroe Mom. She's proud of hers, so what's wrong with you? It was complicated, but I moved ahead working on these films because I loved being a filmmaker. It was like this job was made for me. Luckily, in the beginning, for the most part, all the crew knew each other. They had to, because it was an underground production, and then we found people by word of mouth. Someone said there was a help-wanted ad for College Couples in the Emerald. I believed it, when I saw it, but I couldn't believe how open minded

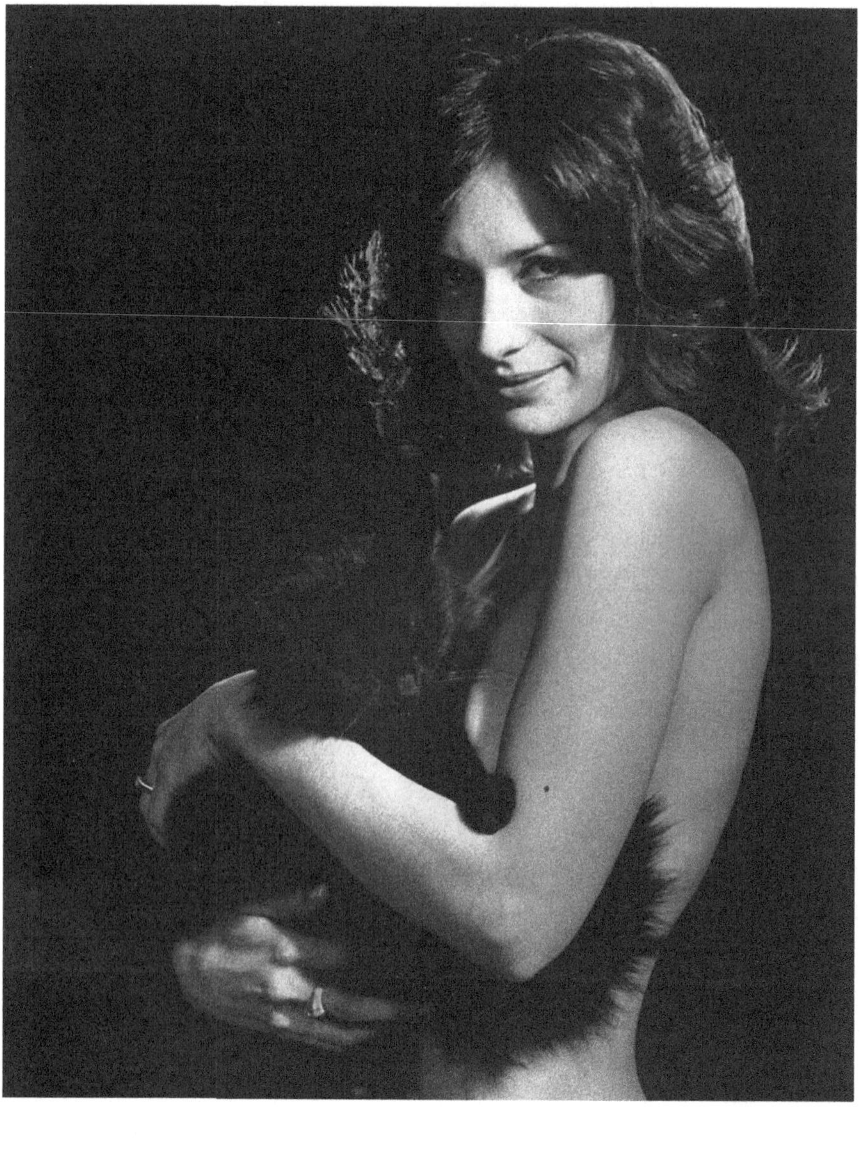

they were about the whole thing. But the film crew and I were old film friends, so I felt right at home. Given the $1.00 an hour minimum wage, I made more then, in one day, than when I was working for a whole month at Bob's Hamburgers in high school, because the money was under the table, and there were no taxes or fees taken out. I was feeling very guilty about what my Parents and Grandparents would think, but at the same time happy to be creative. Truth be told, I never let that stop me from doing anything I believed in. I just wasn't sure if I believed in this or not. Part of me had embraced the free love ethic of our generation, I was in an "Open marriage," a Commune based feeling of sharing and loving. I felt it wasn't wrong to exercise my God-given powers. But the complicated part was that the incest made me feel as if somehow, as a child, I had betrayed someone. And the deep shame surrounding that marred my ability to understand myself, or to believe in "the God of my father," who seemed, like my father, capable of wrath. My Mother was who I first worshipped, she even looked like a goddess. A Blonde and Blue-eyed Danish goddess. One whose beauty caused severe problems in her marriage to my Dad, as it was to cause in mine.

But my husband was practicing a sort of Pygmalion on me; (he was my student teacher in high school) and then became the Arthur Miller to my Marilyn Monroe, my Prankster nick-name from Ken Kesey. Jay appreciated my intelligence, which is why I married him. He was also in San Francisco in the early sixties and was entrenched in their ideals. But he was also an accountant at heart, and $300 a weekend was a huge amount of money. And he never asked questions when I brought it home after filming all day. He was very pragmatic about it all. And I was very indigenous about sex. I would choose who and when. I also found it very humorous, and sacred. My girlfriends from the reservations and I would giggle about things my white girlfriends would never, ever, even talk about. Patriarchal sex is very different than Matriarchal sex. The first is about control, the second is about the joys of love and *life*.

We filmed on the U of O Campus. You have to understand, that compared to *what was normal* in those wild days, this movie was TAME! I have a scene with a Professor that was so ho-hum I didn't even remember I had done it. But you can imagine how I felt when I realized one of my professors at the U of O had seen it!

Then a third film came, called *Swinging Ski Girls*. Old friends from *Street Girls*, like musician Jimmy Smith, did a scene at a Ski Lounge in Bend with me, and I danced for this one. But my girlfriend Lucretia stole the show, in a scene at Berg's Ski Shop with Rick Cassidy, and the Film Director "Bob Gilbert" fell madly in love with her. Next thing I know, she and I were spending a lot of time at his place on 13th and Lawrence, because he wanted her and I to start writing the stories for these films. And we did. Twelve of them. Somewhere I read that one of the financiers of these films saw that making films for women by women was the future. But back then, we just took people at face value, and besides, we had a real repertoire film company back then too, who were happy to get the work, and didn't care. When we made these films, we never dreamed they would see the light of day. We were told that they were only shown at the "Pussycat Theaters" in San Francisco. I knew there was a woman there, in "The City" as we called it, who showed quality erotica at her theater, Sutter Cinema. Her name was Arlene Elster, one of Janis Joplin's best friends from high school, and was "one of us." A Flower Child, who ran an international erotic film festival. Like her, because we were poetic cinema filmmakers, we couldn't help but project a little art in our films. Now they call them the "Classical or Golden Age" of Adult film, because they had story lines, were shot on real film, and had real characters and great locations. I am proud of them.

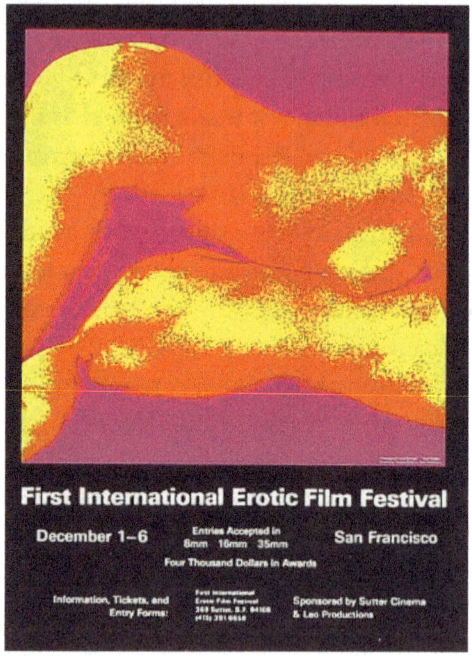

So far, my story is pretty bizarre for a woman who never wanted to be a filmmaker. And as time went on, and when all my poetic cinema films were lost, I never thought these films would still exist, either, until a few years ago. I had contacted an old acquaintance, Ken Fobes, the former Press Secretary for Oregon Governor Tom McCall; for a quote for Vol. I of this book, about how I became the liaison to the set for *One Flew Over the Cuckoo's Nest* in 1975. All these years later, he was researching the Adult Industry for a book, and had found me – on the Internet. Like all over the place. Imagine my shock when he also told me that it was the Producers of *Cuckoo's Nest* who had recommended me to the Governor to replace the 86'd film commissioner. He also remembered that when he had called me in to meet with him, at the request of the Governor, his intention was for an informal interview for the recommended position on *Cuckoo's Nest.* I had no idea. I thought he had called me in because at the time I was lobbying the Governor's office for funding the Indigenous film crew. He also said I had mentioned working on 14 color motion pictures. And now he knew what 14 films I was talking about, because there I was, in them. Back in 1975, when he asked me about them, evidently I had told him. My first reaction was "Oh My God," I am so glad I never participated in any real sexual encounters on camera. Just this last year, I found a Lobby Card with me on it. They made up anonymous names for us in postproduction. That's me on the top part of the Lobby Card, with a photoshopped top on.

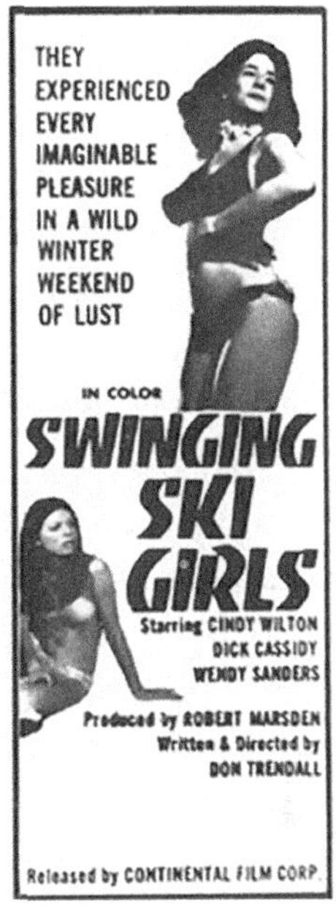

Lucretia and I were now partners-in-film, since *Cinderella Liberty;* and close friends, but not lovers. However, we agreed that guys love the idea of two women together, so we simulated being lesbians. The first one was called *Welcome Wagon Girls.* And we women were the stars *and* the writers. We got to explore what we wanted to see on the screen. We were in control of the male gaze on our bodies. As a matter of fact, we reversed the roles. We became the gazers, and that was so incredibly strange, because it's men for the large part who respond to visual stimuli, and women who respond to the emotional. We gave our audiences both, which made them rather poetic. It was such a hit, that headquarters asked for more from us. And then the word got out, and more people kept showing up to be a part of it. Evergreen, the local film company, processors of slides and high-end poetic cinema 16 mm film, now started processing these films. A local production company loaned their editor out to cut these films. And we cranked out six more films in half a year, before May; when I was discovered by a Hollywood director.

> "Pornography as a genre, is a literature of Eros – the formulation of love's mythology. In classical cultures that formulation was by and large coherent, incorporated into religion and the mainstream of cultural life. In modern cultures that mythology has lost coherence, become obscene. Phallic worship (or even curiosity) has become something to be oppressed, and consequently a source of shame."[240]

"In modern cultures that mythology has lost coherence, become obscene…" is exactly what my generation and Yeats were talking about. But on an Easter Sunday shoot, we were introduced to a new kind of Phallic God, a Hollywood star: Johnny "The Wad" Holmes, who like an Easter Bunny brought all of us girls Easter gifts. And we shot a scene where two of the local actress/topless dancers argued about who got on top of him first. They kept saying, "No, after you..." to each other for so long the whole cast and crew broke out laughing. He really was that big. But I can't say that most of us girls were not just a little bit curious. Johnny taught me a lot. I found it is imperative to an actress to have someone with some skill to bounce off of, in dialogue. And I had become so comfortable with Hagen and my friends as crew, that I had allowed myself to be photographed in the nude.

In early May of 1973, my photographer Dan Webb, who was still paying me $25 an hour to model for him, disappeared, which he did off and on. Next thing I know, I am getting a phone call that I thought was a prank. Lucretia was at my house, no doubt we were getting ready to go somewhere, when the phone rang. I was in the tub, and she answered it for me. Then she came into the bathroom and told me a Hollywood director was on the phone and wanted me to be in his next movie, I said, "Yeah, right. It's the Merry Pranksters. Hang up."

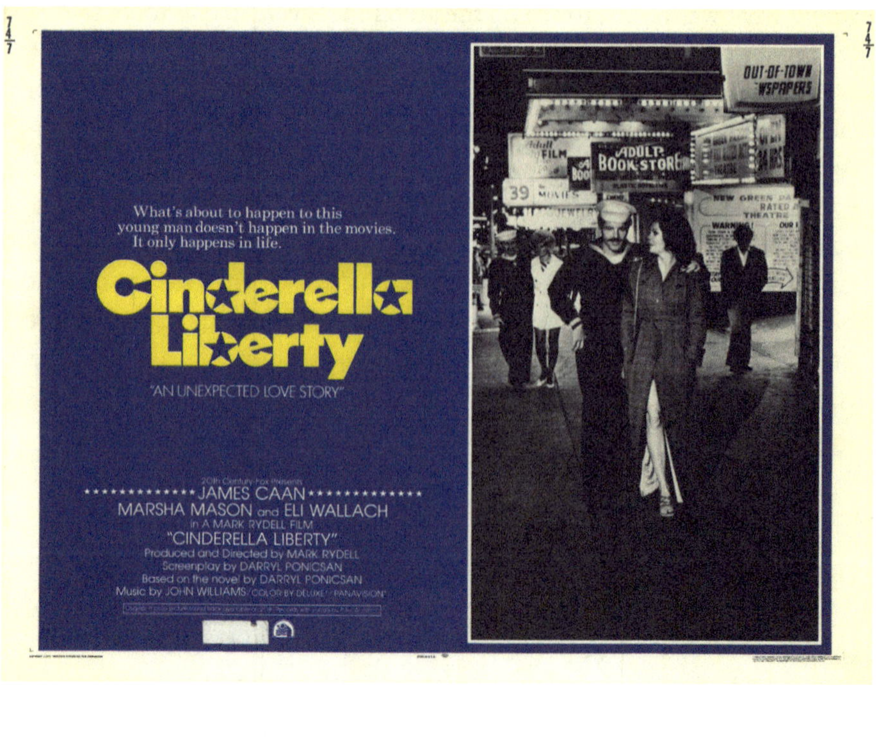

To make a long story short, it was Mark Rydell, the director of *The Fox* ('67) *The Reivers* ('69) *The Rose* ('79) *The Cowboys* (72) and eventually *On Golden Pond* ('81). He called back later that evening, a little chagrined. "Do you want this part or not?" he said. He was filming in Seattle, a movie called *Cinderella Liberty*, with James Caan, Eli Wallach, and Marsha Mason. He would buy me a plane ticket, send a limo to get me, put me up in the "Above the Line" Mansion on Queen Anne Hill, and pay me per diem and Screen Actors' Guild wages. About $500 for one day's work. He told me that if I flew up the next day, I could attend as his guest, the Premiere of John Wayne's Premiere of *Cahill, U.S. Marshall.* And I said yes. And that Premiere changed my life forever. As we arrived at the Red Carpet in the limo, John Wayne was in a tussle with some American Indian Protestors on the dais above the sidewalk that led into the theater. Marlon Brando had snubbed the Oscar's just a few months earlier, by sending Sacheen Littlefeather to turn the Oscar down on his behalf, and to raise awareness about what had happened at Wounded Knee, when my friend Russell Means and other traditional Hunkpapa Sioux had occupied the small town to protest the rigged system on the reservation, where even the BIA was complicit in its extreme poverty. This was not long after American Indians had occupied Alcatraz.

I remember now where I had seen one of the signs that was at the U of O Longhouse a few years ago. It said, "Caution: Hollywood Still Shooting." I had seen it first on a protestor's cardboard sign at that premiere. John Wayne was not happy. He took it personally, when it was really about how Indians were depicted. I think that seeing "Sonny Corleone" (James Caan) get out of the limo stopped it. *The Godfather* was all the rage then.

John Wayne's attention was riveted away from the protester's anyway, as Rydell was a dear old friend from *The Cowboys,* and after they hugged, we all went into the lobby. At the private reception, champagne flowed and Rydell soothed Wayne's feathers. I was wearing a slinky floor length dress that Lucretia had loaned me, with matching stacked heels. I knew Wayne was feeling better when he sidled up to me and drawled all over me.

How this changed my life was that for the first time I saw young American Indians with a Great Spirit instead of a broken one. I saw them stand for the Truth. And the truth is that the American Cowboy Archetype embodied by John Wayne as *icon,* was part of a dialectic where denigrating American Indians was what you did when you wanted to elevate the whites. And why do the whites need elevating? Because the people who will hate you the most are the people who have greatly wronged you.

And American Manifest Destiny, based on a 1492 Papal Bull called The Doctrine of Discovery, made it legal to take an Indigenous people's land by putting a flag on it, and declaring the ownership in the name of the Queen and/or King; wherein you own everything, including the original people themselves. Furthermore, you call them savages and make them not human, not worthy, and deem them simply as chattel. That is how you rationalize your own behavior.

And what is worse, is that you feel threatened by them and don't know why. But as a bicultural I can tell you this ... it was understandable that Rydell would side with his old friend that he directed in *The Cowboys*. But Wayne was threatened by the Indians, and later on in the shoot, Rydell was threatened by a Black extra I was talking to on the dock. Both the Indians and I, and the Black man and I, had a camaraderie that goes beyond skin color. We recognize each other as kindred spirits. It is a soulfulness I can't quite explain yet, but I am beginning to think it is because we resonate vibrationally and even speak the same syntactical language. The white woman in me is totally confused by it and doesn't understand it yet, either. But I think the threatening part of a lot of systemic racism is sexual. And deep down, besides the hidden guilt for generations of wrongful subjugation, is the knowledge that the White man's way of worshipping money and going to any length to acquire more is coming to an end; and that their ways will not work anymore in the New Age. Neither will pursuing a career for money when your heart craves love. Which was Rydell's message in *Cinderella Liberty*, and why my scene was so crucial, and why he needed an "exotic" girl, one with Indigenous genes.

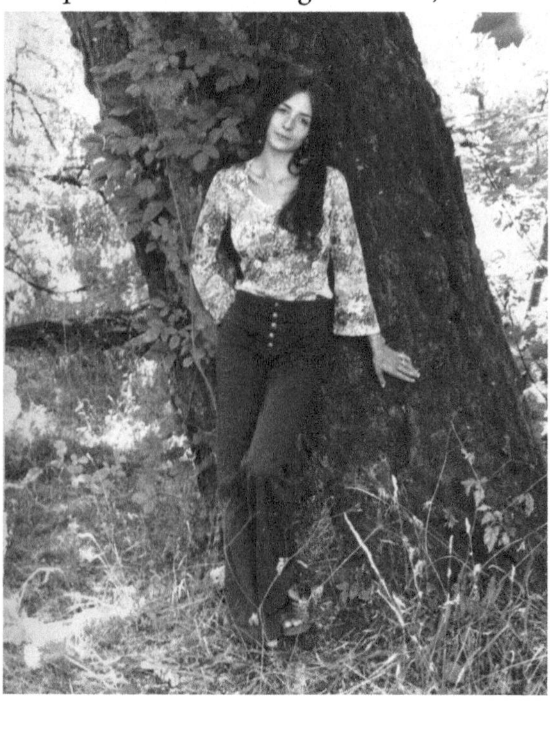

Since then, Mark and I have been lifelong friends. The last time I saw him, in 2009, we had dinner and sat by the pool of The Sunset Towers and talked for hours. Finally I

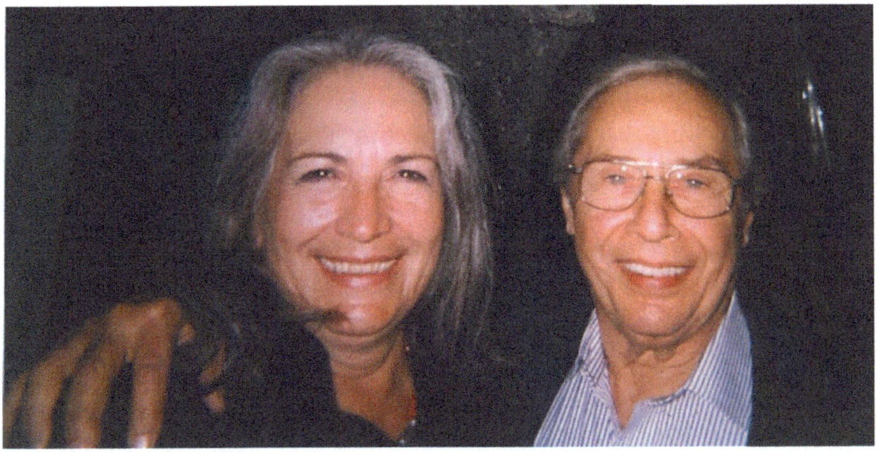

got my nerve up, and asked him if he remembered why he had hired me sight unseen for that role in 1973, some 36 years before. He said he was attending a luncheon at the Seattle Film Conference with Vilmos Zsigmond, when a disabled man came up to them and just put a picture in front of them. Of me. And then he turned it over and said, "There's her phone number." Rydell had looked through Lola Holliwell's Talent files in Seattle, but wasn't happy, evidently. When he and Vilmos saw my photo, they went "HER." It was a nude medium shot of me. And it launched my Hollywood Career. But back then, at first, I had to learn many things.

I had to learn how to get to the airport on time, and how to even fly in an airplane; which was my first, among these many other firsts: how to ride in a Limo, how to attend a Premiere, how to talk to a movie star, how to handle yourself when you first meet a Hollywood director, all in the same day. As I wrote in Vol. I; I missed the plane, hence missed the limo; which had to be sent again; and regarding limos, you are to sit in the back seat, not the front. You are to talk to a movie star only when talked to, at first; (easy for me because I really had a fear of talking too much and now, was terrified by the whole experience; especially since the limo driver let me know he didn't appreciate having to drive twice in one day to SeaTac, so I didn't want to say a word, *anyway*) and you *especially* are *not* to trip on the Turkish Runner and fall down on your face the minute you walk in the front door to meet the director. But it broke the ice, and everybody jumped up, concerned. I'll never forget Rydell asking me if I was hurt. And when I said "No. Just mad." everybody laughed, and we became instant friends. I guess that was my audition, because my role was not to be shot until the end of the film, a month later. And I was welcomed to stay as the film's guest in the meantime. When Rydell asked me if there were any other girls like me in Oregon, ones experienced in film, he then told me to bring my girlfriend Lucretia up too, to be in the scene with me. And I did.

During that summer that we worked in Seattle on *Cinderella Liberty,* Lucretia and I were cast in very small roles as "Dance Hall Girls." The premise of this film was that a Navy Seaman (James Caan) was stranded in Seattle when his ship left, and was waiting for the next time it arrived, in order to leave again. But in that short amount of time, he found himself falling in love with a hooker (Marsha Mason) who had a Mulatto son (Kirk Calloway). Sound Western? You bet. "Dance Hall Girls" instead of "Strippers. "The white Male" who comes into a situation to save The Whore with the Heart of Gold and her Mulatto, downtrodden son." But with a twist.

The third act turning point consisted of the Navy Seaman, on *Cinderella Liberty* (allowed on shore until midnight) now that his ship had returned and was having to decide what to do before the ship left the next day; either try to make it with the hooker and create a family with her son (and go AWOL); or leave with the ship, like a good cowboy would do.

This was the scene that I was in. An old Navy Salty Dog (Eli Wallach) had retired and was a "barker" in Post Alley for a "Girly Show"; and James Caan was keeping him company and hoping for some advice until "Lights Out," when the Dance Hall Girls came out of the Stage Door to head home. Wallach tries to grab two of them for himself and Caan, but the girls don't want to have anything to do with them. Essentially, the scene portrayed that not even "Strippers" wanted to have anything to do with them. And Caan decides he doesn't want to be like Eli Wallach when he gets old.

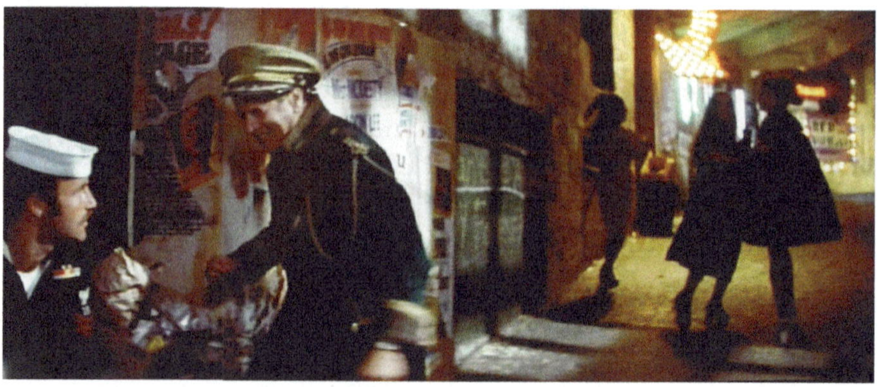

For this scene, the writer Darryl Ponicsan had the girls very scantily dressed in the script, with stacked high heels. The wardrobe woman, Rita Riggs (*Marnie, The Birds*) was faithful to the script, and dressed me as a stripper. But once on the set, Rydell took one look at me and yelled at her, and told her to put a full cape over me. And I did my scene, but it didn't make sense anymore. James Caan was to decide that he didn't want what Eli Wallach had, and would choose to stay and make a family, after realizing he didn't want to grow old and be a barker in the alley, alone with sleazy Dance Hall girls who didn't even want him. But now there was no motivation. The girls were not lascivious enough. The Male gaze was thwarted. And all of these statements by critic Laura Mulvaney came true, that broke the Patriarchal spell, because: "There was no gaining control and possessing of the woman within the diegesis,"[241] "there was no voyeuristic fantasy,"[242] There was no "watching in an active controlling sense, an objectified other,"[243] There was no established "guilt" of the women.[244] And my personal favorite, there was no being "tied to her place of bearer, not maker, of meaning."[245]

Somehow, not being sexualized in that scene created an alternative meaning, one that created agency for women, and that was amazing to witness. I think Marsha Mason had enlightened the director (who had previously made D.H. Lawrence's *The Fox*) at the "Family Style" Sunday Dinners at our Crew Hotel (the Mansion on Queen Anne Hill) where we would dine and then sip Watergate Whiskey (that Eli Wallach had brought from D.C.) and talk politics and feminism. And Marsha Mason would reign with her keen intellect about Watergate, and Eli admired her for it, and she became my new heroine. But that wasn't all. James Caan and his brother Ronnie and I stayed friends, and they would take me to The Whiskey a Go Go to dance when I was in town. Rydell and Zsigmond even brought me to LA. and took me out to dinner to fun places like Mus-

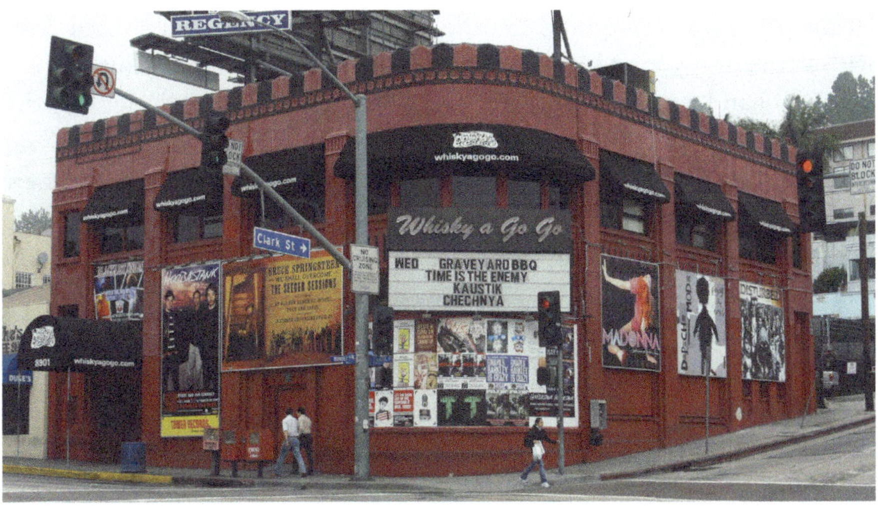

so and Frank's and introduced me to the very famous Hollywood Casting Director Lynn Stalmaster, which changed my life.

Just like my disastrous entry into Rydell's life, my first audition for Hollywood's most famous Studio Casting Director of all time, Lynn Stalmaster *the Master Caster,* was a disaster. He was the Casting Director for many of Mark Rydell's movies, and Mark had heard about and talked me into auditioning for the lead role in an upcoming 20th Century Fox film called *Vrooder's Hootch* aka *The Crazy World of Julius Vrooder* (1974) with "star" Timothy Bottoms, one that Lynn was casting.

On the plane down to Hollywood for the audition, I had flown with my girlfriend Lucretia, who had been with me in the scene with Eli Wallach and James Caan for Rydell, earlier that Spring in Seattle. And on the plane Lucretia had befriended some Execs next to us, and talked them into letting us stay at their place in Century City. They were heading to New York later that night on the Red Eye, so I thought that would be a great idea because it would save us both extra cab fare from LAX to Hollywood, and hotel lodging.

The problem was, before my audition with Stalmaster later the next day, I had tried to kill two birds with one stone and had gone to another appointment with Marilyn Grabowski, a photo editor for *Playboy Magazine* on Sunset Blvd; and had accidently locked the key to the Century City apartment inside. When I got back there, and went to the front desk, the managers of the complex didn't believe that Stuart Diamond, the original apartment renter had ever given me a key, because it was against the rules to let people stay there that were not on the lease, especially without them there; and consequently wouldn't let me in. I knew they wouldn't let me go upstairs now, so I left the front desk to go out the main door with a toss of my long hair for effect (as in hmpf! "I am so insulted, I am leaving!") and ran around the back to the parking garage and snuck up the back stairs to wait for Lynn Stalmaster to pick me up. My nail polish was chipped, I needed a shower from sweating bullets in the prior interview with *Playboy*. That particular audition was for Playmate of the Month early the next year, and I had negotiated until I was finally offered $3000 without even having to drop my drawers. It was the 70s all right, and the truth was that I made about that much *working for a whole year* at Cinema 7 in Eugene. So that was quite a coup, if I do say so myself. But all I could do now, locked out from my luggage, was to apply a spot of lipstick and perfume I found in my purse, and sit in the hallway and wait for Mr. Stalmaster to come and take me to dinner, hopefully still wanting to audition

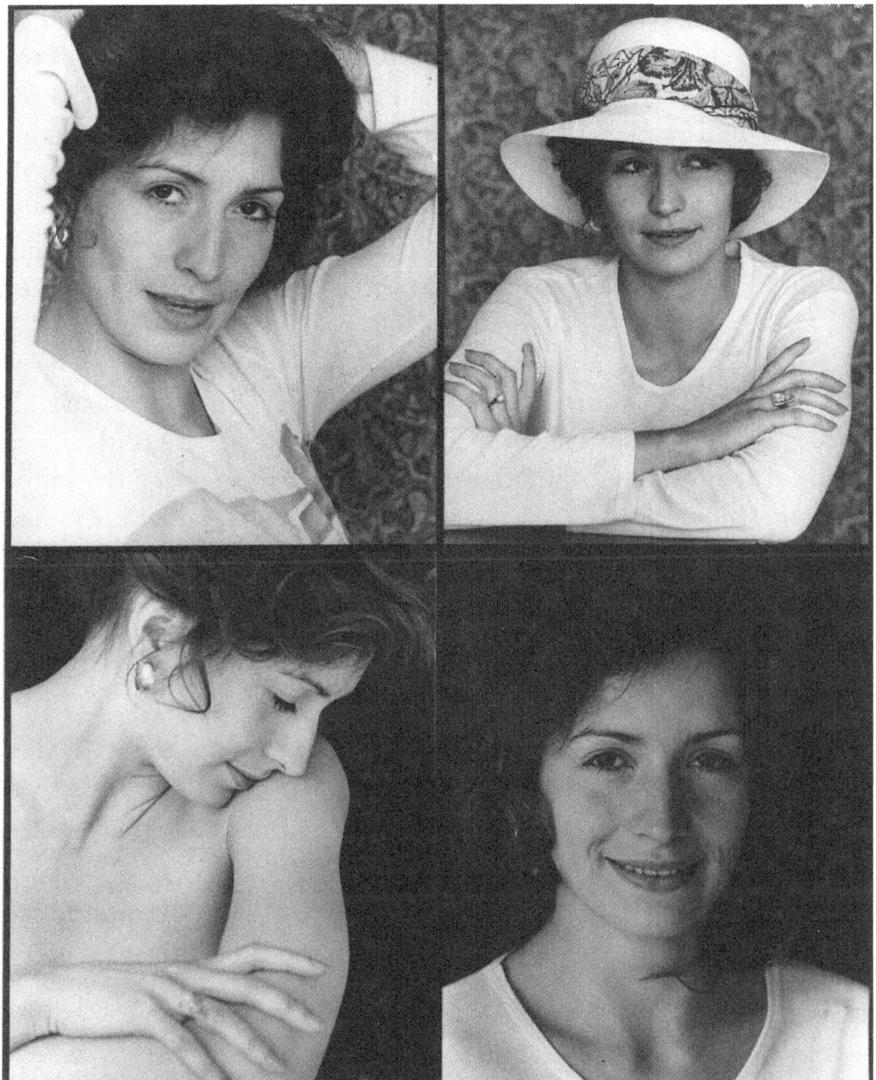

From Katherine Wilson's Portfolio. Photos by Silver Fox Studios.

me after seeing what a wreak I was. The truth was I was terrified, about where Lucretia was, and how could I get ahold of her to tell her we were locked out? And where would I be able to stay without any luggage? It might have been the hippie-dippie loosey-goosey 70s in Oregon, but in Hollywood decorum was everything. Any small hint that you might be a hooker, (like having no luggage) would slam shut many doors that were otherwise open.

I had to learn this again a few years later when I had a celebratory drink at the Polo Lounge with Michael Murphy, an Oregon Producer, after we had successfully pitched his project to Jack Nicholson. After I went to my hotel to change in order to return to Jack's house for dinner, the Polo Lounge would not let me back in to find my phone book with Jack's address. For dinner at Jack's house I had shed my Polyester business suit for a low-cut black sweater with jeans and black boots. That outfit was *not* allowed in the Polo Lounge. Finally, not knowing what else to do, I just sat and waited in the lobby of the bar until I could talk some doctor into going in there for me, which happened, and then he found and brought me my little black book. Needless to say, I was late for dinner at Jack's house!

But here I was again, locked out of where I needed to go, and inappropriately dressed for my evening audition in a daytime business suit. As Lynn walked down the hallway to where I sat on the floor, I could tell he was more than a little surprised and wondering about me and the whole situation. I promptly burst out in tears and told him the truth, I had locked myself out, was so sorry I was such a mess, and we immediately became friends. He took me to dinner, and then to his house where he let me take a shower, pull myself together and offered to let me stay in his daughter's room. And then he gently led me into my motion picture audition, (my Hollywood first!) by telling me the story of *Vrooder's Hootch* and about the character I was auditioning for. When I was ready he read with me, playing the character of Timothy Bottoms. Just like riding a bicycle, my old training from South Eugene Drama Teacher Ed Ragazzino came back, and remembering what he had said about acting for film, I delivered my lines in a very understated way. When we were through my audition, Lynn he told me I was "a natural actress;" the very words Ed had used. And I had been elevated to the next step, which was a meeting with the Producer of the film at the Studio. Now that was all settled, I could relax over a glass of wine, and I told him the whole story of my day, including the offer from Marilyn Grabowski and *Playboy* Magazine. He advised me very gently to turn it down, because he said I had real chance at a real career as an actress in LA; and the *Playboy* gig would be "the kiss of death' for my career. And I believed him. These guys had gone all out to help me. So I turned it down.

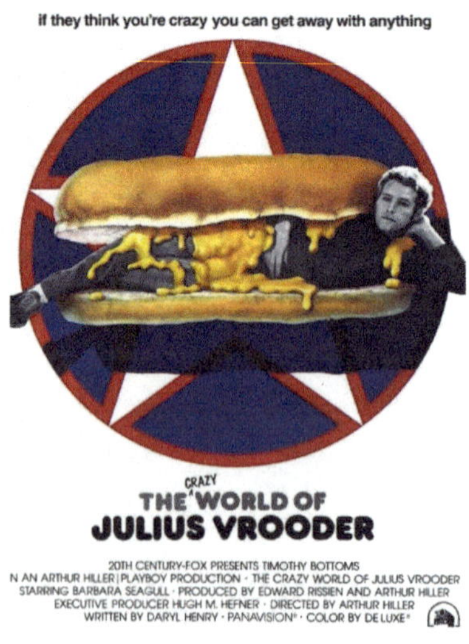

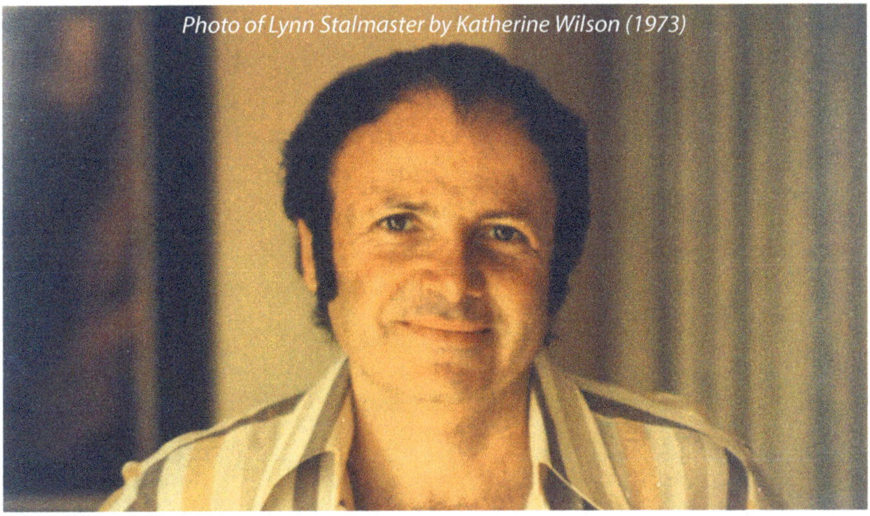

Photo of Lynn Stalmaster by Katherine Wilson (1973)

He also wanted me to change my last name back to my maiden name, too; but I could not do that for many reasons. But I stayed with him for three days until I found Stuart Diamond had returned from New York and luckily Lucretia, too, who was back at the apartment. In the meantime I went to Lynn's office with him every day and watched him work. We would then have dinner and talk over the day's auditions, and maybe even go disco dancing at the Candy Store. He had also set up my "lunch" with Producer Michael Gruskoff at Fox, as I was his recommendation for the part in *Vrooder's Hootch*. He and Mark Rydell had also set me up with the Dean at USC Film School, and I was amazed when the Dean promised me admission and even a scholarship, just based on their word. And then it all fell apart. Not because of Grabowski, or Rydell, or Stalmaster. It fell apart because of me. When I went to the meeting at Fox for lunch with an Executive there, the Executive made it clear that I was lunch, if I wanted the role in the film. And I told him no. I'm happy to play sexy roles, I loved to do that for film, with lots of make-up and hair stylists and even be a scantily-clad-clothes horse, but sex was sacred. I was the one who decided if I felt something deeper than what was in my reptilian brain. That was worthy of sacred sex. And I packed my bags and came home to Oregon, vowing to create my own kind of industry.

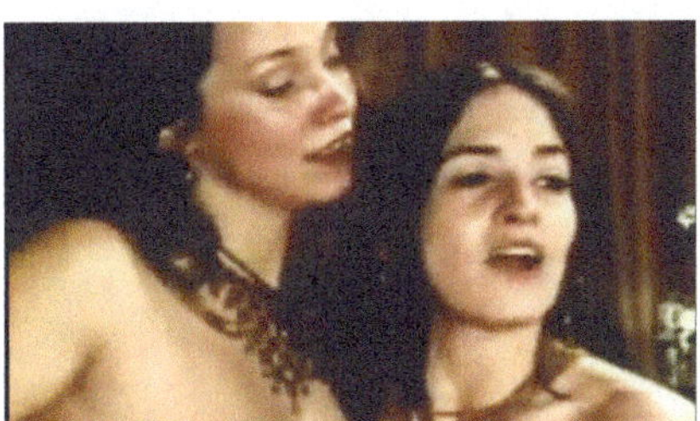

So this all inspired me to create a more integrous industry here in Oregon. And what I came back to Oregon with was an incredible gift from

Lynn Stalmaster. He had not only taught me how to audition when he guided me in my interpretation of the character, but showed me how it was done repeatedly in his office, and had inadvertently given me a crash course in how to be a Casting Director. That became my bread and butter for the next 20 some years on 30-some films (a few even Oscar nominations and Blockbusters) and National commercials. And we stayed in touch. I was so sad to hear he passed away this year.

Years later, after I was able to finally work at my true love, which was Screenplay Writing, I hired other casting directors to help package my films for me. I'll never forget the day my friend and colleague Lana Veenker, as my casting director, took me to Vancouver BC to meet one of the *Twilight* Wolfpack boys for the lead role in my screenplay *Blanket of the Sun*. As Stalmaster had done with me, and as I had done with over 100 starring and featured roles that I had cast in films over the intervening years, I led him through the story line into the character. His audition became electrifying. And Lana and I looked at each other with such incredulity, that we got to create and experience such great timeless moments. Thank you, Lynn; for this incredible gift. Because I don't think I would ever have been able to continue to be a filmmaker as just an actress.

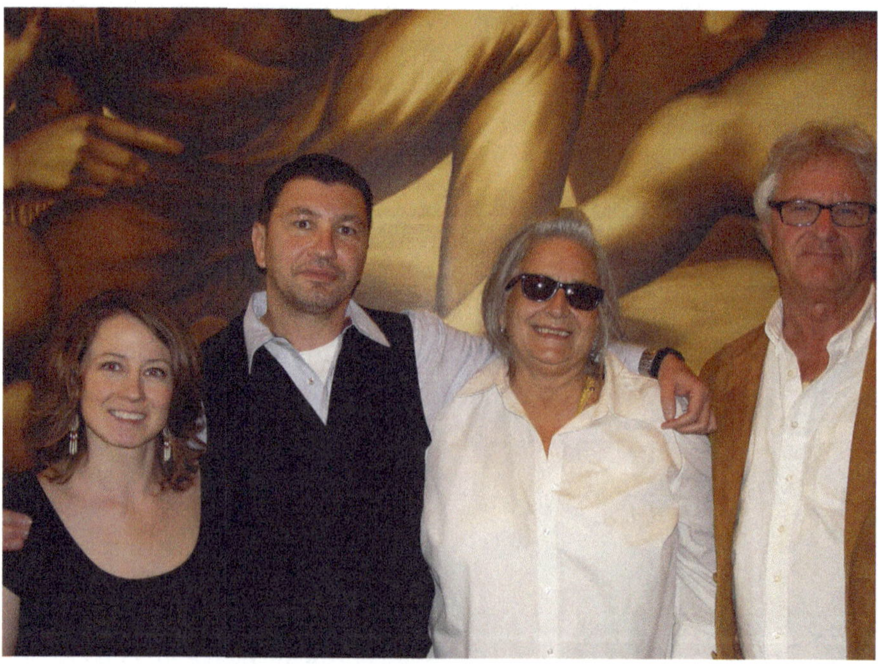

But it wasn't until I attended the U of O again, at 69 years of age; that I realized why; and that was when Professor Pyle was teaching me, about me, in his class; when we were studying Literary theorist Laura Mulvaney and her Essay "Visual Pleasure and Narrative Cinema," (1973) he stated: "her analysis of the "looked-at-ness" of the figure of the woman -- her status as "object to be seen" -- tells us why this reduces women, and it is essentially because (as stated on page 15 of her Essay) she is "*tied to her place of bearer, not maker, of meaning.*"[246] This one sentence alone, for me, is full of the agency of language, as it evokes *bondage* with the word "tied," evokes *powerlessness and patronizing* condescension with "her place," as in "putting her in her place;" and evokes also the painful *labor* of childbearing and a terrible weight with the word "bearer." The sentence also implies that the "bearing"; is not voluntary, it is a *burden* forced to be taken, as if women were originally created for and defined as "*beasts of burden.*"

In other words, God created women as he created Eve, such as found in the Olde English Genesis: (... and as a punishment for partaking of the tree of good and evil) God says to Eve: "You shall be under male rule, tightly restricted in awe of man, and abject shall you suffer the error of your ways, await death, and in weeping and lamentation give birth to sons and daughters in the world through great sorrow."[247] But it is in the words "...of bearer, not maker, of meaning," that we find not only is woman a bearer, and she is indeed "under male rule" like a mule; but the sentence implies that men, like Adam, is God-like in that he can create meaning; but she cannot. What does this mean? The word, meaning? It is a noun. It is an adjective. For me, it means *choosing the agency of language in order to be heard.*[248]

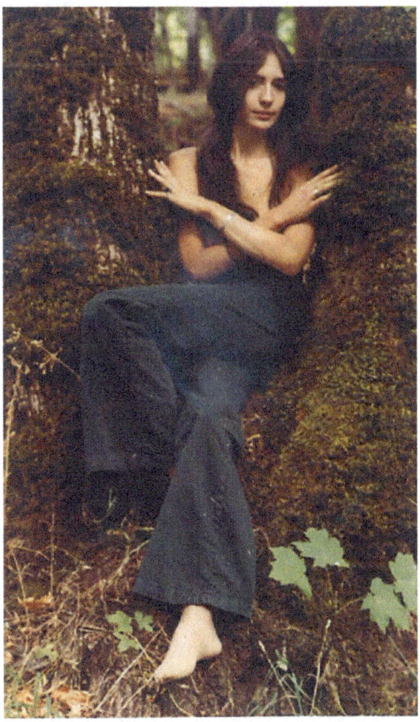

In Part III, on page 19, of her Essay; Mulvaney cuts to the chase. Cinema has become the poster child for this interplay between sender and receiver: "Women displayed as sexual object is the *leitmotif* of erotic spectacle she holds the look, (with her *to-be-looked-at-ness*) and plays to and signifies male desire."[249] So the male is the sender and the female the receiver of the Male Gaze, which is how meaning is created. And women bear *the-to-be-looked at-ness.* In other words, woman cannot even convey information or concepts. They are only the receiver, and even though they can bear children, they cannot create them; they are only the receptive vessel of the male/God's life-giving power to create human beings through Apollonian Arrows shot into the receptive Dionysian by the phallus. The terms Apollonian and Dionysian are from Friedrich Nietzsche in *The Birth of Tragedy.* However, I certainly agree with whomever "Faculty" is at Florida International University:

> Using these terms we can see that Platonism and Neo-Platonism clearly advocated Apollonian values and denigrated the Dionysian. It is also worth mentioning that the Dionysian values are often associate(d) with females and the feminine. Keep in mind that "female hysteria" was a common medical diagnosis, made exclusively in women, which dates back to ancient Greece. Women have long been portrayed as more sensitive, emotional and more "physical" (limited and/or determined by their bodies) then men.[250]

So how can women ever turn back the clock to Plato where this all started? Essentially, as Laura said, "We can't." But she infers we can transcend it, "the first blow ... is to free the look of the camera in its materiality into time and space." And that is invoking the need for women behind the lenses, creating their own omniscient view of story, and not just behind the lenses, but as Directors who chose the story, clothing and dialog; and therefore will be as close as we will probably ever get to the time when God was a Woman.[251]

And she was right, because I returned to Oregon with a vengeance. I wanted to create a Film Industry in Oregon that honored integrity. And it took me almost 20 years, but I did it. And I wanted to produce films from stories about women, like John Barth's *Chimera,* (1972) that reimagined the ancient *1001 Nights* through the eyes of Scheherazade and her little sister Dunyziad. I almost convinced Michael Douglas to film it, when he was looking for romantic and erotic films for women a few years later! And I did make a toast at dinner at Jack Nicholson's house taken from this book, too. More on that in the next Chapters. But I ended up having to work with what I had at the time, which was a local film crew, my girlfriend Lucretia and her beau Don Gilbert, and his financer. And we worked really hard to make romantic and sexy films from a woman's point of view, for the next 6 months; when once again I got a call from a director, one that Dan Webb had also instigated for me, and it was for a much larger budget film to be shot in Portland.

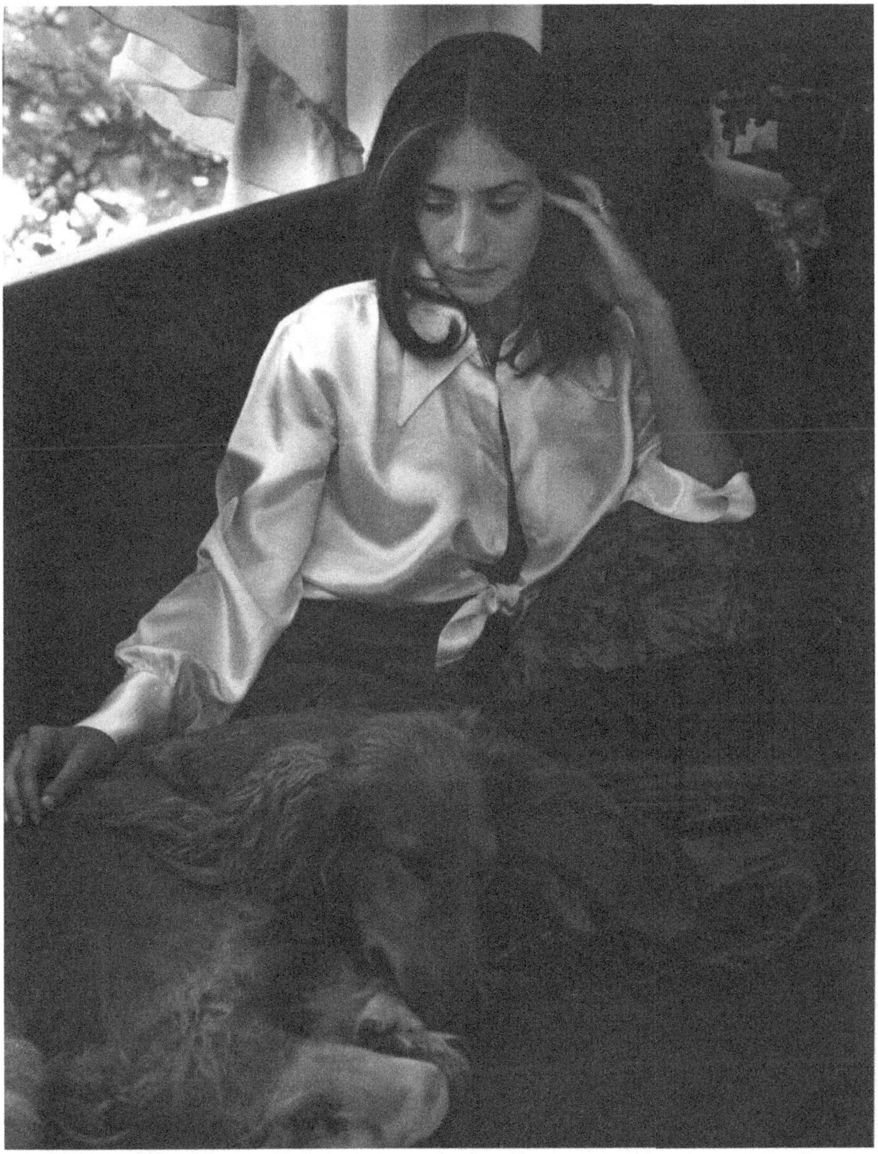

Katherine Wilson in 1973 with Larry the Dog. Photo by Dan Webb.

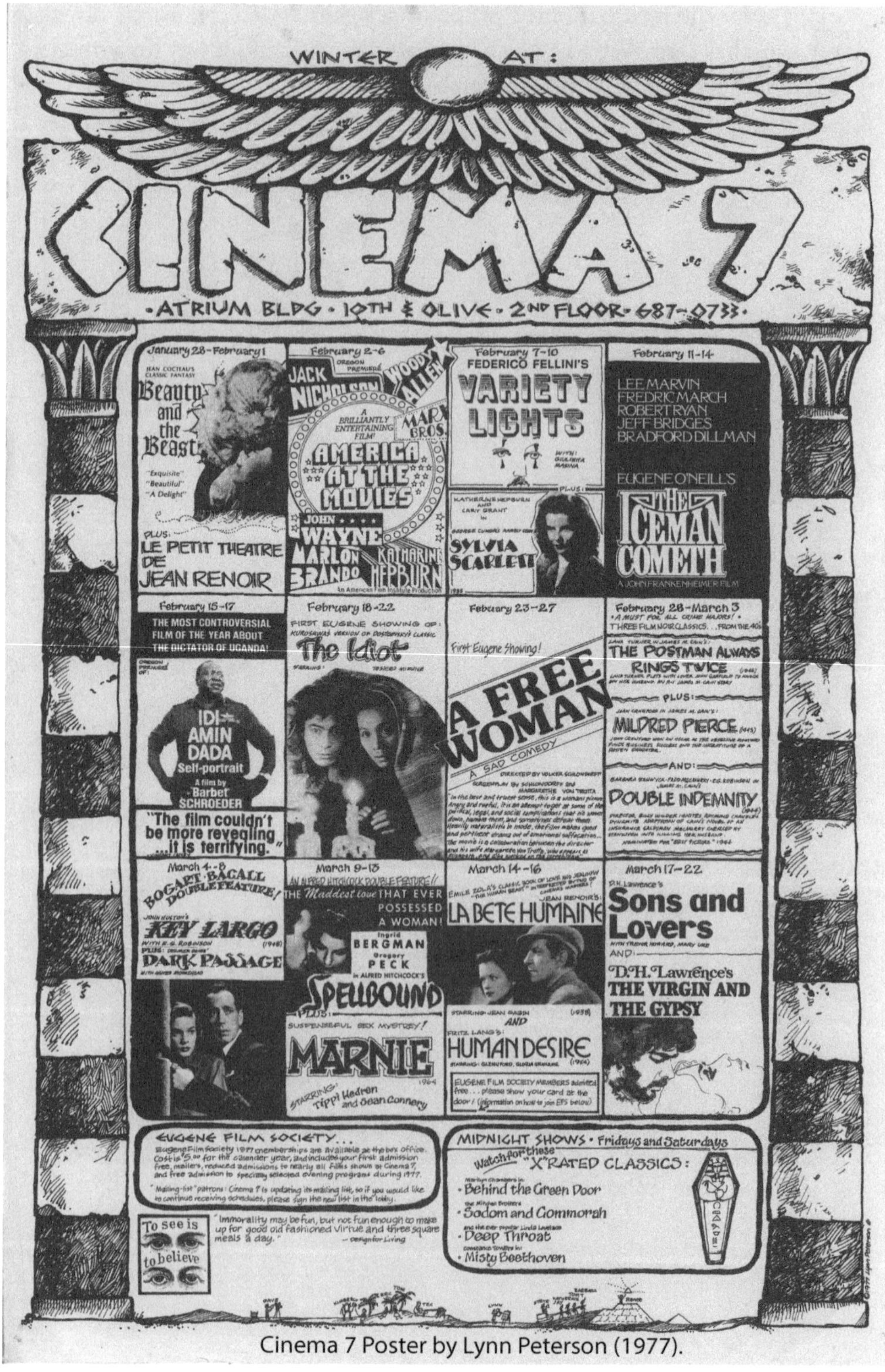

Cinema 7 Poster by Lynn Peterson (1977).

Chapter 9

Neither Earth Or Air Or Fire Or Water ~1974

> It is said that analyzing pleasure or beauty destroys it. That is the intention of this article.[235]
>
> – Mulvaney's "Visual Pleasure and Narrative Cinema"

So essentially, Mulvaney helped define exactly what gave me the creeps regarding "weaponized women," "the male gaze" and "the patriarchal" film. And we women, Lucretia and I, in 1974, now had the lights, the cameras and the action; we had all this power and did not know what to do with it. The closest we would come was to put women in control of their bodies in our movies, and/or maybe reverse the role-playing. There was no manual for how to be a young woman in the 1970s, either; so instinctively we looked to the tribes, who had inspired us with their matriarchal societies in the early 60s. According to Doug George-Kanentiio:

> "In our society, women are the center of all things. Nature, we believe, has given women the ability to create; therefore it is only natural that women be in positions of power to protect this function. We traced our clans through women; a child born into the world assumed the clan membership of its mother. In all countries, real wealth stems from the control of land and its resources. Our Iroquois philosophers knew this as well as we knew natural law. To us it made sense for women to control the land since they were far more sensitive to the rhythms of the Mother Earth. We did not own the land but were custodians of it. Our women decided any and all issues involving territory, including where a community was to be built and how land was to be used. The men are chiefs and the women clan-mothers. As leaders, the women closely monitor the actions of the men and retain the right to veto any law they deem inappropriate. Our women not only hold the reigns of polit-

> ical and economic power, they also have the right to determine all issues involving the taking of human life. Declarations of war had to be approved by the women, while treaties of peace were subject to their deliberations."[252]

This was also true of my beloved Nez Perce, whose ancient Clan mother said not to kill Lewis and Clark. Imagine what this world would be like without unnecessary violence and war? And imagine also our land protected from corporate greed and war against Mother Nature? It was time that Plato's feminine Khôra was redeemed as an equal, and not inferior to the male. Plato needed to come out of his own cave in this regard. And the New Age was about to do just that for him:

> And just as Marranos (biculturals) are oblivious and unsure of their past and identity, impure and contaminated, universally despised, yet precisely because of that masters of survival, so is khôra: treated by Plato as being metaphysically inferior.... It signifies another desert: not the one of a raging jealousy of the One God who cannot stand any rivalry, but the one of an original contamination, heterogeneity, always already 'more-than-one,' subtle and generous potentiality that is not yet formed into rigid identities, of a 'still life', but nonetheless always surviving, living-on, always there, in the dark silent background, hidden and secret.[253]

Was Plato keeping Khôra outside of the Gates of Athens for this reason? Because of her perceived inferior Dionysus-like Femininity to the superior Masculine Apollyonic-like Logic? If so, that's how he got away with disembodied rhetoric, logic and reasoning. And Plato is much to blame for what happened to our world. Because a world without heart, even if the heart makes us crazy, is a world that is dangerous without the Feminine properties of intuition and regeneration. However, whenever things get this far out of Balance, the Aeon gyre is at hand to right all its predecessor's wrongs.

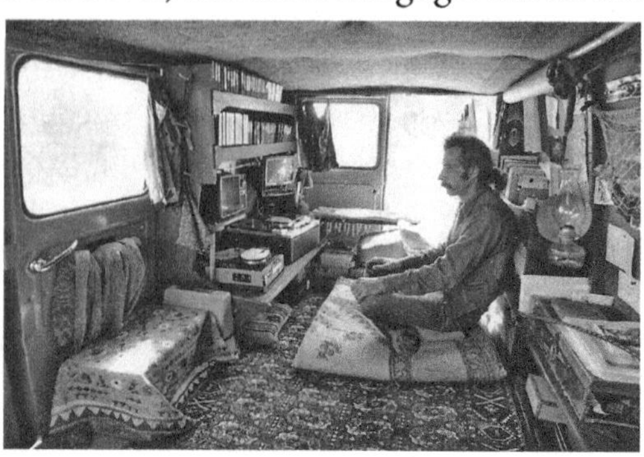

Meanwhile, back at the ranch, it was around this time that Loren Sears was filming the tribes of Northern California. Alcatraz had been held by the Natives for

19 Months, and Leonard Peltier was just going to trial. The American Indian was in the national consciousness. Kesey was still trying to edit the bus footage, and I was still on call for modeling and commercials with the Pranksters. But now I was bringing my girlfriends along as extras.

And we were still cranking out 16mm erotic films. I remember making one up called something like "Shirley and Sherlock Holmes," where we girls were spies for our boss "Shirley," and John Holmes was our, well *Sherlock Holmes*. There was another one I wrote about a "Miss Kitty" who kept the law and order. I remember doing a strip tease dance on the table at White Horse Tavern, actually two of them, one with a contemporary crowd about Lumberjacks who in the story messed with some girls, and then were snitched on. After the good guys talked to the same matriarchal woman who played "Shirley" in the other film, but was now "Kitty" in a similar role; the bad guys got beat up for it in the tavern. The other was a very slow strip tease for my Existential Western, without a contemporary crowd, but it was also a film with John Holmes. We often used the same location for two films if we were shooting them at the same time, because they were hard to obtain.

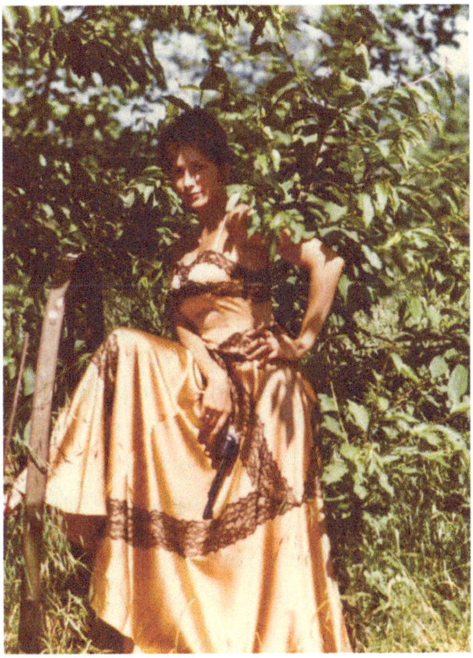

In these three particular films, women were the judge and jury; and as the Iroquois spokesman said, consulted "the women (who) closely monitor the actions of the men" as they once did, in the tribes. Even in a modern-day film, like *Dances With Wolves*, the Chief, Kicking Bird, asks his wife what it is that the "people" say about the relationship regarding Kevin Costner and The Chief's adapted white daughter. I was taught to always talk to the wives of the Chiefs. If I wanted to talk to the Holy Man Horace Axtell, I would call Andrea. If I wanted to talk to Soy Redthunder, I would call Sharon, and if I wanted to call Sabe Redthunder, I would talk to Atwice Kamiakun. Remember when I said Indian people have a great sense of humor about sex? Well, Atwice jokingly calls me Wife #2.

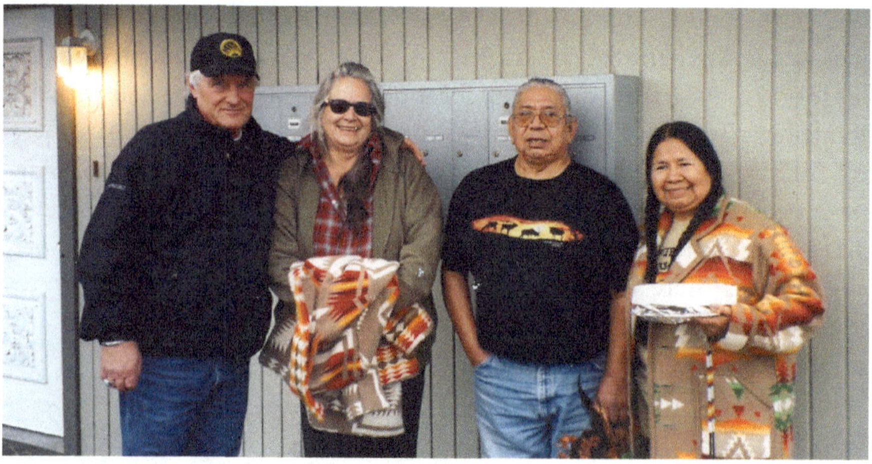

My husband Philip, myself, Chief Sabe Redthunder, Clanmother Atwice Kamiakun

> Friedrich Engels, in 1884, claimed that, in the earliest stages of human social development, there was group marriage and that therefore paternity was disputable, whereas maternity was not, so that a family could be traced only through the female line, and claimed that this was connected with the dominance of women over men or a Mutterrecht, which notion Engels took from Bachofen, who claimed, based on his interpretations of myths, that myths reflected a memory of a time when women dominated over men.[254]

And this new feminist kind of film was possible because there was a new Sheriff in town. A new form of consciousness that was feminine. And a new religion, with new rules. Like my people, we made new rules, based on our hearts, not on our minds:

> "... indigenous peoples' long histories of basing citizenship on kinship: acting as a community member, facing hardships together and adopting family members informally. Kin-based citizenship has a far longer history than citizenship based on nebulous ideas of "blood quantum," wherein ancestry is determined by phenotype and ancestral math."[255]

It was like America's gene pool had reached a critical mass of biculturality in the 60s and 70s. This article supports this: "Native American Ancestors Found in the Genes of Many in the U.S."[256] In the article, a researcher named Conley said the following: "When you go out West, that's where you have the most Native American ancestry in European populations." And once again, The Bicultural or Marrano is the closest name for what I would call this, as discussed here:

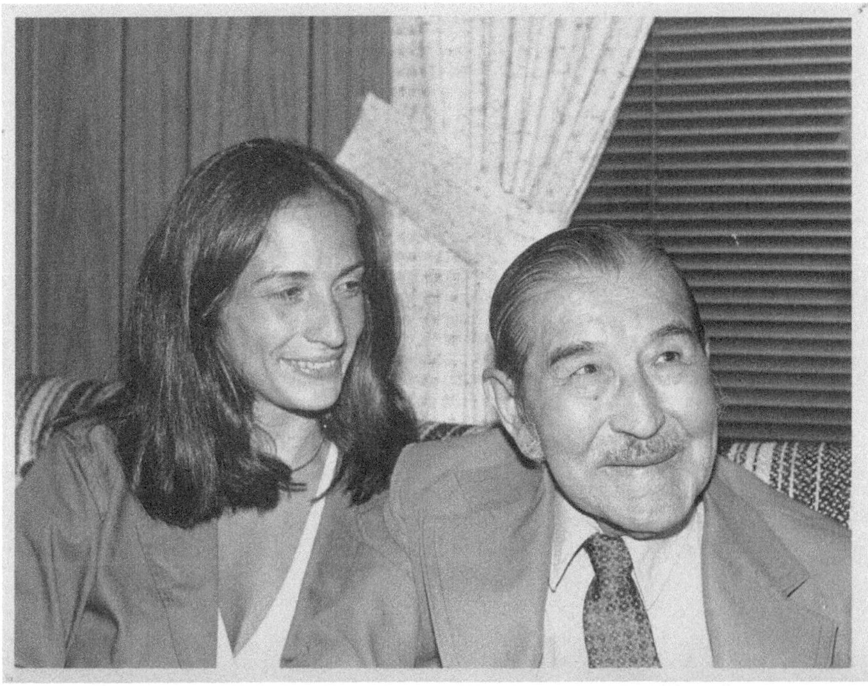

Katherine and Vargas backstage at The Cars "Candy-O" Release Concert, Hollywood Bowl (1979).

> The Marrano context of the modern 'reflecting faith' as being secretly internalized and supported only by the 'inner heart', itself also prone to forgetting, was spotted very aptly by Yirmiyahu Yovel: "For them [Marranos] authentic religion had been deinstitutionalized and privatized, ...depending on the inner heart as its almost sole support.[257]

But the language of the heart has to be nurtured, and as John Trudell stated, *remembered*... "There were, of course, supporting fragments of memory and custom, and the sense of secret fraternity.... In the end, and all along, the person had to face the most important religious truths – decisions about value, and about personal fate in this and the next world – within a private 'inner forum..."

And so we heard the call from the Divine Feminine, we had learned what not to do from religion:

> Just as Marranos exited all forms of institutionalized religions, being now neither Jewish nor Christian, so does khôra remain outside: "*It will never have entered religion and will never permit itself to be sacralized, sanctified, humanized, theologized, cultivated, histori-*

> *cized. Radically heterogenous to the safe and sound, to the holy and the sacred, it never admits of any indemnification.*[258]

The new spiritual sheriff in town, Khôra, allowed us to engage in its Dionysia & Bacchanalias. It out-pictured everywhere, unofficially, in lyrics of Rock and Roll, paintings, and films. Of course, San Francisco took it to new levels.

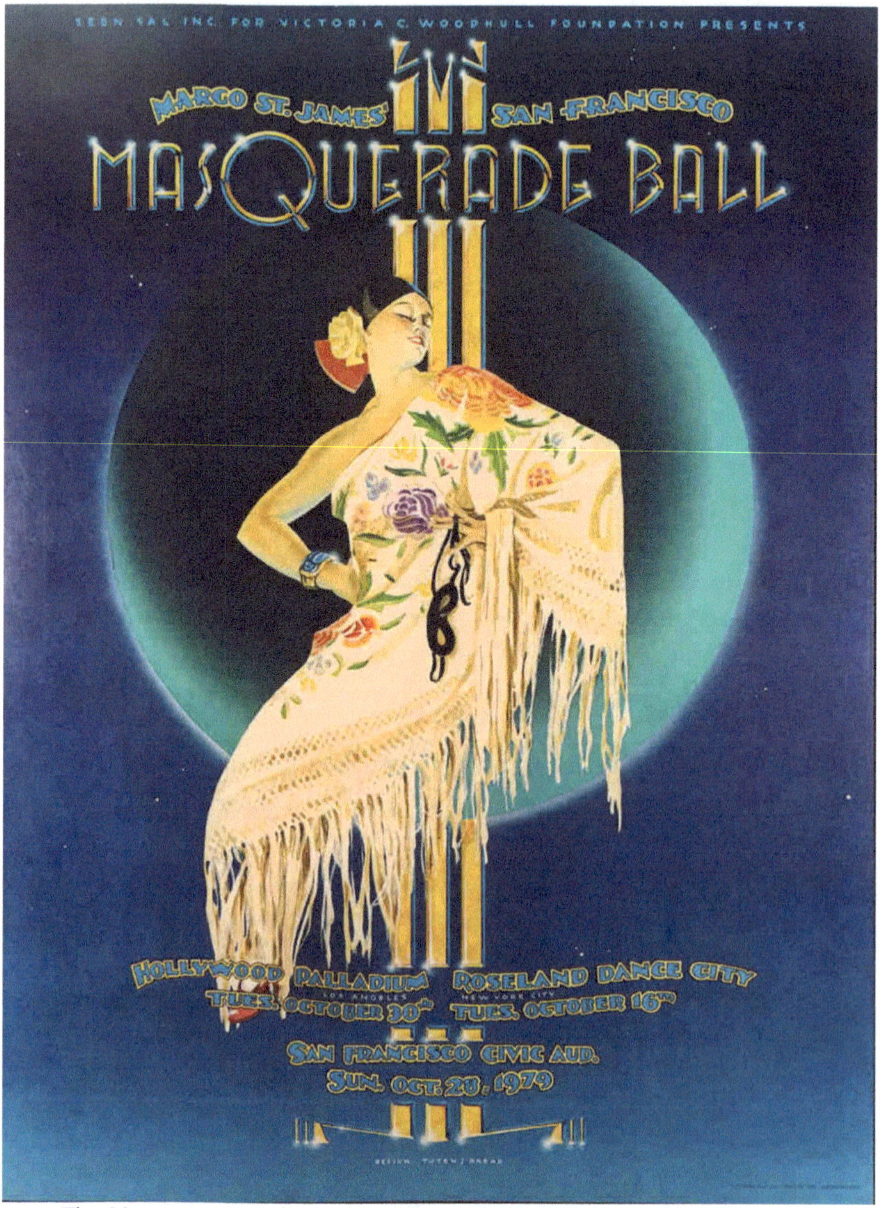

The Masquerade Ball Morphed from The San Francisco Hooker's Ball

> In 1972, a sex-positive activist and former prostitute named Margo St. James founded a very unique activist organization called "COYOTE." The name is an acronym that stands for "Call Off Your Old Tired Ethics." COYOTE was an organization that fought for the rights and protection of sex workers, including porn stars, prostitutes, and pimps alike. The goal of the organization was to challenge how much power the state had to interfere in the sex lives of its citizens. COYOTE went on to start a series of newsletters called Coyote Howls (formerly entitled Coyote Growls), in which they kept their readers up to date on the lawsuits and protests that worked to gain rights for all kinds of sex workers. The majority of the writers for Coyote Howls belonged to a new branch of feminism called Sex-positive feminism. These feminists were men and women who fought for total sexual liberation and sex lives that were free from government intervention.[259]

Many of their lawsuits sought to eliminate police brutality against prostitutes and to decriminalize prostitution. Other goals of the sex-positive branch of feminism included better sex education, "free love," and the general acceptance of all sexualities. Carol Queen, a sex-positive feminist and self-proclaimed sexologist offered this definition of sex-positivity:

> Sex-positive, a term that's coming into cultural awareness, isn't a dippy love-child celebration of orgone – it's a simple yet radical affirmation that we each grow our own passions on a different medium, that instead of having two or three or even half a dozen sexual orientations, we should be thinking in terms of millions. "Sex-positive" respects each of our unique sexual profiles, even as we acknowledge that some of us have been damaged by a culture that tries to eradicate sexual difference and possibility. It's the cultural philosophy that understands sexuality as a potentially positive force in one's life, and it can, of course, be contrasted with sex-negativity, which sees sex as problematic, disruptive, dangerous. Sex-positivity allows for and in fact celebrates sexual diversity, differing desires and relationships structures, and individual choices based on consent. [260]

Of course Stan Brakhage was getting away with making all sorts of films with nudity and depicting all sorts of sexuality. But that was Art. What we were making was closer to Melodrama. But it still was experimental. And it still was an answer to a call to create. But you had to be called. Kesey was a trailblazer for us when he responded to the call to write

One Flew Over the Cuckoo's Nest. 1962 was indeed the era of "pre-emergence" from which all else emerged.

Raymond Williams' said it beautifully "... this condition of pre-emergence, ... we need to explore the concept of structure of feeling (127.)" And even de Man's "Word" and Benjamin's "aura" all indicate there is a *je ne c'est quoi* at work in art; that is ephemeral. My favorite quote of Williams was this: "One way of putting this is to note that these experiences often may help me to identify what it is I already know but have yet to figure to myself as knowledge."[261]

I love this quote because I believe all of these literary criticism articles are important for just that reason, they give us a language. Remembering that without language we have no culture, we even have no memories; I am reminded of what it was like to come back to film school after being a filmmaker for years. Walter Murch, Coppola's editor said it best, and I paraphrase, "we just intuit where to cut to create a way to deliver what the film is saying." In other words, artists are intuitive, they interpret what the "Universe," for lack of a better word, is saying. They are expressing the agency of Aura, of The Word, of the Feeling; but don't have a language to express it in, well, language; except the language of the aura, the word or the feeling in film, paint, poetry, sculpture, etc. So I believe what came first was emanation and then we struggled to describe it. Films gave me a language to describe what we were all feeling, just like English gave me the words to describe things like alliteration; and it is that emanation of aura through feeling that gives us language. For example, Faye Kesey, Ken's wife said in one of my favorite quotes about Ken: "He was trying to make the whole page move, so it would convey something beyond what the words themselves could say."[262]

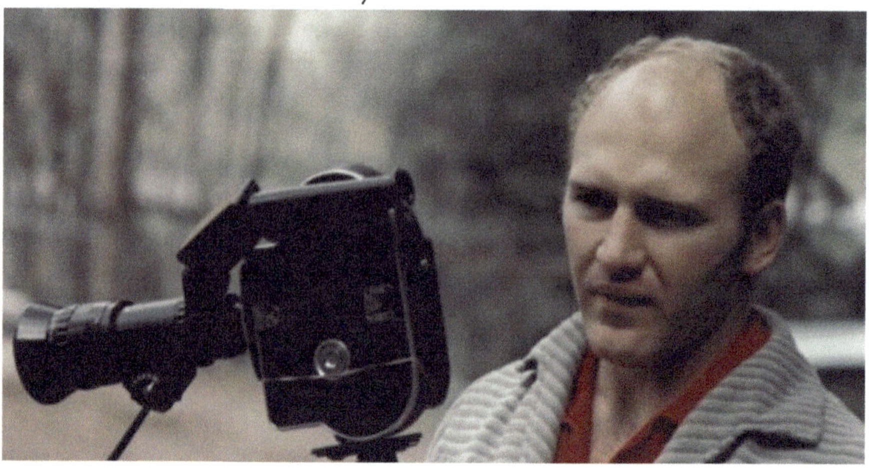

And Kesey said it, too: "...and if I ever get the call to write something else, I will. But the call must come first. I will not write just for the money."[263] And speaking of "the call," the first question I asked my current interviewees is, what called you to the counterculture? Invariably it is the same thing. In an interview with Perry Hyde, a Blues and Rock Promoter from Portland, I asked him what brought him to this line of work. He said that it was clear to him as a child that something was really wrong. To come home from school and to watch your president assassinated on television, then watch someone murder the alleged murderer. "It hit me so hard and so fast... we (our generation) knew that all of it was a lie, and we know that we are still paying to cover it up. Just like the Vietnam war. It started as an accident, but they covered that up, too. And kept killing people. It made me so fucking angry."

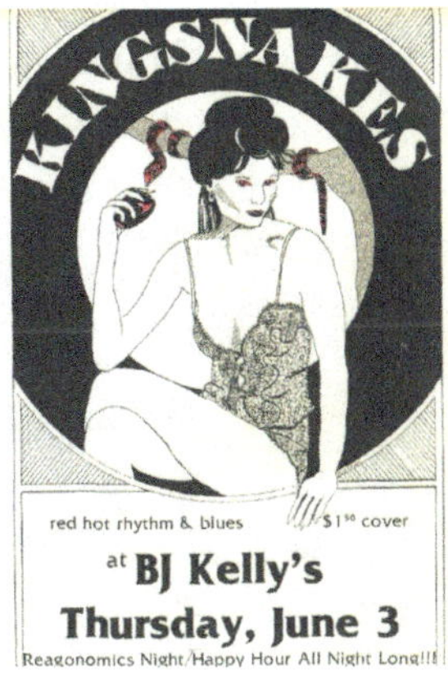

Perry luckily became involved with BJ Kelly's, a wonderful bar and restaurant with music venue as an investor, and booked It's a Beautiful Day in the 70s; and then B.B. King into the new Hult Center for the Performing Arts in the early 80s. He eventually moved to Portland to continue his craft of promoting.[264]

His brother, Tom Hyde, started attending the U of O on the GI Bill in 1970. He went all the way through to getting his Master's in Media Studies and Communication in 1976; and eventually returned to get his Doctorate Degree in 1988. He saw UO Professor Bill Cadbury giving a lecture on a close reading of The Beatles album *Sgt. Pepper's Lonely Heart's Club Band.* "Bill's lecture was at the EMU, as I remember, and his focus was on analyzing the lyrics; at least, that was what caught my attention."[265]

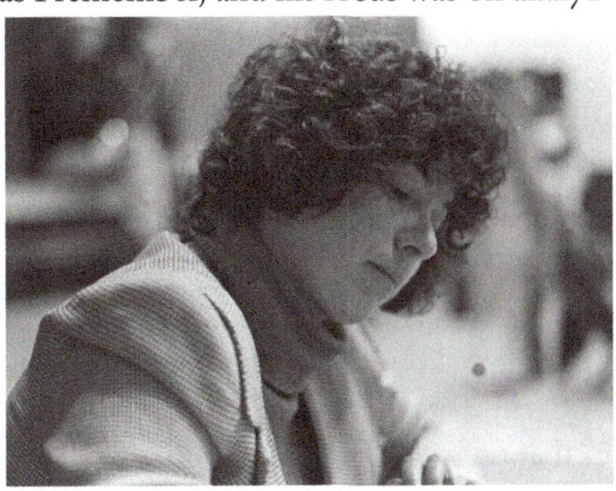

Alice Blanchard at *Animal House* Extras Casting Call. Photo by Gregg Thurlow Weed

While pursuing his degree, he and my friend Alice Blanchard (who would get an Internship on *Animal House* which in turn allowed her into the Director's Guild of America as a 2nd AD) were Graduate Fellows working with Professor Bill Cadbury.

Bill was teaching two film classes, a Monday & Wednesday Class, and a Tuesday & Thursday Class; and screened films for each day's classes. Alice and Tom led the discussions each week, and then continued to show Foreign films on the weekends. It felt like the whole community was showing up, and my friend Lynn Peterson collected small fees from us non-students.

In the meantime, our mutual friend Steve Bove, who was showing films everywhere he could, from 150 Science to the WOW Hall; had successfully navigated the Small Business Administration's paperwork thanks to my husband at the time, Jay Wilson's accounting skills; and according to Dr. Peter Alilunas,[266] (who has a whole binder of research on Cinema 7); we opened our doors on March 18th, 1974. He also had a blueprint of the place, but didn't have any images, so Lynnie and I made him a diorama of it. And gave him the Cinema 7 t-shirt Lynnie made.

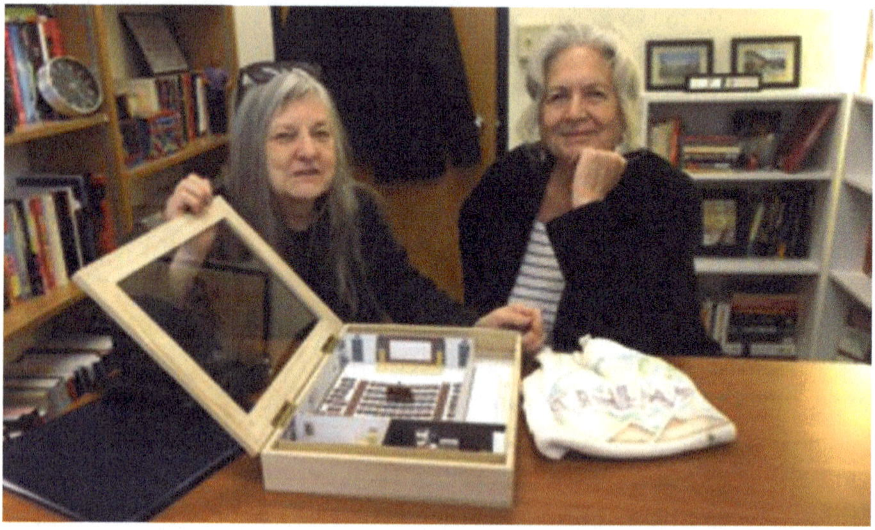

Back then, it was the 70s and I don't remember anything, it seems, except how all of this felt. It felt pre-ordained and I was just along for the ride. Cinema 7 was the 7th Cinema in Eugene- Springfield at the time. I was so grateful to be a part of it. We showed "Art Films" from any country and any era; as long as it was ART. The Venue was in the Atrium Building, a new building because the City was a long way into bulldozing Eugene's Old Victorian Downtown with all the Neon and the wooden balloon-framed buildings. They said they were a fire hazard. But I found out from the Fire Marshall in 2003; that 100-year-old clear fir would petrify in that time, and was not flammable! The truth was, the City Fathers and Mayors were threatened by all the "Hippies" starting businesses in the old Victorians downtown. So they, some say, illegally rezoned the most fertile

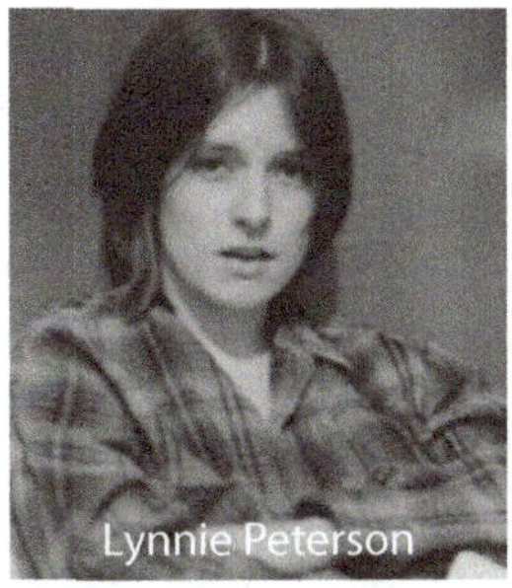
Lynnie Peterson

delta farmland in the county for a shopping mall, so they could bulldoze downtown, shut down the streets to create a Southern California kind of Mall; and built massive concrete post-modernist bomb shelter-like buildings. Cinema 7 was in one of the least obnoxious; The Atrium had growing trees in the lobby with skylights. And we recycled the seats for our venue from the old Heilig Theater.

Lynn Peterson was the Art Director for the interior, and in homage to the great Egyptian Theaters of days gone by, created a wonderful ambiance of the Interior.

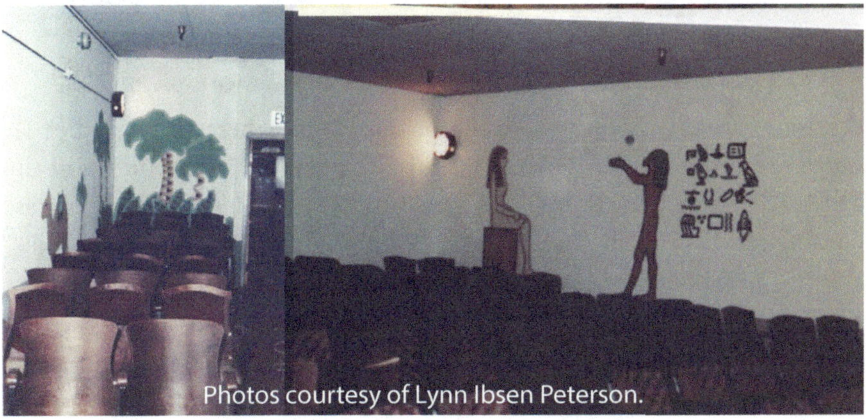
Photos courtesy of Lynn Ibsen Peterson.

And she created all of the World-Famous Posters. Jack Nicholson was on the mailing list, and told us it was one of the finest "Art Houses" in the world. During the filming of *Cuckoo's Nest*, even Academy Award winner Louise Fletcher came down to see a film she was recently in, called *Thieves Like Us*. She was so taken with Cinema 7 "she wanted to party with us afterward."[267]

We only served organic Genesis Apple Juice, popcorn and organic Wha Guru Chews at first. Then due to customer demand, started adding other things, like brownies. I worked four nights a week, Wednesday

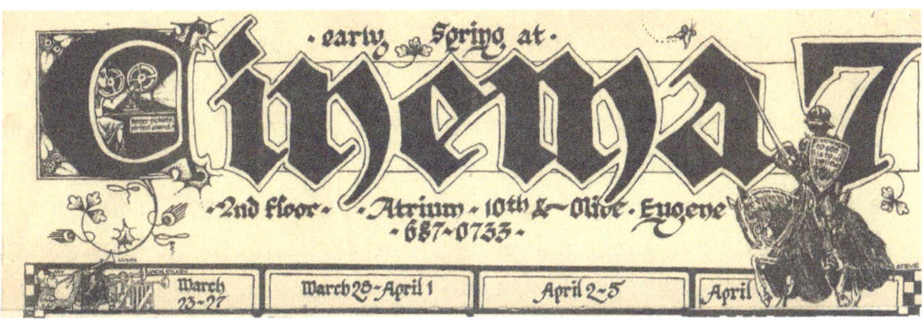

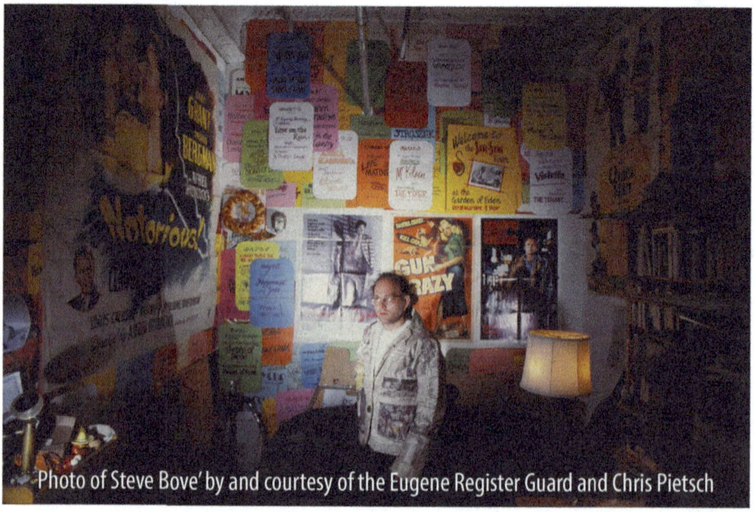

Photo of Steve Bove' by and courtesy of the Eugene Register Guard and Chris Pietsch

through Saturday; which were the prime nights where we would order out from Poppi's Anatolia and would always have a large bottle of the Queen on hand, (Bombay Gin) for visiting "Dignitaries and Filmophiles" coming to kvetch in the back room. The back room was notorious for discussing film, politics, culture, drugs, sex, rock and roll, and even Debussy.

The theater had a nautical-hatch window that could open in the door, so that Steve could monitor the lobby. We could also monitor the theater through the projector windows. Everybody in the back was quiet during the reel changeovers while we held our collective breath, because we were perfectionists. Our motto was "Better images, perfect sound."

Of course it wasn't long until the multiplexes came, to compete with the theaters.

But the worst part was another Art House opened, closer to campus. And we ended up doing what the grand old movie theaters did, we started midnight shows, and when that didn't work, we had to throw caution to the wind and become the first theater to show X-rated films. It is not that X-rated film was some kind of pariah. We showed films that were X- rated and had won Academy Awards, like *Midnight Cowboy*. However, even *Klute* and *Don't Look Now* had some serious sexual mojo going on... but it was the legalities. The defining fine line was "gratuitous sex, with no redeemable social value." And from what I understand, even making these "alternative films" was illegal in Los Angeles County, since 1972, which is why they were making them here in Oregon. We were pushing the envelope, we knew, even making them here. But it was up to a regional theater board to determine the final answer about local theaters, and the district attorney to enforce that and manufacturing adult cinema. So we wrote a letter to the local DA, Pat Horton, and asked him if he would arrest us if we showed *Deep Throat*. We didn't hear from him, so we went ahead and ordered it. But on the night that we had advertised we were first going to show it, we all went to dinner before show time at Leslie's Mandarin Restaurant, and were prepared to go to jail.

We had a normal Cinema 7 billing that Friday night, but as soon as that showing got out, we opened the doors for either the police or the midnight show. Suddenly we saw what seemed like half of Eugene out there, but no cops. There was a line that went down the hall, around the corner, down the stairs and outside the building. I'll never forget the shocking sight of my gynecologist with two girls on his arms buying tickets from me.

But we had to turn most of them away. That night, and the next night, and for the Friday and Saturday night Midnight shows over the following weeks, it was insane. The Cinema was saved. And as the crowds petered out for *Deep Throat*, it started all over again for *Behind the Green* door. In an interview with Cinema 7's Steve Bove', Lloyd Paseman (The Eugene *Register Guard* Film Critic) interviews him for the Register Guard Newspaper in 1981. Steve states he kept Marilyn Chambers (the star of *Behind the Green Door*) around "to help with rising expenses."[249] I never watched them. Except I was exposed to one scene in *Deep Throat* while trying to find someone in the audience who had an emergency at home. And I thought the scene was kind of funny. "Do you mind if I smoke while you eat?" Even as a serious filmmaker, right? But I still had problems with it because of the incest, sexual harassment, and the violent near rape I experienced, creating the creeps because of the male "bearer of meaning." And I hated *Green Door's* opening soundtrack song called "Bubbles," which we could hear in the lobby when people opened the door to get in, because waiting in line had made them late. Mostly because there was absolutely no romance or love tied to the sex act. That was against my religion. The religion of Peace, Love and Understanding. Nor any reciprocal pleasure.

Both of these X-rated films came out in 1972, the year I first started in that industry. But by 1974, it had gone Baroque, just like Dave Getz said about Haight/Ashbury. Here is a great quote from "Snowyb" about all of that on a *Woodstock* Blog by "All That is Interesting";

> I lived in the Haight (Frederick St.) in 65-66 at the height and during the "Summer of Love." Unlike many there, I had a job and laid off drugs for the most part. What I saw was all the "hippie tourists" flocking there not to gain spiritual discovery or an alternative lifestyle, but to get high, laid, and be able to brag back home. By

> 67' like all my friends I'd moved to the woods.... Woodstock, like today's "Burning Man" was just a party, not significant or original except to underline the longings of youth for a lifestyle most can never muster the commitment and hope to gain.[268]

And that is when I decided to quit the "Alternative Cinema" industry, because it wasn't about seduction anymore, it was about kidnapping women and other very patriarchal fantasy kinds of stuff. I wasn't necessarily against it, I believed people should be free to watch what they wanted. But then the perfect "out" for me appeared, a call from Dan Webb, about going to Portland to make a film with some people up there, one of them an Emmy Award winner for "Sign News" in LA. His name was Peter Wechsberg. His mother was a Ballerina in the Royal Ballet Company, whose plane was bombed leaving Berlin after a Recital. The explosion was so loud that Peter was born deaf as a result, but it never stopped him. After winning his Emmy, he recruited old friends from Gallaudet University to help him make a film.[269] They hired me, because like Peter, I was an underground filmmak-

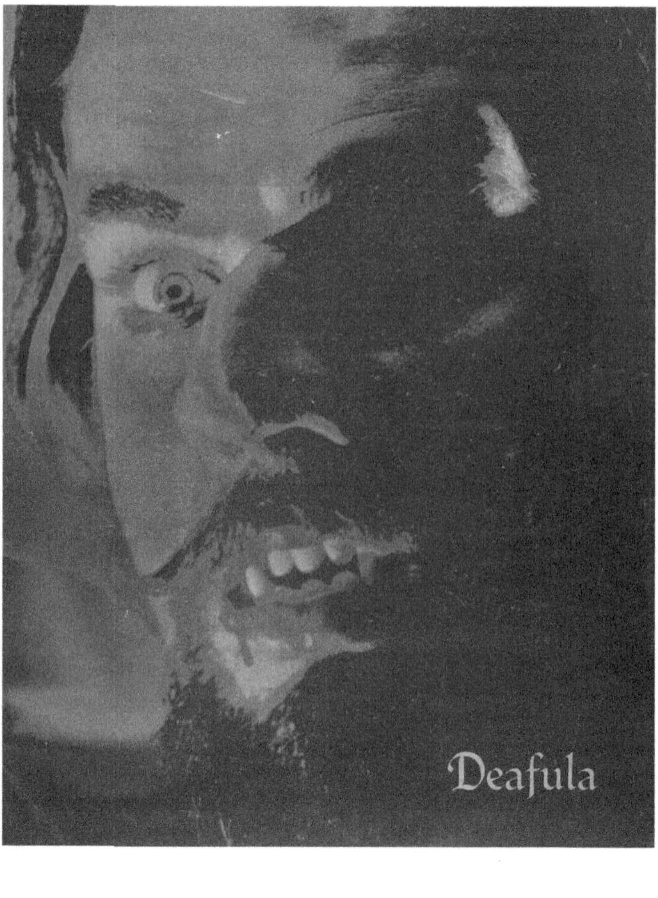

er, who had learned nearly every craft required to make a film. I did some acting, set design, location scouting as well as Make-up and Hair, which took me nearly 3 hours to transform Peter's normally blonde/blue-eyes into dark Count Dracula and his son *Deafula*.[270]

It was the first film ever made for the deaf. We shot it in Portland with J. Wilder Mincey, a fairly good cinematographer. And with some of Will Vinton's film crew. They later helped me get work as a Set Designer in Portland; so much so, that I was a commuter catching the Amtrak Train to Portland only blocks from my house. My favorite part about *Deafula* was learning sign language. Nearly the whole cast was Deaf, and so was my character, Deafula's Mom, who was married to a Minister, but has an affair with Count Dracula, and becomes pregnant with Deafula as a result. Once again, a woman was the Villain in the Drama. Like Eve, she fell for a Snake. This one offered a huge diamond ring, however. What is a girl going to do? She becomes grateful to have at least some interesting costumes to wear. And man, did we have incredible locations as well. They put me in charge of set decoration for one of them. The others were, like most of the independent 70s films, shot in people's houses that were already decorated by the owners.

One of these locations was the Pittock Mansion out West Burnside Blvd. in Portland, and it was already decorated incredibly well as a "period" Victorian. The other was a cabin, I think on the way to Mt. Hood. But there was one location that I wanted to personally interpret with set design. It is where Count Dracula's Coffin is, and where *Deafula*, now as an adult, goes to kill him. There he finds me, now an ancient Hag; his mother, the woman that allegedly had died giving birth to him; but she is among the undead, now, in the cave. The cave was near Grants Pass, Oregon; and was part of the Oregon Cave National Monument. As we set up the HMI lights, the bats were crazed by the activity and the hot lamps of the lights. I knew that normally they wouldn't bite if they didn't get entangled in your hair. I was so glad I had a hooded cape to wear.

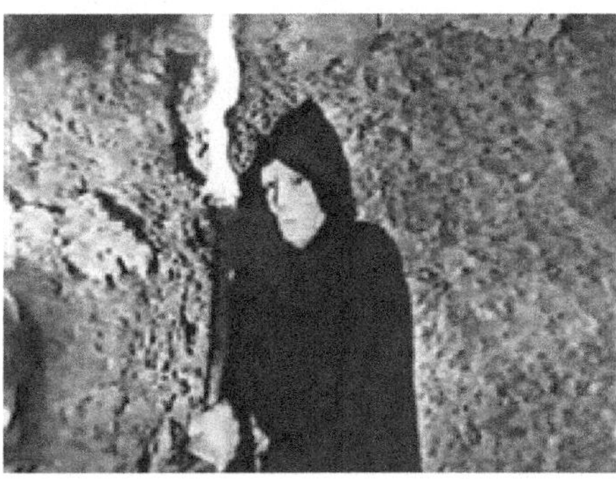
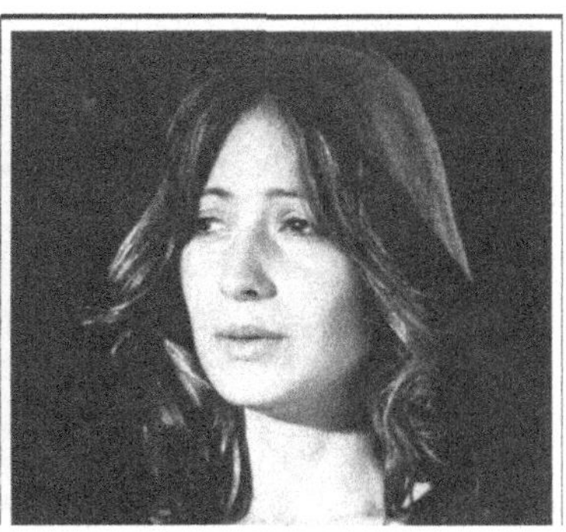

As for the set, I loved the cave as it was, and didn't want to take away from it. So, I very simply added two 4 ft. tall Victorian Candelabras on each side of the coffin.

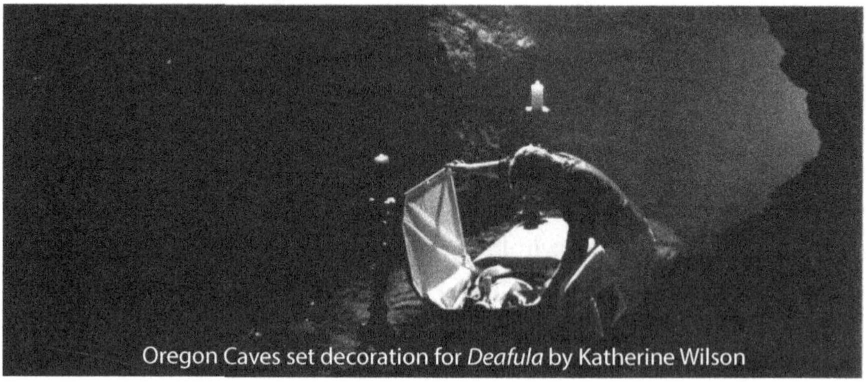

Oregon Caves set decoration for *Deafula* by Katherine Wilson

When we were being interviewed by the *Oregon Journal* newspaper a few days earlier in Portland, I was on the phone with mortuaries trying *to rent* a coffin for that scene. The reporter overheard me and found that hilarious.

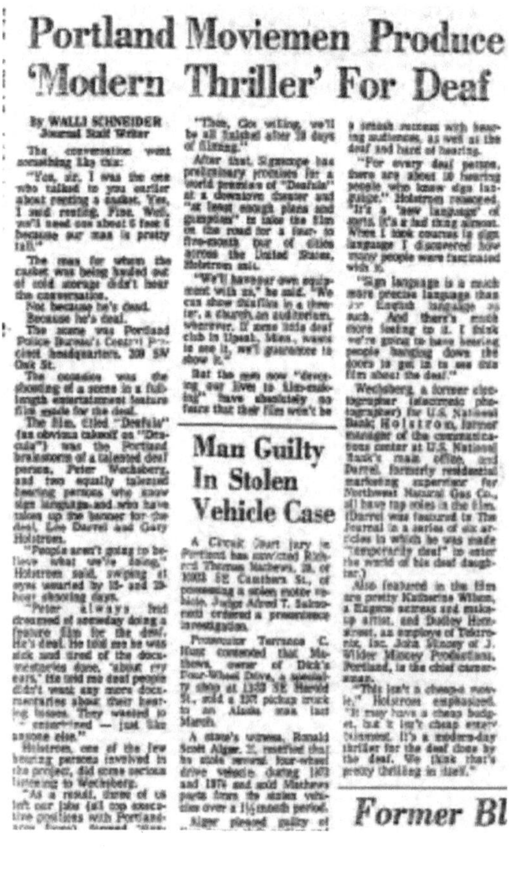

Portland Moviemen Produce 'Modern Thriller' For Deaf

By WALLI SCHNEIDER
Journal Staff Writer

Man Guilty In Stolen Vehicle Case

Former Bl

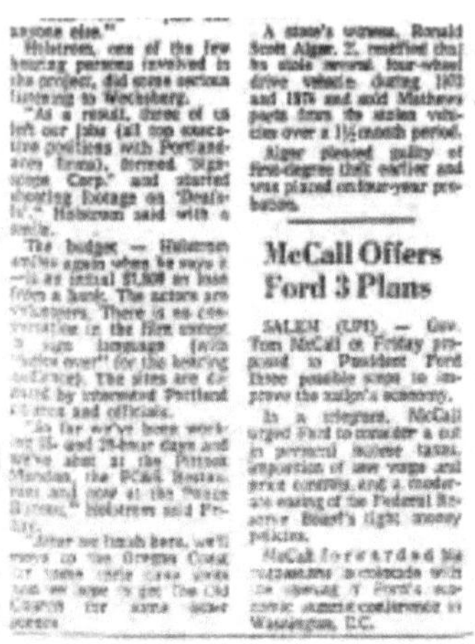

McCall Offers Ford 3 Plans

Oregon Journal, Portland, Oregon 1974.

It was the first time I had ended up in the newspapers related to films. I felt like I had finally arrived. And the coffin was perfect. And so was their hair and make-up.

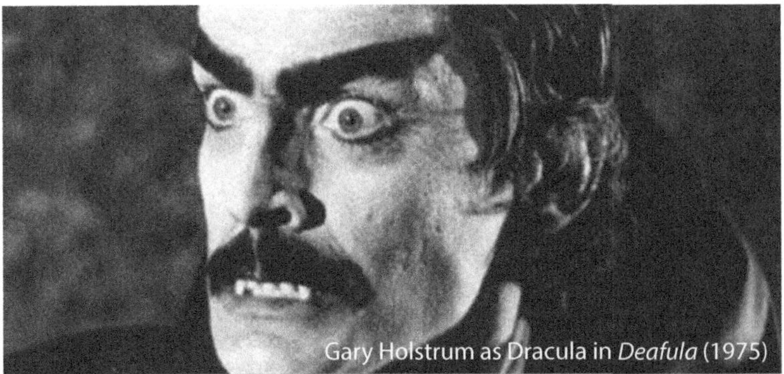

Gary Holstrum as Dracula in *Deafula* (1975)

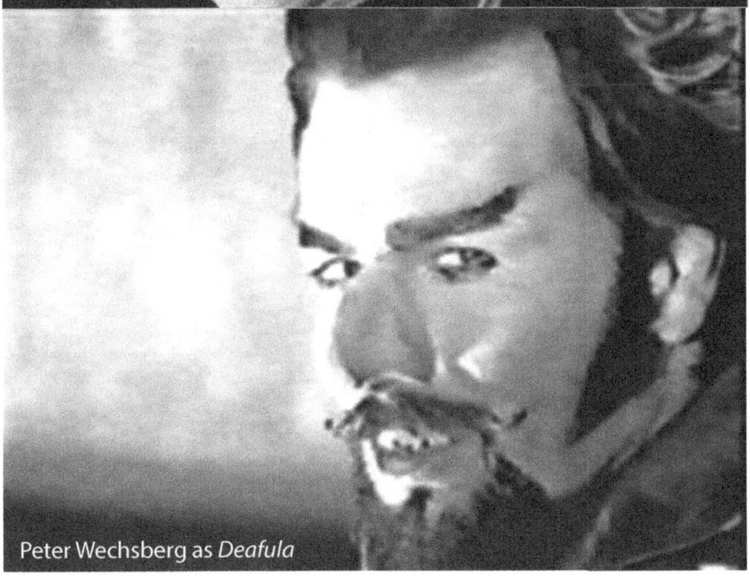

Peter Wechsberg as *Deafula*

It ended up having a Cult following, and one of the fans created these memes of me:[271]

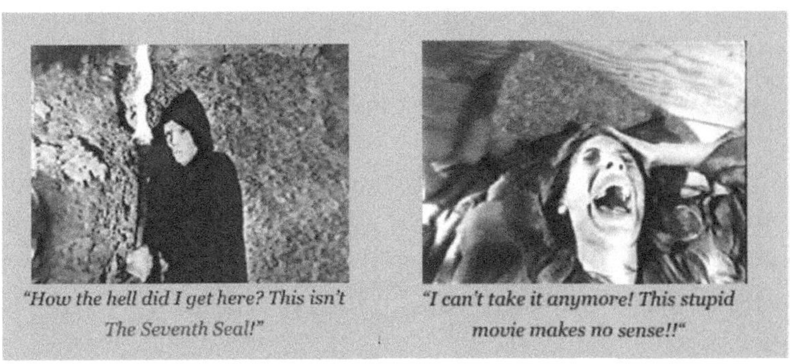

"How the hell did I get here? This isn't The Seventh Seal!"

"I can't take it anymore! This stupid movie makes no sense!!"

But it was the very first movie for the deaf, and the first film I actually got a call sheet on.

CALL sheet

PRODUCTION #______ DATE ______________

TITLE DEAFULA

DIRECTOR ______________

SHOOTING CALL: FRIDAY 1 PM SEPT 27th

RAIN OR SHINE / WEATHER PERMITTING

cast - bits - talent	in makeup	in wardrobe	on set	set - location - scene
Inspector	12:30	12:45	1:00	222 S.W. PINE
Assistant	12:30	12:45	1:00	PORTLAND ORE
				Portland Police Bureau
				Scene 22

CREW CALL

cameraman		operators	
asst. cameraman		asst. cameraman	
sound mixer		recorder	
grips		stage men	
makeup men	1 pm	cable men	
wardrobe		pa operator	
property men		camera effects	
green men		special effects	
electrical operators		laborers	
stillman		police/firemen	

day	date	description of set	actor	set#	location	d/n
		Police office	Lee Hadley	Scene 22		d

Deafula Callsheet, September 24th, 1974.

The Premiere was amazing, too, in late January 1975. But I was praying, to what I've come to believe is something deep inside me, to help me *create* a living wage film industry for myself and my friends and especially for my beloved Oregon; and I was answered with a very synchronous event. A call from the Oregon film commissioner Warren Merrill: "Would you please bring someone to the set of *One Flew Over the Cuckoo's Nest* for me?"

At first I said no, because I heard things weren't going well on set as far as Kesey was concerned; but then I consulted the *I Ching*, and it essentially said: The Creator is always giving, but you need to be gracious enough to receive the gifts. You need to be receptive. And so I said Yes.

> I Ching Hexagram #2 *The Receptive*: Only because nature in its myriad forms corresponds with the myriad impulses of the Creative can it make these impulses real. Nature's richness lies in its power to nourish all living things; its greatness lies in its power to give them beauty and splendor. Thus it prospers all that lives. It is the Creative that begets things, but they are brought to birth by the Receptive.[272]

$$\begin{aligned}\mathcal{L}_{\mathrm{Y}} = &-\lambda_u^{ij}\frac{\phi^0 - i\phi^3}{\sqrt{2}}\bar{u}_{\mathrm{L}}^i u_{\mathrm{R}}^j + \lambda_u^{ij}\frac{\phi^1 - i\phi^2}{\sqrt{2}}\bar{d}_{\mathrm{L}}^i u_{\mathrm{R}}^j \\ &-\lambda_d^{ij}\frac{\phi^0 + i\phi^3}{\sqrt{2}}\bar{d}_{\mathrm{L}}^i d_{\mathrm{R}}^j - \lambda_d^{ij}\frac{\phi^1 + i\phi^2}{\sqrt{2}}\bar{u}_{\mathrm{L}}^i d_{\mathrm{R}}^j \\ &-\lambda_e^{ij}\frac{\phi^0 + i\phi^3}{\sqrt{2}}\bar{e}_{\mathrm{L}}^i e_{\mathrm{R}}^j - \lambda_e^{ij}\frac{\phi^1 + i\phi^2}{\sqrt{2}}\bar{\nu}_{\mathrm{L}}^i e_{\mathrm{R}}^j + \mathrm{h.c.}\,,\end{aligned}$$

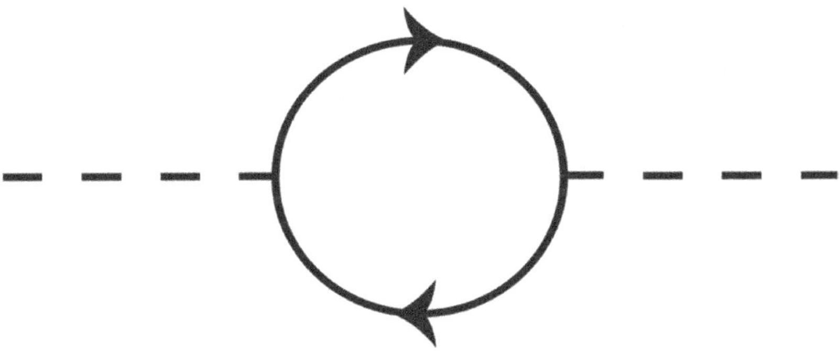

The God Factor: Quantum Mechanics' Higgs-Boson. Wikipedia.
Originally uploaded by JabberWok

> So likewise it is right that the substance which is to be fitted to receive frequently over its whole extent the copies of all things intelligible and eternal should itself, of its own nature, be void of all the forms. Wherefore, let us not speak of her that is the Mother and Receptacle of this generated world, which is perceptible by sight and all the senses, by the name of *earth or air or fire or water,* or any aggregates or constituents thereof: rather, if we describe her as a Kind invisible and unshaped,all-receptive, and in some most perplexing and most baffling way partaking of the intelligible, we shall describe her truly.[273]

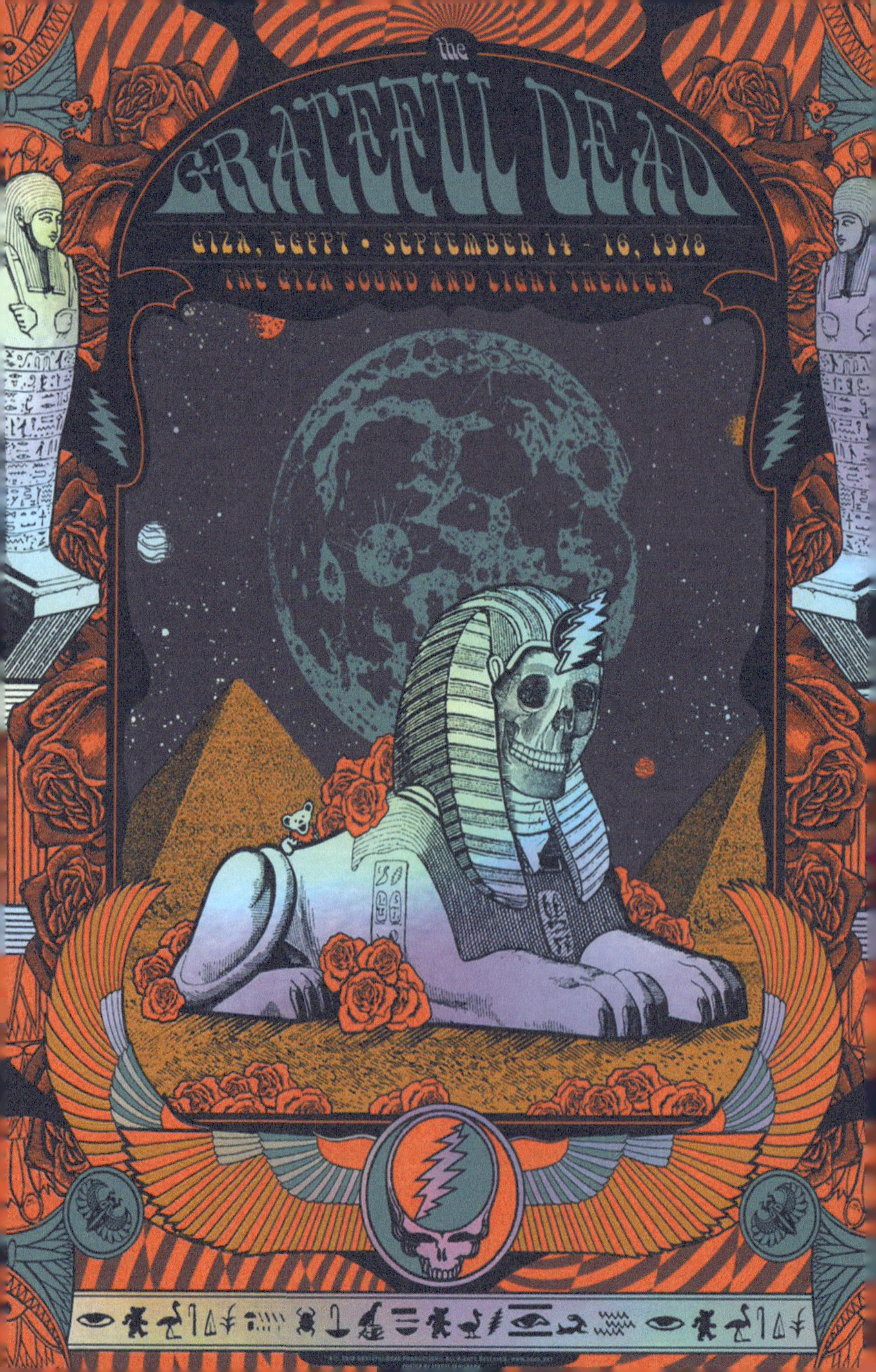
the
GRATEFUL DEAD
GIZA, EGYPT • SEPTEMBER 14 - 16, 1978
THE GIZA SOUND AND LIGHT THEATER

Chapter 10

Downward Causation of the Word ~ 1975

> Kesey further explained to Burt Wolfe his decision to quit writing novels. "Well, like take McMurphy. He was just there, like antimatter. I didn't have to create him; the patients built him for me. But the Indian was different. I don't own the soul of that Indian. He just appeared while I was on peyote, and the first chapter of that book was written by him. So, that makes me wonder am I as talented as I might think or as others think? Or am I an instrument picked to make a statement, and after the statement is made, should I assume I've got the right to make endless statements?... See, I know now that the Indian in *Cuckoo* was not my Indian. *He was brought into being by some higher power* to tell America where it's at.
>
> – Rick Dodgson *It's All a Kind of Magic: The Young Ken Kesey*

Kesey's quote seems to allude to a critical literary theory that I recently wrote about for Professor Pyle's class at the U of O: "we can see how the 'agency of language' is something other than an 'instrument of an author's intentions or expressions' when it is not a relationship between it and it, and not temporal, but eternal, like when the poet creates *Odes to a Grecian Urn* or *The West Wind*; and personifies in them "Thou"-like qualities, when the I-it 'contains the potential of becoming I-Thou,' and according to Buber, it is 'the situation in which man's true personality emerges within the context of his world.'"[274]

And not only that, but truly is "(...) the only I-Thou situation that man can sustain indefinitely." This is the goal, according to Roland Barthes: "We know that in order to restore writing to its future, we must reverse the Myth; the birth of the reader must be requited, by the death of the author."[275]

Furthermore, in the Chapter called "Return to Philology" from *Theory and History of Literature*, Volume 33 by Paul de Man, I found a quote that, as I told my professor, Kesey would also say was very psychedelic: "Close reading ... cannot fail to respond to structures of language(,) which it is the more or less secret aim of literary teaching to keep hidden."[276]

It was thrilling, and indeed hinted at what Emile Benveniste has written, that "...the creative power of language, which establishes an imaginary reality, animates inert things, reveals what does not yet exist, and recalls to the present what has disappeared."[277]

This is all a very Quantum kind of language.

I know how to create structure for screenplays like 1st act, 2nd act, and 3rd act turning points. I know how to structure scenes within the three acts, so a reader doesn't burst out laughing at the worst possible place because the high tension was kept up too long without a "down" scene. Therefore, I am trusting that the structures of language are like the structures of a screenplay, and in essence are like a blueprint that *shows how the sentence would work in a 3-dimensional way* through images. The first six words in de Man 's quoted sentence tells us that "*close reading cannot fail to respond.*"[278] This indicates that the properties of close reading have magical properties of responding to our efforts, much like what Benveniste tells us in *Problems of General Linguistics*: "...the creative power of language, which establishes an imaginary reality, animates inert things, reveals what does not yet exist, and recalls to the present what has disappeared."[279] In the former sentence, "close reading" does all three: by "establishing an imaginary reality" of words responding to us, because they "animate(s) an inert thing" such as letters on a page; and "reveals what does not exist" which is the hidden layer of meaning.

And speaking of a hidden layer of meaning, "which it is the more or less secret aim of literary teaching to keep hidden;" for me, this brings to mind an allegory of the Professor as High Priest; as in that one has to go through them, an intermediary, like some have to do with the Priests in the churches, to talk to God. The use of the "more or less" is similar in scope to different branches of organized religion, some are "more" adamant about keeping to the hierarchical structure, demanding sometimes that one prays to the Mother Mary to then intercede in talking to Jesus, who then talks to God for us; while others are "less" in that they allow one to talk straight to God.

But now, with the High Priests of Literature allowing us to go straight to "The Word," the "death of the author;" truly allows us to commune with the "higher power" that Kesey alludes to. The Creator is who I always have talked to, and avoided the middleman.

Like Spinoza, the Pastoral Pagan believes that they, the rocks, the trees and the earth and all other living things *are* God; and find it silly to go through intermediaries, in giving that very important task to the human symbolic representatives of God, especially since they are human just like we are, and therefore fallible. The "secret aim" of course, is easy to understand, if one follows the money. Churches, Popes and Priests are venerated with huge cash flows for their intersessions. And that brings me to another incredible understanding of the statement by de Man, and that has confirmed my deepest hopes about being a writer, and that definition is regarding someone or something, who can make a living from channeling the symbols and meter, the *un-words* pressing for expression during high moments of inspiration or sorrow, to reveal the words of the Universe that pre-existed before humans, time and space, and in a quantum mechanics sort of way, created downward causation of the word into matter. But the most important words of all, relating to Kesey's quote about a "Higher Power" writing the book, are these: "recalls to the present what has dis-

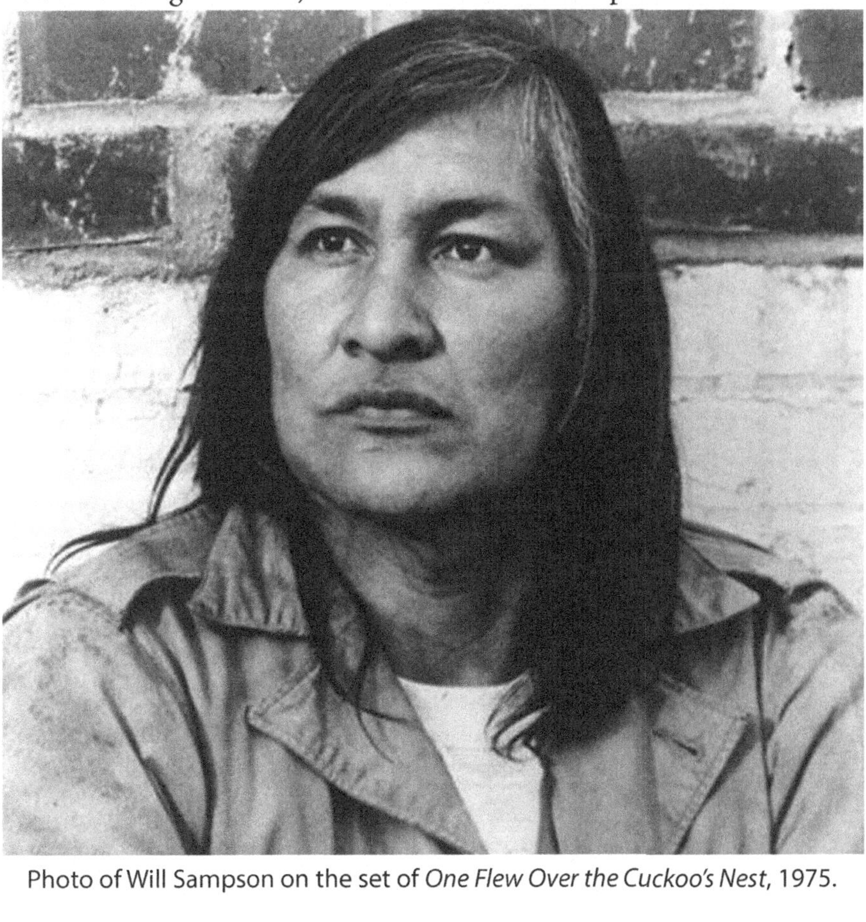

Photo of Will Sampson on the set of *One Flew Over the Cuckoo's Nest*, 1975.

appeared."[280] Which is right out of Leslie Fiedler's *Return of the Vanishing American.*[281] Because in essence, what Kesey did, when he created The New Western, was he animated the "Cigar Store Indian" and made the Noble Savage *human, by giving him a voice,* albeit a bicultural voice, a voice that created stories out of constellations, symbols out of stars, pictographs out of life. Most people don't remember that Will Sampson's character in Kesey's book was a mixed race, white and Native, like so many people. And that we bicultural, mixed races *suffer* from navigating between the two or more cultures in our own minds, hearts and bodies.

When I met Will on the set, during the basketball scene, he gravitated toward me alone on a bench. We didn't need to talk, all he said was 'nice bracelet." We were skin – we were kin. We resonated on the same frequency and didn't need words. Susan Sontag calls it a "proto-futurist aesthetic of the extreme" in American Lit:

> Eighty years after its publication, Susan Sontag described D.H. Lawrence's *Studies in Classic American Literature* as "the most interesting book ever written about American culture (n. pag)…. Indeed, Lawrence identifies in the American classics a proto-Futurist aesthetic of the extreme: "The furthest frenzies of French modernism or futurism have not yet reached the pitch of extreme consciousness that Poe, Melville, Hawthorne, Whitman reached. The European moderns are all trying to be extreme. The great Americans I mention just were it."[282]

I know that Ken was a huge fan of *Moby Dick,* and we both loved Whitman's *Leaves of Grass.* If I was able to, I would try to trace the influences of what Lawrence called "ancient cosmic theories" in their work. However, Kesey's love of Keats and Yeats, I can ascribe to his Irish heritage, too; but more importantly to his biculturality found within *The Return of the Vanishing American* by Fiedler. Because as Lawrence says, a biculturality of Irish and Native American are all about "science and religion" being in "accord."

"But what Lawrence called his new science should be understood as an attempt to approximate those 'ancient cosmic theories' in which 'science and religion were in accord,' and thereby to reconcile belief systems or kinds of knowledge which modernity judges to be antithetical.[283] In this regard, the first version of Studies is akin to W.B. Yeats's *A Vision* (1925; 1937), which also purports to be a new science, albeit one in which, as Kathleen Raine explains, "not matter but mind-consciousness-is the ground of reality as we experience it."[284]

So, this brings us full circle to Chapter One, again, but on a higher level, like a spiral; because once you rail against the "intellect/ego" to deflate itself, you can get both intellect and heart in balance.

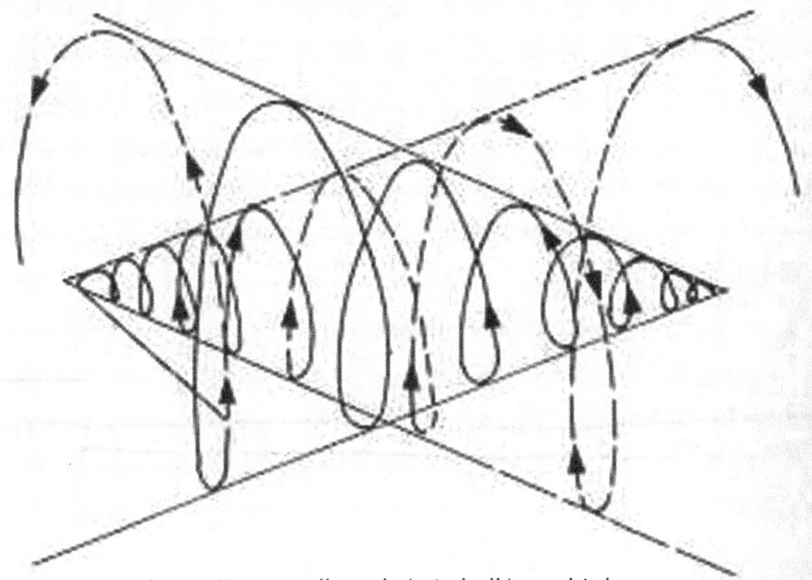

https://www3.dbu.edu/mitchell/yeatshis.htm

However, I digress. Kesey was a World Class author, yes. He was a Pioneer of archaic drug-induced consciousness, as out-pictured with the decolonized Indian in *One Flew Over the Cuckoo's Nest.* But Ken always wanted to be a filmmaker, first, last and always. And because of his living his dream, I got to be one, too. And I was also the one who got to be there, on the set, almost against my will; because I was aware that he wasn't happy with the production, and like my fellow Taurus' Mountain Girl and Jack Nicholson, I was extremely loyal. Especially to Ken. But the Universe conspired against me, when someone I owed a favor to begged me to step in and go to the set. It was the Oregon film commissioner, and it turns out it was to replace him, to actually replace the Oregon Film Commissioner. In the end, I was also Ken's eyes and ears there, especially when it came to Producer Michael Douglas. Because by the end of the filming, and for the next two years, including Ken's lawsuit against him, I was very close to Michael.

And that was how I was appointed by Governor Bob Straub to the set of the film adaptation of *One Flew Over the Cuckoo's Nest* in 1975. I had made friends there while lobbying his office and the legislature for the Indigenous Film Crew of Oregon, because we crewmembers, who were working for Bob Gilbert in Eugene, and for Will Vinton in Portland; were really getting good, and we didn't want to see the movie jobs go to people from out of state, if possible. This appointment was before I knew anything about the film really, except what Kesey had said about it. And I knew he was quoting the *I Ching* when interviewed about it back then. He said that Book Publishers and now the Film Producers were like "Pump Salesmen" and he was "The Well." The Well is Hexagram #48. I knew he wasn't happy with them, because they didn't use his screenplay, told through The Indian's Grandmother, I think; nor their casting choices, as he wanted Kirk Douglas to play McMurphy; and had left the pre-production after about 2 weeks in, about the end of January.

But Kesey was Bicultural, and so was I. I understood exactly how he felt. The way of collaboration, of "Barn Raising"; of everyone working together to create something is often usurped by linear capitalistic bottom lines. And the integrity of the project is compromised by profit. We just don't get that. But even more integral in this situation is the dilemma of the bicultural, and that is the "third language" we have to create to bridge the two cultures in our own minds. And that I think, is why he was so metaphorical. Sometimes I think the "agency of language" intercedes and we don't even know what it is we are saying. And

Cuckoo's Nest Premeire for Inmates, Dec 7, 1975, Aurore Duvedant and Milos Forman

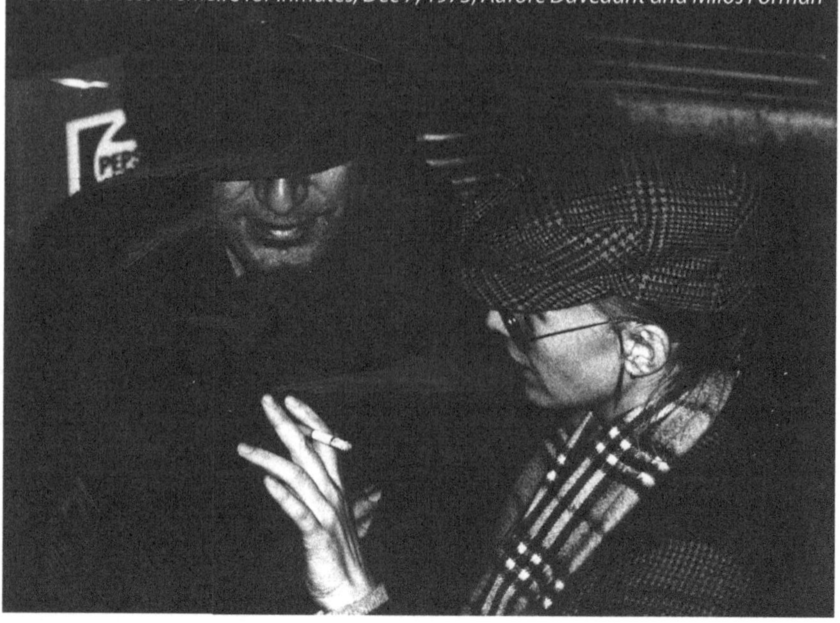

it takes the "death of the author" and a "miracle artist"; a Czechoslovakian Subterfuge Cinematic Poet like Director Milos Forman to unpack it. From outside of our own culture. Because of the Russian Occupation of the Czech Republic, Forman developed a "Marranism"[267] – the 3rd Voice of Biculturalism. So, Forman's visual metaphors, like the bright antiseptic operating room-like white sets, where germs and other living things could never survive, including humanity, reigned; the omniscient camera angles where the Big Nurse had ordered McMurphy "murdered" into a vegetative state; where The Big Nurse's low voice and rational speeches give you the creeps, representing the absolute void of femininity; where no sign of sexuality or passion appears even when McMurphy is throttling her, intent on killing her. And especially this image, where through the window, she makes it clear that her patients are never really heard:

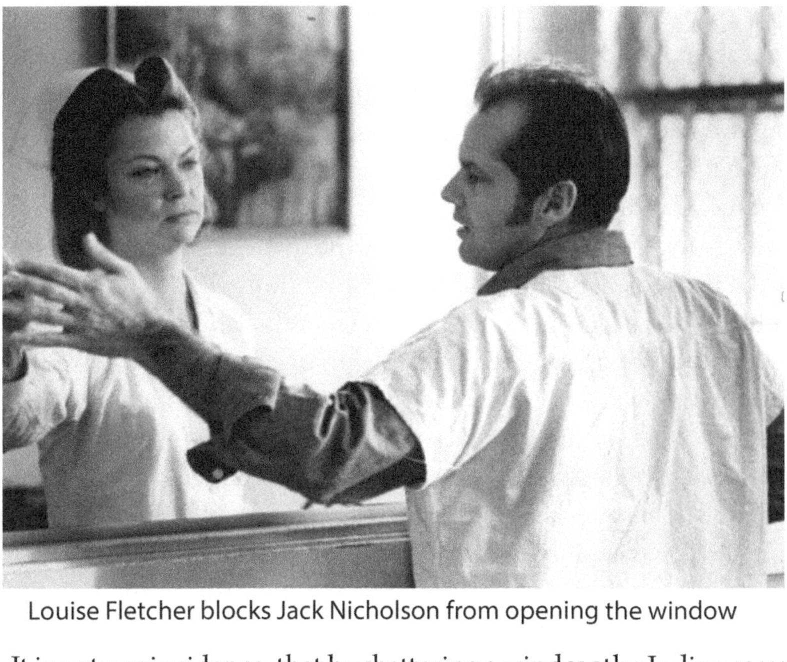

Louise Fletcher blocks Jack Nicholson from opening the window

It is not a coincidence, that by shattering a window the Indian escapes. And it is not a coincidence that windows represented vision but not really sound, especially around this "Machine" of a woman; reminiscent of the automaton women, like Maria in Fritz Lang's *Metropolis* and Olimpia in Hoffman's *The Sandman*.[285]

I was there for all of these scenes. Not only that, this movie is so important to me that I wrote 5 Chapters about it in Volume I of *Echoes from the Set (1967-2017)*. For that book I also wrote that Ken Kesey's champion as an undergrad was literary critic Leslie Fiedler, who fought hard for him to get the Woodrow Wilson Fellowship to Stanford.

Fiedler's book is fully titled *The Return of the Vanishing American*. In it he discusses John Barthes *Sot-Weed Factor*, where, if I remember right, he learns about the hallucinogenic effects of Sot-weed (as in besotted) the original American Indian high-powered tobacco. Also known as what is put into the "Peace Pipe." The designated carriers of Pipes in a tribe know they have to be very strong to carry those pipes. I had a friend who had to give one back, because she didn't feel that she was strong enough to "carry" it, and to deal with its power. I had the same thing happen to me, when a 3000-year-old artifact was given to me by a 108- year-old Mexican Curandera. And Ed Edmo, my Shoshone Bannock friend, also a friend of Kesey's, said that the North American Church's Peyote Ceremonies require many things, including that there has "not been anger in the last 5 days of its participants"[286] and requires a special ceremony before imbibing in the archaic drug.

So when Kesey said that "The Indian wrote the first Chapter of the book," we know what that really means. It is an intense journey. And we know that archaic drugs access the past *and* the future. Because Life is a circle, and a Medicine Wheel. The Prophet says the Creator moistens with his own tears, our medicine. What was the medicine that Kesey brought through his book? Through the Indian? And through the window? In Kesey's book, The Indian is bicultural. (So was Will Sampson.) He is a mixed blood, whom we assumed was deaf, and/or dumb. "...it wasn't me that started acting deaf; it was people that first started acting like I was too dumb to hear or see or say anything at all."[287]

Bromden metaphorically represents the wooden and silent Cigar Store Indian. For me, he also represents the speaker of this metaphorical 3rd language created by Biculturalism. The broom he holds in both his hands anchors him to the ground, while his mind thinks about the Combine. The Combine is a machine whose name "derives from its combining three separate harvesting operations – reaping, threshing, and winnowing – into a single process."[288] The Combine is also a machine that killed Celilo Falls, when it was dammed in 1957 to create hydro-electric power. The turbine engines also had three separate functions: to generate power for electricity, to regulate water levels in case of floods, and to shoot Salmon smelt 600 miles an hour up-river. I can't imagine why they don't think that has something to do with the declining fish count of the whole upper Columbia River Tributary system.

This event was devastating to all of the Columbia Plateau Tribes, who shared Celilo and celebrated there in ceremony all of the Natives fishing traditions for as long as time was old. It could drive an Indian mad to lose this resource in addition to having his land stolen, his people dead from genocide, not to mention his language, and all of his other traditions.

Ed Edmo witnessed the flooding of Celilo Falls, March 10, 1957. This is what he says about it: "How can something so beautiful, so big be taken away? It hurt my heart hard. The thunder of the falls is still in my heart!"[289] Kesey claimed to have once seen a really tall Indian protesting at Celilo, which is a stone's throw from the I-84 E. Freeway to Pendleton. Another time he may have heard of one who put a knife in his teeth and ran screaming into a speeding Log Truck. I know he admired them. What we didn't know was that he could have been one of them. Nor did I know

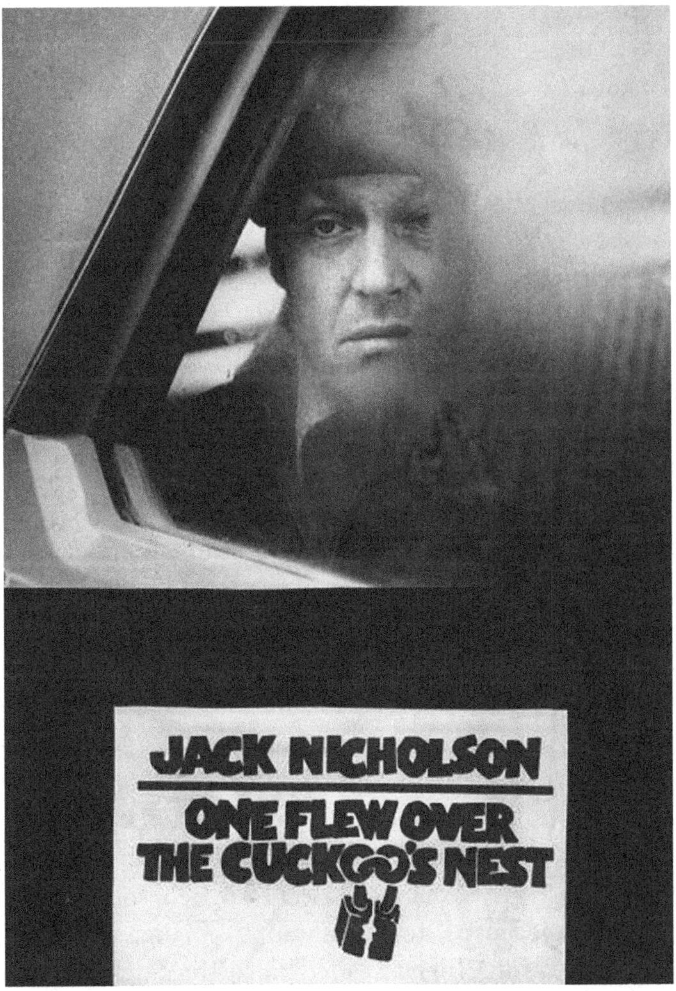

about my heritage at the time. But we spoke the same language. We were comfortable with each other. We understood each other. Bromden was both of us. Bromden is also all biculturals. And Bromden was released from his silence when McMurphy stood up to the Big Nurse, and then the Combine had a monkey wrench thrown into it. McMurphy also treated The Chief just like one of the guys. He wasn't literally put on a pedestal as a Noble or Wooden Indian. He was part of the basketball game, and even more importantly, was heard by McMurphy. For me, *Cuckoo's Nest* released the American Indian from its' stereotype, and opened the door for equality with the freedom to simply be human beings; when its Bromden character, not McMurphy, smashes the window and escapes into the night. It is Bromden who solves the problem of racism in the community, but not with a gun. But by breaking the window that kept people, framed in Stereotypes that creates a barrier from hearing each other, and stuck in seeing just the differences. McMurphy asks us to do the same, so that we can be free, too.

My first day on set was February 11th, 1975. Preproduction was over and filming had begun. The scene was the Electro-shock therapy scene. I was shown a metal chair that was just like all of the ones lining the wall of an ante room, that led into the electro-shock room. Brilliant white and sterile. Jack is wheeled into the other room on a Gurney. Then he is wheeled out, without his shoes on. "Continuity"[273] reminds him to put his shoes back on before the next take. As he does so, he decides to sit a chair closer to me than the one he initially was going to sit in. But it is still across the small room. The crew chuckles. He is wheeled back in, for his take, and is wheeled back out, 10 or 15 times. Each time he sits one chair closer to me to put his shoes back on. Finally he is 2 chairs away from me and the crew is howling. If he was trying to unnerve me, it was working. But the next time he was gurney-ed out, Michael Douglas sent his brother Joel to ask me to cocktails after wrap. I was so relieved to have somewhere to go, away from Jack's up and down arching eyebrows, I said yes. When Jack returned, he sat next to me and asked me if I would like to go to dinner. I said no, but that I had a present for him, and could we go to his trailer, knowing that wrap would take a while. That is when he told me about the Film Commissioner accusing him of smoking pot on the set, and why Warren was 86'ed by the Producers. He had responded, he said, with: "What? Are you nuts?" And I laughed, and said that is what I would have said, because who would want to get high in a place like this 100-year-old looney bin? Then I handed him a Thai Stick. But before I left

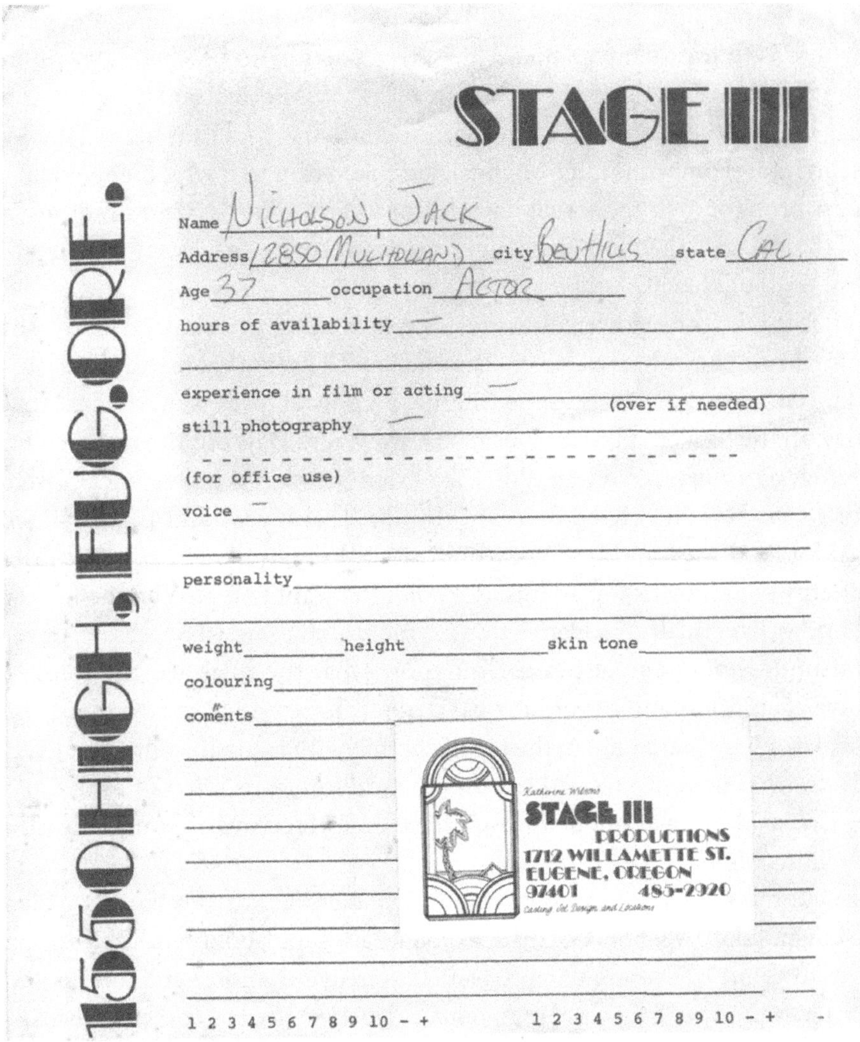

STAGE III

1550 HIGH, EUG. ORE.

Name Nicholson, Jack

Address 12850 Mulholland city Bev Hills state Cal

Age 37 occupation Actor

hours of availability —

experience in film or acting — (over if needed)

still photography —

(for office use)

voice —

personality

weight height skin tone

colouring

comments

STAGE III PRODUCTIONS
1712 WILLAMETTE ST.
EUGENE, OREGON
97401 485-2920

1 2 3 4 5 6 7 8 9 10 - + 1 2 3 4 5 6 7 8 9 10 - +

I had him fill out one of my Casting Files. And tonight, as I was writing this, I just realized he corrected my spelling of "comments." After 45 years of having this file, I just now noticed. Now, Jack has had the last laugh on me; we had many, including on set, at his parties, and when I stayed at his house over the next 7-8 years, until I got sober and had kids. And even now, we still laugh, but on the phone.

February 26th, 1975. The day we filmed the Basketball Scene was the day I got to meet Will Sampson. We were outside and it was a pretty great day, weather wise, for Oregon. I had heard several stories about how they found Will Sampson. No doubt by the Car Salesman who sold cars to the Indians back then. I had already heard stories about similar Reservation car salesmen in Chiloquin. And I also heard they had to helicopter in to where Will was being a "hoe-dad," a tree planter; somewhere way up in the North woods to notify him of an audition. Another said he was at the car lot and the Car Salesman called Michael and told him he had finally seen him, six months after Michael had asked him to start looking. Whatever brought Will there that day was a modern miracle. It was indicative of the "Magic" that happened when anything to do with Kesey happened. We all could feel it.

I think Ken's powerful experience in writing the character brought him from the other world to the dance. That synchronistic dance we danced back then. During the filming, I know all eyes were on Jack that day on the basketball court, because it was Press Day. But the person who came to sit next to me was Will. Like I said before, I was wearing a Native Bracelet. He said, "Nice Bracelet." I said, 'Thank you." but that is all we said. Like Kesey and me. We would sit and say nothing, because of the energy engulfing us was so intense, we didn't want to break the spell. Now I know that it really is a Native thing, a bicultural thing. You feel safe, never misunderstood, and at peace. You know what the rules are, the rules to love each other and never hurt each other. Kesey once said to me, as he took my hand, and held it; during a meeting with a possible film financier: "I know you would never hurt me in a million years," he said, But what wasn't said, yet was implied was, "I have to protect myself from these other kinds of people."

In the documentary, *The Life and Times of the Red Dog Saloon*; Milan Melvin, (aka Sweet Sir Galahad, as Joan Baez sang about him) had a great quote about *US*: (and I paraphrase) "... there were whores and thieves and outlaws ... you know, people you can trust."[290] That is the kind of trust Kesey portrayed in *Cuckoo's Nest*. It is the kind that the inmates had for McMurphy; even when he charged each of them more for renting the boat than it cost, as the Big Nurse pointed out. But he had given them more back, they reasoned, so it was an honest swindle. Evidently, not so with Hollywood types. Ken didn't trust them at all, as a matter of fact, and his good friend Hunter S. Thompson had a great quote about it, that I know Ken liked: "The Film Business is a shallow money trench. A long, plastic hallway where theives and pimps run free and good men die like dogs.

Turning his back on Hollywood for a while, Ken was always creating, and in the summer of 1975, he created the very first Poetic Hoohaw, out at the farm, and invited the people he could trust to participate. Here is a great photo by Clyde Keller of Ken's Kitchen back then:

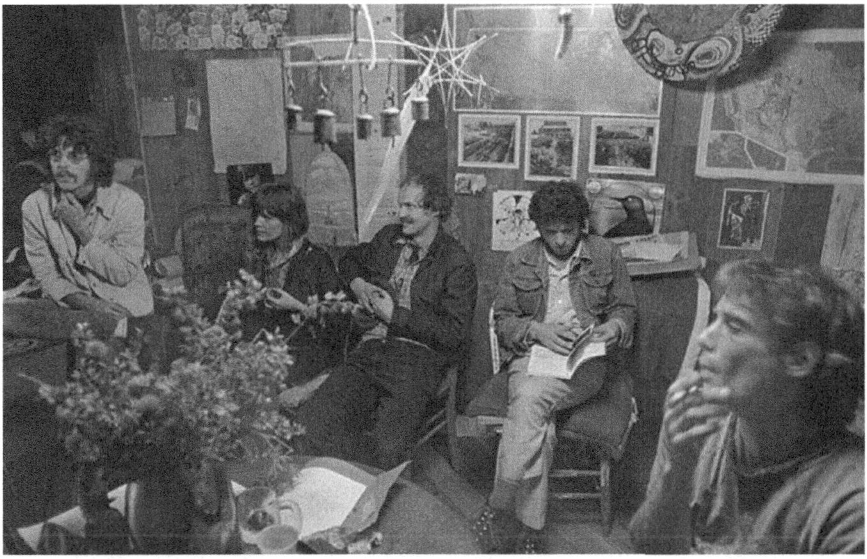

Paul Krassner, Tangerine Steinbrecher, Walt Curtis, Bill Graham and David Butkovitch.

I wanted to use the above photo, at first, for this book cover; because it had iconic representations of the 1960s, especially 70s Politics (Paul Krassner); Art: Tangerine, who was a stained glass artist; Poetry: (Walt Curtis, the Oregon Poet Laureate who wrote Gus Van Sant's first film *Mala Noche*;) and Rock & Roll (Promoter Bill Graham); as well as "Film"[291] with High Speed Camera Operator David Butkovich; (who also worked with Hagen and I). But instead I am using this one, again from Clyde Keller; of the Hoo-Haw, with Steve Christiansen, Bill Murray, Paul Goldshein, Ken Kesey and

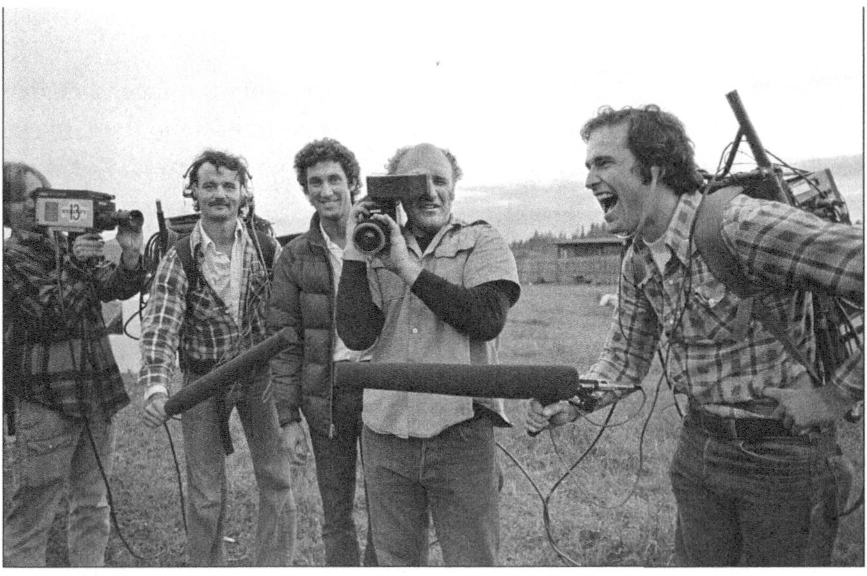

Bill Bradbury. And I am so glad that I am, because we just lost Steve this year, and I wanted to honor him. My pardner in film, Bob Laird, was a really close friend, and found actual footage of this shot in Steve's Betamax Video collection. Laird said he heard that a LA Production Company had created the first video camera and brought it up for Kesey to see, and all these guys from the local TV Stations came to try it out. As you can see, Steve (far left) is holding a local KVAL Channel 13 TV camera in the shot; *but in the video,* it also shows him filming Kesey with one that looks just like the camera Kesey is holding in this photo. The point of all this, is to show how we were back then, everybody sharing techniques and equipment with everybody else. I also found a hilarious blurb about these cameras, and this just about sums it all up about our film gang:

> The Portapak would seem to have been invented specifically for use by artists. Just when pure formalism had run its course; just when it became politically embarrassing to make objects, but ludicrous to make nothing; just when many artists were doing performance works but had nowhere to perform, or felt the need to keep a record of their performances; just when it began to seem silly to ask the same old Berkleean question, 'If you build a sculpture in the desert where no one can see it, does it exist?'; just when it became clear that TV communicates more information to more people than large walls do; just when we understood that in order to define space it is necessary to encompass time; just when many established ideas in other disciplines were being questioned and new models were proposed – just then the Portapak became available.[292]

Radically New Film equipment wasn't the only advancement that summer, either; the house band for The Merry Pranksters, the *Grateful Dead,* was coming out of a creative hiatus with a whole new way of being the *Dead,* and this time its name wasn't coming out of Merriam Webster's dictionary, like the first one. So many had thought the Dead's name came out of the *Egyptian Book of the Dead,* that by Quantum reasoning, it became the truth. What does Kesey's character Chief Bromden say? "But it's the truth even if it didn't happen." And Ken would say: "Don't ever ruin a good story with the Truth." But the truth is, the Dead started to create a whole new sound:

> *Blues for Allah* was the group's highest-charting album until 1987s *In the Dark*... (where) a discernable Middle Eastern theme

> emerged, supported by Robert Hunter's lyrics. Non-Western time signatures on some of the material added to the concept, as well as experiments with instrumentation, such as flute on the Bach-inspired "Sage & Spirit" (named for manager Rock Scully's daughters). Garcia said he was "creating scales that generated their own harmony in ways that weren't symmetrical in regular, classical major-minor relationships."[293]

That sound carried them all the way to Egypt, a few years later. But mostly I mention it because of its relationship to the gestalt of our generation, both the biculturality and the Quantum Mechanics gestalt, of the New Age.

Because this Chapter is indeed Chimeric and a full circle like we found with Yeats, it becomes a spiral staircase when bassist guitar play Phil Lesh states this new sound was partly inspired by a poem by Percy Blythe Shelley:

> Jerry brought in a strange, almost atonal melodic entity that would evolve into the title song and sequence for the album, and I had sketched out a little Latin-flavored, seven-beat instrumental number inspired by Shelley's poem "Ozymandias" called "King Solomon's Marbles" Besides "Crazy Fingers," his marvelous essay in

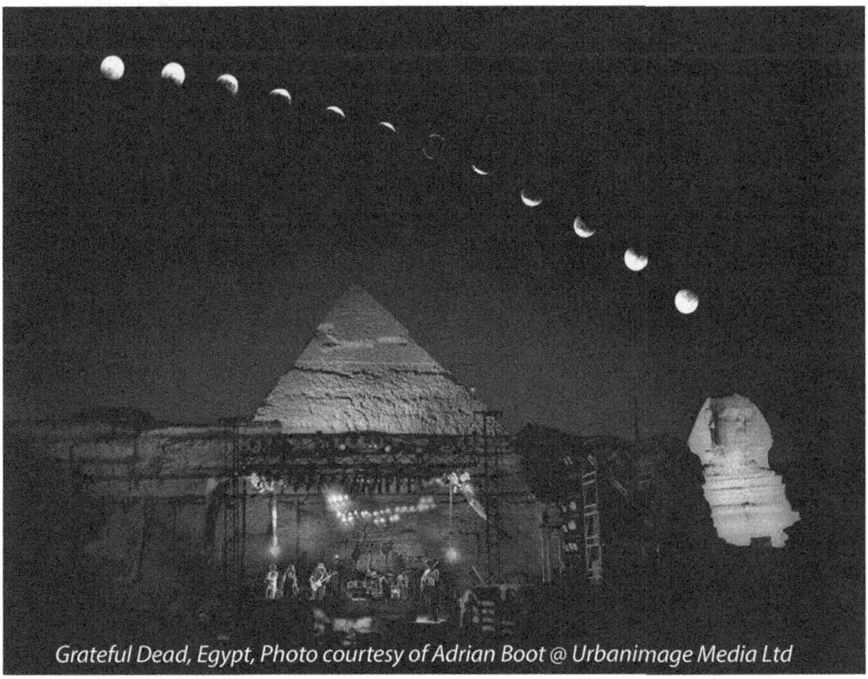

Grateful Dead, Egypt, Photo courtesy of Adrian Boot @ Urbanimage Media Ltd

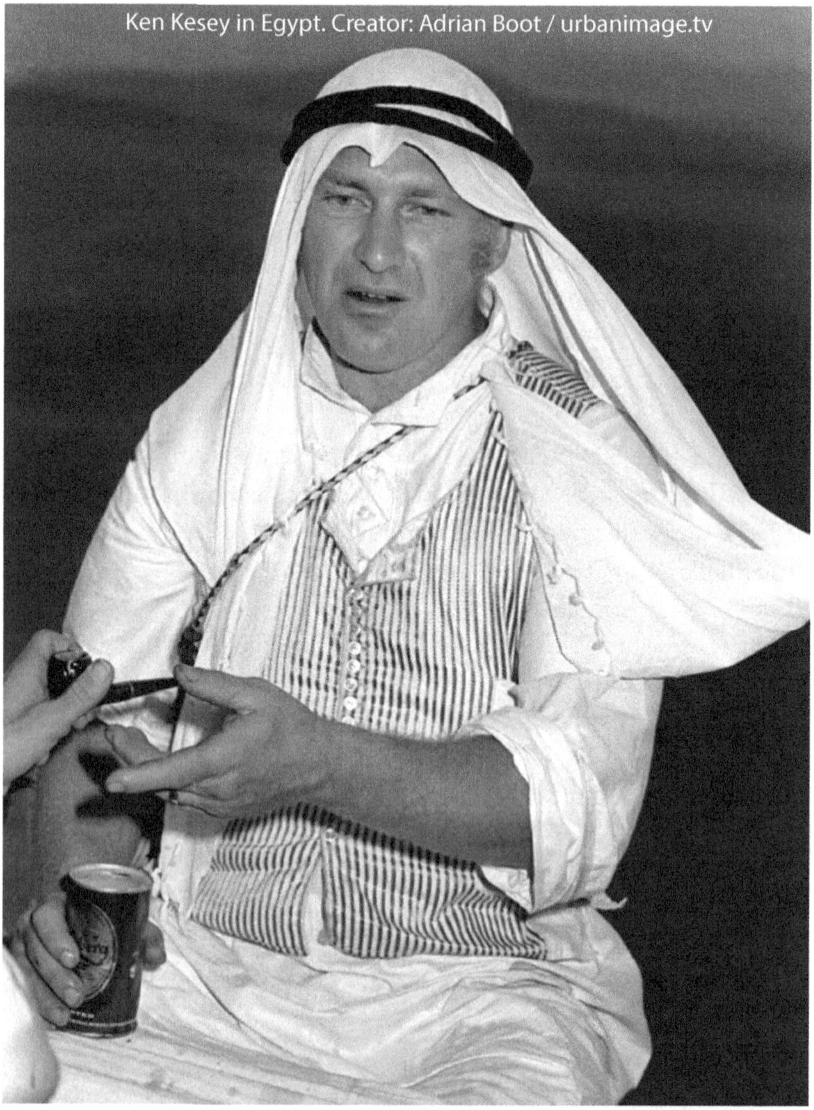

Ken Kesey in Egypt. Creator: Adrian Boot / urbanimage.tv

> smoky ambiguity, Jerry also contributed a triptych of already written tunes ("Help on the Way," "Slipknot," and "Franklin's Tower") that would become, in live performance, one of our finest exploratory vehicles. Bob had a beautiful guitar instrumental, "Sage and Spirit," and one of his stompin-est self-congratulatory rockers, "Music Never Stopped," to round out the album.[294]

"Consideration was given to naming the album after the Enlightened King Faisal of Saudi Arabia, who was assassinated after recording began. [8] The band had been told that he was a fan of the Grateful Dead. Ultimately, Robert Hunter considered his lyrics for the title track a *requiem for the ruler*. The song also references *One Thousand and One Nights*."[295] Drummer Bill Kreutzmann recalled:

> Once we started performing them live … we turned a corner and it was a whole other ball game. Those songs are among our very best and they lived up to their potential. We had to play them live in front of an audience in order for that to happen. Once we let them outside and started taking them for walks, they each had a growth spurt during which they really discovered themselves. The album also contained a group of really experimental songs ("Stronger than Dirt," "Unusual Occurrences in the Desert") that bordered on acid jazz composition. Wild stuff. Deep cuts."[296]

And speaking of *One Thousand and One Nights,* about that same time, I would try to talk Michael Douglas into producing *Chimera,* a book written by John Barth, which was a feminist version of the *1001 Nights*. Later, I would even make a toast from it: "The Key to the Treasure is the Treasure Itself" to Bernardo Bertolucci, Jack Nicholson, and other guests at dinner one night, at Jack's House.

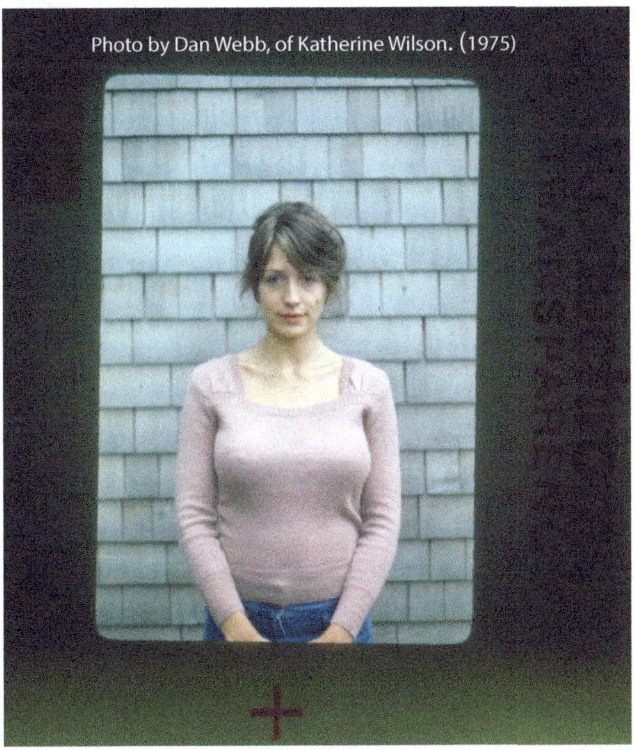

Photo by Dan Webb, of Katherine Wilson. (1975)

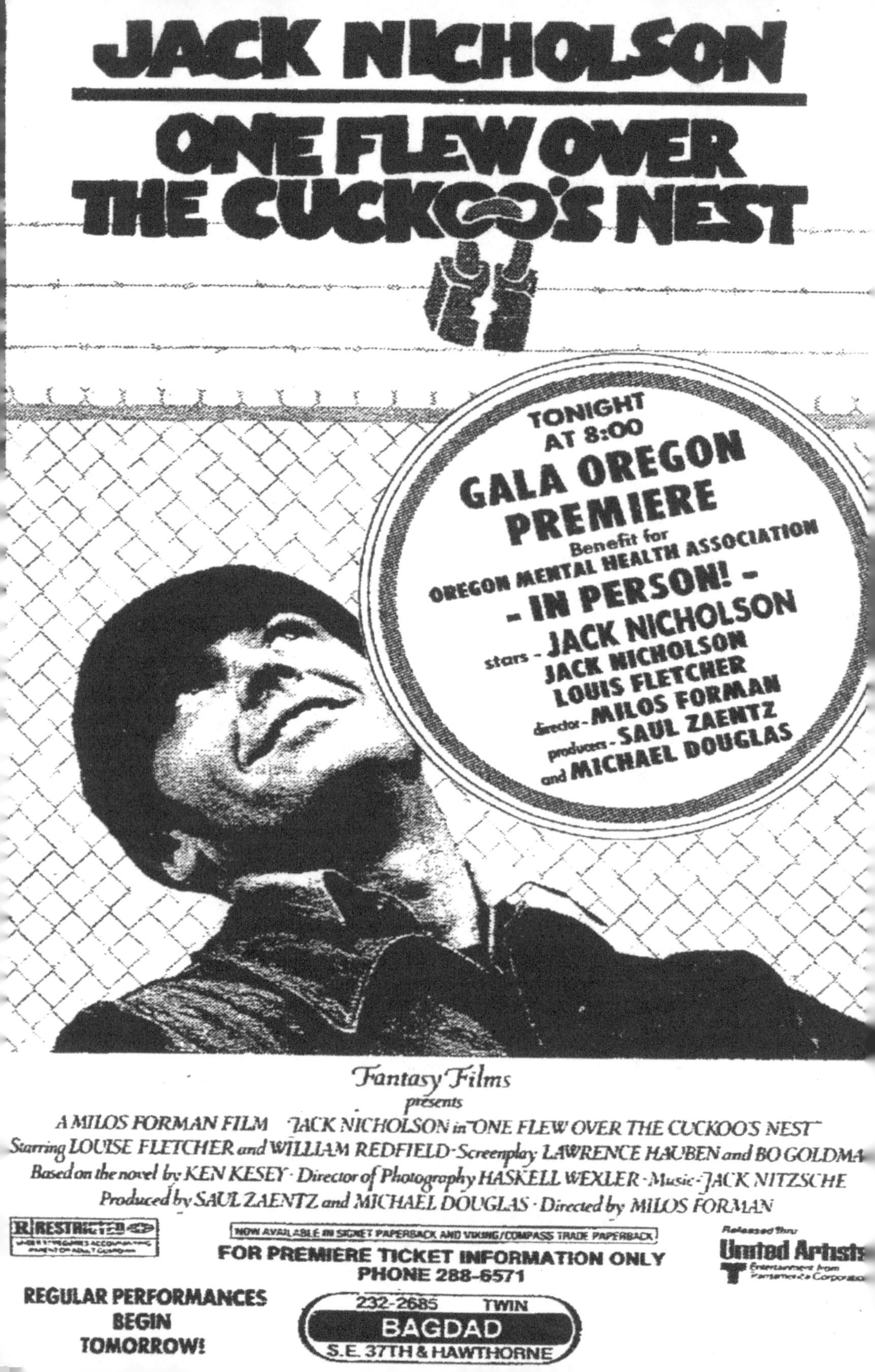
JACK NICHOLSON
ONE FLEW OVER THE CUCKOO'S NEST
TONIGHT AT 8:00
GALA OREGON PREMIERE
Benefit for OREGON MENTAL HEALTH ASSOCIATION
- IN PERSON! -
JACK NICHOLSON
stars - JACK NICHOLSON
LOUIS FLETCHER
director - MILOS FORMAN
producers - SAUL ZAENTZ
and MICHAEL DOUGLAS
Fantasy Films
presents
A MILOS FORMAN FILM JACK NICHOLSON in "ONE FLEW OVER THE CUCKOO'S NEST"
Starring LOUISE FLETCHER and WILLIAM REDFIELD · Screenplay LAWRENCE HAUBEN and BO GOLDMA
Based on the novel by KEN KESEY · Director of Photography HASKELL WEXLER · Music · JACK NITZSCHE
Produced by SAUL ZAENTZ and MICHAEL DOUGLAS · Directed by MILOS FORMAN
R RESTRICTED
NOW AVAILABLE IN SIGNET PAPERBACK AND VIKING/COMPASS TRADE PAPERBACK
FOR PREMIERE TICKET INFORMATION ONLY
PHONE 288-6571
Released thru
United Artists
REGULAR PERFORMANCES
BEGIN
TOMORROW!
232-2685 TWIN
BAGDAD
S.E. 37TH & HAWTHORNE

Chapter 11

The Wound of Khôra
~ 1976

The cut does not constitute a manifestation of the romantic desire to leave a trace, but takes the form of a wound and refers to the other. It is itself a trace of the other, to which we can be faithful only in this fissuring; thus not making from this wound a sacrifice which has any general idealistic aim."

–Urszula Idziak-Smoczynska, Ph.D.
The Theological Turn Of Postmodernity

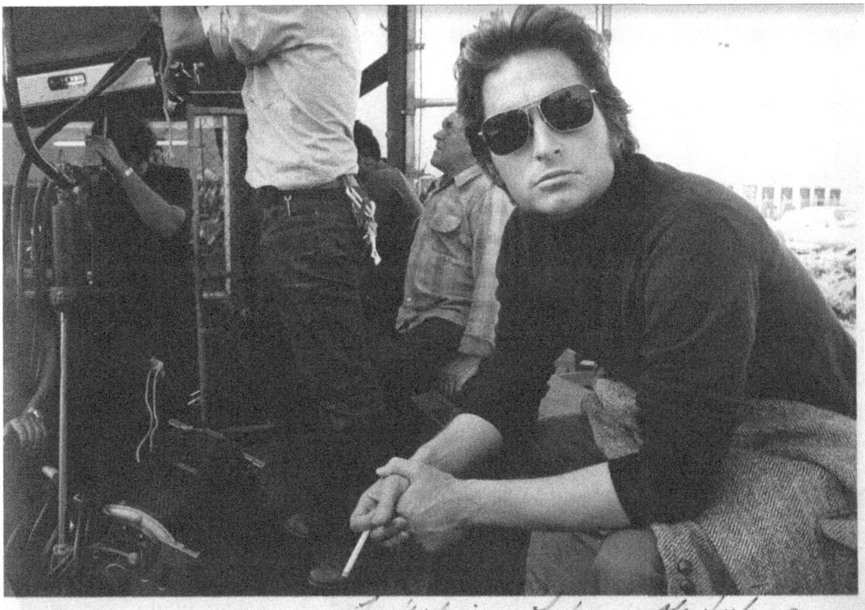

Photo of Michael Douglas by Jim Marshal, taken for Katherine Wilson on the set of *Streets of San Francisco*

1975 had ended with the Premiere of *One Flew Over the Cuckoo's Nest* in Portland at the Baghdad Theater; and then shown again the next day just for the inmates, cast and crew in Salem at the Elsinore Theater. I had never known such powerful moments in my life as I attended both

Premieres as Michael's guest, and was honored by his seating me next to former Governor McCall Friday night; the next day riding in the limo with just him and Jack from Portland to Salem, where Governor Bob Straub and Dr. Dean Brooks reigned at their Salem Premiere; and then to the Airport to see them and Milos off. On the way, Michael and I took Christmas presents to the women of Ward 84, the Homicidal Lockdown Ward of the Institution we had filmed in. Just remembering the looks on their faces as they saw him bringing them gifts brings tears to my eyes. I had never experienced so much unconditional love ever before. For me, this was the pinnacle of the whole movement that started in the 1960s. Nor had I ever experienced this level of romancing before. Michael was a gentleman who always opened the car doors for me, was always protecting me, feeding me, and telling me how wonderful I was. And Jack was the third entity in our relationship, always providing comic relief when things got too serious. I was already married, and Michael was in a relationship with Brenda Vaccaro. However, we lived in the moment and let what may happen, happen; because as Khalil Gibran's *The Prophet* says, "... think not you can direct the course of love, for love, if it finds you worthy, directs your course."[297] And because of this love, the world was broken open for me. So in 1976, we found ourselves immersed in the last great days, the absolute "Crown of Creation":[298] of sex, drugs and rock and roll of the 60s and 70s.

On March 29th, 1976 when the Academy Awards were presented, Michael, Saul, Jack, Louise and Milos swept the Oscars for the first time since the film *It Happened One Night* in 1934, *42 years earlier!* And then jetted around the world for a year promoting the hell out of it. I got a postcard from Michael in July; they were staying at the Otani Hotel in Tokyo. I knew he and Brenda had broken up in January, even though she was his guest at the Academy Awards. She had earned it, from living through years of Development Hell with Michael.

I was so proud to be a part of it. And the film inspired me, by what happened on *Cuckoo's Nest,* to have a professional casting file for the next time Michael or any other filmmaker would come to Oregon, to avoid the embarrassment of them seeing signs on telephone poles downtown, like their Casting/Car Salesman had made: "*Do you have a face that scares Timber Wolves? If so, call this number.*"

As luck would have it, I found out that Pierre Dunne from the *Willamette Valley Observer* had been asked by Dennis Hopper to collect head shots for him, so I was all over that, contributing some from my meager files. Allegedly, Dennis was coming back to Oregon to make *Trask* by Oregon Author Don Berry. In the 60s, Don Berry wrote incredible historical fiction novels about Oregon's Mountain Men and their relationships with the Indians, and the Indian's relationships to Nature.

Jack was also slated to return to Oregon that summer for his own Don Berry project, *Moontrap*. In this *New York Times* article by Bill Davidson, on October 12th, 1975, Jack talks about it.

> He spoke dispassionately and professionally about the script for *Moontrap*, which he had just finished writing, and he discussed his plans for directing the film next June. "I should have directed a lot of other pictures by now," he said, "but I think back to the days when I was broke and then somebody offers me a million dollars to act in a picture – and I'm chicken about turning it down. No one would pay me anywhere near that much for directing. But *Moontrap* is my own, so it's different."[299]

But because of the Academy Awards, this little film *Cuckoo's Nest*, financed by Jazz Distributor Saul Zaentz, one that didn't even have a theatrical-release deal six weeks into shooting, was now the hottest project in five decades. Also, they all had ownership point-wise, and the more they promoted it, the more money they made. And on United Artist's dime, I might add, for a whirlwind tour of the world, showing their film.

So the production of Jack's *Moontrap* was pushed the summer that he was in Europe with Michael, and has never been made, and I don't think it ever will be. And *Trask* has had so many people try, including me, (well, on both of them) because they were two of the finest (albeit bicultural) stories I have ever read. Back then, there were so many to choose from, like Rick Steber's *From New York to Nome*, that superstar Paul Newman had optioned: Rick's collection of bicultural stories in *Rendezvous*, including one that I have optioned off and on for 26 years about Chief Joseph's Nephew, Jackson Sundown.

The New Hollywood had also been making *Little Big Man*, with Dustin Hoffman; and Paul Newman was making *Buffalo Bill and the Indians, or Sitting Bull's History Lesson*. All of these 60s and 70s movies were made only after Ken Kesey freed the American Indian from the Wooden Indian stereotype in his book published in 1962. And what came out of Dennis Hopper's *Trask*? The casting files he asked Pierre Dunne to collect were given to me, because the film was not made; and just in time. They soon after became a huge asset for me with The Oregon Film Factory, a new company formed by members of the Original Merry Pranksters; and they needed help getting talent for the local commercials they were doing. They said, “the talent includes you.” But my going fee was $25 an hour, in the days of less than $2.00 an hour minimum wage. That price was a little steep for them, so I traded my hourly rate for an Office in the Garage, which was $25 a month.

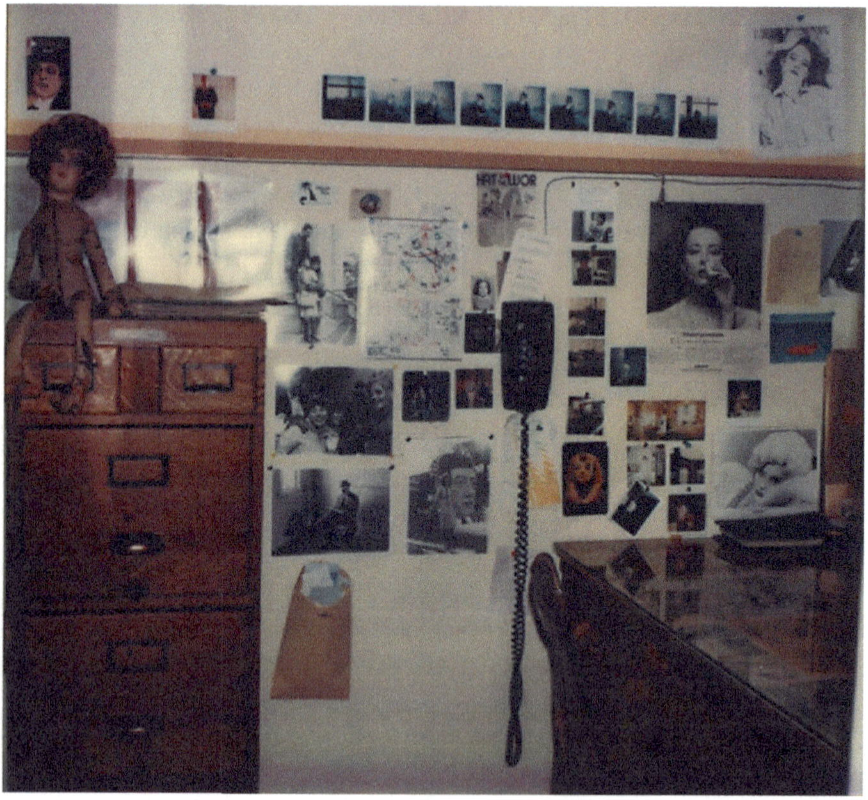

It was a really good trade for them, because they eventually got a phone call from the Bobbsey Twins (which is what I called Bobby Miller and Bobby Steinbrecher in LA) who were working on commercials, too. They said that the drought in California had made it impossible for a company from New York to film there, and they needed to find a greener location, really quick. I know the production company was uncomfortable about moving away from their California support system, like all of the equipment rental houses, the casting directors and the talent agencies; but because we were independent filmmakers, a lot of us could do 5 different jobs at once, (I had learned to write content, location scout, cast, do make-up, hair, set design and change film in the bag for a film camera) and so we all were well rounded in all aspects of film production. They were blown away.

And when their production manager, Terry Donnelley flew up to see the location, he wanted to see our casting files. And because of Dennis Hopper, I had some. And because I had some, we brought a commercial production to town that left around $250,000 in the community; and because it was such a huge success, it also brought another $117,200 in residual payment to the actors. Plus, we got 10% of it for putting it all together. At first, I was nervous. It's one thing to put together a couple of girlfriends for a local Joe Romania car commercial; and totally another thing to bring in 2700 actors for a national one to audition; because that is the ratio they told me they needed, 100 auditions for each part, a total of 27 parts in the commercial which equaled 2700 interviews in two weeks. But they were so relieved to not have to cancel the shoot, that they taught me what to do. Lynn Stalmaster had taught me how to audition actors. But they taught Bob Laird and I how to become powers of attorney for each actor we cast, to get our fee.

They said we would never see it if the talent got the checks first. By the time we were to start shooting, we had our final picks, including Kesey's Grandmother Ophelia in a scene at the Skinner's Butte Victorian Mansion, being pushed by an elderly gentleman in a swing; we had all ages and all ethnics, including the cutest little black boy with his dad for a food eating scene, and with some others for a skateboarding scene; we had a young couple for the scene of riding a horse; we had kids for fishing with a dog on a wooden raft scene; we had a marching band from Sheldon High School (one of my many Alma Maters) who ended up being able to go to Europe to compete in a Continental Marching Band contest with the money they made; we had kids for splashing in the rain; a little girl who hugged a sheep, another one who was being taught to play croquet by her Grandfather; a Chinese girl and others at a Ballet class; and even an American Indian cowboy with a horse saddle on his shoulder. But we could not find the perfect American archetypal John Wayne Cowboy. I was frantic, because I had let them down. Me, a sixth generation Oregon Pioneer and Indian Rodeo girl who had hundreds of relatives in town. In desperation, I called the Lane County Sheriff's Mounted Patrol; which on which their website said "continues the tradition of patrols on horseback by Western sheriffs. The Mounted Patrol supports special initiatives that call for a mounted deputy, like crowd control, civil unrest and search and rescue." I remember it was after dark when a tall Sheriff knocked on the

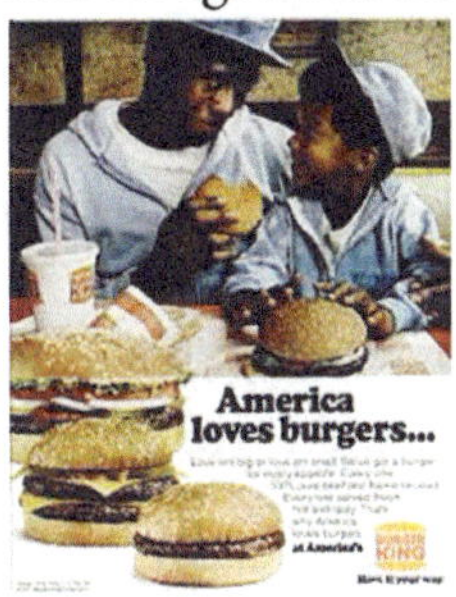

door of our office in a cowboy hat and riding gear, fresh off the trail. He was just like John Wayne, and he hesitated, framed in the doorway like a John Ford movie; because we were all jumping up and down screaming "that's him!" His name was Gene Terpenning, and suddenly I had earned the right to be a legitimate professional Casting Director. My J. Walter Thompson and Oregon Film Factory comrades were quite pleased with me. And this is how, in 1976, during the country's Bi- Centennial, America finally made a *mainstream bicultural commercial.* You can see it where the links are, on the last page of the book.

Meanwhile, Cinema 7 continued to thrive, and after the Burger King commercial, I continued to work 4 nights a week. We were showing Ron Finne's works in mini film festivals, and showed Don Cato's Cannes' Silver Award-winner short called *Skinner's Beaut.* Oregon's own Will Vinton, winning an Oscar for his animated short *Closed Monday,* had inspired every filmmaker I knew.

At Cinema 7, I continued to watch so much film there it affected my vision, but I couldn't get enough. And Steve Bove, Barbara Embree and I made our own film. It was called *Tangles,* and we shot it in B&W 16mm at Yachats, on the Oregon coast. I played a Mermaid who was dying in the Tide pools because her jealous sister had poisoned her, and took her magic Hair Combs. The final scene was Barbara Embree, as my sister, in front of a mirror, trying on the hair combs, and they immediately made her turn into an ugly Hag. I was so proud of it that Mark Rydell set up a screening of it at Fox. And it was a beautiful film, up on the big screen at last, one that I was a part of. It is now considered a "lost film."

I had also visited Rydell on the set of *Harry and Walter Go to New York;* and became friends with Elliott Gould. While there, I taught Elliott Gould how to do "The Hustle," which is why he gave me a rolled up "Movie Money" (printed for *Butch Cassidy and the Sundance Kid*) and signed it with this: "to spend this you gotta do a hustle."

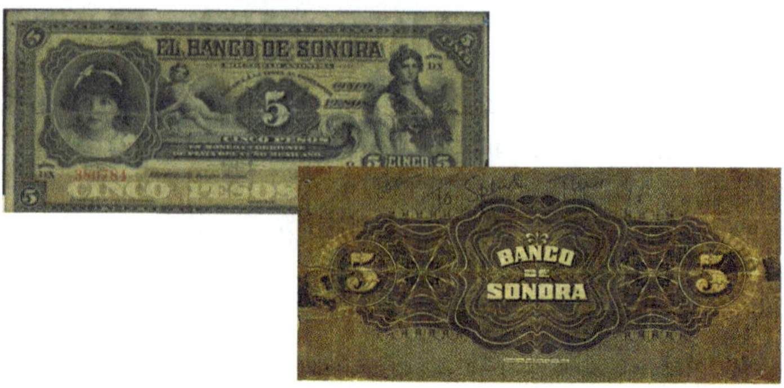

He then volunteered to take me home, which was to Michael Douglas' house on Cold Water Canyon. He couldn't get over the fact that I knew Michael, nor that I was from Eugene. But when Michael answered the door he was convinced.

And the Oregon Film Commissioner couldn't believe it either, when I showed up with Michael for a location scout meeting in the Governor's Office in October. Michael was on a new project called *China Syndrome*. Even though Warren had access to the Governor's airplane, I was Michael's favorite location scout now, and I would even scout for him again in 1983. But on this day, he also wanted my input about what women would want in a film, *especially since he had seen me one night in an Adult film*, while filming *Streets of San Francisco*. He said he and the crew were holed up in a motel in San Francisco, watching TV, when a show about *Welcome Wagon Girls* was playing. Suddenly, he said, he saw me, stood up and told the crew "I know that girl! Her name is Katherine." And the crew said, "Nah .... No way you know that girl." And then I turned to the camera and said "Hi, I'm Katherine," which is how he saw me, playing right there on the TV screen.

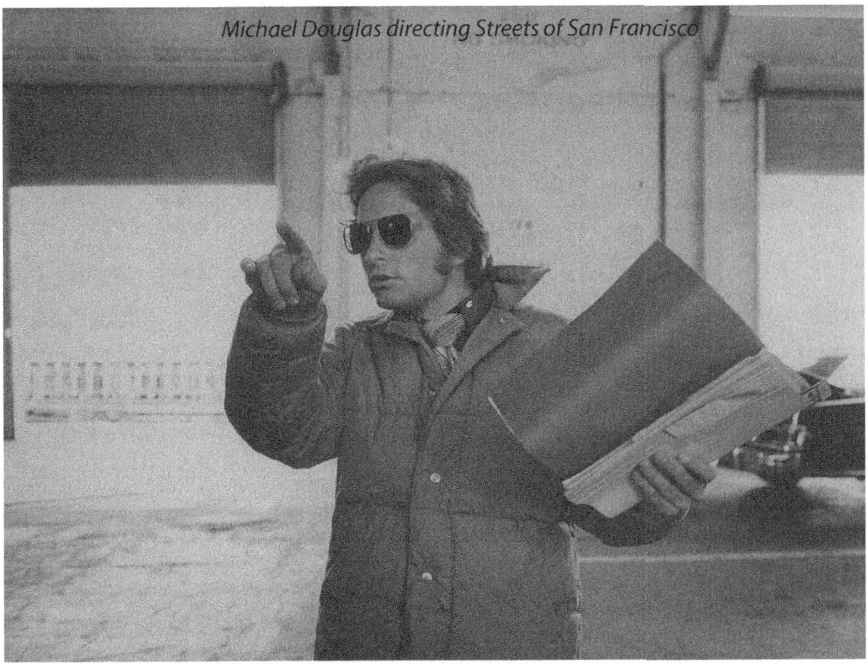

Michael Douglas directing Streets of San Francisco

I told him that the book he gave me, *Fear of Flying* by Erica Jong was right. *"A woman's erogenous zone is in her mind."* I told him about *Chimera* by John Barth. Imagine how incredible it was that he succeeded in producing *Romancing the Stone* in only eight years, as opposed to the twelve years *Cuckoo's Nest* took. Hollywood certainly didn't want Crazy, Indian, or women's voices, but he did it, and then he made *Jewel of the Nile*. I so love him for that, for making these two romantic films with strong women.

I need to add that in the 70s the whole decade was about sex. "A new, sexualized popular culture pervaded American life in the 1970s, and it seemed that everyone wanted to be part of it. Watching a porn film at the local theater, flipping through a sex advice manual in line at the grocery store, dancing the hustle at a glittery discotheque – all were markers of sexual sophistication."[300]

> The sexual revolution was considered by many to be the most shocking social trend in the 1970s. It cast aside traditional sexual restraints and began a decade of alternative eroticism, experimentation, and promiscuity. In part facilitated by the development of the birth-control pill and other contraceptives, Americans in the 1970s broke many sexual taboos. Interracial dating, open homosexuality, communal living, casual nudity, and dirty language all seemed to indicate a profound change in sexual behavior. Sexual activity among the young especially increased. Surveys during the 1970s reported that by age nineteen, four-fifths of all males and two-thirds of all females had had sex. Fashion designers promoted a new sensuality, producing miniskirts, hot pants, halter tops, and formfitting clothes designed to accentuate women's sexuality.[301]

"The 1970s were truly the golden age of the porno. *This is the only time in the history of cinema where pornographic films were semi-legitimized.* 'Porno chic' was in full effect– *Behind the Green Door* was shown at Cannes and *Deep Throat* was raking in untold millions, and big-name celebs like Jack Nicholson and Johnny Carson were in line to see these films. Legislation was extremely permissive at this time, and pornographic theaters and bookstores were popping up everywhere."[302]

> *Deep Throat* was released in 1972 and was made for about $23,000. The movie quickly became the most profitable movie of all time (and still is today), pulling in over $600,000,000! In the 1970s, it was a commonly expressed belief that the porn industry would actually meld with Hollywood. Bob Hope was even making jokes about it...[303]

The author calls this "Porn Chic." Not sure I would agree with that, but I agree with him here:

> ... sexual revolution certainly began prior to 1970: the pill actually hit the scene in the 1960s, Hugh Hefner's playboy lifestyle before that, and the infamous Kinsey Report before that ... you could even go further back to Sigmund Freud and Margaret Sanger in the early 1900s. In fact, you could probably keep tracing it back and back and back – every trend had an origin somewhere, and that origin had its origin somewhere else, and so on.[304]

The origin of the 60s and 70s Cultural Revolution was like a good screenplay, 4 or 5 things happening at the same time. In this book, we tried to show the implications of certain theories about our generation, as well as including certain *Forces from the Underground influencing Cinema*. Underground music, books and paintings, and what we saw in the Plato-cave-like syndrome in our parents; the calling: whether you call it Khôra, Collective Consciousness and/or with Archaic drug use; Quantum Mechanics, Biculturalism, protests against the war in Vietnam, Ken Kesey, the Red Dog Saloon, the Beats, Yeats, Shelley, Nietzsche and even the Atom Bomb, were all prevalent forces.

But I personally saw more of a reaction against, than I saw a striving for, because none of us really knew what was emerging, except what we were turning against. And a big part of it was Post-modernism. Post-modernism was ear-marked by dialectics. We felt it failed to create a collective consciousness, like the one we experienced on LSD; the one we experienced when we really *loved*. That was what our art, music and lifestyle was about, until it went dominant in the national consciousness and culture and became a commodity. And then, of course, it turned in on itself.

Post-modernism failed, because like the Age of Reason that spawned it, it was simple rhetoric, not rhetoric like in figures of speech, but debate-like rhetoric in Plato's logic. In other words, a rhetoric without emotion, academics without a "structure of feeling."[305] A language without a "radical aesthetic"[306] or words for The Sublime. I can't believe how many words have become the opposite of their original etymological meanings, which have created ambivalence because people were overwhelmed by its didactic logic. By the time we got to German Expressionism, Cubism and Dadaism, just words were insufficient to express our existential anxiety, our feelings. Because The Word was no longer The Creative. The word became the Tower of Babel all over again. A sign that the end of the Old Age is at hand, thank God, just like 2000 years ago. An example of where this post-modernism led us, is a painting by Max Pechstein. I was asked to go see it and write about it for a class I was taking last winter. A class I suffered through, but now I understand why

The Jorden Schnitzer Museum's description card for this painting tells us that it is an "unusual" painting and wonders if it was because of the death of Max Pechstein's and his wife's newborn son in 1912. It is unusual because he "tended to paint nudes, portraits, or scenes of urban nightlife, not domestic genre scenes."[307]

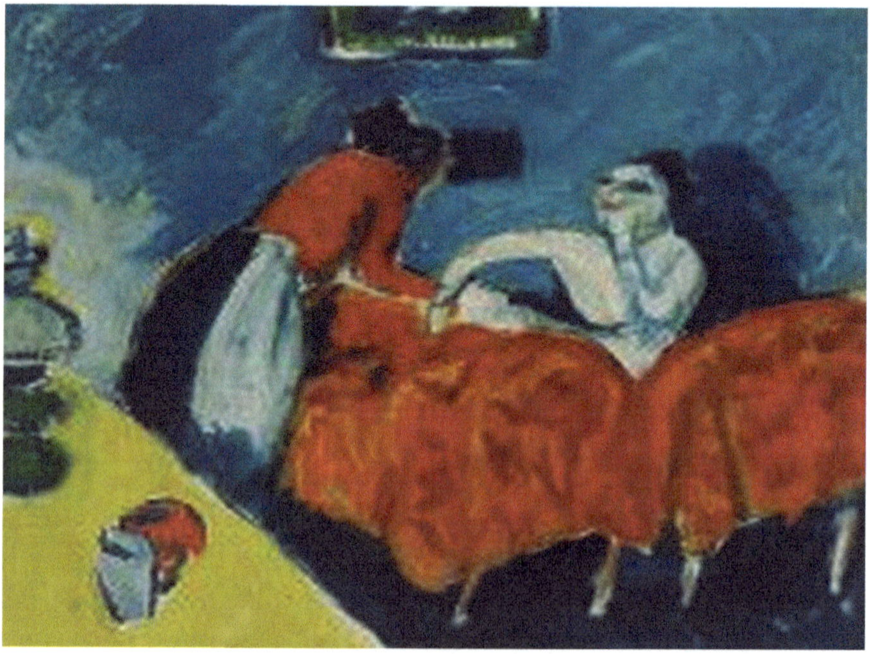

At first glance it could appear to be a painting of a midwife with a cloth washing a woman in bed before or after the act of childbirth. But upon a closer look, perhaps not. This closer look begins with looking carefully at the choices of the Painter's colors, the applications of his brush, and then closely examining the Mise en Scene of the objects, the lighting, the poses of the characters, and the painting on the wall.

Max Pechstein's painting at first appeared to be evoking a Blaue Reiter painting because of the incredible blue colored background, like the "The Blue Rider" Painting by Wassily Kandinsky with its powerful blues; however, Pechstein was really part of the group Die Brücke (The Bridge) in Dresden.

In *Max Pechstein: the Rise and Fall of Expressionism* by Bernhard Fulda and Aya Soika; they state what *The Bridge* movement was about: "The idea was to produce spontaneous sketches, capturing the models' natural movements, so to avoid the laboured poses and rigid norms of academic style."[308]

The blue background has a texture like a stucco wall, but the woman on the right's distorted arm quickly draws the eye as if pointing to the vivid red color, which looks like a thick fabric over chairs, because of the angle of chair-like legs.

However, the position of the woman makes the likelihood of chairs impossible and created dissonances in perspective with the legs at an odd angle and the perspective of her position in the painting. What may be more easy to rationalize is that she is in a bed, or twin beds pushed together, which may have been done to facilitate childbirth. The position of her right arm indicates 'Melancholy,' as coded by the famous engraving *Melencolia* by Albrecht Dürer;[309] but she has no solid surface or table to prop her elbow on, which makes her gesture appear awkward. However, she has a smile on her lips, which creates additional dissonance. Perhaps the smile is in embarrassment, of needing the other woman's help.

Furthermore, the Table Lamp 'Light' (that the painting's title mentions) creates odd-shaped shadows, one is colored black (of the woman with the apron) and in the form of a square; while the woman in the bed's shadow is more bluish and more natural. There are black shadows under the bed, but none of the objects on the table in the circular light arc have shadows, as if they are not really there, but a phantom of the subconscious of the other woman. The woman on the left of the painting appears older and is wearing an apron and a cap on her head, indicating servant status. The angle of her arm imitates the position necessary for setting a heavy tray down. But there is no tray. And what could have been *on the tray,* appearing to be a coffee or teacup and a saucer or a small plate with a bun on it, is still on the table. Eerily, the painting on the wall seems to have white crosses in the foreground, with green grass in the background, and more blue paint, evoking a Christian graveyard. An incredible contradiction in a birthing room. In Donald Gordon's *Content by Contradiction,* he states: "Ambivalence – the presence in a single work of art of two or more mutually contradictory meanings – was Nietzsche's bequest to the German Expressionists."[310]

Even the name of the Dresden painters that Pechstein became a part of, "The Bridge" was named after a quote from Nietzsche: "What is great in man is that he is a bridge and not an end: what can be loved in man is that he is an overture and a going under. I love those who do not know how to live, except by going under, for they are those who cross over."[311]

And there are many contradictory meanings in this painting highlighted with the use of Primary colors. The first is the color blue (considered a spiritual color by the Blaue Reiter) against the passionate blood red colors of the bedding. The yellow of the lamp is painted with the same yellow as the table, but the only reflection of this light is one of a flesh-tone color on the one distorted arm coming out of the woman's right breast, and the hands of the other woman, indicating human warmth between the women where they almost touch. No other form of illumination exists except this reflection and the shadows. That tells us it is not the FACT of the woman bringing a tray to her in bed (as evidenced by the lack of tray and coffee and plate) but the ACT of caring for her in this way.

In *Max Pechstein: the Rise and Fall of Expressionism,* again by Bernhard Fulda and Aya Soika, they state: "Expressionism grew out of a common European tendency of the 1880s that Robert Goldwater called a 'desire to make emotion meaningful.'"[312]

The Fact of a melancholic gesture with the woman's left arm (subconscious) is in direct contrast and contradiction to her smile, (a conscious Act of Feeling). Perhaps the other woman's act of stooping with a heavy tray (subconscious) is in reality her subconscious wish she was serving breakfast in bed as opposed to her feelings of cleaning the woman after childbirth.

> Expressionism viewed emotion with the traditional German ambivalence towards mind/body experience. More-over, Symbolist feeling was indirect, evocative and generally subordinated to pictorial form, while Expressionist feeling could be direct to the point of formlessness. To this extent, Symbolism fostered esthetic experience, Expressionism real experience. Symbolism stood for esthetic distance, Expressionism for the examined life.[313]

Expressionism in this painting does indeed examine not only the conscious life of the women, but also their *subconscious* life. Furthermore, another layer of contradiction in the painting could be a sexual one, in that "The Die Brücke (The Bridge) artists (in Dresden) kept a house-book, inscribed *Odi profanum vulgus,* in the spirit of the 1886 Nietzsche, and celebrated sex in their art just as Nietzsche had in his late notes published as *The Will to Power* (1901)."[314]

The ambivalence of Life-Death creates a third meaning (like the oxymoron of Love/Death in Tristan and Isolde); but here instead, sexual love creates human life in pregnancy, but pregnancy can also create the death of the child and even the mother. So indeed, this painting titled Two Women in Lamplight may express this incredible oxymoron of not Liebestod, (Love Death) as in Gordon's work; but Eros/Thanatos or jouisssance/stasis, (Life/ Death) in Max Pechstein's Painting. The use of primary colors in this painting indicates a kind of primitivism; and the "content by contradiction" creates a third meaning: "Primitivism is a word that describes the condition or quality that belongs to something crude and unrefined. When this word primitivism is applied to the arts, such as the visual arts or music, it can be described as simple ideas juxtaposed with each other forming new ideas, new images, and new sounds."[315]

This definition rings all of my bicultural bells. It's as if the Universe knew it was going to take the bicultural human to straddle the gap between the Archaic and the Quantum Future, which is what happens every 26 thousand years or so when the widening gyre of Pisces meets the widening gyre of Aquarius; and comes full circle like a Medicine Wheel; and this is so important I am including a whole page of definitions, many from those theorists I have relied on in this book. This concept all but requires the Bridge between objectivity and subjectivity, between Apollo and Dionysus, between linear and circular, in order to grasp the love created by "the wound of Khôra."[316]

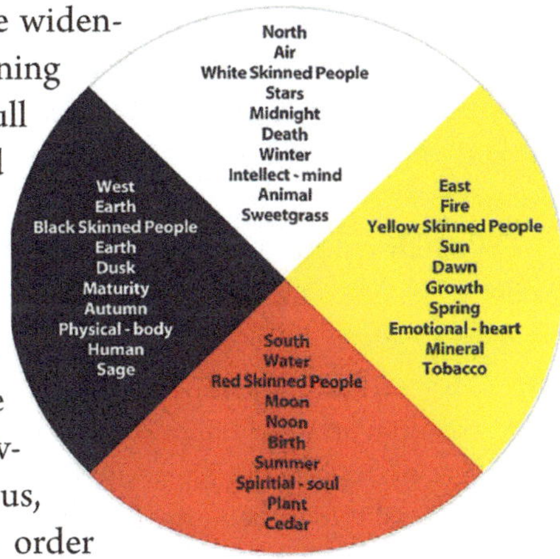

So no wonder we instinctively turned to sex. Sex is what imitates the wound of khôra. Sex was what created biculturalism in its own way. Sex was the answer to symbolism vs. semioticism, it was more than a physical bridge, it was emotional, mental, and cultural connection between polarized worlds. And all that reptilian brain obsession with sex from encountering annihilation from Post War, Post Nuclear, and Postmodernism created millions of us, to appear as the 7th generation of the great end and beginning of the alpha and the omega – the Great Word and the Great Symbol, a bicultural marriage so to speak. We are the 7th generation.

When Post-modernism killed the most important feeling in the world, which is love; it created this puritanical "intellect" that we were revolting against, with Yeats and Shelley and Kesey; and this is why we embraced their symbolism and metaphors, and embraced feeling because we were so starved for it and starved for the feeling of Spirit:

> The Polish born Berlin author Stanislaus Przybyszewski ... was a Symbolist writer who tried to interpret Nietzsche as a Symbolist by changing the Nietzschean concept of sex into the most un-Nietzschean idea of "spirit." This was a particularly bohemian strategy, because it took what the German middle-class mind saw as a source of the greatest evil and presented it as an exemplum of the greatest good.... In his 1892 *Psychology of Individuation: Chopin and Nietzsche*, Przybyszewski argues that a mere bodily function can be transmuted, with the German philosopher's help, into an idealizing "holy way": Also accessible to art in this macrocosmic view [exemplified by Zarathustra] ... will be The Sexual: that never satiated lust which displays only the eternal joy of creation, everlasting self-affirmation, and a big "yes" to all the will's instincts for personal immortality, for propagation; those spasms of passion, considered as the deepest instinct of life, as the holy way to life's future, to life's eternity.[317]

Even Donald E. Gordon, the incredible author of *Content by Contradiction* wondered about this particular time:

> How did it happen? Why were Romantic hopes for spiritual or material progress replaced by a late 19th-century ambivalence and fear of decline? And how did Expressionist hopes for spiritual and cultural renewal emerge from this pessimistic turn-of-the-century atmosphere? While the metaphysician may cite a Zeitgeist in answering these questions, the historian must provide causal explanations.
>
> Without in any way denying the existence of multiple contributing factors, I would nonetheless claim that the chief model for ambivalence in Expressionist art was the influential philosophy of Friedrich Nietzsche. I mean primarily the later and not the earlier Nietzsche, not so much the Wagner-inspired romantic who thought that "art represents the highest task and the truly metaphysical activity of this life"(1872), but the un-illusioned realist whose self-imposed task was "to look at science in the perspective of the artist, but at art in the perspective of life (1886).[318]

And the only way to do that is to *marry* science and art, and art and life, with aesthetics, a structure of feeling and therefore create a third understanding with a bicultural language. Nietzsche himself said this: "Everything perfect and beautiful works as an unconscious reminder of ... this aphrodisiac bliss (Physiologically: the creative instinct of the artist and the distribution of the semen in the blood). The demand for art and beauty is an indirect demand for the ecstasies of sexuality communicated to the brain."[319] This sounds so much like Yeats in his later years, too.

Even the dark sexual energies of both Nietzsche and Yeats can be beautifully expressed by the symbolic Hindu Goddess of Death, Kali. Her "...iconography, cult, and mythology commonly associate her not only with death but also with sexuality, violence, and, paradoxically, in some later traditions, with motherly love."[320]

If you ever met a Grizzly Bear Mama with her cub, this would not seem to be a paradox. Grizzly males are known to kill their cubs in order to engage the female into ersatz and breeding. She will take him on and win, because there is no violence like violence caused by deep love. Love can make you lift a car off of your daughter, if needed. Love can make you kill, lie, cheat and steal. Love can make you write love songs, become a poet, put your life in a 9 to 5 job if need be. Love is the only true power there is. But you have to risk it, you have to put your heart "under the claw," you have to appear to be foolish, a clown, a joker, a fool. If you don't believe me, go listen to 60s love songs.

But in 1976, it wasn't just for me, this love, this fizzure, this "Wound of Khôra," that broke both my heart and the heart of the world open, and allowed women's logic and voice back into this world where they belonged. She was reflecting the New Age everywhere, like a magic mirror. Case in point, on the 8th of March, 1976 there was a United Nations Statement by the Secretary-General marking International Women's Year as now an International Decade. There were even international women leaders in power, like Isabella Peron and Indira Ghandi. This was because our generation, worldwide, seemed to be born to see right through thinly veiled heteropatriarchy-like rationalizations to control our commitment to love, sexuality, as well as to male dominated rationalizations for war:

> What is not well known is that the Blaue Reiter's eschatological concerns (e.g., Kandinsky's I 909-13 images of Deluge and Last Judgment, Marc's 1913-14 Animal Destinies and Fighting Forms)

were presaged by the late Nietzsche's concept of creation through destruction, also from 1901:

> The desire for destruction, change ... becoming can be the expression of an overfull power pregnant with the future (my term for this, as is known, is the word "Dionysian"); but it can also be the hatred of the ill-constituted, disinherited, underprivileged, which destroys, has to destroy, because what exists, indeed existence itself, all being itself, enrages and provokes it.[321]

And *this* is what the revolution was all about in my generation, because the Cultural, Sexual, Political, and Musical revolutions all came about by hearing the call, trying to express it, and marrying together the bicultural Quantum of Space and the Atom with the Primitive and Archaic. Which once again, really brings us back full circle to Chapter O. The Fool. Therefore, a perfect example for the next Chapter for the next year, 1977; is *National Lampoon's Animal House*; because where do you go after completing a cultural cycle that Raymond Williams called "pre-emergence, dominant and then residual? You parody it. And mock all of that ages' sacred cows with the advent of Disco, Polyester Bell Bottoms, Long Hair and Sideburns on Republicans, and Mass Production of all of the 60s Icons to create and sell these empty shells of their spiritual intent for the masses, who didn't even care about the spiritual calling we experienced that made our generation. But we *now* know that this was just a window in time anyway, a presage of what was to come in the 2000s, but at the time we didn't know that. A lot of us started "drinking heavily" as Belushi put it in *Animal House*, to try to replicate the "love vibration" that seemed to go away by 1978. But I am happy to report that I was able to experience it coming back again in 1987, for just 3 days during the Harmonic Convergence, and to experience it now as it has returned again, and it is getting so much stronger that it now feels like the energy of the 60s have returned with a vengeance, this time for 2000 years. Perhaps now, with

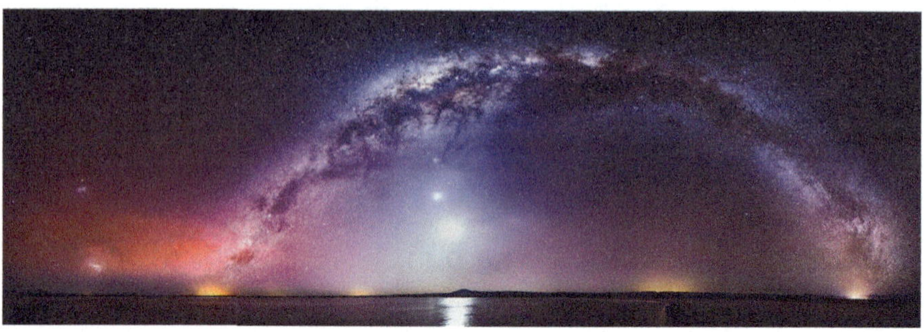

women Philosophers, such as the one below, we can come into balance: She says, "...we discover in Derrida's work a new logic of life.... It corresponds to the neutrality of Khôra, to the balanced relationship.... Therefore this logic will be feminine. Her rebellion will be only a revolt against the suffering.... And her desire will be so pure that it is incapable of being decently implemented. (Dionysus anyone?) The life of which she will be the figure ...accepted like the flowers of the desert – 'resurrected.'"[322] I say it's about time.

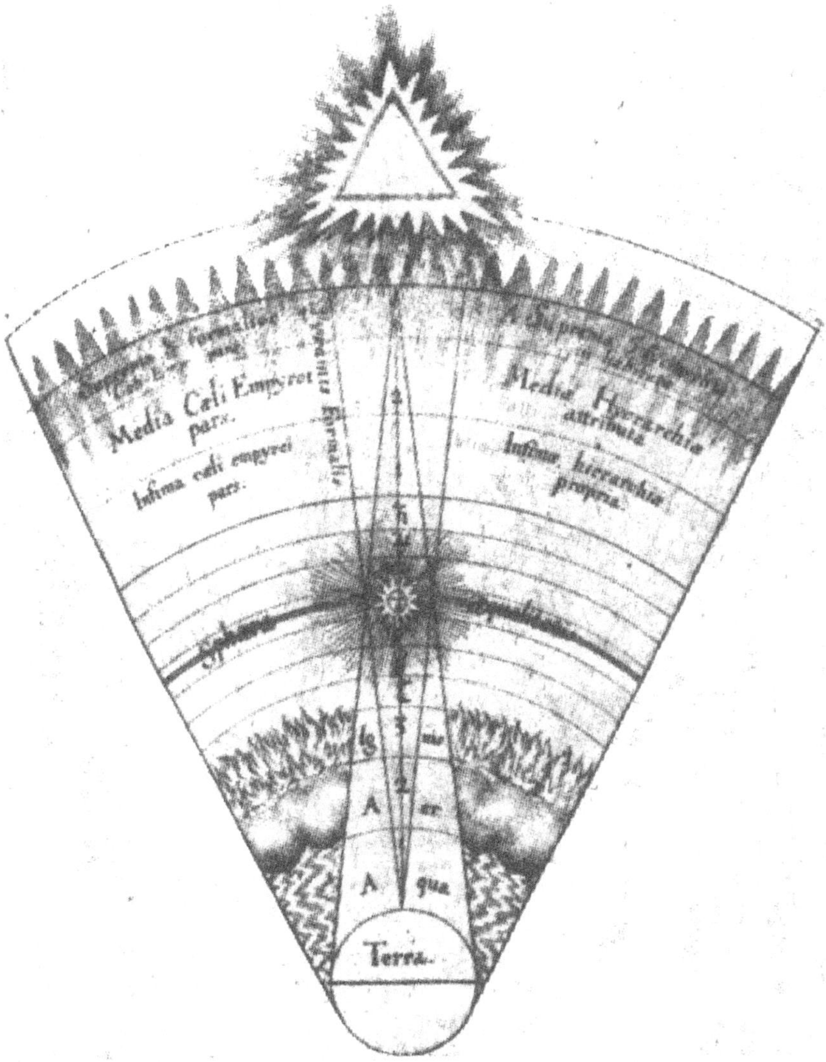

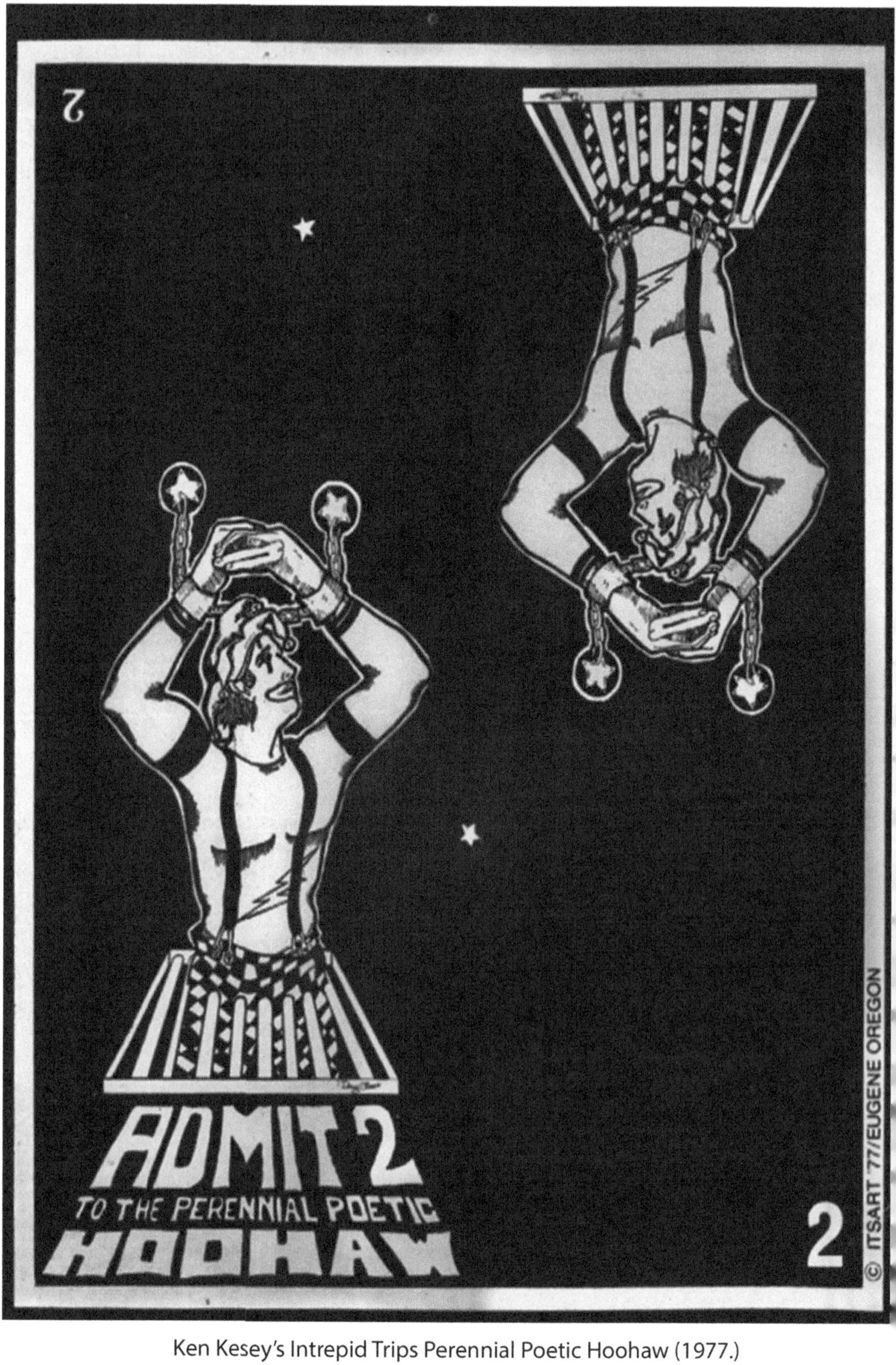

Ken Kesey's Intrepid Trips Perennial Poetic Hoohaw (1977.)

Chapter 12

Parody Not Pastiche
~1977

> The fool is the breakthrough of the absolute into the field of controlled social orders. Almost all non-literate mythology has a trickster-hero of some kind. And there's a very special property in the trickster: he always breaks in, just as the unconscious does, to trip up the rational situation. He's both a fool and someone who's beyond the system. And the trickster represents all those possibilities of life that your mind hasn't decided it wants to deal with. The mind structures a lifestyle, and the fool or trickster represents another whole range of possibilities. He doesn't respect the values that you've set up for yourself, and smashes them.
>
> – Joseph Campbell,
> interviewed by the late Michael Toms

If this doesn't sound like the plotline for *National Lampoon's Animal House,* I don't know what does. Oh wait! That also sounds like the Merry Pranksters! How could I ever forget, that the connections between this film and The Merry Pranksters were so huge that I undertook a 7-year process to make a documentary about it all.[323]

And that we have returned to Chapter O (again). The Fool. In the movie *Animal House,* the protagonists step off the cliff everyday as creative problem solvers. "We can do anything we want! We are college students!" And don't forget Yeats' edict, "to revolt against the intellect." Because if anything, you can get *that* out of this film. Just look at the war between Dean Wormer and the Deltas. Let's explore this... "Furthur."

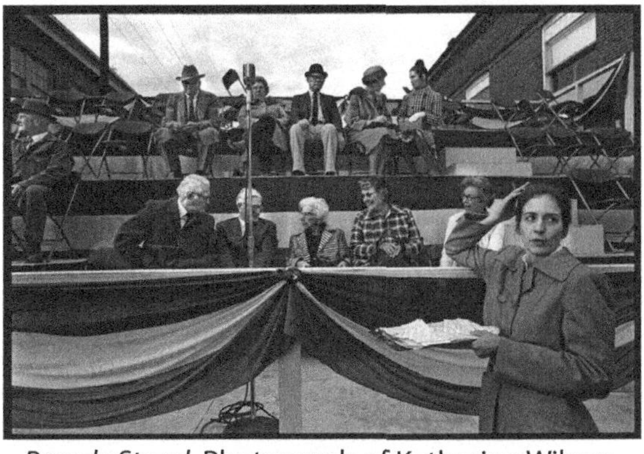

Parade Stand. Photograph of Katherine Wilson by John Bauguess (1977).

Of course it helped that I worked on the film, that I was friends with the Producers and Writers, as I tell you all this. And I was on the bus when the film first came into my life.

Let's take a look at what happened in 1977 in the world at large. It was the last good year of the 60s and the 70s. As David Getz said about Haight/Ashbury, the early years were Medieval, the next were Classical, and then the whole thing went Baroque by 1969. By 1978, when this film came out, the whole culture had gone Baroque. Here are a few examples of why, in this poster, under the headings of *70s Slang* (dictionary) and IN *Style*:

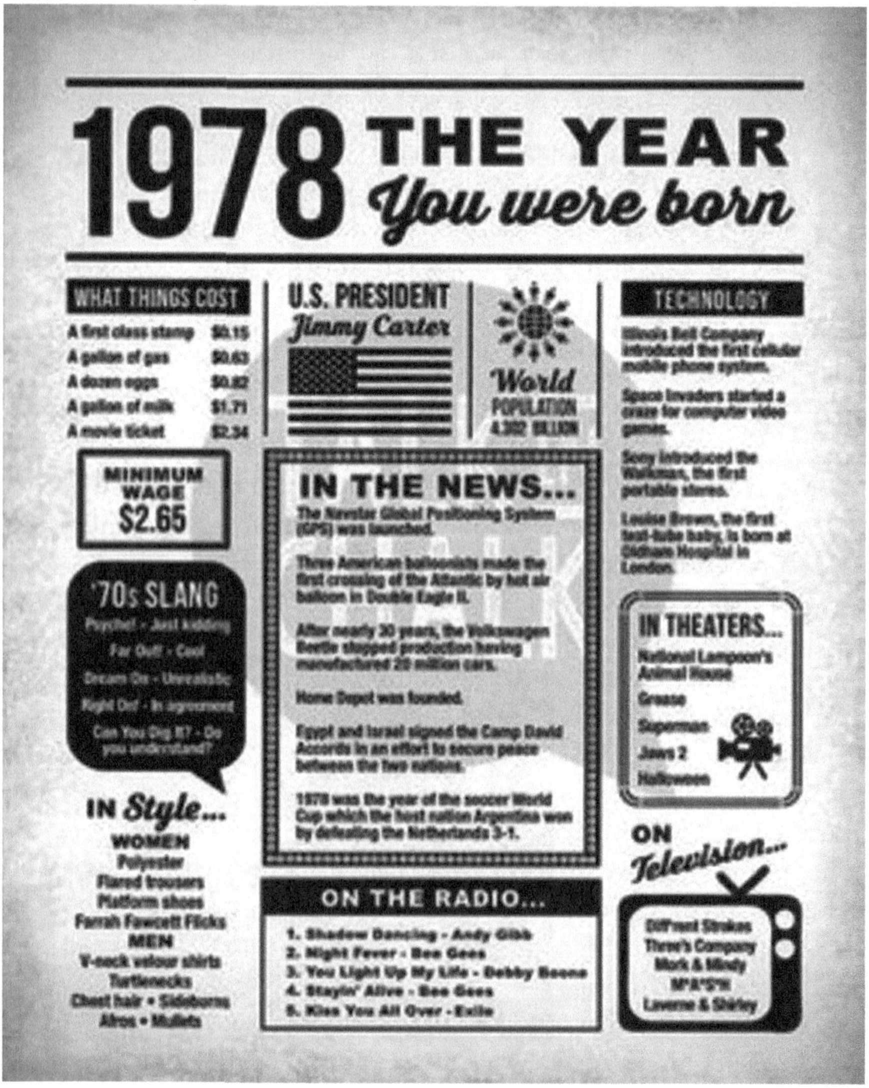

Wikipedia Memes for each year

And when I say Baroque, I mean Parodied… Mocked. Because whatever the 60s were about, spiritually; was lost in the sudden Mass Consumerism of the Culture.

A perfect example was in Boulder, Colorado, when a Monk named Trungpa Rinpoche, who had undertaken a flight to freedom from Tibet under Chinese Communism, and walked over the Himalayas to a refugee camp in India. From there he was sponsored to attend Oxford, and then moved to Boulder to begin an Ashram. By 1978, his Holiness had devised a new Buddhism that attracted Beat Poet Allen Ginsberg to create, with Anne Waldman, The Jack Kerouac School of Disembodied Poets. University of Oregon Alumni Jerry White writes about that:

> Stan Brakhage, the filmmaker, told me of how he'd been asked in 1977 to show his work at a benefit for Naropa poets whose salaries hadn't been paid. 'I told them I'd do it, but only on condition the proceeds went absolutely to the poets, and not to buy a golden pillow to grace the buttocks of the guru,' Brakhage said. 'They said fine, I showed my films, and later found out that the poets' salaries still hadn't been paid, but that $200,000 had been spent to bring in a New York public relations consultant to do a PR campaign for Trungpa."[324]

A perfect example of the commodification of the Peace Love and Understanding generation, yes? But before the awful 80s were over, Trungpa's disciples were dying of Aids. Perhaps this is why the writers of *Animal House* returned to 1962 for their film, the last year of "American Innocence" to Lampoon our generation. Because I think they knew 1962 was the year our generation really began with the publication of Ken Kesey's *One Flew Over the Cuckoo's Nest*. And one of its major tenets was "Question Authority," as if in answer to the Yeatsian question of how to "revolt against the Intellect." This is just like in the film *Getting Straight*, where Elliot Gould explodes regarding the insipid intellectualism in his Master's Thesis Committee Meeting, and again in Jack Nicholson's defense of the attack by Intelligentsia of Karen Black in *Five Easy Pieces*. Yeats' revolt against the Intellect was played out in *Animal House*. And I will happily show you how.

I was once asked to defend the film on NPR, after some rather scathing articles came out against it around its 40th Anniversary, of course from Academe, right when the community had spent nearly six-figures to create a celebration of the film in Cottage Grove, Oregon. I called my defense: "Harvard, Dartmouth and National Merit Scholars Write a Script to Lampoon Academia and Corporate Fraternities: *National Lampoon's Animal House*." The first item of my defense was the National Lampoon's own manifesto: "To nationally criticize someone or something by using irony, ridicule, sarcasm and satire." So, I reasoned, *Animal House* is a lampooning of these 'higher learning' institutions. And it poked huge fun at their "sacred cows." No wonder the University of Oregon tries to live down its notoriety as the location of the film. But it wasn't really aimed at the U of O; it basically came down to this: *It made fun of everybody.* Because, honestly, we humans need to laugh at our-selves once in a while. We have been taking ourselves much too seriously.

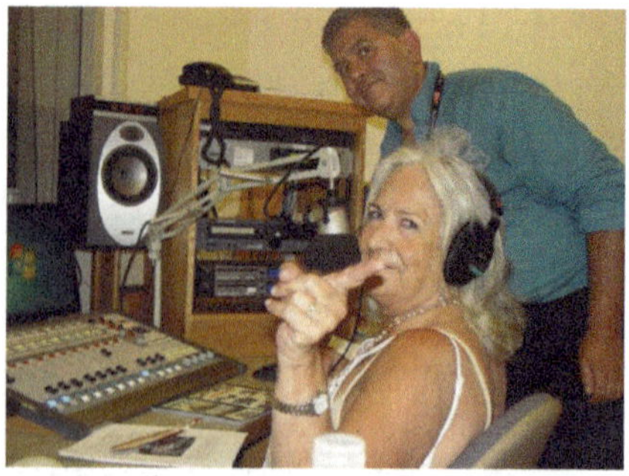

Brian Bull, technician; & guest Katherine Wilson, in the Booth @ NPR

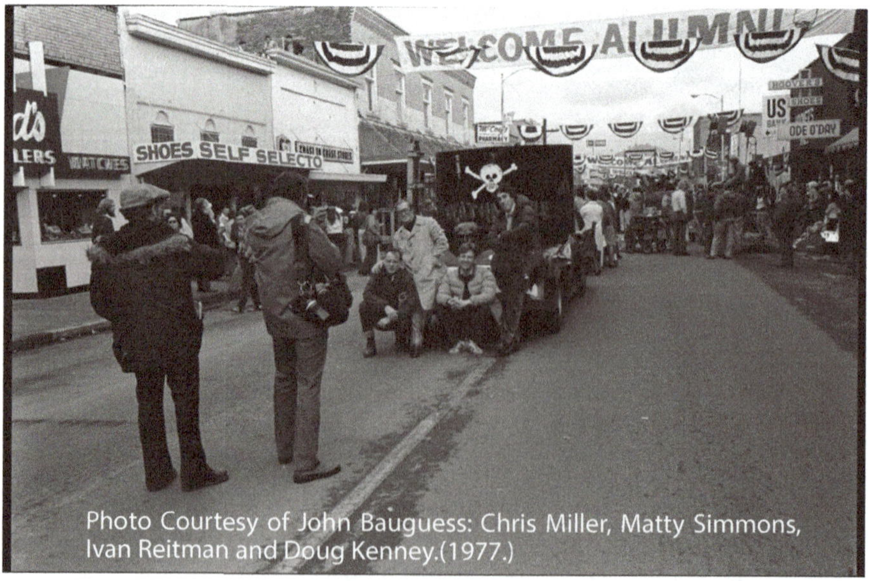

Photo Courtesy of John Bauguess: Chris Miller, Matty Simmons, Ivan Reitman and Doug Kenney.(1977.)

My second defense was that I knew one of the writers, Chris Miller. It was Chris who came on board and changed *National Lampoon* writers Doug Kenney and Harold Ramis' screenplay *Laser Orgy Girls* from a high school to a collegiate comedy called *Animal House*. Harold Ramis didn't want to be just an extra on set, so he didn't come. But I knew Doug Kenney from working on the production of *Animal House*; but not as well as I knew Chris, who returned to Eugene as my guest in later years. Chris was the one who told me that his fraternity at Dartmouth were huge fans of Ken Kesey's.

But East Coast colleges would not allow them to film the screenplay there, plus they were even *protested against* in the Bible Belt. Which is why they ended up calling me at the 11th hour in the late summer of 1977. They had 3 days to find a new location or the movie was to be 'pushed.' As in, off a cliff. When the U of O President finally said 'Yes,' they were floored. Why did the U of O say yes? I told them it was because the U of O had esteemed alumni: This was the home of Ken Kesey and the Merry Pranksters.

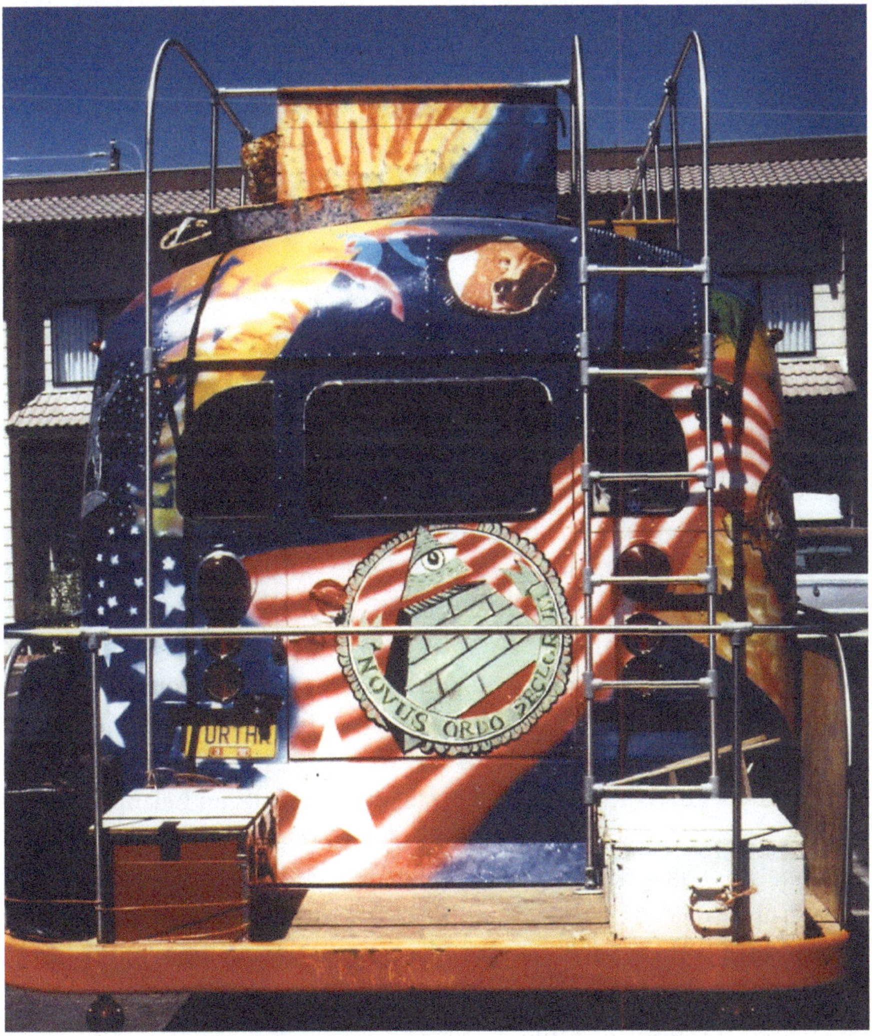

Photo of Kesey's Psychedelic Bus by Katherine Wilson

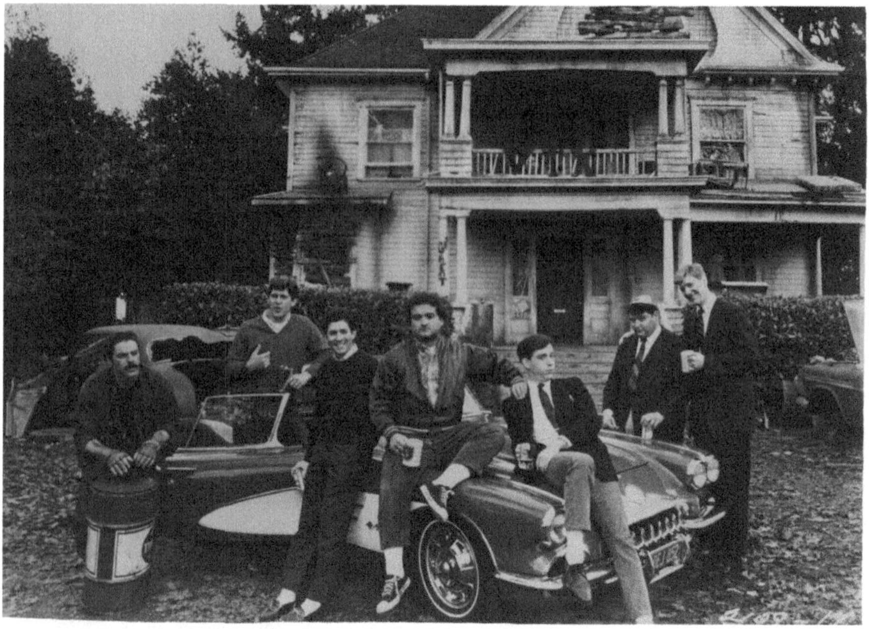

The Animal House with The Animals. Photo courtesy of USL. (1977)

As noted, 1962 was the year *One Flew Over the Cuckoo's Nest'* was published to enormous critical acclaim. And its author greatly influenced *Animal House* writer Chris Miller. By 1964, when Chris was in his last year at Dartmouth College, Kesey was on his psychedelic bus going to New York with his Merry Pranksters. The literary, social and political world has not been the same since. But at the time, Ken was simply on his way to celebrate the publication of his second novel, *Sometimes a Great Notion* at a Publishing Convention back East. Fresh off the press from months spent writing on the Oregon coast, this was Kesey's Magnum Opus about the edge of the "ortidal bore" frontier. Where do you go when the end of the frontier starts turning back on you? You turn back on yourself, you go within. Because consciousness is now the new frontier.

In 1964, Kesey was also on his way to wrestle the minds of the "East Coast" intellectuals, much like his protagonists Hank and Leland did with each other. Kesey was an Oregon individualist who wanted to take on the machine of civilization's pseudo-intellectualism. He demanded authenticity from everyone. He said, 'Spirit is the only currency.' I say, Truth. "But many a truth is spoken in jest." To me, he was the Fool of the Tarot Deck, the Joker, the Prankster of Love. And the first image of this particular chapter was drawn by him for his Perennial Hoohaw. In 1976, 10,000

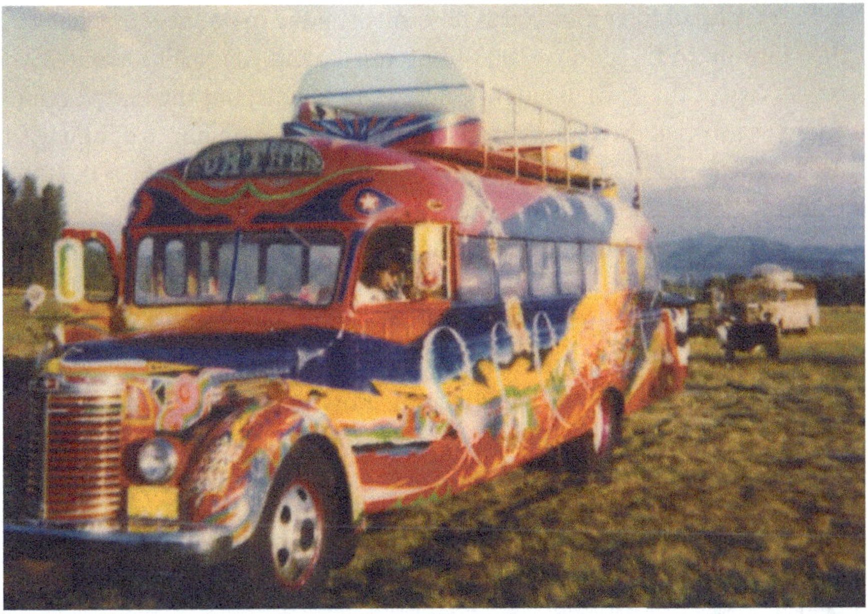

Photo by Katherine Wilson of Kesey's Farm of New Bus and Original Bus, Circa 1990.

people came to celebrate poetry, music and art with him at Mac Court at the U of O. He had a lot of people following him, including Chris Miller, the writer of the original story that also became *Animal House*, which was back then called *Night of the Living Fires* – Chris' Dartmouth fraternity's answer to Tom Wolfe's 1968 *Electric Kool-Aid Acid Test* about Kesey and his Merry Pranksters in 1964.

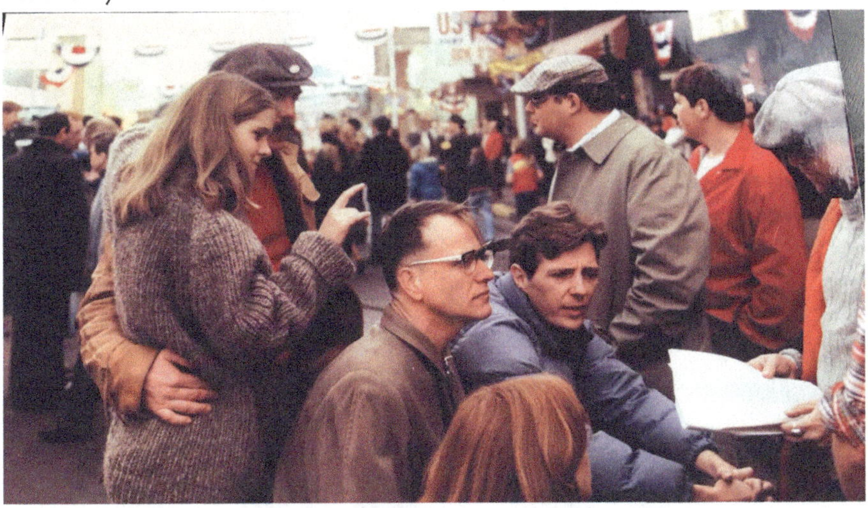

Writers Doug Kenney and Chris Miller in Cottage Grove, Oregon; with D-Day and Clorette DePasto looking on. Photo courtesy of Jonathan Schwarz. (1977)

Later, Chris Miller told me his fraternity wanted to be "beer pranksters." I flew him up to Oregon in 2003 to be our Grand Marshall for our 25th Anniversary of the *Animal House* Celebration Parade, but the first thing he wanted was to visit the Pranksters. He once showed me a photo of him with Kesey at the Dexter Lake Club during filming. In an interview here in 2003, he talked about *Animal House* archetypes, and how we all knew a Bluto, an Otter, a Boon. And I might add a Casanova, a Don Quixote, and a James Dean. But the correlations in the script to the Merry Pranksters was ironic. First of all, the very HOUSE itself was once a hang-out for Prankster Mike Hagen and rented by his side-kick Jackie Springer (and others) because someone had accidently burned down their own fraternity house. This was in 1957, but by the time *Animal House* came to town, it was a half-way house for Parolees going to College. *Truth is stranger than fiction.*

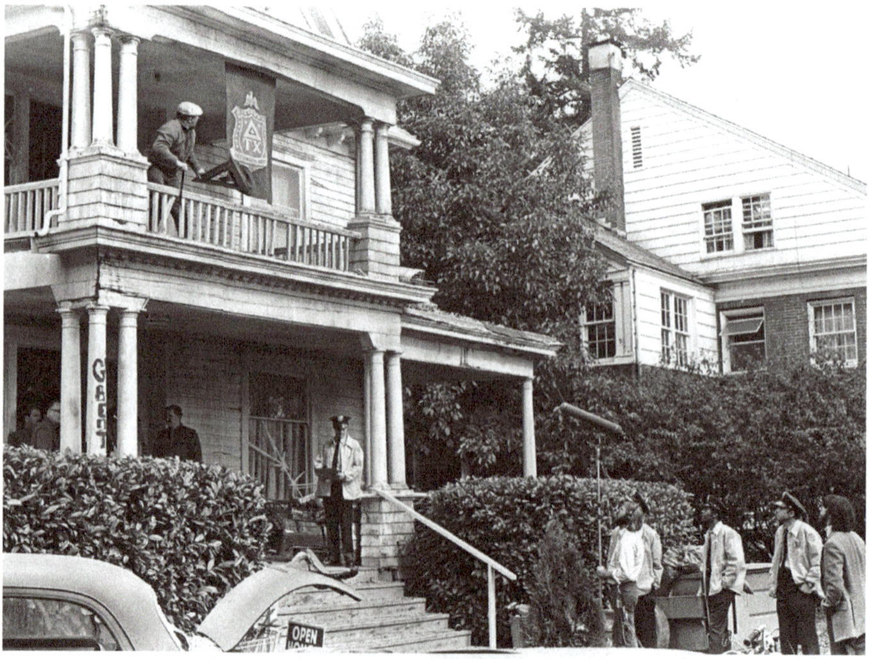

Cast and Crew filming the "They dropped the bar!" scene.
Photo by Gregg Thurlow Weed.

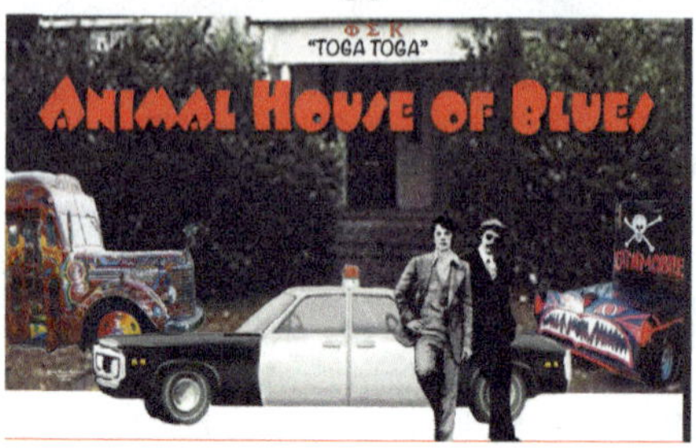

Here are Some other Correlations Between Animal House and the Merry Pranksters:

- Otter says to Flounder: "You %$#@&* up. You trusted us." ('Never Trust a Prankster.')

- They held a "Toga party" much like the Bay area "Acid Trips" in 1966 with Owsley and the early Grateful Dead.

- The Donald Sutherland scene in the bathroom with drugs: "The Universe in a Thumbnail" THAT came right out of Tom Wolfe's book about Kesey and the Pranksters, in *The Electric Kool-Aid Acid Test.*

- The Road Trip, which was first created by Beat Poet Jack Kerouac in *On the Road.*

- Creations of painted vehicles like the Psychedelic Bus and The Deathmobile were NEW!

- Other Ironies: Belushi's first improv coach at Second City in Chicago was Del Close, who was an original Merry Prankster on the Bus.

- Belushi wanted Kesey to play the professor in *Animal House* before Donald Sutherland agreed to do it, and went out to the Farm to visit him, with Landis.

- It was Kesey's Arriflex 16mm camera that created Oregon's first modern film crew. His thousands of feet of footage brought many filmmakers to the area, who were exactly what the Production needed for Location Scouts, (and who shot the locations with Kesey's 16mm camera) Location Production Assistants and Location Casting Directors.

- But more importantly, *Animal House* was written with the same cinematic literary voice as Kesey's, one that Milos Forman called 'subversive.' As was the Anti-heroic, and New Hollywood, comic-book type of storyline.

- Doug Kenney, who played 'Stork' with a slide-rule, was the author of the anti- establishment plot, and the total Lampoon of academia and its corporate brethren, the Fraternities. If you unpack *Animal House,* you will find in the Betas, minds as narrow as their ties, in crewcuts and starched shirts.

- As we see in the ending, the Deltas were the "Alpha Males" because Belushi won in the end when he ran off with the "Queen" of the Cheerleaders. So did Ken Kesey with Faye.

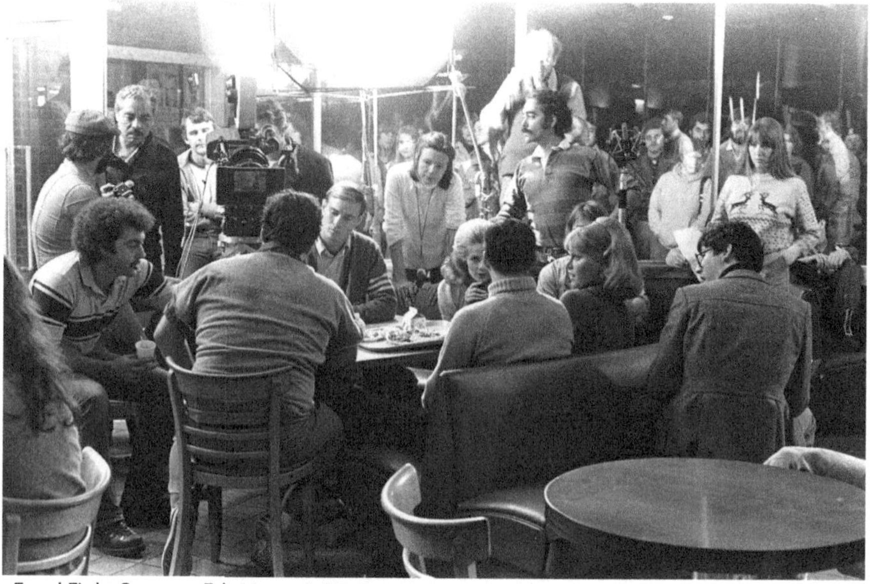

Food Fight Scene @ Erb Memorial Union, University of Oregon. The Betas vs. the Deltas w/ the help of John Belushi. Photo by Gregg Thurlow Weed. (1977.) Used by permission.

In the opening scene, we follow two 'fraternity pledges' across campus as they arrive at the 'Beta House.' We are introduced to Niedermeyer, who slams the door in the face of Kent Dorfman. He mocks civility as he introduces them to the Swim Team Captain, the Sorority Girls, and the Editor of the *Daily Faberian*. He and Greg Marmalard sequester them away with the Blind guy, the Muslim and the Arab/East Indian on the Cast-off's couch. A black waiter passes out refreshments on a tray, a status symbol of past slave-owners, much like Mayor DePasto's 'black servant' statue in the yard. All while classical music is playing under the footage as a soundtrack. Next, we follow them over to "The worst (Frat) house on campus." And they get hosed by Belushi taking a leak. They shake it off and follow him in. Belushi wears a Letterman's Jacket and reminds us of some great athletes, strong & versatile and also stereotypical large and dumb. But when the 'going gets tough,' he gets the Delta's going. Not so dumb. And gets the girl. He's a leader, who later becomes a Senator.

Here our white racist culture is lampooned when our Deltas are relegated to the "Rejects Corner" replete with the mix of races, a Black Man with a Turban, far left; next to him is an Arab/East Indian, then a Jew, and far right, a Handicapped/Blind White man.

It's interesting that the Deltas were immediately pegged by the upper echelon of Fraternal Life and their "Greeter Girls;" and then brought

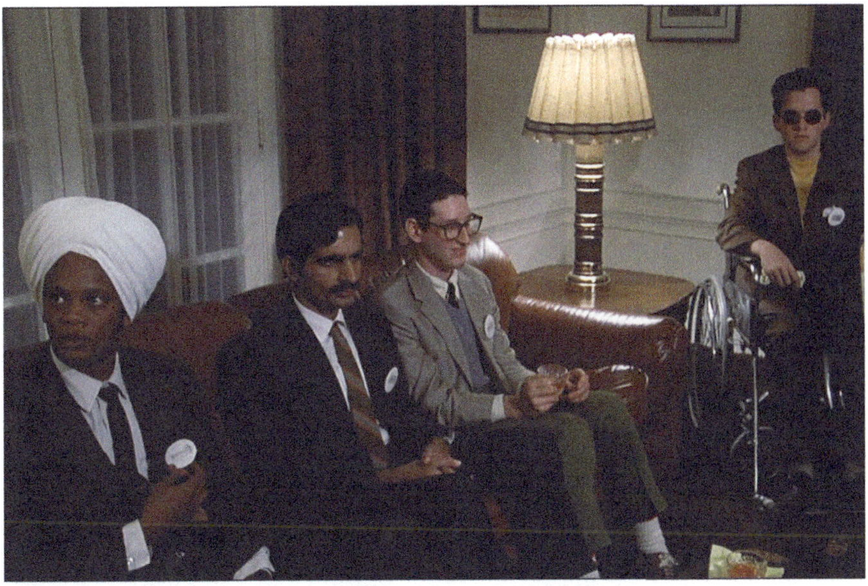

Fraternity Rejects on a Couch. Photo Courtesy of Universal Studios Licensing.

to this corner, because back in the 60's, we flower children were also eschewed by this culture as rejects. We were named freaks, and were so happy to find anyone at all like us. That is why we started things like the Renaissance Fair, in order to find each other within the post-industrial culture, because we just didn't belong to society, as it was then. This tells me what I surmised about the members of Animal House being a parody of our 60s generation, but not a pastiche; because the film doesn't just lampoon Fraternal and Corporate racism, it made fun of *all* of us. Interestingly enough, though, there is one pastiche present, and that is represented by Belushi's costume in the Parade Scene, when he heroically rescues nearly nude Mandy Pepperidge by swinging off the top of a building Tarzan-style; dumping her into a stolen convertible and riding away with her like on a magic steed, wearing a Pirate outfit. If we look closely at his costuming (which in this photo is his identically costumed stunt double, Al Mauro) we see a pastiche or conglomeration of styles. Unpacking from top to bottom, we see a "hippie" bandana-like scarf on his head; then on his upper body, from the inside out, we see

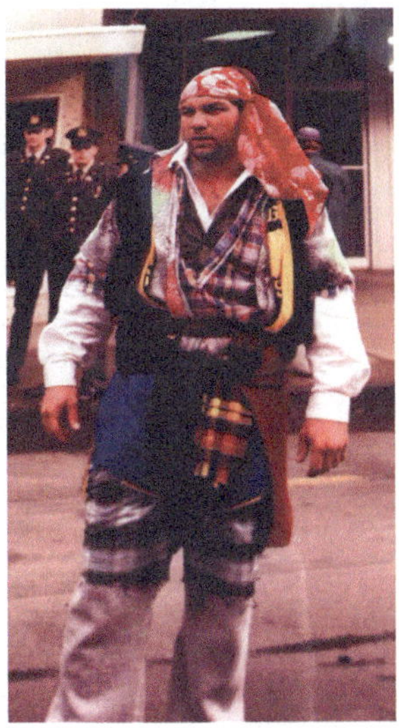

Al Mauro by Jonathan Schwarz (1977).

a 50s era white "starched 'stiff's' shirt," covered by what looks like a 60s Madras-style surfer shirt, then a 70s Polyester Brown shirt, covered by his rather psychedelic "tie-died" shirt he wore in the Louie Louie-singing scene. On top of all that is a bright yellow and plaid scarf, with a black zippered vest. Holding it all together around his waist is a red pullover with black sleeves, giving him a "Indian loincloth" effect.

To finish everything off, we have athletic sweatpants, covered by torn-off-at-the-knees flannel pajama bottoms, covered with track-style running shorts. This man is everyman, and we all root for him when he gets the girl. A Hero with a 0.0 GPA. Talk about railing against the intellect! I love the shot of him flying through the air in his Converse Flyers, too, which you can also see in the image below:

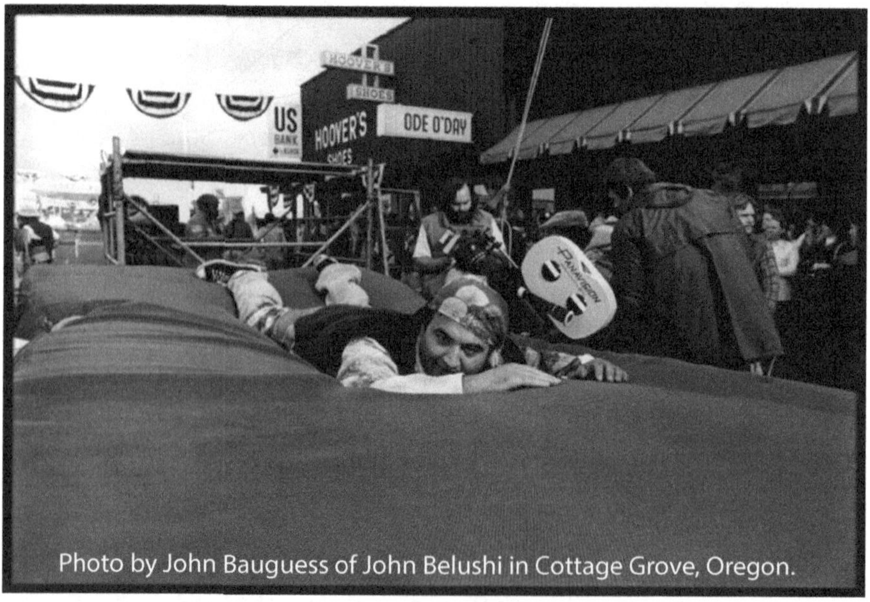

Photo by John Bauguess of John Belushi in Cottage Grove, Oregon.

The other Deltas are dressed more collegiately, like Otter, who anticipates a deep religious ecstasy with his date, (sound familiar? He's just like Prankster Mike Hagen) and Boon, who is reading a *Playboy* magazine and living somewhat vicariously through Otter's prowess, while 'his girl' is downstairs pouring beer for the new pledges in front of a lit mermaid with breasts made of goldfish bowls. Katie, Boon's girlfriend, eases the young "rejected" pledge's nervousness with an unthreatened quip about 'nice fish.' She is a modern woman who is the voice of reason until she doesn't know what to say when caught by Boon sleeping with her professor. She echoes "a woman's mind is her erogenous zone" with this act. But then again, she is a proto-feminist and saves Boon from the police at the end of the film. But Boon is shaken up by this, as the tables are turned now, and then, learning his lesson, he remains loyal to his girl. Otter is more like a goddess worshiper, as evidenced by his "anticipation of a religious experience"; Flounder has good motives with his childhood girlfriend from Harrisburg, the girl he hopes to marry, but hopes he gets "lucky" with one of the Emily Dickenson girls, representing the Madonna/Whore complex. Hoover, however, is a brain, sweet and naive, and sexless, and becomes an attorney. D-day is more interested in mechanical things, represents the 50s with his ducktail hairdo, kind of like Page Browning in the Merry Pranksters; and even Pinto goes with his good conscience when his date passes out undressing. How anyone can call this sexual assault is beyond me, a #MeToo survivor, by the way. The thirteen-year-old date, Clorette DePasto, seems to be like myself and my girlfriends at that age, just young girls, who stuff tissues in their bras to look sexier, testing their powers in and trying their hand at seducing older boys. We were the sexually overt ones, and sometimes it created consequences. But in *Animal House*, in what was clearly consensual before she passed out, was our sweet Pinto who even took her home.

Then, in the Emily Dickenson college lobby as Edith Piaf sings in the background, Otter whistles the song "Peter and the Wolf" as he pranks some Emily Dickenson College girls into coming with him and his friends on the Road Trip. Consensual as well. Girls like Otter.

They arrive at the Dexter Lake Club (a Roadhouse) where Boon's favorite musicians, Otis Day and The Knights are playing. Could there be a greater reference to the polarization of Black and White races? Even the

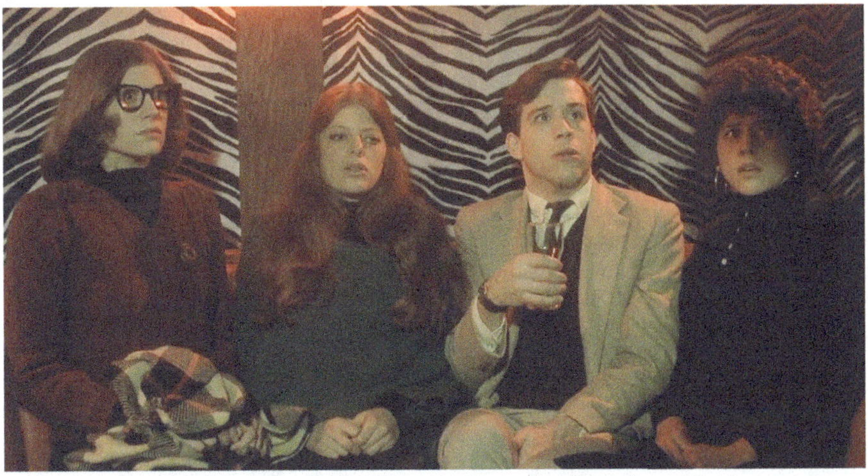

Emily Dickenson Girls: Noreen, Brunella, (Pinto) and Beth.
Photo courtesy of Universal Studios Licensing.

Studio was afraid of instigating riots of racist outcry, when Richard Pryor told them it was funny as hell and 'white people are crazy.' But is it really the Deltas who are racist? Or is it perhaps Brunella, the girl who claims she is majoring in Academia's "Primitive Cultures"?

For me, this scene reminds me of the time in the 60s when my girlfriends Edie, Mary and I went to Berkeley to have lunch at a "Soul Food" Restaurant called *Albertines*, in an all-black neighborhood. When we walked in, the whole place went quiet, and the waitress looked at us like Otis did to our Deltas. Like we weren't even there. The old Indian Reservation stare. I said hello to everybody, but we were not served. Who is racist here? I might add us Indians think "white people are crazy," too, with their hang-ups about sex. I laughed at the scene with Clorette DePasto, because teenagers are encouraged to explore their sexual curiosity in many of the non-colonialized tribes around the world like the Trobriander Tribe in Papua, New Guinea. As a third-generation feminist, I see the young girl initiating sexual innuendo every time we see her, not Pinto. This was indeed my experience in the 60s. We young women were suddenly pursuing who we wanted to have sex with, not the other way around. Even Donald Sutherland, the Professor, seems to be representative of our generation, a Bohemian who smokes pot and sleeps with his students. That happened a lot in the 60s and 70s. So much so we included it in one of our "adult films." I kid you not.

But aren't the true villains here the socially approved Dean Vernon Wormer, the figurehead of Academia; and Niedermeyer, the figurehead of ROTC, and Greggie, the figurehead of the University Fraternity system?

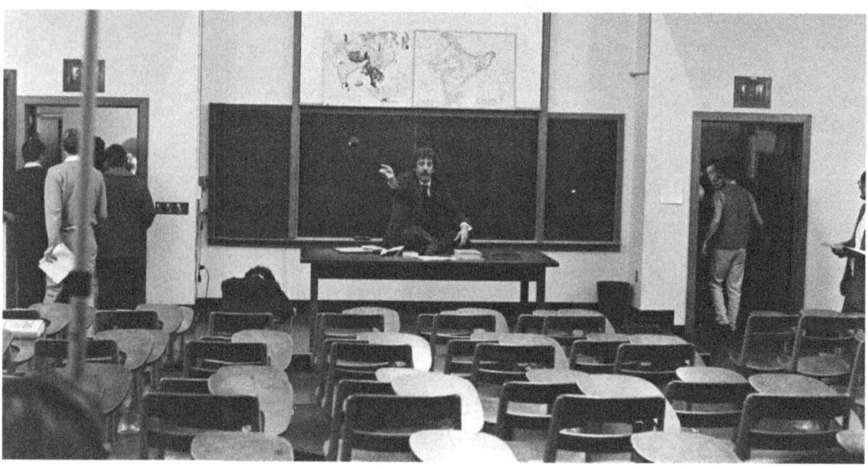

Photo courtesy of Gregg Thurlow Weed (1977).

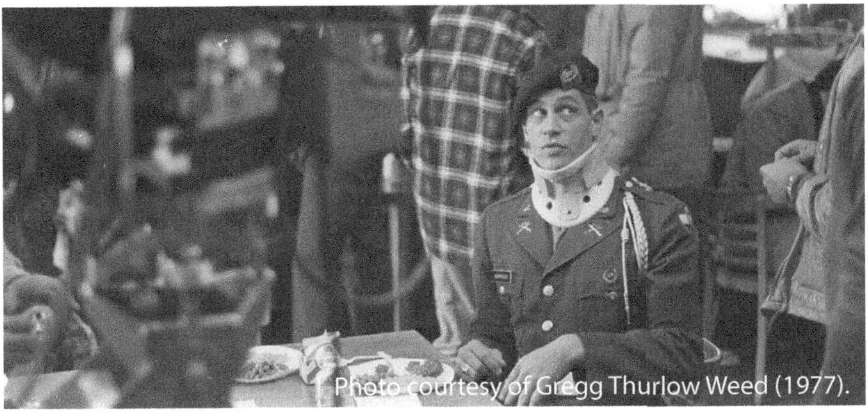

Photo courtesy of Gregg Thurlow Weed (1977).

Are they not the sneaky, underhanded, manipulative, coercing, paternalistic and impotent characters who resort to threats, incarceration and violence to solve their problems? And aren't the Deltas much more creative to solve theirs?

Otter sums it all up in a soliloquy at the end. Yes, the Deltas were created by a system of exceptionalism, stereotypical generalism, labeling, rigidity and control, which in itself is an indictment of the whole fraternity, educational and societal system, but he is not going to let them badmouth the USA, the land of the free.

Even the log-line tells us this: 'It was the Deltas versus the Rules. The Deltas won.' And we came away celebrating that fact: "To Mr. Ramis, the fact was, that "comedy is inherently subversive."[325]

Student Court Scene, *Animal House*. Photo courtesy Gregg Thurlow Weed

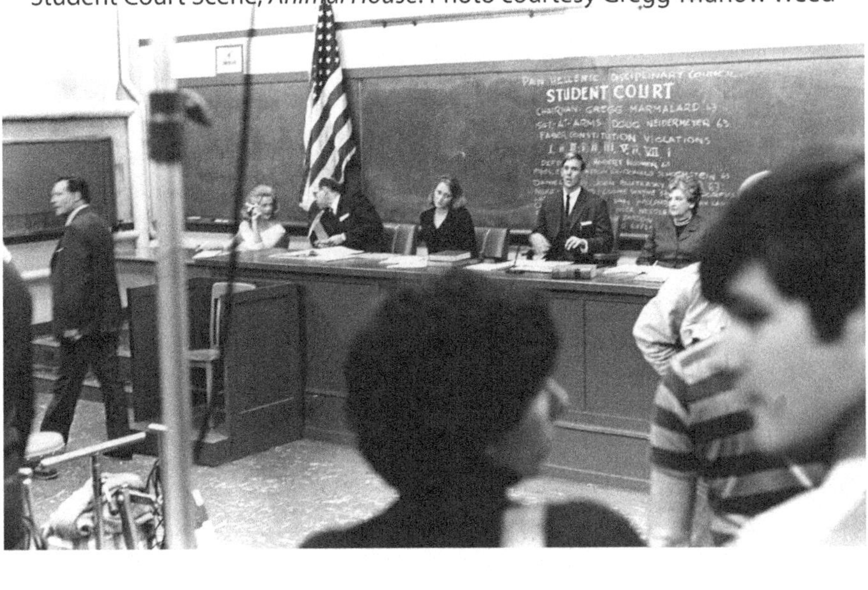

> "We represent the underdog as comedy usually speaks for the lower classes," Mr. Ramis once said. "We attack the winners." He made ... his film acting debut ... in *Stripes,* a comedy about military life that he wrote with Dan Goldberg and Len Blum. The film is an example of his ability to be simultaneously silly and subversive."[326]

"At one point (Bill Murray) even exhorts his fellow soldiers by yelling: "We're not Watusi! We're not Spartans – we're Americans! "That means that our forefathers were kicked out of every decent country in the world. We are the wretched refuse. We're the underdog. We're mutts. Here's proof." He touches a soldier's face. "His nose is cold."[327]

And being mutts, being bicultural, being penal colony progeny, rebels, revolution-aries, the world's tired and poor, and refugee's, in this Cultural Mosaic of America, is what created our greatest strength, diversity. Because we also came here seeking religious freedom, we have a base-line history of Marranism. We, as the bi- and tri-cultural children of the 60s, were the liminal generation. That is because a critical mass of us were lucky enough to realize: "One must submit to Dionysian madness in order to attain the state of primordial unity, a state beyond social barriers and narrow thinking."[328]

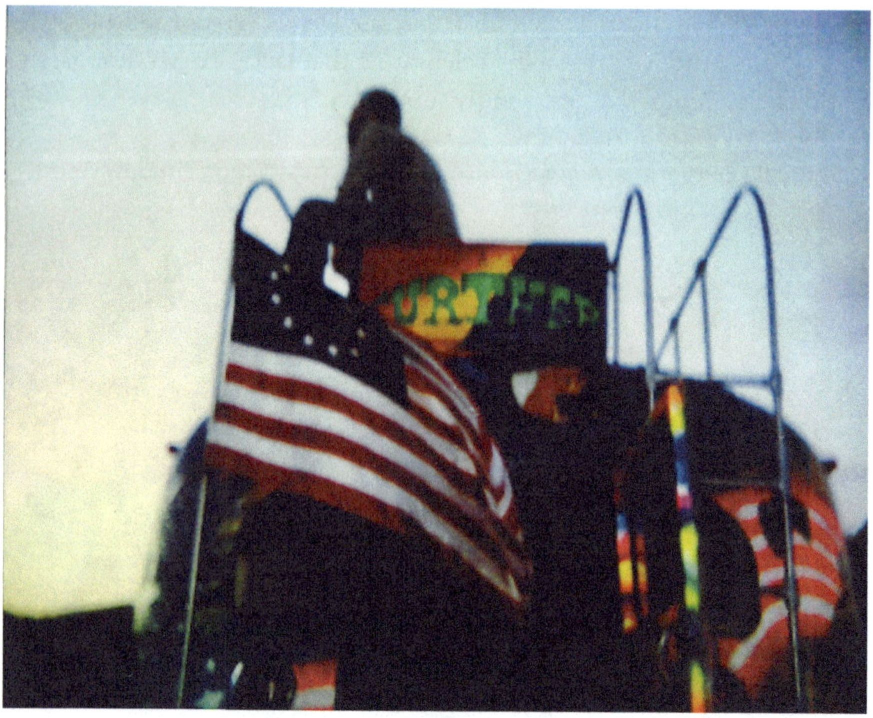

And because of our ancestors, we also came here seeking religious freedom, so we also have a base-line history of Bicultural Marranism. America is a microcosm of the world, working things out.

I will never forget the day I first really knew I wanted to be a filmmaker for the rest of my life. It was in November of 1977; I was at the Dexter Lake Club scene, watching the door while they filmed. Suddenly the scene before me seemed like a messianic one. The stage was lit with red lights, Otis and the Band were lip sinking to *Shama Lama*. As the light

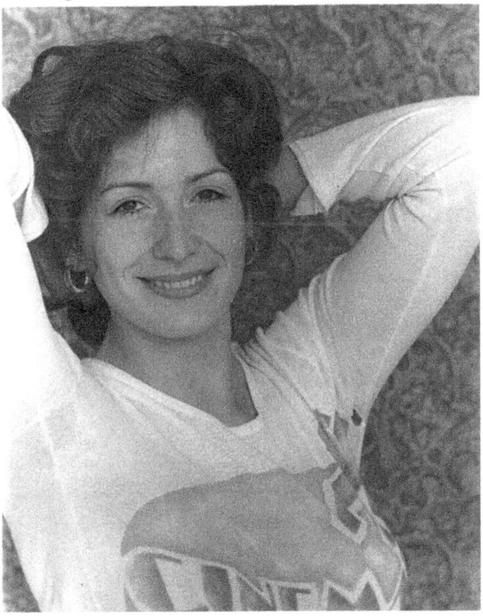

spilled off the stage, you could see that the dancers were dancing, farther out in the darkness, the camera and crew were doing their job. No one had to say anything, because we all caught the Vision. Extras were at the tables in even more darkness, holding their breath, too, in admiration of the Art being created that night. And it reminded me of a Manger Scene; because of everyone's contribution and concentration on the center of light. It was a magical feeling. This shot was in the groove, and a miracle was happening, and as I looked at the scene, I realized we were all there together, black and white, extra and star, Jewish and Christian and Pagan; all equals in the moment contributing to the scene. And I knew that I would spend the rest of my life trying to recreate that moment. When we were all one.

The End

Afterword

As Jung predicted, synchronicity became the hallmark of the New Age, and has been the guiding principal in my life as a bi-cultural woman and as a filmmaker. Our independent film company that began with Kesey's camera in 1964, blossomed on *Animal House* and eventually led to a State-wide Industry. My husband Philip went on to work on over 50 Major Motion Pictures and TV series with Oregon's A-team crew; while I stayed home with my kids and wrote screenplays to be made in Oregon. The same synchronistic force that conspired to put me on Kesey's bus in July of 1969; returned again and again to create miraculous events, whenever I would be open to it. The first one I remember after *Animal House* was running into Belushi in LA a year later. He lived in New York, I lived in Oregon, but one day I was visiting Peter Wolf in LA, when we went to Irv Azoff's house. Irv lived with his Mom despite being the manager of The Eagles, Linda Ronstadt, and the J. Geils Band, among many others. I walk in the door and suddenly I hear "Legs! Legs! What are you doing here!!!!" It was Belushi, yelling the nick-name he gave me in Eugene.

A series of events, including Belushi's death, conspired to bring me into sobriety. I was then led to find my friend Philip again, whom I had not really seen since high school, after over 20 years of being at the same functions and parties, but never at the same time. A synchronistic event also led to buying our first house on Campus, where I was working at the U of O between film jobs; which were, in the first decade, few and far between, until 1991. While working at the U of O in the Continuation Center I was invited, all expenses paid, to attend the Harmonic Convergence with the Grateful Dead in Telluride, Colorado. This was a 3-day event in the summer of 1987 that heralded the opening portal to the Age of Aquarius, and I experienced, 3 years sober, mental telepathy with my friends in Eugene, and birds, rocks and trees talking to me. When I returned to Eugene, I knew the Great Spirit wanted me to return to film, and it just "so-happened" there was a TNT movie coming to the U of O that needed me as Location Scout and Casting Director, and Philip as a Transportation Coordinator, called *Finish Line*. Afterward, we moved to Bainbridge Island, WA. hoping to break into the work in Seattle, but there was a lot of resistance to us. A Quantum Mechanics prayer practitioner intervened and we were offered three jobs within 3 days. I ended up first working on an ABC movie after intuiting I needed to call Barbara Claman in LA, who just so happened was looking for me; and then a River Phoenix film called *Dogfight*, and was also asked to be a consultant for Native American talent on *Northern Exposure*, which led to Elaine Miles from the Rez near Pendleton, Oregon being hired. Philip was also hired on *Crossing the Rubicon*. A series of synchronistic events led us back to Eugene, where I worked with Mike Hagen and Ken Kesey on their screenplay *Last Go 'Round*. After a Grateful Dead show on a Sunday, Kesey was bemoaning the fact the liquor stores were closed, when I just happened to remember that Hoyt Axton had put a 4-pack of his Moonshine-filled fruit jars in my trunk. You can imagine how miraculous Kesey thought that was! The Kesey film project led to another, where I had to research the Nez Perce Tribe. I just "so-happened" to meet a man at a coffee-shop in Eugene who was the founder of the Chief Joseph Circle of Friendship, and he invited me to Tamkaliks in the Wallowas. It just "so-happened" the tribe had lost their First-Aid EMT/Medic due to a death in their family; and it just "so-happened" my partner in the film, Rick Wadkins, was an EMT/ Movie Medic; who showed up within hours. Later, it just "so-happened" that I was in LA looking for American Indian "name talent" to package the screenplay with, and Keanu Reeves came right up to me and talked to me in a restaurant, and Indian Bob came up to me at the American Film Market. Hollywood wasn't ready yet for a film narrated through Indian eyes, but the film, by bringing me to Tamkaliks in the Wallowas, brought me to find my own unknown tribal heritage, and my best-friend-forever, Etta Conner. Years later, wanting to attend our religious Washat Ceremonies closer to home, I found a Buddhist woman in red robes walking and carrying what looked like Potluck fare downtown Cottage Grove. I asked her if she needed a ride, and she said yes. It just "so-happened" she was walking out to the Rodeo Grounds for a Washat Ceremony. After I lost Etta to cancer in 2016, I just didn't have the heart to continue the never-ending development hell of my film projects, and just "so-happened" to be invited to present at Dr. Rust's Introduction to Film class at the U of O. While there, five young filmmakers needed a professional to mentor them in order to graduate. They just "so-happened" to want to film a documentary on *Animal House*, and I just "so-happened" to have written one recently. We went on to win two "Best" awards at the same film festival. And it just "so-happened" that my former pardner at the Oregon Film Factory had just moved back to Eugene, as well as one of my extras who was now a well-known director. They both lent their skills to help the student's film, which brought it up to the high standards of the Corporation for Public Broadcasting, and it was picked up and aired on OPB in May of 2018 to the highest Nielson Ratings in the country during Prime Time. It just "so-happened" that Cottage Grove needed to advertise their "Guinness Book of World's Records Largest Toga Party" and so they paid all the fees. As I had my whole career, I loved working with young filmmakers, and decided to return to the U of O to finish my degree so I could mentor professionally. It just "so happened" that I ended up in a class with a Professor who was a fan of my first book, and before I knew it I was so deeply committed to the U of O that I applied on the year and half-long waiting list for U of O houses. In the meantime, Dr. Rust supported me to write this sequel to my first book over the summer as an English Class, and the English Department gave me an award for expenses. I only had 3 months to write a book that had taken me two years to complete before, so I really had to push myself, and finished it on the Friday of Dead Week, a week early. But it just "so-happened" that finishing it early was a miracle, because we became homeless due to the Holiday Farm fire; and immediately the U of O gave us a house to live in, because I "just so happened" to be on the list. I then got accepted to Grad School and awarded a Graham Fellowship. Then I won a Sigma Tau Delta award. For me, this has all been the Divine Intervention of the Age of Aquarius. All I have ever done is to just answer the call. What is calling you?

Khôra Terminology

There must be circumcision of the word, writing, and it must take place... can only be poetic, an incision in the body of language... It opens the word to the other, and the door, it opens history and the poem and philosophy and hermeneutics.

- Jacques Derida,

Julia Kristeva deploys the term as part of her analysis of the difference between the semiotic and symbolic realms, in that Plato's concept of "khôra" is said to anticipate the emancipatory employment of semiotic activity as a way of evading the allegedly phallocentric character of symbolic activity (signification through language), which, following Jacques Lacan, is regarded as an inherently limiting and oppressive form of praxis. Julia Kristeva articulates the khôra in terms of a pre-signifying state: "Although the khôra can be designated and regulated, it can never be definitively posited: as a result, one can situate the khôra and, if necessary, lend it a topology, but one can never give it axiomatic form."[3]

Jacques Derrida uses khôra to name a radical otherness that "gives place" for being. Nader El-Bizri builds on this by more narrowly taking khôra to name the radical happening of an ontological difference between being and beings.[4] El-Bizri's reflections on "khôra" are taken as a basis for tackling the meditations on dwelling and on being and space in Heidegger's thought and the critical conceptions of space and place as they evolved in architectural theory and in history of philosophy and science, with a focus on geometry and optics.[5] Derrida argues that the subjectile is like Plato's khôra, Greek for space, receptacle or site.

Plato proposes that the khôra rests between the sensible and the intelligible, through which everything passes but in which nothing remains. For example, an image needs to be held by something, just as a mirror will hold a reflection.

For Derrida, khôra defies attempts at naming or either/or logic, which he "deconstructs". See also Derrida's collaborative project with architect Peter Eisenmann, in Chora L Works: Jacques Derrida and Peter Eisenman.[6] The project proposed the construction of a garden in the Parc de la Villette in Paris, which included a sieve, or harp-like structure that Derrida envisaged as a physical metaphor for the receptacle-like properties of the khôra." (https://en.wikipedia.org/wiki/Kh%C3%B4ra)

Live Links to Content

Podcast Interview with Steve Rust and Katherine Wilson about Echoes Vol. I~ (2019):
https://www.splittoothmedia.com/podcast-oregon-film-history-through-katherine-wilsons-echoes-from-the-set/

OPB Version of Animal House of Blues: (2018):
https://vimeo.com/495846734/222df9ea42

EMU Ballroom Casting Call for Animal House: (2019):
https://vimeo.com/400122172/8de7c92b45

Animal House Set & House History: (2019):
https://vimeo.com/401735276/4367deb178

The EMU Food Fight from Animal House: (2019)
https://vimeo.com/399570228/6eab0a62f7

Cinema 7: (2019)
https://vimeo.com/401805694/0167ee0cc3

KEZI Interview of Katherine Wilson Part 1 (1998)
https://vimeo.com/352406178

KEZI Interview about Animal House Part 2 (1998)
https://vimeo.com/352574322

OPB Trailer for Animal House of Blues: (2018)
https://vimeo.com/261167151

Governor's Office of Film and Video Executive Director Tim Williams Interviews Katherine Wilson (2019)
https://vimeo.com/453748115/27f5861e4e

Burger King Commercial: (1977)
https://www.youtube.com/watch?v=pJ3ugB74UNU

Link to Echoes From the Set VOL. I (2019)
https://www.dropbox.com/s/90f6gwvc8cjcy8p/A%2B%20Echoes%20From%20the%20Set%20low%20rez.pdf?dl=0

U of O Research Symposium Session with Dr. Rust and Dr. Alilunas: (2019)
https://vimeo.com/429422032

KJO Radio Interview about Echoes from the Set Vol I: (2019):
https://www.dropbox.com/s/z7eobakfov2q0yn/0827%20Katherine%20Wilson.mp3?dl=0

Vietnam protest Wikipedia:
https://sunsetgun.typepad.com/sunsetgun/2021/03/the-rebel-rousers-psych-out-.html

File: Launching of the ferry "Issaquah," 1914 (MOHAI 6470).jpg." Wikimedia Commons, the free media repository. 19 Nov 2020, 03:53 UTC. 26 Apr 2021, 02:33:
https://commons.wikimedia.org/w/index.php?title=File:Launching_of_the_ferry_%22Issaquah,%22_1914_(MOHAI_6470).jpg&oldid=513417401.

Bibliography

Agape https://usatoday30.usatoday.com/life/2001-11-05-agape.htm.

Alexander, Hartley B. "PLATO'S CONCEPTION OF THE COSMOS." The Monist, vol. 28, no. 1, 1918, pp. 1–24. (JSTOR, www.jstor.org/stable/27900668. Accessed 23 June (2020).

American Film Institute's Program for Jack Nicholson's Lifetime Achievement Award. (1994). In the Katherine Wilson Special Collection at the Knight Library. University of Oregon.

Anleyork, Daniel. Old Testament Narratives, edited and translated. HVP 2011 (pg. 69).

Apollo and Dionysian: https://faculty.fiu.edu/~harrisk/Notes/Aesthetics/Apollonian%20Dionysian%20Dichotomy.htm.

Arendt, Hannah, and Karl Jaspers. 1992. Hannah Arendt/Karl Jaspers Correspondence, 1926–1969. Edited by Lotte Kohler and Hans Saner. Translated by Robert, and Rita Kimber. New York: Harcourt Brace Jovanovich. First published 1985. York: Harcourt Brace Jovanovich.

Arendt, Hannah. 2007. *The Jew as Pariah: A Hidden Tradition. In Jewish Writings.* Edited by Jerome Kohn andRon H. Feldman. New York: Schocken Books.

Arendt, Hannah. *The Jew as Pariah: A Hidden Tradition.* 2007. From the Marrano Phenomenon.

Axmaker, Sean. "Walter Hill: "Operate on your instincts." *GreenCine Daily* (2005).

Babbs, Ken, Re: Kesey *From Cronies*, unpublished manuscript; permission granted Dec 23, 2020.

Barthes, Roland Manteia (1968.) *Roland Barthes and the English Tradition*. Philip Thody, Ed. University of Leeds. First Published May 1, 1977 Research Article https://doi.org/10.1111/j.1467-954X.1977.tb03230.x. Volume: 25 issue: 1_suppl, page(s): 57-67. (May 1, 1977).

Beardsley, Eleanor. NPR. "How we got here." 1968 Protests.

Benveniste, Emil. *Problems of General Linguistics.* University of Miami Press. (1973)

Bernard, Jeff. Associated Press. Interview of Faye Kesey. Jan 18, 2004.

Bicultural Identity: www:https://en.wikipedia.org/wiki/Bicultural identity.

Bielik-Robson, Agata. Special Issue Editor. *The Marrano Phenomenon.* The University of Nottingham, U K. Editorial Office M DP I St. Alban-Anlage 66 4052 Basel, Switzerland. This is a reprint of articles from the Special Issue published online in the open access journal Religions (ISSN 2077-1444) from 2018 to 2019 (available at: https://www.mdpi.com journal/religions/specialissues/marrano).

Bielik-Robson, Agata. The Marrano God: Abstraction, Messianicity, and Retreat in Derrida's "Faith and Knowledge." Department of Theology and Religious Studies, the University of Nottingham, University Park, Nottingham NG7 2RD, UK; agata. bielik- robson@nottingham.ac.uk Received: 14 November 2018; Accepted: 17 December 2018; Published: 29 December 2018. Bielik-Robson, Agata.

Bloom, Harold. *New Edition of Ken Kesey's One Flew Over the Cuckoo's Nest*. Edited, Published by, and with an introduction by Harold Bloom. Published February 1, 2008.

Boot, Adrian/urbanimage.tv. Copyright: (c) 2020 Adrian Boot /urbanimage.tv.

Bordwell, David. *Film History: An Introduction*. McGraw Hill. pg. 451. Quote from Brakhage's Metaphors on Vision. ed. P. Adams Sitney. (New York: Film Culture, 1963).

Campbell, Joseph. Interview by the late Michael Toms in *An Open Life*, p. 39. Harper Perennial Publication. New York. (May 23, 1990).

Cato, Don: https://www.queensworldfilmfestival.com/about/.

Christensen, Mark. Ken Kesey Interview: Burton Wolfe. From *Acid Christ* Pg. 159. Schaffner Press. (2010).

Christianson, Mark. *Acid Christ*. Quote from Burt Wolfe via U of O Professor Bob Williams Page 202-205. Schaffner Press. (2010).

Colman Smith, Pamela. 1909 Tarot card scanned by Holly Voley. (http://home.comcast.net/~vilex/) for the public domain, and retrieved from http://www.sacred-texts.com/ https://en.wikipedia.org/w/index.php?curid=31022204.

Corkin, Stanley. "Cowboys and Free Markets: Post-World War II Westerns and U.S. Hegemony" JSTR.

Corkin, Stanley. Professor University of Connecticut. Letter to Katherine Wilson. August, 2020.

Davidson, Bill. The conquering antihero. *NYT* interview. October 5th, 1975. Pg. 267. https://www.nytimes.com/1975/10/12/archives/the-conquering-antihero-his-portrayals-of-losers-and-misfits-allow.html.

de Bolla, Peter. *Art Matters*. Harvard University Press. Cambridge, Massachusetts. London, England. (2001).

de Man, Paul. "Return to Philology" from *Theory and History of Literature*, Volume 33 (Page 24).

Derrida, Jacques. Essay: "Faith and Knowledge: An Essay on Faith, Reason, and Human Nature. The two sources of 'religion' at the limits of reason alone. p. 34. (1981); p. 100. (1994); p. 262 (1999).

Derrida, Jaques. "Faith and Knowledge." (pg. 58). In The Marrano Phenomenon edited by Agata Bielik-Robson.

Dodgson, Rick. *It's All a Kind of Magic: The Young Ken Kesey*. University of Wisconsin Press (2013).

Donald E. Gordon. *Content by Contradiction*. (Pg. 78) (Pg. 80-83). Essay of Unknown Origin.

Donnelly, Michelle. *Pioneering Women in Screenwriting* (2015) The Script Lab.

Driscoll, Matthew W. *Ken Kesey And Literary Shamanism*. University of North Carolina. Wilmington, DE.

Dürer, Albrecht. Melencolia: https://en.wikipedia.org/wiki/Melencolia_I#/media/File:Albrecht_D%C3%BCrer_-_Melencolia_I_-_Google_Art_Project_(_AGDdr3EHmNGyA).jpg. http://ebookcentral.proquest.com/lib/uoregon/detail.action?docID=894139.

Engels, Friedrich (1984). Der Ursprung der Familie, des Privateigenthums und des Staates. Im Anschluss an Lewis H. Morgans Forschungen (in German). Berlin: Dietz.

Faculty @ Florida International University: "Apollonian" and "Dionysian" are terms used by Friedrich ... https://faculty.fiu.edu › ~harrisk › Notes › Aesthetics.

Fiedler, Leslie. *Return of the Vanishing American*. Stein and Day. New York. (1967).

frankfob2@yahoo.com. *The Broken Land* (1962) synopsis, written by and published on IMDBPro.

Freher, Dionysius Andreas - http://pikabu.ru/story/vopros_znatokam_3702182, Public Domain.

Freud: https://www.geneseo.edu/~easton/humanities/Freud.html.

Frye, Northrup. *An Honoured Guest: New Essays on W. B. Yeats*. United Kingdom, Edward Arnold, 1965. St. Martin's Press, (1966).

Fulda, Bernhard, and Aya Soika. *Max Pechstein: the Rise and Fall of Expressionism,* De Gruyter, Inc., 2012. ProQuest Ebook Central: Created from uoregon on 2020-02-22 16:35:32 http://ebookcentral.proquest.com/lib/uoregon/detail.action?docID=894139.

Galloway, Stephen. *The Hollywood Reporter*. March 29th, 2017.

George-Kanentiio, Doug. *Iroquois Culture & Commentary,* New Mexico, Clear Light Publishers, 2000, Pgs. 53–55. U of O Knight Library.

Gibran, Kahlil. *The Prophet.* Pg. 18 Project Gutenberg. https://www.gutenberg.org/files/58585/58585-h/58585-h.htm#link1.

Ginsberg: https://en.wikipedia.org/wiki/Howl.

Godwin, William: https://en.wikipedia.org/wiki/Anarchist.

Greene, Liz. (PHd. History) & PHd.(Theology) "C.G. Jung's Vision of the Aquarian Age" *Quest* 106:2, pg. 19, 25.

Gwyther, David. Collection of Vietnam Protest Era Documents. (1969): *The Emerald*

Harris, Keith & Richard Gehr, *Rolling Stone Magazine*. August 28th, 2019.

Hegel, G. W. F. *Faith & Knowledge*. Translated by Walter Cerf and H. S. Harris.

Hermine, Freed (1976). "Where do we come from? Where are we? Where are we going?". In Ira Schneider & Beryl Korot (ed.). *Video Art: An Anthology* (1st ed.). New York: Harcourt Brace Jovanovic.

Hoffmann, E.T. A. *The Sandman, The Golden Pot and Other Tales*. Translated by Ritchie Robertson. Oxford: Oxford UP, 2009.

Holmes, Ernest. *The Science of Mind,* 1926. Holmes, Ernest. Living Without Fear: Penguin Publishing Group E-book pg. 113 ISBN:9781101442685, 1101442689. Published: September 2, 2010

Hopi Prophesies: https://www.crystalinks.com/hopi2.html

Hume, Kathryn. "Brautigan's Psychomachia." *Mosaic: An Interdisciplinary Critical Journal* Vol. 34, No. 1 (March 2001), pp. 75-92 (18 pages) Published by: University of Manitoba.

Hutchinson, Pamela. British Film Institute: https://www2.bfi.org.uk/news-opinion/news-bfi/features/where-begin-early-women-filmmakers.

Idziak-Smoczynska, PhD, Urszula. The theological turn of postmodernity. To be alive again. Accessed through: Article in Approaching Religion · July 2013 DOI: 10.30664/ar.6752. From://www.researchgate.net/publication/326298442_The_theological_turn_of_postmodernity_to_be_alive_again/link/5b90d-5f7a6fdcce8a4c8031b/download.

IMDBPro. Http://imdb.com Summary of Drive, He Said.

IMDBPro.com Http://Imdb.com. Bob Rafelson. Bio.

Jefferson Airplane. "Crown of Creation "(1968). BMI

Jenkins, Lee M. Studies in Classic American Literature and American Studies (Quote from Susan Sontag.) https://www-jstor org.libproxy.uoregon.edu/stable/pdf/45176310.pdf?refreqid=excelsior%3Acb5bd4e64962fd07f18ba119c8e4dffa.

Jong, Erica. *Fear of Flying*. Henry Holt and Company New York. (1973).

Jung on God https://carljungdepthpsychologysite.blog/2020/04/18/carl-jung-on-god-quotations/#.X-1k-elKh8w.

Jung, Carl. *Researches Into The Phenomenology Of The Self* (1959) By Bollingen Foundation Inc. Y. Pantheon Books Translated from the first part of Aion: Untersuchungen zur Symbolgeschichte (Psychologische Abhandlungen, VIII), published by Rascher Verlag, Zurich, 1951.

Kesey, Ken. *Kesey's Jail Journal*. Penguin Group / Viking. Publication date: November 1, 2003.

Kesey, Ken. *One Flew Over the Cuckoo's Nest*. Viking. ISBN 0-606-04239-3 (prebound, 1962):

Khôra: https://en.wikipedia.org/wiki/Kh%C3%B4ra.

Kittredge, William. *Owning It All*. Essays: "Silver Bullets". Grey Wolf Press. 1987 Pg. 155.

Levine, Elana. *Wallowing in Sex: The New Sexual Culture of 1970s American Television*. (2007) *American Decades: 1970-1979: Vincent Tompkins, Judith Baughman, Victor Bondi, Richard Layman* (1995) https://flashbak.com/the-decade-of-decadence-a-quick-look-at-the-sexual-revolution- 29469/.

Marranism: https://www.infoplease.com/dictionary/marranism.

Marx, Karl & Friedrich Engels. *The Communist Manifesto*. New York: Signet, pg. 49. 1998).

Michael Beckwith https://en.wikipedia.org/wiki/Michael_Beckwith#:~:

Michaelson, Peter. *The Aesthetics Of Pornography*. Herder and Herder New York. (pg. 19).

Miller, Eddis N. Kantian *Transpositions: Derrida and the Philosophy of Religion*. 28: pg. 82- 92.

Mitchell, Joni. "Woodstock" (1969) BMI

Moretti, Franco. "Dialectic of Fear," in F. M., *Signs Taken for Wonders: Essays in the Sociology of Literary Forms*. Translated by Susan Fischer, David Forgacs, and David Miller. London: Verso, I988, pp. 83-108.

Morris, JM. *The Remembered Years.*

Mouse, Stanley, Poster for The Sierra Club," April 7–9, 1967, offset lithograph, 20 x 13 3/4 inches, AOR 2. 365, collection of Gary Westford, Salem, Or. Photo: Dale Peterson.

Mulvaney, Laura. "Visual Pleasure and Narrative Cinema" 1973: (page 16, I.)

Naas, Michael. Derrida, *From Now On* Bronx, NY: Fordham University Press, 2008

Native Genes: Georgia Tech. http://www.rh.gatech.edu/news/626646/native-american-ancestors-found-genes-many-us.

Nietzsche: https://www.goodreads.com/author/show/1938.Friedrich_Nietzsche. Nietzschean Theory: "God is Dead."

Note on Carl Jung: "The sending of the Paraclete has still another aspect. This Spirit of Truth and Wisdom is the Holy Ghost... He is the spirit of physical and spiritual procreation who from now on shall make his abode in creaturely man. Since he is the Third Person of the Deity, this is as much as to say that God will be begotten in creaturely man."

Note: Eros and Thanatos – "Freud identifies two drives that both coincide and conflict within the individual and among individuals. Eros is the drive of life, love, creativity, and sexuality, self-satisfaction, and species preservation. Thanatos, from the Greek word for "death" is the drive of aggression, sadism, destruction, violence, and death."

Note: Director Kelly Reichardt's term for Leslie Fiedler's "New Psychedelic Western" is "New Age Western."

Oregon Encyclopedia, The. https://oregonencyclopedia.org/articles/ernest_haycox_189 9_1950_/2006.

Oxford English Dictionary.

Paseman, Lloyd. Interview with Steve Bove'. Cinema 7. The *Eugene Register Guard* Newspaper, Sect. D. Pg. 1, 3. Nov. 27th, 1980.

Peter Wolf/ *Deafula*. http://www.peterwolfproductions.com/about-us.html.

Peterson, Elizabeth U of O Film Studies Timeline.

Plato, *Timaeus,* 51a 254 Plato, www.perseus.tufts.edu. Retrieved 2020-07-20. Roberts, Alaina E. University of Pittsburgh.

Plotinus. *The Six Enneads* Written 250 A.C.E. Translated by Stephen Mackenna, The 6th Ennead, page 350. Neoplatonism's "Emanations from the Universe." JSTOR.

Pyle, Forest. Phd. Academic terminology: "radical aesthetic" from his book: *Art's Undoing: In the Wake of a Radical Aestheticism*. Forest Pyle. Copyright Date: 2014. Published by: Fordham University Press. Pg: 328.

Quantum Mechanics https://commons.wikimedia.org/wiki/File:One-loop-diagram.svg.

Raine, Kathleen. *Yeats, the Tarot, and the Golden Dawn.* The Sewanee Review, Winter 1969, Vol. 77, No. 1 (Winter, 1969), pp. 112- 148 Published by: The Johns Hopkins University Press. https://www.jstor.org/stable/27541704?seq=1.

Ramis, Harold: https://www.nytimes.com/2014/02/25/movies/harold-ramis-who-helped-redefine- what-makes-us-laugh-on-screen-dies-at-69.html.

Ramis, Kenney and Miller. *National Lampoon's Animal House.* (1977).

Religious Use of Peyote: https://www.law.cornell.edu/uscode/text/42/1996a.

Sears, Loren: https://www.lorensears.com/.

Shelley, Mary: https://en.wikipedia.org/wiki/Mary_Shelley.

Simon, Alex. Robert Evans: "The Hollywood Flashback Interview." University of Oregon Knight Library. Oregon Films collection, (1929-1983). Stable URL: http://www.jstor.com/stable/27541704.

Tanner, Steven L. *The Western American Context of One Flew Over the Cuckoo's Nest.*

The BBS Story. https://www.criterion.com/boxsets/769-america-lost-and-found-the-bbs-story.

The I Ching https://divination.com/iching/lookup/48-2/.

The *Oregon Journal* Indictment of Local Draft Boards 13; 14. (now defunct.) Written by Kip Morgan. From the David Gwyther Collection. The *Oregon Journal,* Portland, Oregon. (now defunct.)

The Third Voice: https://knowledgeworkx.com/articles/global-intelligence/423/how-to-use-the-third-voice-in- intercultural-coaching How to use the third voice when coaching in an intercultural setting.

Thompson, Kristin. David Bordwell. *Film History, an Introduction.* McGraw Hill. pg. 209.

Washington Post May 4, 1990 "The Harmonic Convergence Revisited." https://play.google.com/books/reader?id=81koDwAAQBAJ&printsec=frontcover&pg=GBS.PT196.

Weiss, Daniel H. Faculty of Divinity, University of Cambridge, Cambridge CB3 9BS, UK; 7 March 2019.

Weller, Sheila. "Suddenly that Summer" *Vanity Fair* article, July 2012. https://archive.vanityfair.com/article/2012/7/suddenly-that- summer?fbclid=IwAR-3SAue3K5UviJtqzSypSqWyTa3kXpaagZHi_uV pOA0Re8DiTuAj QIi LYcA.

Whitmer, Peter 0. "Ken Kesey's Search for the American Frontier ," *Saturday Review,* May- June 1983: pp. 26, 27.

Wikipedia for definition of Linguistics.

Wikipedia. Feminist influences then and now. Erica Jong and Fear of Flying. 1973. Wikipedia https://en.wikipedia.org/wiki/Leigh_Brackett#:~:text.

Wikipedia. The Grateful Dead/"Blues for Allah."

Williams, Raymond. *Marxism and Literature.* Oxford, New York. Oxford University Press. (1977). Accessed through: http://lchc.ucsd.edu/MCA/Mail/xmcamail.2012_11.dir/pdfm9zBHlJ6w8.pdf.

Wilson, Katherine. Interview with Dale Kesey, 2020.

Wilson, Katherine. Interview with David Butkovitch (August 2020).

Wilson, Katherine. Interview with Ed Edmo. (August 2020).

Wilson, Katherine. interview with Gail Lee from the Bookmine. (202).

Wilson, Katherine. Interview with Loren Sears, (July 2020).

Wilson, Katherine. Interview with Lyllye Reynolds Parker. (2020).

Wilson, Katherine. Interview with Lynn Peterson. (July, 2020).

Wilson, Katherine. Interview with Perry Hyde. (July, 2020).

Wilson, Katherine. Interview with Philip Krysl, (July 10, 2020).

Wilson, Katherine. Interview with Rick Johnson. (June 2020).

Wilson, Katherine. Interview with Stanley Corkin (August 6th, 2020).

Wilson, Katherine. Interview with Terry O'Conner. (August 2020).

Wilson, Katherine. Interview with Tom Hyde. (July, 2020).

Wilson, Katherine. Interview with Mike Hagen, (July 2020).

Wilson, Katherine. Recorded Interview with Dale Kesey. (July 2020).

Wilson, Katherine. Interview with David Gwyther (2020).

Wilson, Katherine. Interview with Bob Laird (2020).

Wilson, Katherine. Interview with Ron West (2020).

Wilson, Katherine. Interview with Mike Dilley (2020).

Wilson, Katherine. Interview with Ron Finne (2020).

Wolf, Peter. Deafula. http://www.peterwolfproductions.com/about-us.html.

Woo, Elaine. "Bert Schneider dies at 78; 'Easy Rider' producer" *Los Angeles Times* Dec. 14, 2011 12 AM PT.

Works, Mary. T*he Life and Times of the Red Dog* David Getz Interview.

Works, Mary. *The Life and Times of the Red Dog Saloon* DVD (1993)

Works, Mary. *The Life and Times of the Red Dog Saloon*. Milan Melvin interview.

Wright, Brett. Article on Kelly Reichardt. Split Tooth Media.

Yeats Poem: Second Coming. Poetry Foundation: https://www.poetryfoundation.org/poems/43290/the-second-coming.

Yeats, William Butler. Letter to John O'Leary, July 1892 [Yeats' spelling], in Letters, 1865 95, Vol. I, OUP 1986, p. 303.

Zeyl, Donald and Barbara Sattler, "Plato's Timaeus", The *Stanford Encyclopedia of Philosophy* (Summer 2019 Edition), Edward N. Zalta (ed.), URL = <https://plato.stanford.edu/archives/sum2019/entries/plato-timaeus/>2001 Space Odyssey

FILMOGRAPHY

1. *2001 Space Odyssey*
2. *A Few Notes on Our Food Problem*
3. *Agnes of God*
4. *Aliens*
5. *Animal House of Blues*
6. *Atlantis Rising*
7. *Behind the Green Door*
8. *Beverly Hills Cop*
9. *Bob and Carol, Ted and Alice*
10. *Bring Me the Head of Alfredo Garcia*
11. *Bringing Up Baby*
12. *Buffalo Bill and the Indians, or Sitting Bull's History Lesson*
13. *Butch Cassidy and the Sundance Kid*
14. *Cahill, Us Marshal*
15. *Cheyenne Autumn*
16. *China Syndrome*
17. *Chinatown*
18. *Cinderella Liberty*
19. *Close Encounters of the Third Kind*
20. *Closed Mondays*
21. *Daisies*
22. *Dance Hall girls*
23. *Dances With Wolves*
24. *Deafula*
25. *Deep Throat*
26. *Diamonds Are a Girl's Best Friend*
27. *Dixie Lanes*
28. *Don't Come Knocking*
29. *Don't Look Now*
30. *Drive, He Said*
31. *Easy Rider*
32. *El Dorado*
33. *Fatal Attraction*
34. *Five Easy Pieces*
35. *Flash Dance*
36. *Flight to Fury*
37. *Gentlemen Prefer Blondes*
38. *Getting Straight*
39. *Hair*
40. *Harold and Maude*
41. *Harry and Walter Go to New York*
42. *Have Gun Will Travel*
43. *Heaven and Earth Magic*
44. *Hell On Wheels*
45. *His Girl Friday*
46. *Hombre*
47. *How Old Is Water*
48. *How to Beat the High Cost of Living*
49. *Indecent Proposal*
50. *It Happened One Night*
51. *Jewel of the Nile*
52. *King of Marvin Gardens*
53. *Klute*
54. *Little Big Man*
55. *Lonely Are the Brave*
56. *Love Story*
57. *Lumberjacks*

58. *Magic Trip*
59. *March on Washington*
60. *Marnie*
61. *Meek's Cutoff*
62. *Midnight Cowboy*
63. *Ms. Sherlock Holmes*
64. *My Darling Clementine*
65. *National Lampoon's Animal House*
66. *Olive Trees of Justice*
67. *On Golden Pond*
68. *One Flew Over the Cuckoo's Nest*
69. *Only Angels Have Wings*
70. *Personal Best*
71. *Psyche-out*
72. *Rashomon*
73. *Red Dog Saloon*
74. *Red River*
75. *Reel Injuns*
76. *Return to Lonesome dove*
77. *Ride the Whirlwind*
78. *Rio Bravo (1959),*
79. *Rio Lobo*
80. *Romancing the Stone*
81. *Romeo and Juliet*
82. *Scarface*
83. *Sergeant York*
84. *Skinner's Beaut*
85. *Smoke Signals*
86. *Sometimes a Great Notion*
87. *Stand By Me*
88. *Star Wars: Episode V - The Empire Strikes Back (1980)*
89. *Street Girls*
90. *Sunshine Daydream*
91. *Swinging Ski Girls*
92. *Swinging Sorority Girls*
93. *Tamanawis Illahee: Rituals and Acts in a Landscape*
94. *The Big Sleep (1946)*
95. *The Birds*
96. *The Broken Land*
97. *The Cowboys (72)*
98. *The Fortune*
99. *The Fox ('67)*
100. *The Godfather*
101. *The Graduate*
102. *The Kid is All right*
103. *The Kid Stays in the Picture*
104. *The Last Samurai*
105. *The Lone Ranger*
106. *The Reivers ('69)*
107. *The Rifleman*
108. *The Rose ('79)*
109. *The Searchers*
110. *The Shooting*
111. *Butch Cassidy and the Sun-dance Kid*
112. *The Trip*
113. *The Way West*
114. *Thieves Like Us*
115. *Thunder Alley*
116. *Thunder Island*
117. *To Have and Have Not*
118. *Top Gun*
119. *Tribal Home Movies*
120. *Twentieth Century*
121. *Twilight*
122. *Two Lane Blacktop*
123. *Untitled Girl*
124. *Vrooder's Hootch aka Crazy world of Julius Vrooder*
125. *Welcome Wagon Girls*
126. *Woodstock*

Endnotes

1 Dionysius Andreas Freher. Public Domain. https://commons.wikimedia.org/w/index.php?curid=57449504.

2. Wheel designed by Katherine Wilson; Graphics by Lynn Peterson

3 Malcolm X. Diary entry, 24 September 1964.

4 Carl Jung on God. April 18, 2020

5 Liz Greene, "C.G. Jung's Vision of the Aquarian Age" *Quest* 106:2, pg 19-25

6 *Ibid.*

7 Samael Aun Weor Astrological Chart: https://www.gnosticmuse.com.

8 https://www.crystalinks.com/hopi2.html

9 https://www.poetryfoundation.org/poems/43290/the-second-coming

10 Paraclete/Holy Spirit/The Comforter Ether, the 5th Element /Goddess.

11 Rusty Goldman Interview by Katherine Wilson.

12 Katherine Wilson Interview with Honey Green August 25th, 2020

13 "Tribal Home Movies" News clip. Eugene *Register Guard* 4/13/2007. Pg. 15. Courtesy of Loren Sears.

14 David Bordwell. Film History An Introduction. Mc Graw Hill. pg. 451. Quote from Brakhage's *Metaphors on Vision.* ed. P. Adams Sitney. (New York: Film Culture, 1963), n.p. (Stan Brakhage also quotes Genesis:' first six words of the Bible.)

15 Pamela Colman Smith –Albano Waite Tarot Deck. 0. The Fool.

16 Kathleen Raines. Kathleen Raine. *Yeats, the Tarot, and the Golden Dawn*. The Sewanee Review, Winter 1969.

17 Cover of *Time* magazine, April 8th, 1966.

18 Friedrich Nietzsche https://www.goodreads.com/author/show/1938.Friedrich_Nietzsche.

19 Friedrich Nietzsche https://www.goodreads.com/quotes/22827-god-is-dead-god-remains-dead-and-we-have-killed.

20 Yeats (Letter to John O'Leary, July 1892). *Yeats in Kelly & Domville*, 1986, Pg. 303.

21 Mary Shelley. https://en.wikipedia.org/wiki/Anarchism.

22 Plotinus, *6th Ennead* page 350. Neoplatonism's Emanations from the Universe.

23 Samael Aun Weor, Astrological Chart: https://www.gnosticmuse.com.

Note: Gnostic philosopher Samael Aun Weor declared February 4, 1962 to be the beginning of the "Age of Aquarius" heralded by the alignment of the first six planets, the Sun, the Moon and the constellation Aquarius.

24 Raymond Williams "Structure of Feeling." Oxford Reference. *Preface to Film* (1954). Raymond Williams. n, published by the Oxford Press. Chapter 8. Dominant Residual and Emergent. Pg. 126

25 Gyre and images https://www.crystalinks.com/gyresyeats.html

26 *Ibid.*

27 Raymond Williams "Structure of Feeling." Oxford Reference.

28 *Ibid.*

29 Peter de Bolla, *Art Matters*. Pg. 1.

30 Sheila Weller. LSD, Ecstasy, and a Blast of Utopianism: How 1967's "Summer of Love• All Began. V*anity Fair*. https://www.vanityfair.com/culture/2012/07/lsd-drugs-summer-of-love-sixties

31 Karl Marx.

32 Moretti, Franco. *Dialectic of Fear, Signs Taken for Wonders: Essays in the Sociology of Literary Forms.*

33 Pamela Colman-Smith. Tarot Deck by Albano-Waite.

34 Donald Gordon, *Content by Contradiction* (1962)

35 John Trudell. *The Lion's Roar.*

36 *Reel Injuns*. Interview with John Trudell.

37 Joni Mitchell song "Woodstock."

38 Native American Peyote: 42 US Code Section 1996a. Traditional Indian religious use of peyote.

39 Ken Babbs. *Cronies*. Used by permission from author. Unpublished.

40 Rick Dodgson, *The Young Ken Kesey: It's All a Kind of Magic.* (2013) by University of Wisconsin Press.

41 Kathleen Raine, *Yeats the Tarot and the Golden Dawn*, pg. 112

42 Rick Dodgson, T*he Young Ken Kesey: It's All a Kind of Magic.* (2013) by University of Wisconsin Press.

43 *Ibid.*

44 The Tower Tarot Deck card by Pamela Colman-Smith.

45 Seth Abramson. Attorney. Professor. Journalist. NYT bestselling author. Meta-modernist.

46 Peter Michaelson. Professor of English, Creative Writing, University of Colorado, Boulder. Woodrow Wilson Special Fellowship, University of Chicago; Notre Dame, Northwestern University.

48 Alexander, Hartley B. "Plato's Conception Of The Cosmos."

49 *Ibid*

50 *Ibid*

51 Matthew W. Driscoll *Ken Kesey and Literary Shamanism*

52 Rick Dodgson, *The Young Ken Kesey: It's All a Kind of Magic*

53 Katherine Wilson Interview with Dale Kesey July, 2020

54 Steven L Tanner. "The Western American Context of One Flew Over the Cuckoo's Nest." Article. Pg. 68.

55 Katherine Wilson interview with Dale Kesey, July 10th, 2020

56 *The Oregon Encyclopedi*a.

57 Steven Tanner. The Western American Context of One Flew Over the Cuckoo's Nest." Article. Pg.165.

58 Quoted in Peter 0. Whitmer, "Ken Kesey's Search for the American Frontier ," *Saturday Review*, May-June 1983: pp. 26, 27.

59 *Ibid.*

60 Wikipedia contributors. "Bicultural identity." Wikipedia, The Free Encyclopedia. Wikipedia, The Free Encyclopedia, 26 Sep. 2020.

61 Wilma Mankiller Natives In America An Online Literary Publication For Native American, Alaska Native, & Native Hawaiian Youth.

62 The Quinde Journey | The Guancavilcas

63 *Echoes From the Set Vol. II (1967-1977) Shadows From the Underground: Cinema Under the Influence.* (August 2021)

64 Harjo and Byrd. Introduction, Pg. 2 of *Reinventing The Enemy's language*: Note: Regarding the use of the terms "Indian," "native," and "Native American": Native American is a term invented in academe and is the term of the moment. It was invented to replace the term American Indian. This is a serious misnomer. In our communities we first name ourselves by tribe, but the general term commonly used is Indian in the United States and native in Canada. Canadian tribes also use the term First Nations with which to address their peoples.

65 Arendt, Hannah. 2007. The Jew as Pariah: A Hidden Tradition. In *Jewish Writings*. Edited by Jerome Kohn and Ron H. Feldman. New York: Schocken Books.

66 Agata Bielik-Robson, Editor. The University of Nottingham U K.

67 Peter Alilunas. 2020 *History of the Motion Picture* II Class.

68 Daniel Weiss, Faculty University of Cambridge, Cambridge

69 Jacques Derrida, "Marx & Sons" (Derrida 1999, p. 262).

70 "Return to Philology" from *Theory and History of Literature,* Volume 33 by Paul de Man, (Page 24.)"

71 *Art Matters*. Peter de Bolla. pg. 127

72 Katherine Wilson Contemporary Criticism paper in ENG 419. Spring 2020.

73 Genesis.

74 Percy Blythe Shelley. *Ode to the West Wind*. 1819

75 CN (Nest 10).

76 Ken Kesey. *One Flew Over the Cuckoo's Nest* ('62).

77 Mathew Driscoll. Thesis: *Ken Kesey And Literary Shamanism*

78 *Ibid.*

79 *Ibid.* (Pg. 175.)

80 Leslie Fiedler. *The Vanishing American*.

81 Mary Works. *The Life and Times of The Red Dog Saloon*. Documentary.

82 Katherine Wilson. *Echoes From the Set (Vol. I)* Chapters 5 & 6. (2019

83 William Butler Yeats. The Second Coming. *The Dial* (November 1920) and published in his collection of verse entitled Michael Robartes and the Dancer (1921).

84 W. B. Yeats. *Michael Robartes and the Dancer*. Cuala Press. Pg. 34. (1921).

85 Bohm, Arnd. "Northrop Frye: The Consolation of Criticism." *Monatshefte*, vol. 95, no. 2, 2003, pp. 310–317. JSTOR, www.jstor.org/stable/30154107. Accessed 10 Apr. 2021.

86 *Ibid.*

87 Edith Hamilton. *Mythology: Timeless Tales of Gods and Heroes*, 1942 by Little, Brown and Company.

88 Wikipedia contributors. "Northrop Frye." Wikipedia, The Free Encyclopedia. Wikipedia, The Free Encyclopedia, 6 Apr. 2021.

89 *The Double Vision: Language and Meaning in Religion* by Northrup Frye (1991).

90 Alice Macdonald. Katherine Wilson email conversation. Feb 8th, 2021.

91 Bohm, Arnd. "Northrop Frye: The Consolation of Criticism." *Monatshefte*, vol. 95, no. 2, 2003, pp. 310–317. JSTOR, www.jstor.org/stable/30154107. Accessed 10 Apr. 21.

92 Sheila Weller. LSD, Ecstasy, and a Blast of Utopianism: How 1967's "Summer of Love" All Began. *Vanity Fair*. https://www.vanityfair.com/culture/2012/07/lsd-drugs-summer-of-love-sixties.

93 Mary Works. *The Life and Times of The Red Dog Saloon*. Dave Getz Interview. Documentary.

94 *Film History: An Introduction* (4th Edition) Bordwell and Thompson (Pg. 451). Paraphrases from Brakhage: Metaphors On Vision, ed. P Adams Sitney (New York: Film Culture, 1963) n.p.

95 Bhagavandas. *It's Here Now, Are You?* https://www.last.fm/music/Bhagavan+-Das/+images ('85)

96 Sheila Weller. LSD, Ecstasy, and a Blast of Utopianism: How 1967's "Summer of Love• All Began. *Vanity Fair*. https://www.vanityfair.com/culture/2012/07/lsd-drugs-summer-of-love-sixties.

97 *Ibid.*

98 Andrea Smith (Cherokee intellectual, feminist, and anti-violence activist) *Heteropatriarchy And The Three Pillars Of White Supremacy: Rethinking Women Of Color Organizing.*

99 Philip Deloria. Harvard Professor. *Counterculture Indians and the New Age.*

100 *Ibid.*

101 Yeats, W.B., *Mythologies* (London: Macmillan, 1963), p. 345-346.

102 Philip Deloria. Article: "Playing Indian." Yale University Press. Pg. 158, 170.

103 UCSF Campus news by Nina Bai. Born in the Summer of Love: The Haight Ashbury Free Clinic Transformed Drug Addiction Treatment. Clinic Launched by UCSF Doctor Is Celebrating 50th Anniversary.

104 Wikipedia contributors. "LaNada War Jack." Wikipedia, The Free Encyclopedia. Wikipedia, The Free Encyclopedia, 20 Mar. 2021. Web. 22 Apr. 2021.

105 Angela Aleiss. *Native Americans And Hollywood Movies: Making the White Man's Indian* Pg. 119.

106 Wikipedia contributors. "LaNada War Jack." Wikipedia, The Free Encyclopedia. Wikipedia, The Free Encyclopedia, 20 Mar. 2021. Web. 22 Apr. 2021.

107 Neil Diamond. *Reel Injuns*. Documentary.

108 John Trudell. Interview in documentary *Reel Injun* (85 min). 2009.

109 Yeats, W.B., *Mythologies* (London: Macmillan, 1963), p. 345-346.

110 Wikipedia contributors. "Native Americans in the United States." Wikipedia, The Free Encyclopedia. Wikipedia, The Free Encyclopedia, 20 Apr. 2021. Web. 20 Apr. 2021.

111 Philip Deloria. Article: "Playing Indian." Yale University Press. Pg. 158, 170.

112 *Ibid.*

113 Northrup Frye. *An Honoured Guest: New Essays on W. B. Yeats*. United Kingdom, Edward Arnold, 1965

114 Hopi Prophesy, Wikimedia.

115 Northrup Frye. *An Honoured Guest: New Essays on W. B. Yeats*. UnitedKingdom, Edward Arnold, 1965.

116 Northrup Frye. *An Honoured Guest*. Chapter II. "The Rising of the Moon: A Study of "A Mission". Pg. 15.

117 *Ibid.* Pg. 16.

118 Charles Parnell/Wikipedia

119 Northrup Frye. An Honoured Guest. Chapter II. "The Rising of the Moon: A Study of "A Mission".

120 *Ibid.*

121 Emilie Kutash, Philosophy Department, Salem State University, Salem, MA.

122 Ernest Holmes. *Living Without Fear*. Penguin Publishing Group 1926.

123 Carter, Dr. Lawrence E., Dean of Morehouse College International Chapel (2019).

124 Sheila Weller. LSD, Ecstasy, and a Blast of Utopianism: How 1967's "Summer of Love• All Began. *Vanity Fair*. https://www.vanityfair.com/culture/2012/07/lsd-drugs-summer-of-love-sixties.

125 *Ibid.*

126 Steven L Tanner in his article "The Western American Context of One Flew Over the Cuckoo's Nest" pg. 165.

127 Sora Han, *Bonds of Representation: Vision, Race and Law in Post-Civil Rights America*. Cruz: University of California B Santa Cruz, (2006).

128 Oxford English Dictionary.

129 Plotinus, *6th Ennead.*

130 Eleanor Beardsley. NPR "How we got here."

131 *Ibid.*

132 *Ibid.*

133 https://en.wikipedia.org/wiki/Howl

134 Philip Krysl Interview by Katherine Wilson July, 2020. July 10, 2020.

135 Philip Krysl story written about "John Steinbeck, IV."

136 *Ibid.*

137 *Ibid.*

138 Peter Michaelson *Unspeakable Spectacle, the Movies.* Page 243.

139 *Ibid.*

140 *Ibid.*page 24

141 Peter Michaelson. *Speaking the Unspeakable.* Chapter 2: "Pornographic Ways and Means" page 55.

142 Angela Aleiss. *Making the White Man's Indian Native Americans And Hollywood Movies.*

143 Alex Simon *Robert Evans: The Kid is Alright.*

144 Arthur Grant: *The Cinema Cafe*

145 Robert Evans. *The Kid Stays in the Picture.*

146 *Ibid.*

147 Plotinus. *6 Enneads.*

148 Bill Davidson *NYT* interview: The conquering antihero October 5th, 1975. Pg. 267.

149 William Kittredge *Owning It All* Chapter "Silver Bullets."

150 Stanley Corkin, Ph.D. *Cowboys and Free Markets: Post World War II Westerns and US Hegemony.*

151 Katherine Wilson. *The Frontier Mythology in Sometimes a Great Notion.*

152 Stanley Corkin, Ph.D. Interview via email with Katherine Wilson, dated 8/06/20.

153 From the American Film Institute's Interview 1994.

154 Elaine Woo, *Los Angeles Times.*

155 Dale Kesey Interview by Katherine Wilson July, 2020.

156 Baron Wolman and Lisa Law, Flashing on the 60's. 2000.

157 *The Remembered Years* by JM Morris.

158 Ron Finne: Oregon Films Collection, 1929-1983 University of Oregon Knight Library.

159 https://www.lorensears.com/

160 Loren Sears Interview by Katherine Wilson July, 2020.

161 Don Cato: https://www.queensworldfilmfestival.com/about/

162 *Acid Christ* by Mark Christianson, quote from Burt Wolfe via U of O Professor Bob Williams Page 202- 205.

163 Lyrics to Aquarius / Let the Sunshine In by James Rado and Gerome Ragni, 1967.

164 Long Time Coming by David Crosby.

165 Lynn Hughes. *The Life and Times of the Red Dog Saloon,* by Mary Works.

166 Chan Laughlin. Ibid.

167 Elizabeth Peterson: Addendum to UO Cinema History. and *The Remembered Years* by JM Morris.

168 Mike Dilley Interview by Katherine Wilson.

169 *Ibid.*

170 Ron West, PhD Interview by Katherine Wilson.

171 Bob Laird Interview by Katherine Wilson. July 3rd, 2020

172 *Ibid*

173 Ron Finne Interview by Katherine Wilson. June, 2020.

174 Richard Brautigan. Wikipedia/Brautigan.

175 *Ibid.*

176 Kathryn Hume. *Brautigan's Psychomachia.*

177 Agata Bielik Robson. T*he Marrano Phenomenon: Jewish 'Hidden Tradition' and Modernity.*

178 David Getz, *The Life and Times of the Red Dog Saloon* by Mary Works.

179 Steven L Tanner in his article "The Western American Context of One Flew Over the Cuckoo's Nest" pg. 165.

180 https://pro.imdb.com/name/nm0706182/about

181 Dr. Stanley Corkin letter to Katherine Wilson

182 Bill Davidson. The conquering antihero. *NYT* interview. October 5th, 1975.

183 Raymond Williams *Marxism and Literature.*

184 Writtenby frankfob2@yahoo.com and published on IMDBPro.

185 Carole Eastman Interview: https://www.classicfm.com/composers/mozart/pictures/mozarts-music-movies/mozart-music-movie-five-easy-pieces/

186 Wikipedia contributors. F*ive Easy Pieces.* Wikipedia, The Free Encyclopedia. Wikipedia, The Free Encyclopedia, 24 Apr. 2021. Web. 28 Apr. 2021.

187 *NYT*: Anita Gate.

188 *Ibid.*

189 Film Comment: Bombast: Carole Eastman By Nick Pinkerton on November 21, 2014.

190 Bill Davidson *NYT* interview: The conquering antihero October 5th, 1975. Pg. 267.

191 *Vanity Fair* article. Sheila Weller. Suddenly That Summer.

192 Raymond Williams *Marxism and Literature.*

193 Rick Johnson. Interviewed by Katherine Wilson.

194 Terry O'Conner. Interviewed by Katherine Wilson.

195 Lynn Peterson Interview by Katherine Wilson.

196 Terry O'Conner Interview by Katherine Wilson.

197 Bill Davidson. The conquering antihero. *NYT* interview. October 5th, 1975.

198 *The Marrano Phenomenon* edited by Agata Bielik-Robson.

199 Joni Mitchell. Woodstock.

200 Derrida's 1994 essay, "Faith and Knowledge."

201 *Ibid*

202 Agape. https://usatoday30.usatoday.com/life/2001-11-05-agape.html.

203 Ernest Holmes, *The Science of Mind*, 1926.

204 Michael Bernard Beckwith https://en.wikipedia.org/wiki/Michael_Beckwith#:~:.

205 Derrida 2002. p. 53. (Later on as Faith and Knowledge.)

206 Arendt, Hannah. The Jew as Pariah: A Hidden Tradition. 2007. From the *Marrano Phenomenon.*

207 Arendt, Hannah. The Jew as Pariah: A Hidden Tradition. 2007. From the *Marrano Phenomenon.*

208 Gould's dialog from *Bob & Carol, Ted & Alice*

209 Jacques Derrida, "Marx & Sons."

210 Derrida's 1994 essay, "Faith and Knowledge." pg. 15

211 Nietzschean "God is Dead."

212 Derrida's 1994 essay, "Faith and Knowledge".

213 Hannah Arendt. The Jew as Pariah: A Hidden Tradition. 2007. From the *Marrano Phenomenon.*

214 Lyllye Reynolds Parker Interview by Katherine Wilson. August 2020.

215 U of O Film Studies Timeline Courtesy of Elizabeth Peterson, Knight Library.

216 *Ibid.*

217 Lynn Peterson Interview by Katherine Wilson. July 2020.

218 U of O Cinema Timeline

219 Gail Lee (from the Bookmine) interview by Katherine Wilson.

220 Wikipedia 1973 Feminist influences then and now

221 Kristin Thompson. David Bordwell. *Film History, an Introduction.*

222 Keith Harris & Richard Gehr, *Rolling Stone* magazine. August 28th, 2019.

223 Stanley Corkin, *Cowboys and Free Markets: Post-World War II Westerns and U.S. Hegemony.*

224 Michelle Donnelly *Pioneering Women in Screenwriting*. February 28, 2015.

225 Wikipedia https://en.wikipedia.org/wiki/Leigh_Brackett#:~:text.

226 Ibid.

227 Brett Wright article. *Split Tooth Media.*

228 https://pro.imdb.com/name/nm0102824/about.

229 William Kitteredge. *Owning it All* "Silver Bullets."

230 "Interview with Walter Hill Part 1". Directors Guild of America. 2007.

231 William Kitteredge. *Owning it All.* "Silver Bullets."

232 Stephen Galloway. *The Hollywood Reporter.* March 29th, 2017.

233 *National Lampoon's Animal House.* Written by Ramis, Kenney and Miller.

234 Stephen Galloway. *The Hollywood Reporter.* March 29th, 2017.

235 Sharon Blair Home Movie at *Nestucca Spit*

236 Quote origination is disputed because nobody "was there."

237 Axmaker, Sean (October 3, 2005). "Walter Hill: "Operate on your instincts"". GreenCine Daily.

238 *The Marrano Phenomenon* edited by Agata Bielik-Robson.

239 Pamela Hutchinson. British Film Institute. (2019) https://www2.bfi.org.uk/news-opinion/news-bfi/features/where-begin- early-women-filmmakers.

240 Peter Michaelson *The Aesthetics Of Pornography.*

241 Laura Mulvaney's *Visual Pleasure and Narrative Cinema.* (page 21)

242 *Ibid* ((page 24)

243 *Ibid* (page 17)

244 *Ibid* (page 23)

245 *Ibid* (page 15)

246 *Ibid.*

247 Old Testament Narratives, edited and translated by Daniel Anleyork.

248 Wikipedia definition of Linguistics.

249 Laura Mulvaney. *Visual Pleasure and Narrative Cinema.* Pg. 19. (1973)

250 Faculty at Florida International University "Apollonian" and "Dionysian" are terms used by Friedrich...

251 Laura Mulvaney. "Visual Pleasure and Narrative Cinema" 1973.

252 Doug George-Kanentiio, Iroquois Culture & Commentary, New Mexico, Clear Light Publishers, 2000, pp. 53–55

253 *The Marrano Phenomenon: Jewish 'HiddenTradition' and Modernity.* pg. 127. Edited by Agata Bielik-Robson.

254 Engels, Friedrich (1984). *Der Ursprung der Familie, des Privateigenthums und des States.* In Anschluss and Lewis H. Morgans Forschungen (in German).

255 Alaina E. Roberts. Article in the *Washington Post.* The U.S. District Court for the District of Columbia strikes down the one-drop rule for tribal membership. (J. Scott Applewhite/Associated Press) September 7, 2017.

256 h.gatech.edu/news/626646/native-american-ancestors-found-genes-many-us.

257 Jacques Derrida. Faith and Knowledge. (,p. 58) *The Marrano Phenomenon,* Edited by Agata Bielik-Robson.

258 *Ibid.*

259 Coyote Howls: Sex-positive Feminism. Posted on April 4, 2014 by alysoncrooms

260 *Ibid.*

261 Raymond Williams. Marxism and Literature, published by the Oxford Press. 1978.

262 Jeff Barnard interview of Faye Kesey. Associated Press. Jan 18, 2004.

263 Ken Kesey Interview: Burton Wolfe via U of O Professor Bob Wilson. From *Acid Christ* by Mark Christensen. Pg. 159. Schaffner Press 2010.

264 Perry Hyde interview Katherine Wilson. August, 2020.

265 Tom Hyde, PhD Interview by Katherine Wilson.

266 Via conversation with Dr. Peter Alilunas.

267 Lynn Peterson Interview by Katherine Wilson.

268 All that is Interesting/ Woodstock/ By Natasha Ishak/ comment by Snowyb. Published February 20, 2020.

269 *Deafula* courtesy of Signscope, Inc.

270 http://www.peterwolfproductions.com/about-us.html.

271 https://en.wikipedia.org/wiki/Deafula

272 Richard Wilhelm. *The I Ching*: or *Book of Changes*, p. 11. 1923. Translated into English from the German by Cary F. Baynes, with a foreword by Carl Gustav Jung.

273 Plato, *Timaeus*, 51a. Plato, www.perseus.tufts.edu. Retrieved 2020-07-20

274 Forest Pyle. *Recordings for class.* Spring 2020 U of O.

275 Roland Barth Manteia (1968.)

276 Paul de Man. "Return to Philology" from *Theory and History of Literature*, Volume 33 (Page 24.)

277 Emil Benveniste Benveniste. *Problems of General Linguistics*.

278 Paul de Man. "Return to Philology" from *Theory and History of Literature*, Volume 33.

279 Emil Benveniste Benveniste. *Problems of General Linguistics*

280 Emil Benveniste Benveniste. *Problems of General Linguistics*

281 Leslie Fiedler. *Return of the Vanishing American.*

282 Lee M. Jenkins *Studies in Classic American Literature and American Studies*

283 *Ibid.*

284 Kathleen Raine. *Yeats, the Tarot, and the Golden Dawn.* The Sewanee Review, Winter 1969.

285 Der Sandmann, (1816) is a short story written in German by E. T. A. Hoffinann. *The Golden Pot and Other Tales.* Translated by Ritchie Robertson. Oxford: Oxford UP, 2009.

286 Ed Edmo Interview by Katherine Wilson.

287 Ken Kesey. *One Flew Over the Cuckoo's Nest.*

288 Wikipedia

289 Ed Edmo Interview by Katherine Wilson.

290 Milan Melvin, *The Life and Times of the Red Dog Saloon* by Mary Works.

291 David Butkovitch Interview by Katherine Wilson. (August 2020).

292 Hermine, Freed (1976). "Where do we come from? Where are we? Where are we going?" In Ira Schneider & Beryl Korot (ed.). *Video Art: An Anthology* (1st ed.). New York: Harcourt Brace Jovanovich.

293 Wikipedia. The Grateful Dead/ Blues for Allah.

294 *Ibid*

295 *Ibid.*

296 *Ibid.*

297 Kahlil Gibran. *The Prophet.*

298 Jefferson Airplane, "Crown of Creation" (1968).

299 Bill Davidson. The conquering antihero. *NYT* October 12, 1975, Page 267

300 *Wallowing in Sex: The New Sexual Culture of 1970s American Television* by Elana Levine (2007).

301 *American Decades: 1970-1979*: Vincent Tompkins, Judith Baughman, Victor Bondi, Richard Layman (1995)

302 https://flashbak.com/the-decade-of-decadence-a-quick-look-at-the-sexual-revolution-29469/

303 *Ibid.*

304 *Ibid.*

305 Raymond Williams term.

306 Dr. Pyle term.

307 Donald E. Gordon. Content by Contradiction.

308 Bernhard Fulda, Aya Soika. *Max Pechstein: the Rise and Fall of Expressionism*

309 Albrecht Dürer. Melencolia. 1514.

310 Donald E. Gordon. *Content by Contradiction.*

311 Friedrich Nietzsch. *Thus Spoke Zarathustra* Pg. 5.

312 Bernhard Fulda, Aya Soika. *Max Pechstein: the Rise and Fall of Expressionism.*

313 Donald E. Gordon. *Content by Contradiction.* 'Expressionism's Departure from Symbolism" Pg. 79.

314 Nietzsche. *The Will to Power* (I90l)

315 Wikipedia/ Primitivism.

316 Jacques Derrida, *Faith and Knowledge.*

317 Donald E. Gordon. *Content by Contradiction.* Pg. 19.

318 *Ibid.*

319 Wikipedia /Nietzsche

320 Wikipedia/ Yeats.

321 Donald E. Gordon. *Content by Contradiction.* pg. 83.

322 Urszula Idziak-Smoczynska PhD. The theological turn of postmodernity. To be alive again.

323 Katherine Wilson's *Animal House of Blues.* (2018).

324 Stan Brakhage in Rolling Stock, 1980-1990 -Jerry White. U of O Knight Library.

325 By Douglas Martin. *NYT*. Feb. 24, 2014.

326 *Ibid.*

327 *Ibid.*

328 https://faculty.fiu.edu/~harrisk/Notes/Aesthetics/Apollonian%20Dionysian%20Dichotomy.htm

Index

G

H

Y

Z